For The Security Of

Israel

Find Joseph

(Ezekiel 37:15-22)

Walter James Taylor

Walnut Harvest Media Group

All Scripture quotations, unless otherwise indicated, are taken from the *King James Version* of the Bible.

Copyright © 2011 Walter James Taylor

Second Edition.
All rights reserved under International and Pan-American Copyright Conventions.
Published in the United States.

Published in Walnut Creek, California by
WALNUT HARVEST CHURCH MEDIA GROUP
Walnut Creek, CA, USA • whattimeblog@gmail.com

FOR THE SECURITY OF ISRAEL FIND JOSEPH

ISBN 978-0-9679460-1-6
    1. Bible—Prophecies. 2. Jerusalem in prophecy—International status.
    3. Arab-Israeli conflict. 4. Jerusalem in Christianity. 5. Jerusalem in Islam.
    I. Title

DEDICATION

TO MY CHILDREN

BILLY, ALBERT, JARROD, ELLIOTT

EBONY AND CHARLES

ACKNOWLEDGEMENTS

My sincere and deepest appreciation and thanks to Elissa Stevens and Mark Cameron-Muir for their tireless hours spent in editing the text of this book, so that this message concerning Joseph can be understood and received by both those who know the Bible and those who do not.

Thanks is also given to the guys in my Life Group—Warren, Perry, Mickey and Ron—for their constant input and encouragement as **For The Security Of Israel: Find Joseph** was taking shape as a book.

TABLE OF CONTENTS

FORWARD

This book is written to Israel, the Jews, the nations of the world, the Church, all the natural descendants of Abraham, and to anyone else who has a current or historical interest in the national ownership of the parcel of ground which at various times in history has been known as the land of Canaan, Palestine, or the modern state of Israel. Modern Israel includes the West Bank, which is the area that is proposed to become a Palestinian state.

For the myriad of Christians who will read this book, yes, I know about Galatians 3:14-15 and 29. These Scriptures, however, concern the spiritual seed of Abraham which, I agree, is the Church; but only those in the Church who can also trace his or her genealogy to one of the 12 tribes of Israel are Abraham's natural seed. **Here is a spiritual law**: There can be no fulfillment of a spiritual application of a text if its natural application is not also true. First the natural; then the spiritual[1]. But, my assignment in this book is to focus on Israel's pre-messianic security: not the Church.

The record of the perpetual ownership of this parcel is contained in the Old Testament of the Bible, which at the very least contains the world's most historically accurate account of the nations who formerly occupied the land. Seven Canaanite nations lost this land through conquest based upon a series of promises made by the LORD God Jehovah to Abraham, Isaac, and the twelve tribes of Jacob (whose name God changed to Israel).

By tracing the **Abrahamic Covenant**, that the God of Israel swore in blood to **Abraham and his seed** and confirmed to Isaac and Jacob, it is easy to establish that when the children of Israel finally took the land around 1250 BCE, that their conquest was in fulfillment of Israel's Covenant spoken over 400 years earlier. The record of this conquest is recorded in the book of Joshua, after the children of Israel had spent 400 years in Egyptian slavery. Their 40 years wandering in the wilderness is recorded in the books of Exodus, Leviticus, Numbers and Deuteronomy.

---

1 1 Corinthians 15:46.

1

What is also important to remember in evaluating the turbulence of present day Middle Eastern politics and war, is that national ownership of the land did not change when God sent the northern kingdom of Israel (the 10 tribes) into Assyrian captivity around 722 BCE, nor when Jehovah sent the southern Kingdom of Judah (primarily Jews) into 70 years of exile in Babylon beginning around 586 BCE. Its ownership has also not changed because the Romans, beginning in 70 CE, scattered Jews across the face of the earth. Why? Because the Abrahamic Covenant, like it or not, is an everlasting covenant established by the eternal God.

After 70 years of Babylonian captivity, a remnant of Jews returned to the land, rebuilt the walls of Jerusalem, and consolidated the nation of Israel. These accounts are recorded in the Books of Ezra and Nehemiah. Again, in 1948, another remnant of Jews reestablished the nation of Israel and repossessed this same land that was already theirs through a series of new wars pursuant to these same eternal promises.

It is vital for all to remember that the Abrahamic Covenant is still in full force and effect. It is an eternal covenant that cannot be broken except that the God of Israel would cease to exist. Whether one is a son (or daughter) of Abraham through Isaac; or a son (or daughter) of Abraham through Ishmael; or one of the descendents of Abraham through his marriage to Keturah; or any other descendant of the sons of Noah, the God of Abraham will defend the Abrahamic Covenant and Israel's right to this land because of what He swore to Abraham in **Genesis 12:1-3**:

> *"Now the LORD had said unto Abram, Get thee out of thy country, and from thy kindred, and from thy father's house, unto a land that I will shew thee: And I will make of thee a great nation, and I will bless thee, and make thy name great; and thou shalt be a blessing: And I will bless them that bless thee, and curse him that curseth thee: and in thee shall all families of the earth be blessed".*

Although the Jews have now returned twice to their land of Israel from their Diaspora of the Babylonians and later the Romans, it is now time on God's prophetic calendar for Joseph and Ephraim to also return to their land of Israel—because it is the same land. The Abrahamic Covenant applies equally to all of the descendants of the 12 tribes of Jacob.

Walter James Taylor

Introduction

It is God that created the nation of Israel. He is the same God that divided the Red Sea, parted the Jordan River, smashed the walls of Jericho, and plagued the mightiest nation on the face of the earth—the Egyptians—because Pharaoh would not give freedom to God's people: the children of Israel. How is it, then, that the apple of God's eye— a nation that He both established and resurrected in 1948 according to the prophetic Scriptures—can seek to establish its own peace and security in these troubled times without returning to these same Holy writings to determine whether God has provided the security needed for Israel 2,500 years before she has experienced the threats of today to the land?

This book is written entirely from Old Testament Scriptures, which have been validated as being accurate by the Dead Sea Scrolls[1]. The book simply traces the promises that God made to Abraham, Isaac, Jacob, Joseph, Sarah, Rebekah and Hagar. It then establishes from the writings of numerous Hebrew prophets which prophecies have been fulfilled, where their fulfillment can be found in the world today, and what is yet to be fulfilled—for the sole purpose of making a determination of where the Israel of today is on God's prophetic clock as is revealed in the Bible, itself.

Established on the pages to follow, totally from the writings of Moses and the other Hebrew[2] prophets, is that **God has promised Israel a season of great material prosperity and peace for the days in which we now live: if she only meets one condition**. But, in order to reach this season of abundance, the Jews of the tribe of Judah must come to the realization— however reluctantly—that all of the promises that God has made to Israel and that He will honor and faithfully execute, are promises that He has given to a Hebrew nation, and not to one that is exclusively Jewish.

1 All of the books of the Old Testament have been found and validated to be almost identical to the Hebrew texts we have today, except for the Book of Esther which is yet to be discovered.
2 We do not know the tribes of all of the prophets. Moses, Ezra, Nathan, Jeremiah, Ezekiel and maybe Zechariah were priests of the tribe of Levi. David and Solomon were of the tribe of Judah. Joshua and Samuel were of Ephraim. Hosea is reported to be from either Ruben or Issachar. Nahum came from the area that is now Iraq.

ABRAHAM IS HEBREW AND NOT JEWISH

One of the critical points of this book is that Abraham was Hebrew[3], and not Jewish, and all of the seed of Abraham through Isaac are Hebrews. Every Hebrew alive on the earth today is a full heir to all of the provisions and promises of the Abrahamic Covenant, including the right to possess the land of Canaan. But, only a relative few[4] of the Hebrew natural seed of Abraham, **through Isaac**, are the Jewish heirs of these promises: who presently and therefore rightfully occupy the land of Israel.

The first Bible reference to a "Hebrew" is used of Abram in Genesis 14:13 ... "Abram the Hebrew". God changes Abram's name to Abraham (Genesis 17:5). His covenants of promise are to flow through Abraham's son of promise, Isaac, and Isaac's son, Jacob—whose name God also changes to Israel (Genesis 32:28). Israel had 12 sons. The 12 sons of Israel unquestionably became the 12 tribes of the nation of Israel. One of Israel's sons, Joseph, is described as being a Hebrew (Genesis 39:14, 17 and 41:19). Joseph refers to himself as a Hebrew from the "land of the Hebrews" (Genesis 40:15). His brothers are referred to as Hebrews (Genesis 43:32). The midwives of the house of Jacob[5] (or children of Israel[6]) while in Egyptian bondage are called Hebrews (Exodus 1:15 and 17). The Israelite women giving birth are also described as Hebrews by Moses' sister, Miriam (Exodus 1:19). She calls these new mothers "Hebrews", even though Moses was of the tribe of Levi (Exodus 2:1-7).

When Moses was grown, he became grieved to the point of murder

3 Hebrew, from _eber_, meaning across or from the opposite side. Every reference to a Hebrew in the Bible is a reference to a nation whose roots are from the eastern side of the Euphrates River.
4 There are between 13 and 14 million Jews alive in the world today.
5 The "house of Jacob" in the Bible is always a reference to the 12 tribes of Jacob, who God named "Israel". See a further discussion on the Bible's use of the name "Israel" on page 51.
6 The term "children of Israel" is: (1) sometimes a reference to the 12 tribes of Jacob (the whole house of Israel); (2) sometimes to the 10 tribes of the northern kingdom of Israel, after the reign of David and Solomon; and (3) sometimes represents the "house of Judah" (the tribes of Judah, Benjamin and Levi, together with a representative sample of the other 10 tribes who stayed with Judah after the kingdom was divided)—even after the relatively small number of Israelites (mainly Jews) returned to the land after 70 years of Babylonian captivity under the rebuilding programs of Ezra and Nehemiah.

The best method that I have found to determine which group is referenced by the terms "children of Israel", or "all Israel" is to gain an understanding of the passage under consideration—at the time it was given, and to its primary initial recipient(s)—and to read it as if the same statement was uttered by a television news broadcaster over the nightly news on the same day ... as most of us believe everything we hear on the evening or internet news in localized media talk.

when he saw an Egyptian attacking one of his Hebrew brethren (Exodus 2:11 and 12). Moses gave repeated testimony before Pharaoh of his relationship to the Lord God of the Hebrews (Exodus 3:18; 5:3; 7:16; 9:1 and 10:3). Forty years later, after God had delivered the children of Israel from Egyptian bondage, Moses gave the people commandments from God concerning the purchase of a Hebrew slave (Exodus 21:2); which Moses reiterated after 40 years in the wilderness (Deuteronomy 15:12). Jeremiah confirmed this commandment during the times of a divided kingdom, after the 10 tribes had been carried into Assyrian captivity (Jeremiah 34:9 and 14). Jonah also referred to himself as a Hebrew (Jonah 1:9).

The point of all of this is that the covenant and promises that God gave Abraham must be fulfilled in a **Hebrew nation**, and not one that is solely Jewish. I give deference and honor to the Jews of the world for their struggles and sufferings over the centuries in many lands, as well as to the nation of Israel. I lift up to God the destinies of both. No one, however, can fairly and honestly trace the Abrahamic Covenant to its natural seed, without realizing that **all Jews are Hebrews, but not all Hebrews are Jews.**

This book is neither anti-Israel nor anti-Jewish. On the contrary, its sole purpose is to remind Israel and Jews of the world that Israel's present deliverance is already written in the Hebrew Scriptures. As a Christian, one thing that I have learned about Jehovah, the God of Israel, and about His Jewish Son who is my God, Jesus (Yeshua ben Yosef / Yeshua ben David), is that no person or nation can receive anything that is not first given by God. *A man can receive nothing except it be given him from heaven.*[7] An individual or nation that seeks to secure by human means what God has not promised will add multiplied grief and sorrows to any self-generated "blessing".

ISRAEL'S PROMISED SEASON OF GREAT PROSPERITY AND PEACE

There is a season of great material prosperity and peace now within the grasp of Israel and its people that is hidden in the words of Ezekiel 38.

Ezekiel 38:8-14[8] After many days thou shalt be visited: **in the latter years** thou shalt come into **the land that is brought back from the sword**, and is **gathered out of many people**, against the **mountains of Israel**, which have been always waste: but it is

---

7 John 3:27.
8 All Scripture is from the King James Version of the Bible.

brought forth out of the nations, and they shall **dwell safely** all of them. ... the <u>**land of unwalled villages**</u> ... that <u>**dwell safely**</u> ... **dwelling** <u>**without walls**</u>, and having <u>**neither bars nor gates**</u> [Israel now has walls, bars and gates everywhere]... the **desolate places that are now inhabited**, and upon the **people**[9] that are **gathered out of the nations**, which have **gotten cattle and goods**, that dwell in the midst of the land ... **silver and gold** ... **cattle and goods** ... a **great spoil** ... Thus saith the Lord God; In that day **when my people of Israel dwelleth safely**[10], shalt thou not know it?

But, this season of prosperity and peace, as well as the solution to the Palestinian issues that have plagued Israel since 1948, is not dependent upon the recognition of Israel as an "all-Jewish state"—by the Arabs or by the world—for **Jehovah has nowhere promised an all-Jewish state to the tribe of Judah.**

ISRAEL'S PATHWAY TO GREAT PROSPERITY AND PEACE

Prophetically, then, by the authority of the Hebrew Bible, the prerequisite for entering this season of abundance is for Israel and its Jewish people to return to the destiny that God has preordained for this time—which is that the "stick of Joseph which is in the hand of Ephraim, and the tribes of Israel his fellows" to be joined with the "stick of Judah", as "one nation in the land upon the mountains of Israel" (Ezekiel 37:15-22).

> **Ezekiel 37:15** The word of the LORD came again unto me, saying, **16** Moreover, thou son of man, **take thee one stick**, and write upon it, **For Judah**, and **for the children of Israel his companions** [a remnant of all the children of Israel that are mingled with the Jews of Israel]: then **take another stick**, and write upon it, **For Joseph, the stick of Ephraim**, and **for all the house of Israel his companions** [Ephraim is in the presence of the house of Israel, which is the 10 tribes that were carried into Assyrian captivity]: **17** And **join them** one to another **into one stick**; and they shall become one in thine hand.

---

9 People ... more than just Jews.

10 Ezekiel 38 and 39 also describe further attacks against the nation of Israel, but which result in devastating God-initiated losses for its aggressors. What is generally glossed over by the readers of these chapters, however, is the prosperity and wealth that these invaders are coming to plunder that provokes these attacks. Israel is doing very well economically these days, but not like what is described by a more careful reading of Ezekiel 38.

18 And when the children of thy people shall speak unto thee, saying, Wilt thou not shew us what thou meanest by these? **19** Say unto them, Thus saith the Lord GOD; Behold, **I will take** the **stick of Joseph, which is in the hand of Ephraim** [and has become a multitude of nations in the middle of the earth], **and the tribes of Israel his fellows** [Ephraim has been joined with the 10 tribes of Israel—also in the middle of the earth], and will put them with him, even **with the stick of Judah** [the Jews of Israel], and **make them one stick** [one nation], and they shall be one in mine hand.

20 And the sticks whereon thou writest shall be in thine hand before their eyes. **21** And say unto them, Thus saith the Lord GOD; Behold, **I will take the children of Israel** [Ephraim and the 10 tribes] **from among the heathen** [Ephraim is among Gentile nations with a lost Hebrew identity], whither they be gone, and will gather them on every side, and bring them into their own land: **22** And I will make them **one nation in the land upon the mountains of Israel**; and one king [prime minister for now; Messiah later] shall be king to them all: and they shall be no more two nations [Israel and Judah], neither shall they be divided into two kingdoms any more at all.

These promises of God are immutable. Joseph and Ephraim were not, are not, and will never be Jewish in their ethnicity. They are the son and grandson of Jacob, the Hebrew, and are full-blooded heirs to the Covenant that God made with Abraham. Joseph, over the years, has become a company of nations in the middle of the earth—whose people are as the dust of the earth, stars of heaven, and sand of the sea.

ESTABLISHED BY THE COUNSELS OF HEAVEN

What we will find detailed in the pages that follow, taken entirely from Hebrew Old Testament Scriptures, is both a revelation and an understanding that Moses and the other Hebrew prophets have clearly revealed that:

- Abraham was Hebrew and not Jewish. So were Isaac, Jacob (who God named Israel), Joseph and Moses.

- God changed Jacob's name to Israel. The 12 sons of Israel became the 12 tribes of Israel.

- Israel always has been and always will be a Hebrew nation.

- All of the descendants of the twelve tribes of Israel are Hebrews. They are all heirs according to each of the promises that God gave to Abraham, Isaac, and Jacob.

- All Jews are Hebrews, but not all Hebrews are Jews—and all Hebrews are of the nation of Israel.

- Rebekah has become the mother of billions of Hebrews: the vast multitude of which are hidden somewhere on the earth. These unseen Hebrews are not Jewish, Arab or Christian.

- The natural descendants of Abraham through Isaac have been given a perpetual right to possess the land of Canaan. This right of possession proceeds from Adonai-Jehovah, the God of Israel. The Lord God of Israel swore by Himself, while standing in blood, His Covenant to Abraham to give him and his offspring the land of Canaan / Palestine / Israel forever.

- These promises of God concerning the land of Israel are given to Abraham and flow through Isaac and Jacob, and not Ishmael, Esau nor the sons of Abraham and Keturah.

- All of the descendants of each of the 12 tribes of Israel have the same right to possess the land of Israel, no matter where they are to be found in the world today, and irrespective of whether, at this writing, they have the knowledge that they are Hebrew.

- The natural descendants of Abraham through Isaac and Jacob have already blessed all of the families of the earth.

- Both the birthright and the blessing of Abraham were given by Jacob to Joseph, and not to Judah.

- Ephraim, the youngest son of Joseph, is the Lord's firstborn.

- The greater manifestation of Joseph's birthright and blessing is to be found in the descendants of Ephraim, and secondly in those of Manasseh.

- Ephraim and Manasseh, like Jacob, are called Israel.

- Ephraim and Manasseh, even today, are also to be known as sons of Abraham and Isaac. They are full-blooded heirs to the Abrahamic Covenant.

- Ephraim, through his descendants, has become a strong company of nations in the middle or center of the earth. They are a numberless multitude of people who are as the dust of the earth, stars of heaven, and sand of the sea.

- Manasseh has become a great people, whose descendants are also in the middle of the earth.

- Ephraim has expanded ("pushed the people") to the ends of the earth the Hebrew children of Israel, carrying the blessing of Joseph that is upon them. His descendants have done so without knowing their true identity as a Hebrew people.

- Ephraim (and possibly Manasseh) shall possess, possess now, or have possessed the gate [gateway] of his [or their] enemies.

- There is gargantuan blessing in the area of land that is the "top of the head" or crown[11] of the parcel of land given by Joshua to the tribe of Ephraim. This parcel of ground lies in an area of the West Bank designated as a proposed Palestinian state.

- Although Ephraim has lost his identity as Hebrew, in the latter years he will come alive to his lineage and claim his inheritance in the nation and land of Israel.

- It is time on God's prophetic calendar for the Jews of Israel to allow their Creator to rejoin the "stick of Joseph" with the "stick of Judah", in order to combine these two branches of the houses of Jacob back into one nation upon the mountains of Israel, in fulfillment of the prophecy of **Ezekiel 37:15-22**.

- The stick [heirs] of Joseph is to be found in the hand [descendants] of Ephraim.

---

11 The area of the crown is adjacent to the city of Nābulus [biblical Shechem] and Mount Ebal.

- God has never promised a "Jewish state" to the tribe of Judah, or to the modern nation of Israel.

- In order to align Israel with the center of God's revealed will, it is the prophetic season and time for the Jewish leadership and people of Israel, and Jews across the world, to recognize that as a Hebrew nation God is requiring that many of the descendants of the 12 tribes of Jacob be encouraged to return to the land of Israel, in fulfillment of Ezekiel 37.

- Such an invitation to return requires both the leadership and people of Israel, as well as Jews around the world, to invest the time, energy, and resources to locate Ephraim (and Manasseh)—who vastly outnumber the entire population of Israel as well as all of the Arab nations put together—and invite their brethren back into the land, as is repeatedly prophesied in the Holy Scriptures written by God's Hebrew prophets.

- To return the nation of Israel to the revealed will of God by the pen of these Hebrew prophets is no threat to the viability of Israel as a Hebrew nation, for the sceptre—the right to rule—was not given to Joseph nor to his descendants, but is to remain with Judah until Shiloh (the Messiah) comes; and finally that

- The fulfillment of Ezekiel 37—that Joseph and Ephraim will be joined again with Judah back into one nation—appears to be the last prerequisite to the building of the third temple. I submit that God will not allow Herod's temple of a Jewish nation to be reconstructed, but only Solomon's temple of a unified Hebrew nation of 12 tribes will be resurrected on the Temple Mount. There Abraham offered Isaac; and there David purchased the land from Araunah the Jebusite[12] in order to " ... build an alter unto the Lord ..." [13].

Israel: Find Joseph

Now, then, let us begin the tracing of Jehovah's Covenant with the Hebrew seed of Abraham.

---

12 Genesis 10:16; and 2 Samuel 24:18-25.
13 2 Samuel 24:21.

10

PART I

TRACING GOD'S COVENANT WITH ABRAHAM

12

CHAPTER 1

GOD'S COVENANT WITH ABRAHAM

The Bible introduces us in Genesis 11 to **Abram**[1] **the Hebrew**[2], the eldest son of Terah, who with Abram and other family members left Ur of the Chaldees[3] to go into the land of Canaan. But Terah stopped short of his destiny; and all the Bible records of him is that his days were "two hundred and five years, and Terah died in Haran".

In Genesis 12, at the age of 75, the Lord God Jehovah renews both his command and promise to Abram … "the LORD had said" … that if Abram would get away from his family and their worship of the moon, He would bless him exceedingly and give him the land of Canaan.

HOW TO NAVIGATE THIS BOOK

A word of caution: Many who will read this book will think that they know the Old Testament Scriptures well enough to skip re-reading the foundation of the revelation of this book. I encourage you to resist this temptation, and to lay again in your heart and mind this foundation that God has established in the recorded history of Israel.

The Bible is like a spiritual prism or a cut diamond … full of hidden Wisdom and Light. When one changes the angle of the Light of God that flows through a prism or diamond, there is revealed to the beholder a personal majesty never seen before; and occasionally during the course of history something may be revealed that few, if any, have ever seen before. This majesty was always present, but the angle of Light was never quite right. This is the purpose of this book—to reveal passages of Scripture that countless millions over the millennia have read, but few have seen in quite the way presented here … in the light of current events in the Middle East.

---

1 Genesis 11:26-32.
2 Genesis 14:13.
3 Now called Mugheir. It is on the western bank of the Euphrates River in Iraq.

What is presented here is not Bible "interpretation" ... but Bible *revelation*—something that God is revealing now to the world from His written Word, for His holy purposes ... for such a time as this. Revealed in this book is *truth*: truth not hidden from us, but hidden for us. Here I will give to you the prophetic truths that God has given to me—from the very same source that I found them—hidden on the pages of the Bible.

My commentary concerning these sacred texts is at times contained in **brackets within the texts of the Scriptures presented**, as well as in **footnotes**: which contain a wealth of relevant information. If you skim over these for whatever reasons, you will not hear in your spirit all that God is saying to you in this book. What I say is nothing. What God is saying is everything.

ABRAHAM'S COVENANT OF BLESSING AND CURSING

Jehovah establishes His covenant of blessing and cursing with Abram.

> **Genesis 12:1** Now the LORD had said unto Abram, Get thee out of thy country, and from thy kindred, and from thy father's house, unto a land that I will shew thee: **2** And I will make of thee a great nation, and I will bless thee, and make thy name great; and thou shalt be a blessing: **3 And I will bless them that bless thee, and curse him that curseth thee: and in thee shall all families of the earth be blessed**[4].

> **4** So Abram departed... and they went forth to go into the land of Canaan; and into the land of Canaan they came. **6** And Abram passed through the land unto the place of Sichem, unto the plain of Moreh. And the Canaanite was then in the land. **7** And the LORD appeared unto Abram, and said, <u>Unto thy seed will I give this land</u>: and there builded he an altar unto the LORD, who appeared unto him.

While the Canaanites were still in the land of Canaan—a land subsequently called Palestine and now known as the land of Israel—the Hebrew God, Jehovah, gave the land of Canaan to Abram [Abraham] and his natural seed and offspring. Despite the varied events of the past several thousand years, the land of Canaan—by whatever name one chooses to call it—will forever belong to the natural seed of Abraham through Isaac

---

4 Genesis 18:18, 26:4 and 28:14.

and Jacob. Why? Because what God says He means, and whatever He gives none can take away. It will last forever.

God respects the boundaries of other nations that He has established. The Bible records the generations of Esau (Jacob's brother) in Genesis 36:8 ... *Thus dwelt Esau in mount Seir: Esau is Edom* [the land of the Edomites]. God had given Mount Seir to the Edomites. When the nation of Israel came out of slavery and wanted to cross the land of the Edomites on the way to Canaan, the king of Edom refused them passage. With much distress the children of Israel were required to go around Edom rather than to engage in war with their brother[5]. However, when the king of the Amorites refused the Israelites passage across his land, they killed him and took all of his cities[6]: because the Amorites had no covenant with the Lord.

GOD GIVES CANAAN TO ABRAHAM AND HIS HEIRS FOREVER

God gives the land of Canaan to Abraham and his descendants forever.

Genesis 13:12 Abram dwelled in the land of Canaan ... **14** And the LORD said unto Abram, after that Lot was separated from him, Lift up now thine eyes, and look from the place where thou art northward, and southward, and eastward, and westward: **15** For **all the land which thou seest, to thee will I give it, and to thy seed for ever.**

Forever in every language of the world means *forever*.

ABRAHAM'S SEED AS THE DUST OF THE EARTH

Not only does the Lord God Jehovah promise to give the land of Canaan to Abram and his offspring, but He also promises to make Abram's descendants a numberless multitude ... as the **dust of the earth**.

Genesis 13:16 And I will make thy seed as **the dust of the earth**: so that if a man can number the dust of the earth, then shall thy seed also be numbered. **17** Arise, walk through the land in the length of it and in the breadth of it; for I will give it unto thee. **18** Then Abram removed his tent, and came and dwelt in the plain of Mamre, which is in Hebron, and built there an altar unto

---

5 Numbers 20:14-21; 21:4.
6 Numbers 21:21-25.

the LORD.

ABRAHAM'S SEED AS THE STARS OF HEAVEN

God first promises that Abraham's seed would be as numerous as the **dust of the earth** (Genesis 13:16). He now uses a different metaphor and promises his descendants will number as the **stars of heaven**.

Genesis 15:1 After these things the word of the LORD came unto Abram in a vision, saying, Fear not, Abram: I am thy shield, and thy exceeding great reward. **2** And Abram said, Lord GOD, what wilt thou give me, seeing I go childless, and the steward of my house is this Eliezer of Damascus? **3** And Abram said, Behold, to me thou hast given no seed: and, lo, one born in my house is mine heir. **4** And, behold, the word of the LORD came unto him, saying, This shall not be thine heir; but he that shall come forth out of thine own bowels shall be thine heir.

5 And he brought him forth abroad, and said, Look now toward heaven, and **tell the stars**, if thou be able to number them: and he said unto him, **So shall thy seed be**. **6** And he believed in the LORD; and he counted it to him for righteousness.

GOD'S COVENANT IN BLOOD FOR THE LAND

Because Abraham's mind is still not fully persuaded concerning the magnitude of God's promises to him regarding the multitude of his sons and daughters in future generations, God settles his mind by completing the ceremony of establishing a blood-covenant. In this ceremony God walks a series of figure-eights through the blood of the sacrifice and utters a series of blessings and curses that establish the terms of the covenant[7]. Thus Abraham, as a man of the East, knew that God would back up these promises with His very life—because the penalty for violating a covenant-in-blood is death. The only way that the Lord could **not fulfill** these promises to Abraham would be for God to cease to exist.

Genesis 15:7 And he said unto him, **I am the LORD** that brought thee out of Ur of the Chaldees, **to give thee this land to inherit it. 8** And he said, Lord GOD, whereby shall I know that I shall inherit it? **9** And he said unto him, Take me an heifer of three

---

7 Genesis 12:1-3.

years old, and a she goat of three years old, and a ram of three years old, and a turtledove, and a young pigeon. **10** And he took unto him all these, and divided them in the midst, and laid each piece one against another [a river of blood]: but the birds divided he not. **11** And when the fowls came down upon the carcases, Abram drove them away.

12 And when the sun was going down, a deep sleep fell upon Abram; and, lo, an horror of great darkness fell upon him. **13** And he said unto Abram, Know of a surety that thy seed shall be a stranger in a land that is not theirs, and shall serve them; and they shall afflict them four hundred years; **14** And also that nation, whom they shall serve, will I judge: and afterward shall they come out with great substance. **15** And thou shalt go to thy fathers in peace; thou shalt be buried in a good old age. **16** But in the fourth generation they shall come hither again: for the iniquity of the Amorites is not yet full.

17 And it came to pass, that, when the sun went down, and it was dark, behold a smoking furnace, and a burning lamp [a lamp of fire] that passed between those pieces. **18 In the same day the LORD made a covenant with Abram** [while standing in blood], saying, <u>**Unto thy seed have I given this land**</u>, from the river of Egypt unto the great river, the river Euphrates: **19** The Kenites, and the Kenizzites, and the Kadmonites, **20** And the Hittites, and the Perizzites, and the Rephaims, 21 And the Amorites, and the Canaanites, and the Girgashites, and the Jebusites.

God gave the children of Israel the land of Canaan all the way across today's Jordan to the Euphrates River in modern Iraq … and Israel has been willing to give away **40% of God's land** in return for recognition of Israel as a Jewish state, if satisfactory security guarantees from the Palestinian government were received. Whether Israel will change this position is yet to be seen … but the point of this book is that Israel and her people, Jews and the nations of the world lack the perception of where God is on His prophetic clock. *My people are destroyed for a lack of knowledge* [8].

"The land shall not be divided when Joseph is joined with Judah", saith the Lord.

---

8   Hosea 4:6.

The Genealogy of Abraham

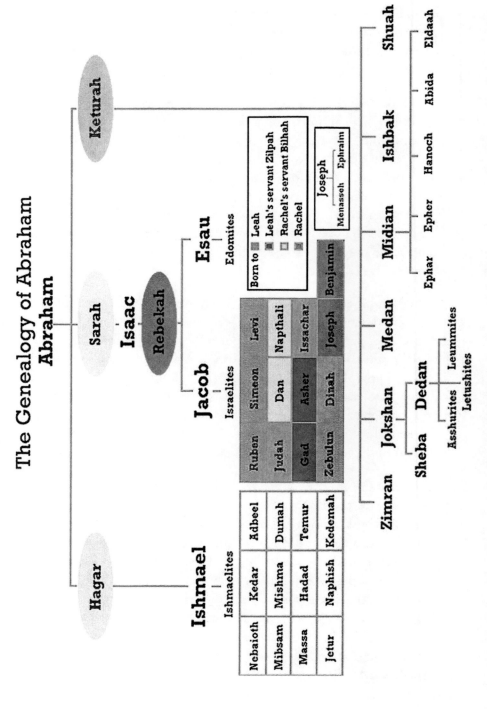

CHAPTER 2

ISHMAEL'S COVENANT WITH GOD

After the passage of time and the promise of God does not manifest itself, Abram [Abraham], like so many of us, begins again to question, and doubt, and wonder … "what if, maybe, I wonder" … whether he should do something to help God bring His promises to pass concerning the birth of a son and heir? Encouraged in this by his wife, Sarai, Abram goes into her handmaid, Hagar, and Ishmael is conceived.

THE HAGARIC COVENANT

God's covenant with Hagar has also produced a multitude of people through Ishmael. Abram is now 85 years old.

Genesis 16:1 Now Sarai Abram's wife bare him no children: and she had an handmaid, an Egyptian, whose name was **Hagar**. **2** And Sarai said unto Abram, Behold now, the LORD hath restrained me from bearing: I pray thee, go in unto my maid; it may be that I may obtain children by her. And Abram hearkened to the voice of Sarai. **3** And Sarai Abram's wife took Hagar her maid the Egyptian, **after Abram had dwelt ten years in the land of Canaan**, and gave her to her husband Abram to be his wife.

4 And he went in unto Hagar, and she conceived: and when she saw that she had conceived, her mistress was despised in her eyes. **5** And Sarai said unto Abram, My wrong be upon thee: I have given my maid into thy bosom; and when she saw that she had conceived, I was despised in her eyes: the LORD judge between me and thee. **6** But Abram said unto Sarai, Behold, thy maid is in thy hand; do to her as it pleaseth thee. And when Sarai dealt hardly with her, she fled from her face.

7 And **the angel of the LORD found her** by a fountain of water in the wilderness, by the fountain in the way to Shur. **8** And he said, Hagar, Sarai's maid, whence camest thou? and whither wilt thou go? And she said, I flee from the face of my mistress Sarai. **9** And the angel of the LORD said unto her, Return to thy mistress, and submit thyself under her hands.

10 And **the angel of the LORD said** unto her, **I will** [God Himself is speaking] **multiply thy seed exceedingly, that it shall not be numbered for multitude**. **11** And the angel of the LORD said unto her, Behold, thou art with child, and shalt bear a son, and shalt **call his name Ishmael**[1]; because the LORD hath heard thy affliction. **12** And **he will be a wild man; his hand will be against every man, and every man's hand against him; and he shall dwell in the presence of all his brethren.**

Hagar Believed In The God Of Abraham

Hagar believed in the Hebrew Lord God Jehovah of Israel.

Genesis 16:13 And **she called the name of the LORD** that spake unto her, **Thou God seest me**: for she said, Have I also here looked after him that seeth me? **14** Wherefore the well was called Beerlahairoi [the well of living after seeing]; behold, it is between Kadesh and Bered. **15** And Hagar bare Abram a son: and Abram called his son's name, which Hagar bare, **Ishmael. 16** And **Abram was fourscore and six years old** [Abraham is 86 years old]**, when Hagar bare Ishmael to Abram** [conceived after 10 years].

The Abrahamic Covenant Flows Through Isaac

Although Ishmael shall and has produced a multitude of people, the Abrahamic Covenant passes through Isaac, and not Ishmael.

Genesis 17:20 And as for **Ishmael**, I have heard thee: Behold, **I have blessed him**, and will make him fruitful, and **will multiply him exceedingly; twelve princes** shall he beget, and I will make him **a great nation. 21 But my covenant will I establish**

---

1   *Ishmael* means *whom God hears*. Ishmael is the first of seven people in the Bible who God names before their birth. His genealogy is recorded in Genesis 17:20; 25:12-18 and 1 Chronicles 1:29-31.

with **Isaac**[2], which Sarah [God changes Sarai's name to Sarah] shall bear unto thee at this set time in the next year. **22** And he left off talking with him, and God went up from Abraham.

23 And Abraham took Ishmael his son, and all that were born in his house, and all that were bought with his money, every male among the men of Abraham's house; and circumcised the flesh of their foreskin in the selfsame day, as God had said unto him. **24** And **Abraham was ninety years old and nine** [Abraham is now 99 years old], when he was circumcised in the flesh of his foreskin. **25** And **Ishmael his son was thirteen years old** [Ishmael's age is important to remember for later], when he was circumcised in the flesh of his foreskin. **26** In the selfsame day was Abraham circumcised, and Ishmael his son. **27** And all the men of his house, born in the house, and bought with money of the stranger, were circumcised with him.

Ishmael Has Become A Great Nation

God again promises that Ishmael shall become a great nation, and this is because he is a son of Abraham. But, as is set forth above, Ishmael is not the promised heir. The Abrahamic Covenant is to flow through Isaac and Jacob, and not Ishmael.

Genesis 21:8 And the child [Isaac] grew, and was weaned: and Abraham made a great feast the same day Isaac was weaned [3 to 5 years after his birth]. **9** And Sarah saw the son of Hagar the Egyptian, which she had born unto Abraham, mocking. **10** Wherefore she said unto Abraham, **Cast out this bondwoman and her son: for the son of this bondwoman shall not be heir with my son, even with Isaac**. **11** And the thing was very grievous in Abraham's sight because of his son.

12 And God said unto Abraham, Let it not be grievous in thy sight because of the lad, and because of thy bondwoman; in all that Sarah hath said unto thee, hearken unto her voice; **for in Isaac shall thy seed be called**. **13** And also of **the son of the bondwoman will I make a nation, because he is thy seed.**

---

2 *Isaac* means *laughter*. God is having a good time because both Abraham and Sarah laughed at the prospect of having a child at the ages of 99 and 90. Isaac is also named before his birth.

14 And Abraham rose up early in the morning, and took bread, and a bottle of water, and gave it unto Hagar, putting it on her shoulder, and the child, and sent her away: and she departed, and wandered in the wilderness of Beersheba. **15** And the water was spent in the bottle, and she cast the child under one of the shrubs. **16** And she went, and sat her down over against him a good way off, as it were a bowshot: for she said, Let me not see the death of the child. And she sat over against him, and **lift up her voice, and wept.**

Hagar cries out to the God of Abraham with tears. But, when Hagar lifts up her voice to God, God hears the voice of Ishmael's destiny.

> **Genesis 21:17** And **God heard the voice of the lad**; and **the angel of God called to Hagar out of heaven**, and said unto her, What aileth thee, Hagar? fear not; for <u>**God hath heard the voice of the lad**</u> where he is. **18 Arise, lift up the lad**, and hold him in thine hand; for **I will make him a great nation. 19** And **God opened her eyes, and she saw a well of water**; and she went, and filled the bottle with water, and gave the lad drink. **20** And God was with the lad; and he grew, and dwelt in the wilderness, and became an archer. **21** And he dwelt in the wilderness of Paran: and his mother took him a wife out of the land of Egypt.

God's covenant with Ishmael is actually derived from His covenant and promises to Hagar, who got caught in the middle of Abraham and Sarah's impatience as to God's infinite wisdom concerning the timing of the fulfillment of His promises concerning Abraham and the multitude of his descendants. God hears her cry and shows her a well of water to keep them alive so that Ishmael could fulfill the destiny that God has spoken over him[3].

Ishmael was 13 years old when he was circumcised (Genesis 17:25), and at this point is now at least sixteen. So, while Hagar is crying out to God a bowshot's distance away from Ishmael, what is Ishmael doing? He is doing what any other hot, tired, hungry and thirsty teenager would be doing under what may have been the only shrub and shade in the desert—he is asleep. When Hagar lifts up his destiny to God, God "hears the voice of the lad", and his provision is supplied immediately. If God would do this <u>for Ishmael, how</u> much more will He fulfill all of His covenant promises to

3 Genesis 16:10-12; 21:13.

all of the descendents of Abraham after the flesh?

THE HAGARIC COVENANT IS PARTIALLY FULFILLED

Even though the Abrahamic Covenant is to be fulfilled through Isaac and not Ishmael, God is yet faithful to His promises to Hagar that Ishmael would become a great nation and begat 12 princes.

> **Genesis 25:12** Now these are the **generations of Ishmael**, Abraham's son, whom Hagar the Egyptian, Sarah's handmaid, bare unto Abraham: **13** And these are the **names of the sons of Ishmael**, by their names, according to their generations: the first-born of Ishmael, Nebajoth; and Kedar, and Adbeel, and Mibsam, **14** And Mishma, and Dumah, and Massa, **15** Hadar, and Tema, Jetur, Naphish, and Kedemah: **16** These are the sons of Ishmael, and these are their names, by their towns, and by their castles; <u>twelve princes</u>[4] **according to their nations**.

> **17** And these are the years of the **life of Ishmael**, an hundred and thirty and seven years: and he gave up the ghost and died; and was gathered unto his people. **18** And **they dwelt from Havilah unto Shur**, that is before Egypt, as thou goest toward Assyria: and he died in the presence of all his brethren.

The historical **Book of Jubillees 20:13** also speaks of Ishmael: *And Ishmael and his sons, and the sons of Keturah [Abraham's second wife] and their sons, went together and dwelt from Paran to the entering in of Babylon in all the land which is towards the East facing the desert. And these mingled with each other, and their name was called Arabs, and Ishmaelites.* From the story of Joseph's enslavement by his brothers, we will learn that the caravan traders that took Joseph to Egypt are referred to as both Midianites[5] and Ishmaelites[6]; and they also dwelt among the Amalekites[7]. Therefore, from the above reference in Genesis 25:18 *"... they dwelt from Havilah unto Shur"* and the Book of Jubillees we understand that the twelve Ishmaelite nations occupied the Arabian Peninsula from Egypt to the Euphrates River.

Ishmael settled in the land of Paran, a region lying between Canaan

---

4 Twelve princes, according to Genesis 17:20.

5 Genesis 15:1-4 (above).

6 Genesis 37:23-36.

7 1 Samuel 15:7 and 27:8.

and the mountains of Sinai. He became a great desert chief. He had twelve sons who became the founders of many Arab tribes or colonies, the Ishmaelites, who spread over the wide desert spaces of Northern Arabia from the Red Sea to the Euphrates (Genesis 37:25, 27-28; 39:1). The sons of Ishmael peopled the west of the Saudi Arabian Peninsula, and eventually formed the chief element of the Arab nations: the nomadic Bedouin tribes. The character of Ishmael and his descendants is vividly depicted by the angel of the Lord: "And he will be a wild man; his hand will be against every man, and every man's hand against him" (Genesis 16:12). These nomads roam the wilds of the desert and are jealous of their independence, quarrelsome and adventurous.

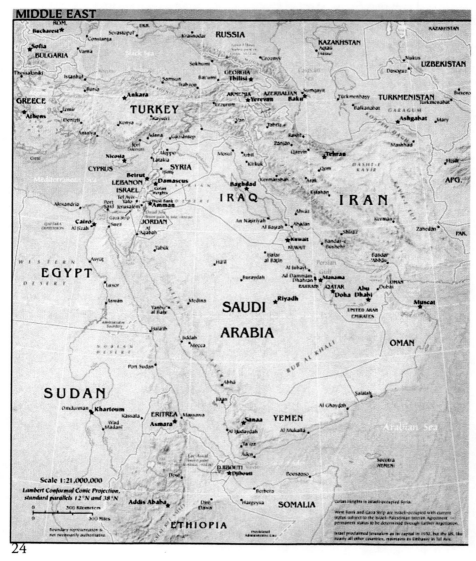

MIDDLE EAST

CHAPTER 3

IN ISAAC IS ABRAHAM'S SEED CALLED

ABRAHAM IS THE FATHER OF ALL ABRAHAMIC NATIONS

God changes Abram's name to Abraham with the promise that his descendants through Isaac [Jacob and Joseph] will become many nations in addition to Israel. These promises have no reference to Ishmael.

> **Genesis 17:1** And **when Abram was ninety years old and nine, the LORD appeared to Abram**, and said unto him, I am the Almighty God; walk before me, and be thou perfect. **2 And I will make my covenant between me and thee, and will multiply thee exceedingly.** 3 And Abram fell on his face: and God talked with him, saying,
>
> 4 As for me, behold, **my covenant** is with thee, and thou shalt be a **father of many nations. 5** Neither shall thy name any more be called Abram, but **thy name shall be <u>Abraham</u>**[1]; for a <u>father of many nations</u> have I made thee. 6 And I will make thee exceeding fruitful, and **I will make <u>nations</u> of thee**, and <u>**kings**</u> [kings of these many nations besides Israel] shall come out of thee.

CANAAN IS GIVEN TO ABRAHAM FOR AN EVERLASTING POSSESSION

The whole house of Israel [the 12 tribes of Jacob] has an eternal covenant to possess the land of Canaan as an everlasting possession. This matter was settled with God when He first spoke it. The tribe of Judah has been having some second thoughts concerning this promise.

Israel: Find Joseph ... And what does Joseph have to say about Judah's negotiations to give away his land?

---

1 *<u>Abraham</u>* means *father of a multitude;* whereas *<u>Abram</u>* means *exalted father.*

Genesis 17:7 And I will establish **my covenant** between me and thee and thy seed after thee in their generations for **an everlasting covenant**, to be a God unto thee, and to thy seed after thee. **8** And **I will give unto thee, and to thy seed after thee**, the land wherein thou art a stranger, **all the land of Canaan, for an everlasting possession**; and I will be their God. **9** And God said unto Abraham, Thou shalt keep my covenant therefore, thou, and thy seed after thee in their generations.

CIRCUMCISION IS THE SIGN OF THE ABRAHAMIC COVENANT

Circumcision is the sign of the Abrahamic Covenant. God swore while standing in blood that He would give the land of Canaan to Abraham and His seed forever … that is His descendants through Isaac and Jacob (Genesis 15:17-18). **Every further act of the shedding of blood when he circumcises his male child by any son of Abraham** regardless of religion (or no religion) **is a further witness-in-blood that the land of Israel belongs in perpetuity to the descendants of the 12 tribes of Jacob**, and none other.

Genesis 17:10 This is my covenant, which ye shall keep, between me and you and thy seed after thee; **Every man child among you shall be circumcised**. **11** And ye shall circumcise the flesh of your foreskin; and it shall be **a token of the covenant** [a witness in blood] betwixt me and you. **12** And he that is eight days old shall be circumcised among you, every man child in your generations, he that is born in the house, or bought with money of any stranger, which is not of thy seed. **13** He that is born in thy house, and he that is bought with thy money, must needs be circumcised: and **my covenant shall be in your flesh for an everlasting covenant**. **14** And the uncircumcised man child whose flesh of his foreskin is not circumcised, **that soul shall be cut off from his people** [God is very serious in this]; he hath broken my covenant.

SARAH IS THE MOTHER OF ALL ABRAHAMIC NATIONS AND KINGS

Here is a quickly forgotten passage of Scripture: **Sarah**[2] shall become the mother of nations, and kings of the people of these nations shall come from her. **Who are these nations? Where are these nations?**

2   *Sarah* means *queen or mother of princes* and is the feminine form of sar., *a prince*. *Sarai* means *princess*.

Genesis 17:15 And God said unto Abraham, As for **Sarai** thy wife, thou shalt not call her name Sarai, but **Sarah shall her name be**. **16** And I will bless her, and give thee a son also of her: yea, I will bless her, and **she shall be a mother of nations** [many nations besides Israel]; **kings of people** [kings of the people of many nations … whose people have become as the dust of the earth, stars of heaven, and sand of the sea] **shall be of her**.

17 Then Abraham fell upon his face, and laughed, and said in his heart, Shall a child be born unto him that is an hundred years old? and shall Sarah, that is **ninety years old**, bear? **18** And Abraham said unto God, **O that Ishmael might live before thee!** **19** And God said, Sarah thy wife shall bear thee a son indeed; and thou shalt **call his name Isaac**: and I will establish my covenant with him for **an everlasting covenant**, and **with his seed after him**.

It is important to note that God's promises to Abraham's wife, Sarah, that she will become the mother of nations and mother of the kings of the people of these nations can have no possible reference to the Arab nations that have come from Ishmael through Abraham's union with Hagar, because Sarah has no blood relationship with Ishmael. Can a woman 90 years old that has never had a child now conceive and give birth? With God, nothing shall be impossible.

THE BLOOD COVENANT FLOWS THROUGH ISAAC

Ishmael is blessed because he is Abraham's son, and Abraham and God love him. But, the Abrahamic Covenant is to be fulfilled through Isaac, not through Ishmael.

Genesis 17:20 And as for **Ishmael**, I have heard thee: Behold, **I have blessed him**, and will make him fruitful, and **will multiply him exceedingly**; **twelve princes** shall he beget, and I will make him **a great nation**. **21 But my covenant will I establish with Isaac**, which Sarah shall bear unto thee at this set time in the next year. **22** And he left off talking with him, and God went up from Abraham.

23 And Abraham took Ishmael his son, and all that were born in his house, and all that were bought with his money, every male among the men of Abraham's house; and circumcised the flesh of their foreskin in the selfsame day, as God had said unto him. **24** And **Abraham was ninety years old and nine**, when he was circumcised in the flesh of his foreskin. **25** And **Ishmael his son was thirteen years old**, when he was circumcised in the flesh of his foreskin. **26** In the selfsame day was Abraham circumcised, and Ishmael his son. **27** And all the men of his house, born in the house, and bought with money of the stranger, were circumcised with him.

SARAH SHALL HAVE A SON

God confirms His promise that Sarah shall have a son.

Genesis 18:1 And the LORD appeared unto him in the plains of Mamre: and he sat in the tent door in the heat of the day ... **9** And they [the Lord and 2 angels] said unto him, Where is Sarah thy wife? And he said, Behold, in the tent. **10** And he said, I will certainly return unto thee according to the time of life; and, lo, Sarah thy wife shall have a son. And Sarah heard it in the tent door, which was behind him.

11 Now Abraham and Sarah were old and well stricken in age [99 and 90]; and it ceased to be with Sarah after the manner of women. **12** Therefore Sarah laughed within herself, saying, After I am waxed old shall I have pleasure, my lord being old also? **13** And the LORD said unto Abraham, Wherefore did Sarah laugh, saying, Shall I of a surety bear a child, which am old? **14 Is any thing too hard for the LORD?** At the time appointed I will return unto thee, according to the time of life, and Sarah shall have a son. **15** Then Sarah denied, saying, I laughed not; for she was afraid. And he said, Nay; but thou didst laugh.

16 And the men rose up from thence, and looked toward Sodom: and Abraham went with them to bring them on the way. **17** And the LORD said, Shall I hide from Abraham that thing which I do; **18** Seeing that **Abraham shall surely become a great and mighty nation**, and <u>all the nations of the earth shall be blessed in him</u>? **19** For I know him, that **he will command his children and his household** after him [this is why God chose Abraham], and they shall keep the way of the LORD, to do justice and judgment; that the LORD may bring upon Abraham that which he hath spoken of him.

ISAAC IS THE SON OF PROMISE

God fulfills His promise to Abraham with the birth of Isaac.

Genesis 21:1 And the LORD visited Sarah as he had said, and the LORD did unto Sarah as he had spoken. **2** For Sarah conceived, and bare Abraham a son in his old age, at the set time of which God had spoken to him. **3** And Abraham called the name of his son that was born unto him, whom Sarah bare to him, **Isaac**. **4** And Abraham circumcised his son Isaac being eight days old, as God had commanded him. **5 And Abraham was an hundred years old, when his son Isaac was born unto him**.

6 And Sarah said, God hath made me to laugh, so that all that hear will laugh with me. **7** And she said, Who would have said unto Abraham, that Sarah should have given children suck? for I have born him a son in his old age. **8** And the child grew, and was weaned: and Abraham made a great feast the same day that Isaac was weaned.

ISHMAEL HAS BECOME A GREAT NATION

God again promises Abraham that Ishmael shall become a great nation.

Genesis 21: 9 And Sarah saw the son of Hagar the Egyptian, which she had born unto Abraham, mocking. **10** Wherefore she said unto Abraham, Cast out this bondwoman and her son: **for the son of this bondwoman shall not be heir with my son, even with Isaac**. **11** And the thing was very grievous in Abraham's sight because of his son.

12 And God said unto Abraham, Let it not be grievous in thy sight because of the lad, and because of thy bondwoman; in all that Sarah hath said unto thee, hearken unto her voice; for **in Isaac shall thy seed be called**. **13** And also of **the son of the bondwoman will I make a nation, because he is thy seed**.

14 And Abraham rose up early in the morning, and took bread, and a bottle of water, and gave it unto Hagar, putting it on her shoulder, and the child, and sent her away: and she departed, and wandered in the wilderness of Beersheba. **15** And the water was spent in the bottle, and she cast the child under one of the shrubs. **16** And she went, and sat her down over against him a good way off, as it were a bowshot: for she said, Let me not see the death of the child. And she sat over against him, and lift up her voice, and wept.

17 And God heard the voice of the lad [when Hagar lifted up her voice to God, God heard the voice of Ishmael's destiny]; and **the angel of God called to Hagar out of heaven**, and said unto her, What aileth thee, Hagar? fear not; for God hath heard the voice of the lad where he is. **18** Arise, **lift up the lad**, and hold him in thine hand; for **I will make him a great nation. 19** And God opened her eyes, and she saw a well of water; and she went, and filled the bottle with water, and gave the lad drink. **20** And God was with the lad; and he grew, and dwelt in the wilderness, and became an archer. **21** And he dwelt in the wilderness of Paran: and his mother took him a wife out of the land of Egypt.

ABRAHAM OFFERS ISAAC ON THE TEMPLE MOUNT

God tests Abraham's faith in His promises by commanding him to offer his son and heir, Isaac, on the Temple Mount.

> **Genesis 22:1** And it came to pass after these things, that God did tempt [try or test] Abraham, and said unto him, Abraham: and he said, Behold, here I am. **2** And he said, Take now thy son, thine **only son Isaac**, whom thou lovest, and get thee **into the land of Moriah**; and **offer him** there for **a burnt offering upon one of the mountains** which I will tell thee of.

Moriah means ... *the chosen of Jehovah.* For God to tell Abraham to go ... "into the land of Moriah; and offer [Isaac] there for a burnt offering" is to literally say to Abraham to offer his son upon ... *one of the mountains or hills that Jehovah has chosen*—or, upon the precise hill in Jerusalem that God had foreordained as a place of sacrifice and offerings. Here on the temple mount Solomon's temple was built, on the spot that had been the threshing-floor of Ornan the Jebusite that King David purchased[3]. This was "the land of Moriah" to which Abraham went to offer up his son Isaac. It has been supposed that the highest point of the temple hill, which is now covered by the Mohammedan Kubbetes-Sakhrah, or "Dome of the Rock," is the actual site of Ornan's threshing-floor[4]. Here also, one thousand years after Abraham, David built an altar and offered sacrifices to God.

> **Genesis 22:3** And Abraham rose up early in the morning, and saddled his ass, and took two of his young men with him, and Isaac his son, and clave the wood for the burnt offering, and rose up, and went unto the place of which God had told him. **4** Then on the third day Abraham lifted up his eyes, and saw the place afar off. **5** And Abraham said unto his young men, Abide ye here with the ass; and I and the lad will go yonder and worship, and come again to you. **6** And Abraham took the wood of the burnt offering, and laid it upon Isaac his son; and he took the fire in his hand, and a knife; and they went both of them together.

Abraham has by now developed such absolute confidence—faith—not only in God's ability to do what He has promised, but in His willingness to do it for Abraham, that he is willing to sacrifice his only begotten son on the alter ... which was his only means of reaching what God has promised him.

> **Genesis 22:7** And Isaac spake unto Abraham his father, and said, My father: and he said, Here am I, my son. And he said, Behold the fire and the wood: but where is the lamb for a burnt offering? **8** And Abraham said, My son, **God will provide himself a lamb for a burnt offering** [God will provide Himself ... a Lamb ... for a burnt offering]: so they went both of them together.

> **9** And they came to the place which God had told him of; and Abraham built an altar there, and laid the wood in order, and **bound Isaac his son** [Abraham commanded and Isaac was obedient to allow his father to bind him on an alter where animals were killed], and laid him on the altar upon the wood. **10** And Abraham stretched forth his hand, and took the knife to slay his son.

> **11** And the angel of the LORD called unto him out of heaven,

---

3   2 Samuel 24:24-25; 2 Chronicles 3:1.
4   1 Chronicles 21:15-27.

and said, Abraham, Abraham: and he said, Here am I. **12** And he said, Lay not thine hand upon the lad, neither do thou any thing unto him: for now I know that thou fearest God, seeing thou hast not withheld thy son, thine only son from me. **13** And Abraham lifted up his eyes, and looked, and behold behind him **a ram** [not a lamb ... yet] caught in a thicket by his horns: and Abraham went and took the ram, and offered him up for a burnt offering in the stead of his son. **14** And Abraham called the name of that place **Jehovahjireh** [my God shall provide]: as it is said to this day, In the mount of the LORD it shall be seen.

GOD SWEARS BY HIMSELF HIS BLOOD COVENANT TO ABRAHAM

The Jews of Israel and the world in number have never been by today's standards as the **stars of heaven**, or as the **sand upon the sea shore**, or the **dust of the earth**. And, in the places where they have been scattered throughout history, Jews have never lost their identity as Jews, and thus have always been available to be counted. Neither has Israel as a nation since its reemergence in 1948, or even in the kingdom of David and Solomon, ever possessed the gates of all its enemies. We, simply, must look elsewhere to locate God's fulfillment of these **blood-covenant promises** to Abraham. Because there is no greater, God can only swear by Himself His promises to Abraham of blessing ... multiplication ... and dominion.

> **Genesis 22:15** And the **angel of the LORD** called unto Abraham out of heaven the second time, 16 And said, **By myself have I sworn**[5], saith the LORD, for because thou hast done this thing, and hast not withheld thy son, thine only son: **17** That in **blessing** I will bless thee, and in **multiplying** I will multiply **thy seed as the <u>stars</u> of the heaven, and as the <u>sand</u> which is upon the sea shore**; and **thy seed shall <u>possess the gate</u> of his enemies; 18** And <u>**in thy seed**</u> shall <u>**all the nations of the earth be blessed**</u>; because thou hast obeyed my voice.

The gate or gateways of a nation are its strategic entrances, passageways or ports[6]. A good example of this for both Israel and Syria is the Golan Heights. Historical examples include Gibraltar, and the Suez and Panama Canals. There is **a hidden Israel** somewhere on the earth today whose <u>people are</u> as stars, sand and dust where these God-sworn promises have

5 Genesis 26:3.
6 C/p. Genesis 24:60.
32

already been fulfilled … **as they must be fulfilled in Abraham before the Messiah comes?**

Israel: Find Joseph

Abraham Offers Isaac On The Temple Mount

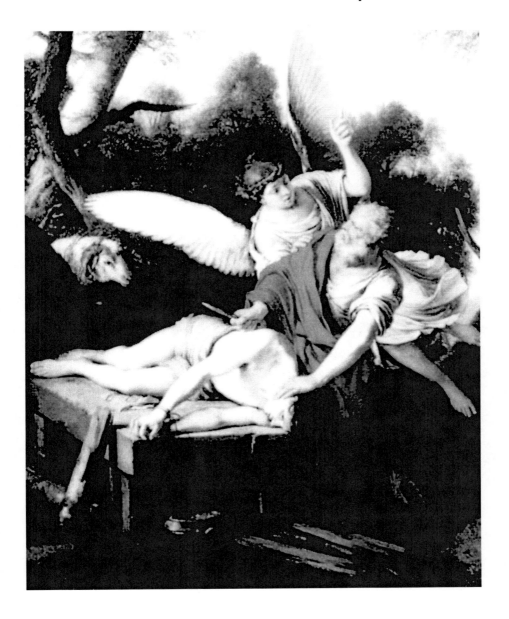

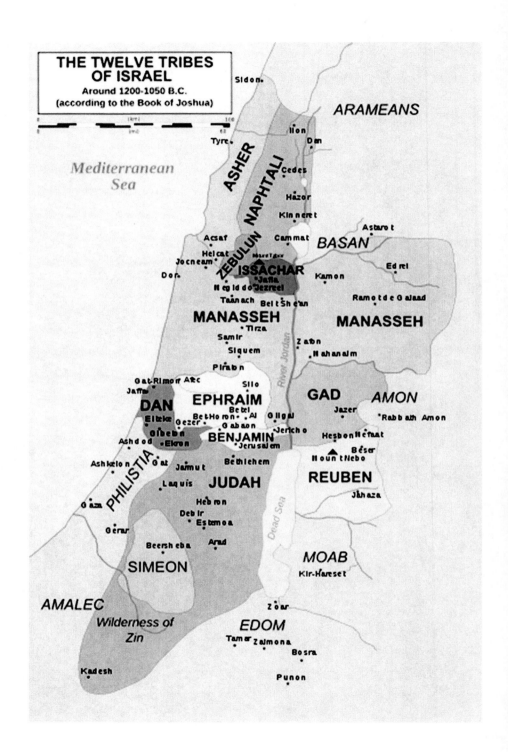

THE TWELVE TRIBES
OF ISRAEL
Around 1200-1050 B.C.
(according to the Book of Joshua)

Mediterranean
Sea

ARAMEANS

Sidon

Tyre
ASHER
NAPHTALI
Ilon
Dan

Cedes

Hazor

Kinneret

Acsaf
Cammat
Astarot
BASAN
Helcat
Jocneam
MoreTabo
Dor
ZEBULUN
ISSACHAR
Kamon
Edrel

Megiddo Jezreel
Jaffa

Taanach
Beit Shean
Ramot de Galaad

MANASSEH
Tirza
MANASSEH

Samir
Zabn

Siquem
Nahanaim

Pirabn

Gat-Rimon Afc
Silo
Jaffa
EPHRAIM
GAD
AMON

DAN
Betel
Jazer
Rabbath Amon

Elteke
BetHoron Ai Gilgal
Gezer Gabaon
Gibebn
Jericho
Hesbon Nefaat

Ashdod Ekron
BENJAMIN
Béser

Ashkelon
Jerusalem
Mount Nebo

PHILISTIA
Gat
Bethlehem
REUBEN

Gaza
Jarmut
JUDAH

Laquis
Jahaza

Hebron

Gerar
Debir
Estemoa

Beersheba
Arad
MOAB
Kir-Hareset

SIMEON

AMALEC
Zoar

Wilderness of
Zin
EDOM

Tamar Zalmona

Bosra

Kadesh

Punon

CHAPTER 4

REBEKAH IS THE MOTHER OF BILLIONS

God's promise that Sarah will be the mother of nations is to be fulfilled in Rebekah.

SARAH'S BONES POSSESS THE LAND

Genesis 23:1 And Sarah was an hundred and seven and twenty years old: these were the years of the life of Sarah. 2 And Sarah died in Kirjatharba; the same is Hebron in the land of Canaan: and Abraham came to mourn for Sarah, and to weep for her.

3 And Abraham stood up from before his dead, and spake unto the sons of Heth[1], saying, 4 I am a stranger and a sojourner with you: give me a possession of a buryingplace with you, that I may bury my dead out of my sight. 5 And the children of Heth answered Abraham, saying unto him, 6 Hear us, my lord: **thou art a mighty prince among us**: in the choice of our sepulchres bury thy dead; none of us shall withhold from thee his sepulchre, but that thou mayest bury thy dead.

7 And Abraham stood up, and bowed himself to the people of the land, even to the children of Heth. 8 And he communed with them, saying, If it be your mind that I should bury my dead out of my sight; hear me, and intreat for me to Ephron the son of Zohar, 9 That he may give me the **cave of Machpelah**, which he hath, which is in the end of his field; for as much money as it is worth he shall give it me for a possession of a buryingplace amongst you.

10 And Ephron dwelt among the children of Heth: and Ephron the Hittite answered Abraham in the audience of the children

---

1   Heth is a son of Canaan (Genesis 10:15).

of Heth, even of all that went in at the gate of his city, saying, **11** Nay, my lord, hear me: the field give I thee, and the cave that is therein, I give it thee; in the presence of the sons of my people give I it thee: bury thy dead. **12** And Abraham bowed down himself before the people of the land. **13** And he spake unto Ephron in the audience of the people of the land, saying, But if thou wilt give it, I pray thee, hear me: I will give thee money for the field; take it of me, and I will bury my dead there. **14** And Ephron answered Abraham, saying unto him, **15** My lord, hearken unto me: the land is worth four hundred shekels of silver; what is that betwixt me and thee? bury therefore thy dead.

16 And Abraham hearkened unto Ephron; and Abraham weighed to Ephron the silver, which he had named in the audience of the sons of Heth, four hundred shekels of silver, current money with the merchant. **17** And the field of Ephron, which was in **Machpelah**, which was before Mamre, the field, and the cave which was therein, and all the trees that were in the field, that were in all the borders round about, were made sure **18** Unto Abraham for a possession in the presence of the children of Heth, before all that went in at the gate of his city.

19 And after this, **Abraham buried Sarah his wife** in the **cave** of the **field of Machpelah** before Mamre: the same is **Hebron** in the **land of Canaan**. **20** And the field, and the cave that is therein, were made sure unto Abraham for a possession of a burying place by the sons of Heth.

A BRIDE FOR ISAAC

Abraham, before he dies, secures for Isaac a bride from his own family who were worshipers of the moon, but now know the God of Abraham.

Genesis 24:1 And Abraham was old, and well stricken in age: and the LORD had blessed Abraham in all things. **2** And Abraham said unto his eldest servant[2] of his house, that ruled over all that he had, Put, I pray thee, thy hand under my thigh: **3** And I will make thee swear by the LORD, the God of heaven, and the God of the earth, that thou shalt not take a wife unto my son

---

2 Eliezer of Damascus (Genesis 15:2).

of the daughters of the Canaanites, among whom I dwell: **4** But thou shalt go unto my country [now living in Syria], and to my kindred, and take a wife unto my son Isaac. **5** And the servant said unto him, Peradventure the woman will not be willing to follow me unto this land: must I needs bring thy son again unto the land from whence thou camest?

6 And Abraham said unto him, Beware thou that thou bring not my son thither again. **7** **The LORD God of heaven,** which took me from my father's house, and from the land of my kindred, and which spake unto me, and that **sware unto me, saying, Unto thy seed will I give this land**; he shall send his angel before thee, and thou shalt take a wife unto my son from thence. **8** And if the woman will not be willing to follow thee, then thou shalt be clear from this my oath: only bring not my son thither again. **9** And the servant put his hand under the thigh of Abraham his master, and sware to him concerning that matter.

REBEKAH IS THE MOTHER OF BILLIONS

In tracing the Abrahamic Covenant, here is another of the most overlooked passages of Scripture in the Bible: by both Jews and Christians—that **Rebekah would become the mother of billions**. This event, I submit, must be fulfilled by the children of Rebekah before the Messiah comes. This event, I also submit, has already happened to the human descendants of Abraham through Isaac. This will become much clearer when we consider the promises of God to the sons of Joseph.

Genesis 24:33 And there was set meat before him to eat [Eliezer has reached his destination and believes he has spotted the Lord's choice for Isaac's wife]: but he said, I will not eat, until I have told mine errand. And he said, Speak on. **34** And he said, I am Abraham's servant. **35** And the LORD hath blessed my master greatly; and he is become great: and he hath given him flocks, and herds, and silver, and gold, and menservants, and maidservants, and camels, and asses. **36** And Sarah my master's wife bare a son [Isaac] to my master when she was old: and unto him [Isaac] hath he [Abraham] given all that he hath. **37** And my master made me swear, saying, Thou shalt not take a wife to my son of the daughters of the Canaanites, in whose land I dwell: **38** But thou shalt go unto my father's house, and to my kindred, and take a wife unto my son ...

Rebekah consents to return with Eliezer to become the wife of Isaac; and the Spirit of God causes Rebekah's family in Syria to speak the same blessing over Rebekah that God spoke over Abraham in Genesis 22:17.

Genesis 24:51 Behold[3], Rebekah is before thee, take her, and go, and let her be thy master's son's wife, as **the LORD hath spoken** [they know the God of Abraham]...**60 And they blessed Rebekah**, and said unto her, Thou art our sister, **be thou the <u>mother of thousands of millions</u>[4]**, and <u>let thy seed possess the gate of those which hate them</u> ... **64** And [having entered the land of Canaan] Rebekah lifted up her eyes, and when she saw Isaac, she lighted off the camel ... **67** And Isaac brought her into his mother Sarah's tent, and took Rebekah, and she became his wife; and he loved her: and Isaac was comforted after his mother's death.

ISAAC RECEIVES THE BIRTHRIGHT

The birthright of the firstborn son is given to **Isaac, heir of God's promises**, and not to Ishmael or to the sons of Abraham and Keturah.

Genesis 25:1 Then again Abraham took a wife, and her name was **Keturah. 2** And she bare him Zimran, and Jokshan, and Medan, and **Midian** [the Midianites], and Ishbak, and Shuah. **3** And Jokshan begat Sheba, and Dedan. And the sons of Dedan were Asshurim, and Letushim, and Leummim. **4** And the **sons of Midian**; Ephah, and Epher, and Hanoch, and Abida, and Eldaah. All these were the **children of Keturah. 5 And Abraham gave all that he had unto Isaac.**

ABRAHAM'S BONES POSSESS THE LAND

Abraham was buried in the land of Canaan. He is still in the land ...

---

3 Abraham's nephew, Bethuel, and grandson, Laban (Rebekah's brother), are speaking. [Bethuel means ... "separated unto God" ... which provides a further indication that Abraham's family have now become worshipers of the true and living God.

4 A thousand times a million is a billion. This is a literal promise for the natural children of Rebekah and not a primary reference to the Church of Jesus Christ.

buried in Hebron, in the area of a proposed Palestinian state. Abraham gave gifts to the sons of his concubines. These unnamed sons of Abraham travel eastward, while Ishmael journeyed to the south.

Genesis 25:6 But unto the sons of the concubines, which Abraham had, Abraham gave gifts, and sent them away from Isaac his son, while he yet lived, eastward, unto the east country. **7** And these are the days of the years of **Abraham's life** which he lived, **an hundred threescore and fifteen years**. **8** Then Abraham gave up the ghost, and died in a good old age, an old man, and full of years; and was gathered to his people.

9 And his sons **Isaac** and **Ishmael** buried him in the **cave of Machpelah**, in the field of Ephron the son of Zohar the Hittite, which is before Mamre; **10 The field which Abraham purchased of the sons of Heth: there was Abraham buried, and Sarah his wife**. **11** And it came to pass after the death of Abraham, that **God blessed his son Isaac**; and Isaac dwelt by the well Lahairoi.

THE HAGARIC COVENANT IS PARTIALLY FULFILLED

Even though the Abrahamic Covenant is to be fulfilled through Isaac and not Ishmael, God is still faithful to His promise to Hagar that Ishmael would become a great nation, and begat 12 princes.

Genesis 25:12 Now these are the **generations of Ishmael**, Abraham's son, whom Hagar the Egyptian, Sarah's handmaid, bare unto Abraham: **13** And these are the **names of the sons of Ishmael**, by their names, according to their generations: the first-born of Ishmael, Nebajoth; and Kedar, and Adbeel, and Mibsam, **14** And Mishma, and Dumah, and Massa, **15** Hadar, and Tema, Jetur, Naphish, and Kedemah: **16** These are the sons of Ishmael, and these are their names, by their towns, and by their castles; <u>**twelve princes**</u>[5] **according to their nations**.

17 And these are the years of the **life of Ishmael**, an hundred and thirty and seven years: and he gave up the ghost and died; and was gathered unto his people. **18** And **they dwelt from Havilah unto Shur**, that is before Egypt, as thou goest toward Assyria: and

5 Genesis 17:20.

he died in the presence of all his brethren.

Two Nations Are Born Of Rebekah

Two nations are born of Rebekah from one set of twins. **Esau and Jacob grew up to produce** two very different peoples, and cultures, and some would even say two races of people. God is beginning to fulfill His promise to **Sarah** that she would be the **mother of nations**[6], and **Rebekah, the mother of billions**[7].

> **Genesis 25:19** And these are the generations of Isaac, Abraham's son: Abraham begat Isaac: **20** And Isaac was forty years old when he took Rebekah to wife, the daughter of Bethuel the Syrian of Padanaram, the sister to Laban the Syrian. **21** And Isaac intreated the LORD for his wife, because she was barren: and the LORD was intreated of him, and Rebekah his wife conceived. **22** And the children struggled together within her [they are still struggling]; and she said, If it be so, why am I thus? And she went to enquire of the LORD. **23** And the LORD said unto her, **Two nations**[8] are in thy womb, and **two manner of people** shall be separated from thy bowels; and the **one people shall be stronger** than the other people; and **the elder shall serve the younger.**

Esau Despises His Birthright

It is the **birthright** that establishes for the firstborn son his right to receive the **blessing** of his father. Esau sells his birthright to his cunning brother, Jacob, for one meal. (At least Jacob knew what he was getting.) **This passage of Scripture is pivotal to the message of this entire book, for as we shall see, both the birthright and the blessing of Abraham will be given by Jacob [Israel] to Joseph, and not to Judah**. Concerning Esau, without the **birthright** of the firstborn son, he has no right to the eternal **blessing** of his father, Isaac, before he dies.

> **Genesis 25:24** And when her [Rachel's] days to be delivered were fulfilled, behold, there were **twins in her womb. 25** And **the first came out red**, all over like an hairy garment; and they called

6 Genesis 17:16.

7 Genesis 24:60.

8 Esau, the firstborn, became the nation of Edom (the Edomites; Genesis 36:1 and 8).

his name **Esau** [hairy red]. **26** And **after that** came his brother out, and his hand took hold on Esau's heel; and his name was called **Jacob** [heel holder or supplanter]: and **Isaac was threescore years old** when she bare them. **27** And the boys grew: and Esau was a cunning hunter, a man of the field; and Jacob was a plain man, dwelling in tents. **28** And **Isaac loved Esau**, because he did eat of his venison: but **Rebekah loved Jacob**.

29 And Jacob sod pottage: and **Esau** came from the field, and he was faint: **30** And Esau said to Jacob, Feed me, I pray thee, with that same red pottage; for I am faint: therefore was his name called **Edom** [red; father of the **Edomites**]. **31** And Jacob said, **Sell me this day thy birthright**. **32** And Esau said, Behold, I am at the point to die: and what profit shall this birthright do to me? **33** And Jacob said, Swear to me this day; and he sware unto him: and **he sold his birthright unto Jacob**. **34** Then Jacob gave Esau bread and pottage of lentiles; and he did eat and drink, and rose up, and went his way: **thus Esau despised his birthright**.

ABRAHAM'S SEED AS THE STARS OF HEAVEN

God promises Isaac the land of Canaan and the surrounding countries. He also confirms His promises to Abraham that his natural descendants through Isaac, and then Jacob, will be as numerous as the stars of heaven, and shall bless all the families of the earth.

Genesis 26:1 And there was a famine in the land, beside the first famine that was in the days of Abraham. And Isaac went unto Abimelech king of the Philistines unto Gerar. **2** And **the LORD appeared unto him**, and said, Go not down into Egypt; **dwell in the land** which I shall tell thee of: **3** Sojourn in this land, and I will be with thee, and will bless thee; for **unto thee,** and unto **thy seed, I will give all these countries,** and **I will perform the oath which I sware**[9] unto Abraham thy father; **4 And I will make thy seed to multiply as <u>the stars of heaven,</u>** and will **give unto thy seed all these countries**; and <u>**in thy seed shall all the nations of the earth be blessed**</u>[10]; **5** Because that Abraham obeyed my voice, and kept my charge, my commandments, my statutes, and

9   Genesis 22:16.
10   Genesis 12:3 and 28:14.

my laws.

God says that He will perform the oath which he swore in blood unto Abraham. These promises require a fulfillment in the offspring of Abraham. Where on the earth have the sons of Abraham through Isaac become as the stars of heaven or blessed all the families of the earth? Someone needs to wake up Israel, Jews, Palestinians, the Church, and the world to the promise that the perpetual ownership of the land of Canaan [Palestine or Israel] was established by God thousands of years ago. If Israel really does understand its Covenant with God, then its leadership and Jewish citizens really do need to start proclaiming this in God's Holy Name.

THE BLOOD COVENANT OF ABRAHAM IS RENEWED WITH ISAAC

The Lord appears to Isaac and renews His covenant of blessing that He swore unto Abraham. Isaac gives an offering to the Lord in the land of his promise. He sows into his destiny: a destiny which God has already fulfilled on the earth.

> **Genesis 26:23** And he [Isaac] went up from thence to Beersheba. **24** And **the LORD appeared unto him** the same night, and said, I am the God of Abraham thy father: fear not, for **I am with thee,** and **will bless thee,** and **multiply thy seed** for my servant Abraham's sake. **25** And he built an altar there, and called upon the name of the LORD, and pitched his tent there: and there Isaac's servants digged a well.

Israel: Find Joseph

CHAPTER 5

JACOB IS ISRAEL

THE BLESSING OF ISAAC UPON JACOB

Jacob secures the blessing of his father by use of trickery to receive what Esau had already sold him when he contracted away his birthright.

Genesis 27:1 And it came to pass, that **when Isaac was old**, and his eyes were dim, so that he could not see, he called Esau his eldest son, and said unto him, My son: and he said unto him, Behold, here am I. **2** And he said, Behold now, I am old, I know not the day of my death[1]: **3** Now therefore take, I pray thee, thy weapons, thy quiver and thy bow, and go out to the field, and take me some venison; **4** And make me savoury meat, such as I love, and bring it to me, that I may eat; **that my soul may bless thee before I die**.

5 And Rebekah heard when Isaac spake to Esau his son. And Esau went to the field to hunt for venison, and to bring it. **6** And Rebekah spake unto Jacob her son, saying, Behold, I heard thy father speak unto Esau thy brother, saying, **7** Bring me venison, and make me savoury meat, that I may eat, and bless thee before the LORD before my death. **8** Now therefore, my son, obey my voice according to that which I command thee. **9** Go now to the flock, and fetch me from thence two good kids of the goats; and I will make them savoury meat for thy father, such as he loveth: **10** And thou shalt bring it to thy father, that he may eat, and **that he may bless thee before his death** [the coveted blessing of the firstborn].

11 And Jacob said to Rebekah his mother, Behold, Esau my

---

1   Isaac lived to be 180 years old (Genesis 35:28). He also lived to see Jacob return to the land of Canaan after 20 years of service with Laban in Syria (Genesis 35:28).

brother is a hairy man, and I am a smooth man: **12** My father peradventure will feel me, and I shall seem to him as a deceiver; and I shall bring a curse upon me, and not a blessing. **13** And his mother said unto him, **Upon me be thy curse**, my son: only obey my voice, and go fetch me them.

Not only does God honor the words of Isaac's blessing of Jacob when he thought he was blessing Esau; but he also honors Rebekah's self-induced curse from the words of her mouth … "Upon me be thy curse, my son." Because of Esau's wrath, Jacob is forced to leave the land for 20 years. Rebekah never again sees her beloved son[2] while she is alive.

Genesis 27:14 And he went, and fetched, and brought them to his mother: and his mother made savoury meat, such as his father loved. **15** And Rebekah took goodly raiment of her eldest son Esau, which were with her in the house, and put them upon Jacob her younger son: **16** And she put the skins of the kids of the goats upon his hands, and upon the smooth of his neck: **17** And she gave the savoury meat and the bread, which she had prepared, into the hand of her son Jacob.

18 And he came unto his father, and said, My father: and he said, Here am I; who art thou, my son? **19** And **Jacob said unto his father, I am Esau thy firstborn**; I have done according as thou badest me: arise, I pray thee, sit and eat of my venison, **that thy soul may bless me**. **20** And Isaac said unto his son, How is it that thou hast found it so quickly, my son? And he said, Because the LORD thy God brought it to me.

21 And Isaac said unto Jacob, Come near, I pray thee, that I may feel thee, my son, whether thou be my very son Esau or not. **22** And Jacob went near unto Isaac his father; and he felt him, and said, The voice is Jacob's voice, but the hands are the hands of Esau. **23** And he discerned him not, because his hands were hairy, as his brother Esau's hands: **so he blessed him**. **24** And he said, Art thou my very son Esau? And he said, I am. **25** And he said, Bring it near to me, and I will eat of my son's venison, that my soul may bless thee. And he brought it near to him, and he did eat: and he brought him wine, and he drank.

---

2 C/p. Proverbs 18:21 Death and life are in the power of the tongue.

JACOB STEALS ESAU'S BLESSING

Jacob receives the **blessing** of Isaac and Abraham on his life.

> **Genesis 27:26 And his** [Jacob's] **father Isaac said unto him**, Come near now, and kiss me, my son. **27** And he came near, and kissed him: and he smelled the smell of his raiment, and **blessed him**, and said, See, the smell of my son is as the smell of a field which the LORD hath blessed: **28** Therefore **God give thee of the dew of heaven,** and the **fatness of the earth,** and **plenty of corn and wine: 29 Let people serve thee,** and **nations bow down to thee:** be lord over thy brethren, and **let thy mother's sons bow down to thee: <u>cursed be every one that curseth thee</u>,** and **<u>blessed be he that blesseth thee</u>**[3].

This story of how Jacob stole both Esau's **birthright** and his **blessing** is recorded in the Bible, in part, **for God to establish for all eternity** how important He has made both the **birthright** and the **blessing of Abraham** upon all who become an heir. As we will see, **both the birthright and blessing of Abraham shall be given to Joseph through his sons.** When it comes time for Jacob [who God named Israel] to bless Joseph's sons before he dies, his primary blessing does not fall upon Joseph's first-born, Manasseh, but upon his youngest son, Ephraim.

For our purposes in this book, the **<u>blessing of Abraham</u>** that Israel needs today and is entitled to by the authority of God's word, **<u>was not given by Israel</u>** [Jacob] **<u>to Judah, but by Israel to Joseph</u>. <u>This blessing is to be found in the hand of Ephraim</u>**[4], and Ephraim is a blessed people.

The **<u>sons and daughters of Ephraim possess or have become some-where in the earth</u>** today:

■ The dew of heaven.

■ The fatness of the earth.

■ Plenty of corn and wine.

■ People that serve them as a company of nations[5].

---

3   C/p. Genesis 12:3 (pg. 14)..
4   Ezekiel 37:15-22.
5   Genesis 35:11; 48:19.

- People as numerous as the dust of the earth, stars of heaven, and sand of the sea.

- Nations that bow down to them and from whom they receive honor in the earth.

- People and nations that exercise dominion.

- People and nations that others will be cursed for cursing; and

- People and nations that others will be blessed for blessing.

Israel: Find Joseph

JACOB RECEIVES THE BIRTHRIGHT AND THE BLESSING OF ABRAHAM

Jacob receives both the **birthright** and the **blessing** of Abraham. This blessing will receive its greatest manifestation over the millennia in the tribe of Judah, with its broad historical footprint, and in Joseph through the generations of his sons: who have achieved greatness in the earth, but are still unidentified as being part of the Hebrew nation of Israel.

Genesis 27:30 And it came to pass, as soon as Isaac had made an end of blessing Jacob, and Jacob was yet scarce gone out from the presence of Isaac his father, that Esau his brother came in from his hunting. **31** And he also had made savoury meat, and brought it unto his father, and said unto his father, Let my father arise, and eat of his son's venison, that thy soul may bless me. **32** And Isaac his father said unto him, Who art thou? And he said, I am thy son, thy firstborn Esau. **33** And Isaac trembled very exceedingly, and said, Who? where is he that hath taken venison, and brought it me, and I have eaten of all before thou camest, and **have blessed him? yea, and he shall be blessed**.

34 And when Esau heard the words of his father, he cried with a great and exceeding bitter cry, and said unto his father, Bless me, even me also, O my father. **35** And he said, Thy brother came with subtilty, and hath taken away thy blessing. **36** And he said, Is not he rightly named **Jacob**[6] for he hath supplanted me these two times: **he took away my birthright**; and, behold, **now he hath**

---

6 Heel holder or supplanter.

<u>taken away my blessing</u>. And he said, Hast thou not reserved a blessing for me? **37** And Isaac answered and said unto Esau, **Behold, I have made him** [Jacob who became Israel[7]] **thy lord**, and all his brethren have I given to him for servants; and with corn and wine have I sustained him: and what shall I do now unto thee, my son?

He or she who is blessed by the Lord is blessed, irrespective of how that blessing was obtained.

God's Prophecy Over Esau / Edom

Although Esau missed out on the blessing of his father, he did receive a word from the Lord.

Genesis 27:38 And Esau said unto his father, Hast thou but one blessing, my father? bless me, even me also, O my father. And Esau [who became known as Edom[8]] lifted up his voice, and wept. **39** And Isaac his father answered and said unto him, Behold, thy dwelling shall be the fatness of the earth, and of the dew of heaven from above; **40** And **by thy sword shalt thou live**, and shalt **serve thy brother**; and it shall come to pass when thou shalt have the dominion, that **thou shalt break his yoke from off thy neck**.

Jacob Is The Heir To The Land Of Israel

By virtue of his receiving both the **birthright** and the **blessing** of Abraham and Isaac, **Jacob becomes heir to God's Covenant with Abraham**.

Genesis 28:1 And Isaac called Jacob, and blessed him, and charged him, and said unto him, Thou shalt not take a wife of the daughters of Canaan. **2** Arise, go to Padanaram, to the house of Bethuel thy mother's father; and take thee a wife from thence of the daughters of Laban thy mother's brother. **3** And **God Almighty bless thee,** and **make thee fruitful,** and **multiply thee,** that thou mayest **be a <u>multitude of people</u>; 4 And give thee the <u>blessing of Abraham</u>, to thee, and to thy seed with thee;** that thou mayest **<u>inherit the land</u>** wherein thou art a stranger, which **God gave unto Abraham. 5** And Isaac sent away Jacob: and he

7 Genesis 32:28.
8 Genesis 36:1 and 8.

went to Padanaram unto Laban, son of Bethuel the Syrian, the brother of **Rebekah: Jacob's and Esau's mother**.

JACOB HAS BECOME A MULTITUDE IN ALL FOUR DIRECTIONS

The **blessing** has caused Jacob to spread in all four directions. While the "house of Jacob" was only one person fleeing from the wrath of his brother, Esau, God reveals to Jacob the gateway of heaven and the ministry of angels. These are his supply line for receiving these blessings in order to reach his destiny. From Bethel, which is in the center of Israel in what is now the West Bank, God confirms to Jacob the Abrahamic Covenant for the land. From the middle of the land of Canaan, God covenanted with Jacob that his descendants would grow in all four directions of the compass to become a vast multitude of people. This multitude far greater than the Jews that are now in the world, or have ever been throughout world history.

> **Genesis 28:10** And Jacob went out from Beersheba, and went toward Haran. **11** And he lighted upon a certain place, and tarried there all night, because the sun was set; and he took of the stones of that place, and put them for his pillows, and lay down in that place to sleep. **12** And he dreamed, and behold **a ladder** set up on the earth, and the top of it reached to heaven: and behold the angels of God ascending and descending on it.
>
> **13** And, behold, the LORD stood above it, and said, **I am the LORD God of Abraham thy father**, and **the God of Isaac: the land** whereon thou liest, **to thee will I give it, and to thy seed**; **14** And **thy seed shall be as the dust of the earth**, and **thou shalt spread abroad to the west**, and **to the east**, and **to the north**, and **to the south**: and **in thee** and **in thy seed shall all the families of the earth be blessed**[9]. **15** And, behold, I am with thee, and will keep thee in all places whither thou goest, and will bring thee again into this land; for I will not leave thee, until I have done that which I have spoken to thee of.

God's presence will be with Jacob through the next 20 years of persecution and affliction with Laban the Syrian. The Lord will be faithful in His promises to Jacob.

---

9 Genesis 12:3 and 26:4.

Jacob is promised to:

- Be blessed by the almighty God.

- Be fruitful and multiply.

- Become a multitude of people with descendants as numerous as the dust of the earth.

- Be the possessor of the blessing of Abraham along with his descendants.

- Inherit the land of Canaan already given by God to Abraham.

- Spread abroad to the west, east, north, and south; and

- Bless all the families of the earth.

All of these promises have already been fulfilled in the 12 tribes of Jacob, who are the sons and daughters of Israel. No honest person can successfully argue that every family in the earth has not been blessed through advances made by descendants of Jews of the tribe of Judah. The life of Albert Einstein should bring closure to any such discussion. In the same manner, once the hidden peoples and nations of Joseph that are descended from the 10 northern tribes of Israel are discovered, the world will also have to acknowledge that the blessing of Joseph that is upon the descendants of his sons, Ephraim and Manasseh, have likewise already blessed all the families of the earth today. No word of God shall ever fail[10].

> **Genesis 28:16** And Jacob awaked out of his sleep, and he said, Surely the LORD is in this place; and I knew it not. **17** And he was afraid, and said, How dreadful is this place! this is none other but **the house of God**, and this is **the gate of heaven**. **18** And Jacob rose up early in the morning, and took the stone that he had put for his pillows, and set it up for a pillar, and poured oil upon the top of it. **19 And he called the name of that place Bethel** [the house of God]: but the name of that city was called Luz at the first.
>
> **20** And **Jacob vowed a vow**, saying, If God will be with me, and will keep me in this way that I go, and will give me bread to eat, and raiment to put on, **21** So that I come again to my father's

---

10 Isaiah 55:11.

house in peace; then shall the LORD be my God: **22 And this stone, which I have set for a pillar[11], shall be God's house: and of all that thou shalt give me I will surely give the tenth[12] unto thee**.

God Calls Jacob Back To Canaan

Jacob now spends the next twenty years in Syria being cheated by Rebekah's brother Laban, who was better at cheating than Jacob was when he stole Esau's birthright and blessing. Nevertheless, the blessing of Abraham that was upon Jacob and his life causes him to become extremely wealthy in spite of and in the midst of all of Laban's persecution. Jacob returns to Canaan with 2 wives, 2 concubines, 11 sons, and 1 on the way, at least 1 daughter, multiplied flocks, herds, servants and other forms of wealth.

Genesis 31:11 And the angel of God spake unto me in a dream, saying, Jacob: ... **13 I am the God of Bethel**, where thou anointedst the pillar, and where thou vowedst a vow unto me: now **arise**, **get thee out from this land**, and **return unto the land of thy kindred** [unto Canaan].

Jacob Reminds God Of His Promise

With the prospects of meeting his brother, Esau, after 20 years, Jacob prays to God in desperation and boldly reminds Him of the destiny that he has inherited as heir to God's blood-covenant with Abraham.

Genesis 32:11 Deliver me, I pray thee, from the hand of my brother, from the hand of Esau: for I fear him, lest he will come and smite me, and the mother with the children. **12 And thou saidst, I will surely do thee good, and <u>make thy seed as the sand of the sea</u>, which cannot be numbered for multitude**.

Jacob Is Israel

God changes Jacob's name to Israel once he is back in the land of Canaan.

Genesis 32:24 And Jacob was left alone; and there wrestled

---

11 The pillar stone of Jacob.
12 A tithe before the law of Moses.

a man with him until the breaking of the day. **25** And when he saw that he prevailed not against him, he touched the hollow of his thigh; and the hollow of Jacob's thigh was out of joint, as he wrestled with him. **26** And he said, Let me go, for the day breaketh. And he said, **I will not let thee go, except thou bless me**.

27 And he said unto him, What is thy name? And he said, Jacob. **28** And he said, <u>**Thy name shall be called no more Jacob, but Israel**</u>[13] **for as a prince hast thou power with God and with men, and hast prevailed**. **29** And Jacob asked him, and said, Tell me, I pray thee, thy name. And he said, Wherefore is it that thou dost ask after my name? **And he blessed him there**. **30** And Jacob called the name of the place **Peniel** [the face of God]: for I have seen God face to face, and my life is preserved.

"Israel" is used variously at least 2,229 times in the Old Testament. In each context, however, the meaning of the name *Israel* is not constant. At various times it stands for the 12 tribes of Jacob; the house of Jacob; house of Israel; and the nation of Israel before 10 tribes were separated, and after a remnant of Jews returned from Babylonian captivity. It also stands for the 10 tribes of the northern kingdom of Israel, both before and after the kingdom was divided: when the southern kingdom had become known as Judah. What is important to remember from **Genesis 32:27-28** is that the promises of the Abrahamic Covenant are resident in "all Israel" ... in all the heirs of Jacob—wherever located, and by whatever national or ethnic identity they are presently called. [See also footnotes #5 and 6, page 4.]

Israel: Find Joseph

ISRAEL RETURNS TO THE HOUSE OF GOD

Israel returns to Bethel where he made his vow to God before his journey to Syria and Laban's house.

> **Genesis 35:1** And **God said unto Jacob**, Arise, go up to Bethel, and dwell there: and make there an altar unto God, that appeared unto thee when thou fleddest from the face of Esau thy brother. **2** Then Jacob said unto his household, and to all that were

---

13 Jacob is transformed from being a "heel holder" or "supplanter" to *Israel*: *God prevails*. He now becomes a Prince with God; Soldier of God; God-wrestling, of God's Prince ... for as a Prince he now has power with God and with man, and has prevailed (Genesis 35:10).

with him, Put away the strange gods that are among you, and be clean, and change your garments: **3** And let us arise, and go up to Bethel; and I will make there an altar unto God, who answered me in the day of my distress, and was with me in the way which I went. **4** And they gave unto Jacob all the strange gods which were in their hand, and all their earrings which were in their ears; and Jacob hid them under the oak which was by Shechem.

5 And they journeyed: **and the terror of God was upon the cities that were round about them, and they did not pursue after the sons of Jacob.** **6** So Jacob came to **Luz**, which is in **the land of Canaan**, that is, **Bethel**, he and all the people that were with him. **7** And he built there an altar, and called the place El-bethel: because there God appeared unto him, when he fled from the face of his brother.

GOD CONFIRMS JACOB'S NAME IS ISRAEL

God confirms the change of Jacob's name to Israel.

Genesis 35:9 And God appeared unto Jacob again, when he came out of Padanaram, and blessed him. **10** And God said unto him, Thy name is Jacob: **thy name shall not be called any more Jacob, but <u>Israel shall be thy name</u>**: and <u>he called his name Israel</u>.

When Jacob and his sons, who become the 12 tribes of Israel, are back in the land of Canaan, God's Divine protection over Israel included protection from the wrath of both Laban and Esau. It also protected Israel from vengeance of any others in the land as a result of the slaying of the men of Shechem[14] by two of the sons of Jacob, Simeon and Levi, as vengeance for the rape of their sister, Dinah. How much more will God protect Israel today when Joseph's descendants return to the land, in the same manner as He did when Jacob and his sons returned to the land.

"When a man's ways please the LORD, he maketh even his enemies to be at peace with him." (Proverbs 16:7)

---

14 Genesis 34.

CHAPTER 6

A COMPANY OF NATIONS IN EPHRAIM

Those who believe in the inerrancy of God in His Hebrew Scriptures must, even reluctantly, accept the fact that Israel—the whole house of Israel / the whole house of Jacob—has become both **a nation** within the land and **a company of nations**[1] outside the land. This company of nations is to be found in the descendants of **Ephraim**, wherever they are today. These Ephraimic nations have grown into a great and numberless people. They have the **birthright** and **blessing of Joseph** upon them. The Holy Scriptures also reveal that this multitude of nations and people are both Hebrew and direct descendants of Abraham through Isaac and Jacob.

ISRAEL HAS BECOME A COMPANY OF NATIONS

These natural descendants of the 12 sons of Israel [Jacob] have become not only the nation of Israel but have also become a company of Ephraimic nations in wherever is the center or middle of the earth. Their kings, rulers, presidents, and prime ministers all have a family tree whose root is in Jacob.

> **Genesis 35:9 And God appeared unto Jacob again**, when he came out of Padanaram, and blessed him. **10** And God said unto him, Thy name is Jacob: **thy name shall not be called any more Jacob, but Israel shall be thy name**: and **he called his name Israel**.

> **11** And God said unto him, I am God Almighty: **be fruitful** and **multiply**; **a nation** [the nation of Israel] and **a company of nations** [the nations of Ephraim and Manasseh] shall be of thee, and **kings** shall come out of thy loins;

---

1 Genesis 48:16-19.

GOD GIVES THE LAND OF CANAAN TO ALL THE SEED OF JACOB

By accepting this simple and straightforward command and prophesy of Jehovah of Genesis 35:11 and 12, it necessarily follows that all of the human descendants of Israel [Jacob] down to the present generation have **the same right to occupy and prosper in the land of Canaan**, which is now the nation of Israel. God spoke these words as part of a perpetual, everlasting, and unchangeable Covenant that He swore in blood to Abraham.

Genesis 35:12 And **the <u>land</u>** which <u>**I gave Abraham and Isaac, to thee I will give it, and to thy seed after thee will I give the land**</u>. **13** And God went up from him in the place where he talked with him. **14** And **Jacob set up a pillar** in the place where he talked with him, even **a pillar of stone**: and he poured **a drink offering** thereon, and **he poured oil** thereon. **15** And Jacob called the name of the place where God spake with him, Bethel.

THE 12 SONS OF JACOB ARE THE 12 TRIBES OF ISRAEL

As in the Bible, I must continually reinforce the fact that the 12 sons of Jacob are the 12 tribes of Israel. Why? Because in tracing the history of God's Covenant people, we will find that vast majority of the descendants of these tribes have an acute case of historical amnesia—and they are not Jewish. Although they are not Jewish, however, they are still sons and daughters of Abraham, and heirs to the covenants of promise that God confirmed in Isaac, Jacob and Joseph.

Genesis 35:21 And **Israel** journeyed, and spread his tent beyond the tower of Edar. **22** And it came to pass, when Israel dwelt in that land, that Reuben went and lay with Bilhah his father's concubine: and Israel heard it [for this his birthright is given to Joseph (1 Chronicles 5:1-2, p. 66-67)]. **Now the sons of Jacob were twelve: 23** The **sons of Leah**; Reuben, Jacob's firstborn, and Simeon, and Levi, and Judah, and Issachar, and Zebulun: **24** The **sons of Rachel**; Joseph, and Benjamin: **25** And the **sons of Bilhah**, Rachel's handmaid; Dan, and Naphtali: **26** And the **sons of Zilpah**, Leah's handmaid; Gad, and Asher: **these are the sons of Jacob**, which were born to him in Padanaram.

27 And Jacob came unto Isaac his father unto Mamre, unto the city of Arbah, which is **Hebron**, where Abraham and Isaac so-journed. **28** And the **days of Isaac** were an hundred and fourscore years. **29** And Isaac gave up the ghost, and died, and was gathered unto his people, being old and full of days: and **his sons Esau and Jacob buried him**.

Esau Is Edom

Esau became known as the nation of Edom (the Edomites). His descendants unto this day have been adversaries to the progeny of Esau's brother Jacob. I wonder how many of today's Palestinians are actually Edomites?

Genesis 36:1 Now these are **the generations of Esau, who is Edom** [the Edomites]. **... 6** And Esau took his wives, and his sons, and his daughters, and all the persons of his house, and his cattle, and all his beasts, and all his substance, which he had got in the land of Canaan; and went into the country from the face of his brother Jacob. **7** For **their riches** were more than that they might dwell together; and the land wherein they were strangers could not bear them because of their cattle. **8 Thus dwelt Esau in mount Seir**[2]: **Esau is Edom**.

Israel Remains In The Land Of Canaan

Israel [Jacob] remains in the land of Canaan ... and returned to the land in 1948, in order to reestablish the nation of Israel.

Genesis 37:1 And **Jacob dwelt in the land** wherein his father was a stranger, **in the land of Canaan**.

Joseph Is Sold Into Egyptian Slavery

Joseph is the the 11th son of Israel [Jacob], by Rachael. His destiny leads him through a path of Egyptian slavery. Judah, the father of today's Jews, is the 4th son of Rachael's sister, Leah. Judah has equal responsibility with his brothers for selling Joseph into slavery. But, to Judah's credit, he speaks up in order to save Joseph's life.

Genesis 37:23 And it came to pass, when **Joseph** was come

---

2 A range of mountains in southern Jordan.

unto his brethren, that they stript Joseph out of his coat, his coat of many colours that was on him; **24** And they took him, and cast him into a pit: and the pit was empty, there was no water in it. **25** And they sat down to eat bread: and they lifted up their eyes and looked, and, behold, **a company of Ishmeelites** came from Gilead with their camels bearing spicery and balm and myrrh, going to carry it down to Egypt.

26 And **Judah** said unto his brethren, What profit is it if we slay our brother, and conceal his blood? **27** Come, and let us sell him to the **Ishmeelites**, and let not our hand be upon him; <u>**for he is our brother and our flesh**</u>. And his brethren were content. **28** Then there passed by **Midianites** merchantmen; and they drew and lifted up Joseph out of the pit, and **sold Joseph to the Ishmeelites for twenty pieces of silver: and they brought Joseph into Egypt** … **36** And the Midianites sold him into Egypt unto Potiphar, an officer of Pharaoh's, and captain of the guard.

JOSEPH PROSPERS IN SLAVERY

The blessing of Abraham on the life of Joseph causes him to prosper even as a slave in Egypt. God is equipping Joseph with the management skills he will need to fulfill his destiny as governor of Egypt.

Genesis 39:1 And Joseph was brought down to Egypt; and Potiphar, an officer of Pharaoh, captain of the guard, an Egyptian, bought him of the hands of the Ishmeelites, which had brought him down thither. **2** And **the LORD was with Joseph, and he was a prosperous man**; and he was in the house of his master the Egyptian. **3** And his master saw that the LORD was with him, and that the LORD made all that he did to prosper in his hand. **4** And Joseph found grace in his sight, and he served him: and he made him overseer over his house, and all that he had he put into his hand.

5 And it came to pass from the time that he had made him overseer in his house, and over all that he had, that **the LORD blessed the Egyptian's house for Joseph's sake; and the blessing of the LORD was upon all that he had in the house, and in the field**. **6** And he left all that he had in Joseph's hand; and he knew not ought he had, save the bread which he did eat. And Joseph was a goodly person, and well favoured ...

Genesis 39:20 And Joseph's master [Potiphar] took him, and put him into the prison[3], a place where the king's prisoners were bound: and he was there in the prison. **21 But the LORD was with Joseph, and shewed him mercy, and gave him favour in the sight of the keeper of the prison.** 22 And the keeper of the prison committed to Joseph's hand all the prisoners that were in the prison; and whatsoever they did there, he was the doer of it. **23** The keeper of the prison looked not to any thing that was under his hand; because the LORD was with him, and **that which he did, the LORD made it to prosper**.

JOSEPH IS HEBREW AND NOT JEWISH

The entire message of this book will be lost if one does not continually remember that Abraham, Isaac, Jacob, Joseph (and Moses) are Hebrews, and not Jews.

THE TESTIMONY OF POTIPHAR'S WIFE

Genesis 39:13 And it came to pass, when she [Potiphar's wife] saw that he [Joseph] had left his garment in her hand, and was fled forth, **14** That she called unto the men of her house, and spake unto them, saying, See, he [Potiphar] hath brought in **an Hebrew** unto us to mock us ... **17** And she spake unto him according to these words, saying, **The Hebrew servant**, which thou hast brought unto us, came in unto me to mock me ...

JOSEPH'S OWN TESTIMONY

Genesis 40:14 But think on me [Joseph speaks to Pharaoh's chief butler] when it shall be well with thee, and shew kindness, I pray thee, unto me, and make mention of me unto Pharaoh, and bring me out of this house: **15** For indeed **I was stolen away out of the land of the Hebrews** [Canaan]: and here also have I done nothing that they should put me into the dungeon.

---

3 Joseph was imprisoned after Potiphar's wife attempted to seduce him and then falsely accuses him when she is rejected...Joseph saying, "...[H]ow then can I do this great wickedness and sin against God?" (Genesis 39:9).

THE TESTIMONY OF THE CHIEF BUTLER

Genesis 41:9 Then spake the chief butler unto Pharaoh, saying, I do remember my faults this day: **10** Pharaoh was wroth with his servants, and put me in ward in the captain of the guard's house, both me and the chief baker: **11** And we dreamed a dream in one night, I and he; we dreamed each man according to the interpretation of his dream. **12** And there was there with us a young man, **an Hebrew, servant** to the captain of the guard; and we told him, and he interpreted to us our dreams; to each man according to his dream he did interpret.

TESTIMONY FROM JOSEPH'S HOME

Genesis 43:26 And when Joseph came home, they [his brothers] brought him the present which was in their hand into the house, and bowed themselves to him to the earth. ... **32** And they set on for him [Joseph] by himself, and for them by themselves, and for the Egyptians, which did eat with him, by themselves: **because the Egyptians might not eat bread with the Hebrews[4]; for that is an abomination unto the Egyptians.**

TWO SONS ARE BORN TO JOSEPH IN EGYPT

God gives Joseph two sons after he became prime minister of Egypt: Manasseh, his firstborn, and Ephraim.

Genesis 41:50 And **unto Joseph were born two sons** before the years of famine came, which Asenath the daughter of Potipherah priest of On bare unto him. **51** And Joseph called the name of the firstborn **Manasseh** [to forget]: For God, said he, hath made me forget all my toil, and all my father's house. **52** And the name of the second called he **Ephraim** [to be fruitful]: For God hath caused me to be fruitful in the land of my affliction.

JOSEPH LOVES AND FORGIVES HIS BROTHERS

Joseph shows great love and forgiveness to his brothers who sold him into slavery. In the hands of the Lord, a slave becomes a father to Pharaoh.

4 In Moses' struggles with Egypt, he refers to "the God of the Hebrews" five times (Exodus 3:18; 5:3; 7:16; 9:1 and 10:3).

Genesis 45:4 And Joseph said unto his brethren[5] ... **I am Joseph your brother**, whom ye sold into Egypt. **5** Now therefore be not grieved, nor angry with yourselves, that ye sold me hither: for **God did send me before you to preserve life. 6** For these two years hath the famine been in the land: and yet there are five years, in the which there shall neither be earing nor harvest. **7** And **God sent me before you to preserve you a posterity in the earth, and to save your lives by a great deliverance. 8** So now it was not you that sent me hither, but God: and **he hath made me a father to Pharaoh**, and **lord of all his house**, and **a ruler throughout all the land of Egypt.**

9 Haste ye, and go up to my father, and say unto him, Thus saith thy son Joseph, **God hath made me lord of all Egypt**: come down unto me, tarry not: **10** And thou shalt dwell in the land of Goshen, and thou shalt be near unto me, thou, and thy children, and thy children's children, and thy flocks, and thy herds, and all that thou hast.

God Makes Jacob The Nation Of Israel While In Egypt

After reunion with his brothers, Joseph sends for his entire family to come to Egypt to be sustained by him during the remaining 5 years of famine. God reconfirms the Abrahamic Covenant before Israel enters Egypt.

Genesis 46:1 And Israel took his journey with all that he had, and came to Beersheba, and offered sacrifices unto the God of his father Isaac. **2** And God spake unto Israel in the visions of the night, and said, **Jacob, Jacob.** And he said, Here am I. **3** And he said, **I am God, the God of thy father: fear not to go down into Egypt; for I will there make of thee a great nation**: **4** I will go down with thee into Egypt; and I will also surely bring thee up again: and Joseph shall put his hand upon thine eyes.

The Abrahamic Covenant Is Kept Alive In The House Of Jacob / Israel

The Abrahamic Covenant is alive to this day in the whole house of

---

5   Joseph speaks to his brothers after they had come the second time into Egypt to buy corn, because there was famine in the land of Canaan.

Jacob. This includes Israel, but has far greater application than to just the Jews of today's Israel. These **70 souls** represent **the whole House of Jacob / the whole house of Israel**. They are natural heirs to the Abrahamic Covenant.

> **Genesis 46:26 All the souls that came with Jacob into Egypt,** which came out of his loins, besides Jacob's sons' wives, all the souls were **threescore and six; 27** And the sons of Joseph, which were born him in Egypt, were two souls: all the souls of the <u>**house of Jacob**</u>, which came into Egypt, were **threescore and ten. 28** And he sent Judah before him unto Joseph, to direct his face unto Goshen; and they came into the land of Goshen.

ISRAEL MULTIPLIES IN THE LAND OF EGYPT

The **house of Israel** multiplies in the land of Egypt. This is a continuation of what God promised Abraham.

> **Genesis 47:27** And **Israel** dwelt in the land of Egypt, in the country of Goshen; and they had possessions therein, and grew, and **multiplied exceedingly. 28** And Jacob lived in the land of Egypt seventeen years: so the whole age of Jacob was an hundred forty and seven years.

ISRAEL MUST BE BURIED IN ISRAEL

Joseph swears to bury his father, Israel, back in the land of Canaan.

> **Genesis 47:29** And the time drew nigh that Israel must die: and he called his son Joseph, and said unto him, If now I have found grace in thy sight, put, I pray thee, thy hand under my thigh, and deal kindly and truly with me; bury me not, I pray thee, in Egypt: **30** But I will lie with my fathers, and **thou shalt carry me out of Egypt**, and bury me in their burying place. And he said, I will do as thou hast said. **31** And he said, Swear unto me. And **he sware unto him**. And Israel bowed himself upon the bed's head.

The bones of Abraham, Isaac, Israel / Jacob, Joseph, Sarah and Rebekah are all buried in the land of Canaan, which is now the modern day state of Israel ... buried on land now proposed as a Palestinian state.

CHAPTER 7

EPHRAIM AND MANASSEH ARE ISRAEL

All of the descendants of Ephraim and Manasseh come from the house of Jacob that make up **the two "Israels"**—the Israel of Jacob, and the Israel of Judah. Stated differently, Jacob is Israel and Israel [Jacob's new name] is Israel; and Judah [the land and the Hebrew people of today's Israel] is also Israel. There is also the ecclesiastical Israel which God created, and the political Israel in which almost 20% of its citizens are Arabs: who are **not heirs** to the Abrahamic Covenant.

The 12 tribes of Jacob are the 12 tribes descended from their father, Israel. The multitude of the Hebrew nations and people of Ephraim—wherever they are—are in open view of all the world. But, they are closed to the knowledge of their Hebrew heritage: as is the world. This vast hidden Israel is as much a part of the historical Israel as are the Jewish Hebrews that occupy the land today. They are brothers separated by disobedience to the commandments of the God that first spoke to Abraham.

EPHRAIM AND MANASSEH BELONG TO ISRAEL

At no time in history, since the 70 souls of the house of Jacob emigrated to Egypt, have Jews from the tribe of Judah been a multitude of people that are numberless by today's standards.

Genesis 48:1 And it came to pass after these things, that one told **Joseph**, Behold, thy father is sick: and he took with him **his two sons, Manasseh** and **Ephraim**. 2 And one told **Jacob**, and said, Behold, thy son Joseph cometh unto thee: and **Israel** strengthened himself, and sat upon the bed. 3 And **Jacob said unto Joseph, God Almighty** appeared unto me at Luz [Bethel] in the land of Canaan, and **blessed me, 4** And said unto me, Behold, **I will make thee fruitful,** and **multiply thee,** and **I will make of thee a multitude of people**; and **will give this land to thy seed**

after thee **for an everlasting possession**.

5 And now **thy two sons, Ephraim** and **Manasseh**, which were born unto thee in the land of Egypt before I came unto thee into Egypt, **are mine**; as **Reuben** and **Simeon** [Jacob's first two sons], **they shall be mine**. **6 And thy issue,** which thou begettest after them, shall be thine, and **shall be called after the name of their brethren in their inheritance** [called after the name of Israel].

All of the descendants of Ephraim and Manasseh belong to Israel, who gives his grandsons by Joseph the same status in their **inheritance in God's Covenant with Abraham for the blessing and the land** as he does for his own natural sons, Reuben and Simeon.

Genesis 48:8 And **Israel beheld Joseph's sons**, and said, Who are these? **9** And Joseph said unto his father, They are my sons, whom God hath given me in this place. And he said, Bring them, I pray thee, unto me, and **I will bless them**. **10** Now the eyes of Israel were dim for age, so that he could not see. And he brought them near unto him; and he kissed them, and embraced them. **11** And Israel said unto Joseph, I had not thought to see thy face: and, lo, God hath shewed me also thy seed. **12** And Joseph brought them out from between his knees, and he bowed himself with his face to the earth. **13** And Joseph took them both, **Ephraim in his right hand toward Israel's left hand, and Manasseh in his left hand toward Israel's right hand,** and brought them near unto him.

EPHRAIM RECEIVES THE BIRTHRIGHT AND THE BLESSING

Joseph receives the blessing of the firstborn through his sons, instead of Reuben[1], who lost it by lying with Bilhah, his father's concubine[2].

Genesis 48:14 And Israel [Jacob] stretched out his right hand, and laid it upon **Ephraim's head**, who was **the younger**, and his left hand upon **Manasseh's head**, guiding his hands wittingly; for **Manasseh was the firstborn**. **15** And **he blessed Joseph**, and said, God, before whom my fathers Abraham and Isaac did walk, the God which fed me all my life long unto this day ...

---

1   Genesis 49:4 and 26; 1 Chronicles 5:1-2.
2   Genesis 25:21.
62

Joseph Is A Multitude In The Middle Of The Earth

Ephraim and Manasseh are of Israel. Over the millennia they have become a multitude in the middle of the earth.

> **Genesis 48:16** The **Angel which redeemed me** [a reference to God] from all evil, **bless the lads**; and **let my name be named on them**, and **the name of my fathers Abraham and Isaac**; and **let them grow into a multitude³ in the midst⁴ of the earth**.

- Both **Ephraim** and **Manasseh** received the **blessing of Israel on Joseph.**

- **Ephraim** and **Manasseh** are **called by the name of Israel**.

- **Ephraim** and **Manasseh**—even to this day—are **sons of Abraham** and **Isaac**, heirs to the Abrahamic Covenant.

- **Ephraim** and **Manasseh** have become **a multitude of people** in the **middle of the earth.**

What does "midst or middle of the earth" mean? How about ... land mass in reference to continents, longitude, latitude, or some other measure? Unlocking this mystery will also unlock the mystery of where Ephraim and Manasseh are today.

Manasseh Has Become A Great People

> **Genesis 48:17** And when Joseph saw that his father laid his right hand upon the head of Ephraim, it displeased him: and he held up his father's hand, to remove it from Ephraim's head unto **Manasseh's** head. **18** And Joseph said unto his father, Not so, my father: for this is **the firstborn** [Manasseh]; put thy right hand upon his head. **19(a)** And his father refused, and said, I know it, my son, I know it: **he** [Manasseh] also **shall become a people**, and **he also shall be great**: ...

- **Manasseh** has become **a great people.**

---

3 Heb.. _rob_, abundance, greatness, multitude.

4 Heb., _qereb_, midst, among, inner part, middle; in the midst, among, from among (of a number of persons).

Ephraim Has Become A Multitude Of Nations

Genesis 48:19(b) ... but truly **his younger brother** [Ephraim] **shall be greater than he**, and <u>**his seed shall become a**</u> <u>**multitude**[5] **of nations**[6]</u>. 20 And **he blessed them** that day, saying, **In thee shall Israel bless**, saying, God make thee as Ephraim and as Manasseh: and **he set Ephraim before Manasseh**.

- ■ Although **Manasseh** has become **a great multitude of people** in the middle of the earth, **Ephraim** has become greater than **Manasseh**.

- ■ The **seed of Ephraim** has become **a multitude of both people and nations**.

- ■ The **fulfillment** of God's promises given to Ephraim will come before Manasseh's, as well as be greater in magnitude.

- ■ **Nowhere** has this prophecy been fulfilled or can be fulfilled solely in the Jewish descendants of the tribe of Judah.

Joseph Has Received The Double Portion

Genesis 48:21 And **Israel said unto Joseph**, Behold, I die: but **God shall** be with you, and **bring you again unto the land of your fathers**. 22 Moreover **I have given to thee one portion above thy brethren**, which I took out of the hand of the Amorite with my sword and with my bow.

Joseph's portion in the blessing and in the land is greater than his brothers, as both Ephraim and Manasseh inherited their own major plots of land[7] in Israel. This is in furtherance of the promises God gave to Abraham and Sarah that they would be the father and mother of nations (Genesis 17:4-6 and 16); and a company of nations (Genesis 35:11). God is speaking here of more than just the nation of Israel; and these prophesies have no reference to Ishmael or Esau because the promises of the Abrahamic Covenant flow solely through the descendants of Isaac and Jacob.

---

5   Heb., _melo_, fullness, that which fills, mass, multitude ... as the dust of the earth, stars of heaven, and sand of the sea.

6   Heb., _gowy_ (_goyim_), nation, people, nations.

7   See map on page 34.

CHAPTER 8

ISRAEL SPEAKS OF THE LAST DAYS

Israel [Jacob], having blessed and uttered amazing prophecies over the sons of Joseph—Manasseh and Ephraim—now, before his death gathers together all of his sons and pronounces a word of blessing (and sometimes cursing) over their destinies in the last days before the coming of the Messiah. We will consider only what the patriarch spoke over Judah and Joseph.

ISRAEL PROPHESIES OF THE LAST DAYS

One of the most important Bible facts to remember about Israel is that as a political entity it is … "not to be reckoned[1] among the nations". Israel is the only nation upon the earth whose history is recorded in advance. It is God's time clock for the nations of the world. Israel is above the daily politics of the world, and cannot be chastised by the nations of the world when its people are in the center of God's will for the nation. The Lord spent the last half of the 20th century reestablishing the nation of Israel, and the Jewish state that **He disbursed** in 70 CE. What He is doing with Israel in the 21st century is to reestablish the Hebrew nation of 12 tribes that was a unified nation during the reigns of David and Solomon. This reunification will reach its fulfillment as the prophecy of Ezekiel 37 comes to pass.

> **Genesis 49:1** And **Jacob called unto his sons**, and said, Gather yourselves together, that I may tell you **that which shall befall you in the last days**. **2** Gather yourselves together, and hear, **ye sons of Jacob**; and hearken unto **Israel** your father.

THE SCEPTRE SHALL REMAIN WITH JUDAH

The right to rule or govern Israel shall remain with Judah. The Messiah

---

1   Numbers 23:9…_Reckon_: to account, count, number, esteem, impute, charge, judge, devise, or plan.

shall also come from the tribe of Judah.

Genesis 49:8 Judah, thou art he whom thy brethren shall praise: thy hand shall be in the neck of thine enemies; thy father's children shall bow down before thee ... 10 <u>The sceptre shall not depart from Judah</u> [the right to rule—the throne—is given to Judah], **nor a lawgiver from between his feet, <u>until Shiloh come</u>**; and **unto him shall the gathering of the people be.**

God's Promises To Joseph Are Fulfilled In Ephraim And Manasseh

Israel's blessing is given to Joseph; but in the last days it is to be fulfilled in the descendants of Ephraim and Manasseh.

Genesis 49:22 Joseph is **a fruitful bough**, even a fruitful bough by a well; whose branches run over the wall: **23** The archers [Joseph's brothers] have sorely grieved him, and shot at him, and hated him: **24** But his bow abode in strength, and the arms of his hands were made strong by the hands of the mighty God of Jacob; (from thence is the shepherd, the stone of Israel:)

Joseph Receives The Birthright And The Blessing

Joseph receives both the **birthright** and the **blessing of Abraham.**

Genesis 49:25 Even by the God of thy father, who shall help thee; and by **the Almighty, who shall bless thee with blessings of heaven above, blessings of the deep** that lieth under, blessings of the breasts, and of the womb: **26** <u>The blessings of thy father have prevailed</u> above the blessings of my progenitors[2] unto the utmost bound of the everlasting hills: <u>they shall be on the head of Joseph</u>, and <u>on the crown of the head</u> of him that was separate from his brethren. [See discussion of this verse and prophecy on pages 74-75.]

1 Chronicles 5:1 Now the sons of Reuben the firstborn of Israel, (for he was the firstborn; but, forasmuch as he defiled his father's

---

2 What Israel is saying to Joseph is this: "The blessings of your father [on you] are greater than the blessing of my forefathers [Abraham and Isaac] on me; and are as lasting as the utmost boundaries of the eternal hills."

bed, **his birthright** was **given unto the sons of Joseph** the son of Israel: and the genealogy is not to be reckoned after the birthright. 2 For **Judah prevailed** above his brethren, and **of him came the chief ruler** [the Messiah]; but **the birthright was Joseph's**:)

Like Jacob, Joseph through his sons has received both the **birthright** and the **blessing of Israel**: which includes all of the promises that God made to Abraham, Isaac, Israel, Sarah and Rebekah. In any search for Joseph, these attributes of his birthright are still to be found in the descendants of his nations and people.

- Blessings of heaven above include well watered lands.

- Blessings of the deep strongly suggest that Joseph's descendants will become fishing and shipping nations.

- Blessings of the breasts and the womb indicate a multitude of offspring in these nations.

- Blessings from the land encompass bountiful crops, minerals, oil and gas.

- Blessing in the governing of nations must accompany all of the above.

THE BLESSINGS OF ISRAEL IS UPON ALL 12 TRIBES

These are the blessings of Israel over His sons, who will grow into the **12 tribes** of the **whole house of Jacob**, and the nation of Israel.

> **Genesis 49:28** All these are **the twelve tribes of Israel**: and this is it that their father spake unto them, and **blessed them; every one according to his blessing he blessed them.**

ISRAEL'S BONES POSSESS THE LAND

All of the blessings and promises of the Abrahamic Covenant are buried with Israel [Jacob] in the land of Israel ... in Hebron, which is proposed to become part of the territory of a new Palestinian state. Yet, each act of interment of a patriarch with the promises of God is a further act of possession by Israel in the land of these same promises.

Genesis 49:29 And he [Israel] charged them, and said unto them, I am to be gathered unto my people: bury me with my fathers in the cave that is in the field of Ephron the Hittite, **30** In the cave that is in the **field of Machpelah**, which is before Mamre, **in the land of Canaan, which Abraham bought** with the field of Ephron the Hittite for a possession of a burying place [in Hebron].

31 There they buried **Abraham** and **Sarah** his wife; there they buried **Isaac** and **Rebekah** his wife; and there I buried **Leah. 32** The purchase of the field and of the cave that is therein was from the children of Heth. **33** And when Jacob had made an end of commanding his sons, he gathered up his feet into the bed, and yielded up the ghost, and was gathered unto his people.

Genesis 50:4 And when the days of his [Jacob's] mourning were past, Joseph spake unto the house of Pharaoh, saying, If now I have found grace in your eyes, speak, I pray you, in the ears of Pharaoh, saying, **5 My father made me swear, saying, Lo, I die: in my grave which I have digged for me in the <u>land of Canaan</u>, there shalt thou bury me. Now therefore let me go up, I pray thee, and bury my father, and I will come again. 6** And Pharaoh said, Go up, and bury thy father, according as he made thee swear.

7 And Joseph went up to bury his father: and with him went up all the servants of Pharaoh, the elders of his house, and all the elders of the land of Egypt, **8** And **all the house of Joseph**, and his brethren, and his father's house: only their little ones, and their flocks, and their herds, they left in the land of Goshen.

9 And there went up with him both chariots and horsemen: and it was a very great company. **10** And they came to the threshing floor of Atad, which is beyond Jordan, and there they mourned with a great and very sore lamentation: and he made a mourning for his father seven days. **11** And when the inhabitants of the land, the Canaanites, saw the mourning in the floor of Atad, they said, This is a grievous mourning to the Egyptians: wherefore the name of it was called Abelmizraim, which is beyond Jordan.

12 And his sons did unto him according as he commanded them: **13** For his sons carried him into the **land of Canaan**, and buried him in the cave of the **field of Machpelah**, which Abraham bought with the field for a possession of a burying place of Ephron the Hittite, before Mamre. **14** And Joseph returned into Egypt, he, and his brethren, and all that went up with him to bury his father, after he had buried his father.

JOSEPH'S BONES POSSESS THE LAND

Joseph was also buried in the land of Canaan, in Hebron.

Genesis 50:22 And Joseph dwelt in Egypt, he, and his father's house: and Joseph lived an hundred and ten years. **23** And Joseph saw Ephraim's children of the third generation: the children also of Machir the son of Manasseh were brought up upon Joseph's knees. **24** And Joseph said unto his brethren, I die: and **God will surely visit you, and bring you out of this land unto the land which he sware to Abraham, to Isaac, and to Jacob**.

25 And Joseph took an oath of the children of Israel, saying, God will surely visit you, and ye shall **carry up my bones** from hence. **26** So Joseph died, being an hundred and ten years old: and they embalmed him, and he was put in a coffin in Egypt.

Exodus 13:19 And Moses took the **bones of Joseph** with him: for he had straitly sworn the children of Israel, saying, God will surely visit you; and ye shall carry up my bones away hence with you.

Joshua 24:32 And the **bones of Joseph**, which the children of Israel brought up out of Egypt, buried they in Shechem, in a parcel of ground which Jacob bought of the sons of Hamor the father of **Shechem** for an hundred pieces of silver: and it **became the inheritance of the children of Joseph**.

Shechem, today's Nābulus, is the place in the "crown of Joseph" where much wealth is hidden for Joseph and Israel … or the Palestinians, if Israel gives away its inheritance. [See pg. 75.]

Moses Reminds God Of His Blood-Sworn Promises To Abraham

While Moses is on Mount Sinai for 40 days receiving the Ten Commandments, his people begin to make their own gods. Moses boldly intercedes for the people by reminding God of what He has promised to Abraham, Isaac and Israel concerning them. During their dialogue God gives the entire nation of Israel to Moses; but Moses has the wisdom to give Israel and its people right back to God.

Exodus 32:7 And the LORD said unto Moses, Go, get thee down; for **thy people**, which thou broughtest out of the land of Egypt, have corrupted themselves: **8** They have ... made them a molten calf, and have worshipped it ... **11** And Moses besought the LORD his God, and said, LORD, why doth thy wrath wax hot against **thy people**, which thou hast brought forth out of the land of Egypt with great power, and with a mighty hand? ...

13 Remember Abraham, Isaac, and **Israel**, thy servants, to whom **thou swarest by thine own self**, and saidst unto them, **I will multiply your seed as the stars of heaven**, and **all this land** that I have spoken of **will I give unto your seed**, and they shall **inherit it for ever**. **14** And the LORD repented of the evil which he thought to do unto **his people**.

The unchangeable God of heaven and earth recognizes no Palestinian right to the land that He gave to Israel. *Forever*, with God, means *forever*.

Even The Fourth Part Of Israel Cannot Be Numbered

Not even one-fourth of Israel can be counted because of its multitude of people—unto this day—because **most of Israel's heirs do not reside in Israel**, and **neither are they Jewish**. This conclusion is inevitable by tracing what God has promised in His Word to Abraham and to his descendants.

Numbers 23:8 How shall I curse [the prophet Balaam is speaking], whom God hath not cursed? or how shall I defy, whom the LORD hath not defied? **9** For from the top of the rocks I see him, and from the hills I behold him: lo, **the people shall dwell alone, and shall not be reckoned among the nations**. **10 Who can**

count the dust of Jacob, and the number of the fourth part of Israel?

ISRAEL HAS BECOME A THOUSAND TIMES MORE THAN THE STARS

Moses, after 40 years in the wilderness, notes that the people of Israel have grown into a multitude as numerous as the stars of heaven. Then to honor the LORD he multiplies even the stars of heaven a thousand times greater. These promises simply cannot be fulfilled in the present nor historical Jewish nation of Israel, because there have never been more Jews upon the earth than could be counted. A literal fulfillment of this multitudes of descendants that God promised Abraham is to be found solely in the promises that God spoke over Joseph and his son Ephraim. This is because these covenants of promise to Abraham and Israel are to flow exclusively through Isaac, Jacob and Joseph; and not Ishmael, Esau or even Judah.

> **Deuteronomy 1:6** The LORD our God spake unto us in Horeb, saying, Ye have dwelt long enough in this mount: **7** Turn you, and take your journey, and go to the mount of the Amorites, and unto all the places nigh thereunto, in the plain, in the hills, and in the vale, and in the south, and by the sea side, to the land of the Canaanites, and unto Lebanon, **unto the great river, the river Euphrates**. **8** Behold, I have set the land before you: **go in and possess the land which the LORD sware unto your fathers, Abraham, Isaac, and Jacob, to give unto them and to their seed after them**.

The prophet Moses declares exceeding increase over Israel's people.

> **Deuteronomy 1:9** And I [Moses] spake unto you at that time, saying, I am not able to bear you myself alone: **10** The LORD your God hath multiplied you, and, behold, **ye are this day as the stars of heaven for multitude**. **11** (The LORD God of your fathers **make you a thousand times so many more as ye are**, and bless you, as he hath promised you!)

> **Deuteronomy 10:11** And the LORD said unto me, Arise, take thy journey before the people, that they may go in and possess the land, which I sware unto their fathers to give unto them. ... **22 Thy fathers went down into Egypt with threescore and ten per-**

sons; and **now the LORD thy God hath made thee as the stars of heaven for multitude**.

Although these and several other passages of Scripture refer to the number of people of Israel as the "stars of heaven" or "sand of the sea", who during the days of Moses or the prophets could have conceived of an earth with over 6 billion people? Which of the patriarchs could have imagined the ever-expanding galaxies and the multiplied billions of stars that the LORD knew about when He gave record to the "hidden Israel" that is alive somewhere today ... which the prophet Moses multiplied by a thousand?

DISOBEDIENCE HAS CAUSED THE STARS OF JUDAH TO BECOME FEW IN NUMBER

Due to Israel's disobedience to the commandments and statutes of God, even the stars of heaven have become few in number. This prophecy of Moses, in the thousands of years since he spoke it, has been realized in the tribe of Judah and its Jewish people: with only between 13 and 14 million Jews alive in the world today. But Joseph, Ephraim, and Manasseh have another set of promises from God. **It is Joseph, then, and not Judah that is the "Israel" that has become as the dust of the earth, stars of heaven, and sand of the sea**.

> **Deuteronomy 28:58 If thou wilt not** observe to do all the words of this law that are written in this book, that thou mayest fear this glorious and fearful name, **THE LORD THY GOD** ... 62 And **ye shall be left few** in number, whereas **ye were as the stars of heaven** for multitude; because thou wouldest not obey the voice of the LORD thy God. 63 And it shall come to pass, that as the LORD rejoiced over you to do you good, and to multiply you; so the LORD will rejoice over you to destroy you, and to bring you to nought; and **ye shall be plucked from off the land whither thou goest to possess it**.

While Satan and the forces of darkness have over the millennia concentrated on destroying Judah and its Jewish population, Joseph with his hidden identity has quietly populated the entire earth. In **Deuteronomy 33:17**, the LORD will prophesy that Joseph will indeed "push the people" of Israel to the ends of the earth. Judah during this same period has also been scattered across the entire earth, but has never lost his identity as being Hebrew and Jewish, as even non-observant Jews at least give lip service to Moses and the Torah (the first 5 books of the Bible written by Moses).

> **Deuteronomy 28:64** And <u>the LORD shall scatter thee among all people</u> [all 12 tribes], <u>from the one end of the earth even unto the other</u>; and <u>there thou shalt serve other gods</u>, which neither thou nor thy fathers have known, even wood and stone.

The multitudes of Joseph and Ephraim not only have lost their identity as Hebrews, but as yet do not know the God of Abraham.

> **Deuteronomy 28:65** And among these nations shalt thou find no ease, neither shall the sole of thy foot have rest: but the LORD shall give thee there a trembling heart, and failing of eyes, and sorrow of mind: **66** And thy life shall hang in doubt before thee; and thou shalt fear day and night, and shalt have none assurance of thy life: ... **68** And the **LORD shall bring thee into Egypt[3] again** with ships, by the way whereof I spake unto thee, Thou shalt see it no more again: and there ye shall be sold unto your enemies for bondmen and bondwomen, and no man shall buy you.

The prophecy in this paragraph has certainly been true for Jews; but Joseph has been hidden because of the blessing spoken over him by Jacob.

MOSES COMMANDS ONLY THE BEST FOR JOSEPH

Before he dies, Moses speaks his **blessing** over the 12 tribes of Israel.

> **Deuteronomy 33:1** And this is the blessing, wherewith Moses the man of God **blessed the children of Israel** before his death. **2** And he said, The LORD came from Sinai, and rose up from Seir unto them; he shined forth from mount Paran, and he came with ten thousands of saints: from his right hand went a fiery law for them. **3** Yea, he loved the people; all his saints are in thy hand: and they sat down at thy feet; every one shall receive of thy words. **4** Moses commanded us a law, even the inheritance of the **congrega-**

---

3 By the time of the Ptolemy kingdom in Egypt which succeeded the reign of Alexander the Great, a multitude of non-Hebrew speaking Jews were so flourishing in Egypt that the Septuagint was commissioned as a translation into Greek of the Tanaka (Hebrew Old Testament Scriptures) for the great library of Alexandria, so that Jews would be able to read Moses, the Psalms, and the Prophets.

tion of Jacob. 5 And he was king in Jeshurun[4], when the heads of **the people** and **the tribes of Israel** were gathered together …

13 And **of Joseph** he said, **Blessed** of the LORD **be his land**, for the **precious things** of heaven, for the dew, and for the deep that coucheth [lies or rests] beneath, 14 And for the **precious fruits** brought forth by the sun, and for the **precious things** put forth by the moon, 15 And for the **chief things** of the ancient mountains, and for the **precious things** of the lasting hills, 16 And for the **precious things** of the earth and fulness thereof, and for the **good will** of him that dwelt in the bush:

When we search for the descendants of Joseph and Ephraim, we must look for the populations of nations in the center or midst of the earth with:

- **Blessed lands** to live in.

- The **precious things** of heaven such as generous rainfall, natural resources, and all other forms of wealth.

- The **dew**, **water**, and all forms of natural resources hidden in the ground: such as oil and gas.

- The **precious fruits** from the sun not only in crops but, perhaps, solar energy, etc.

- The **precious things** put forth by the moon [favorable tides].

- The **chief things** of the ancient mountains such as gold, silver, coal, and other mineral wealth.

- The **precious things** of the everlasting hills

- The **precious things** of the earth and its fullness; and

- The **good will** of him that dwelt in the bush, indicating they will colonize nations and people.

THERE IS IMMENSE WEALTH HIDDEN IN THE CROWN OF JOSEPH

There is something immensely wealthy hidden in the land that makes

4 Heb. Yeshruwn, a symbolic name for Israel, meaning "the upright one".

up the "crown" on the "head of Joseph".

> **Genesis 49:26 ... the blessings ... they shall be on the head of Joseph**, and on **the crown of the head** of him that was separate from his brethren [the blessing of Israel upon Joseph:].

> **Deuteronomy 33:16b Let the blessing come upon the head of Joseph**, and **upon the top of the head** of him that was separated from his brethren [compare the blessing of Moses upon Joseph].

The blessing of both Israel and Moses upon Joseph and his sons both speak of something very noteworthy coming upon the "head of Joseph", and upon the "crown of the head" or "top of the head" of Joseph. In a good map of the parcels of land that Joshua gave to the tribes of Israel, the parcel that was given to Ephraim actually looks like the profile of a king's head with a crown upon it. The area of the crown is adjacent to the city of Nābulus [biblical Shechem] and Mount Ebal—right in the middle of the area designated for a proposed Palestinian state. Israel, as of this writing, may give away this land if its national recognition and security demands were met by the Palestinians.

As both Jacob and Moses prophesied by the foreknowledge of the Spirit of God, there is an immense blessing that is reserved for Joseph and the Israel of today in that area of the crown of his head—be it oil, gas, gold or something else that God has hidden for His nation's use in the latter days.

> *"Therefore, I prophesy by the same Spirit of God that the economy of whatever nation owns this land whenever this blessing manifests will explode like a financial mushroom cloud of an Atomic Money Machine."*

JOSEPH HAS POPULATED THE ENTIRE EARTH

Moses is not through with his **blessing upon Joseph** and his sons. The nations of both Ephraim and Manasseh, by the spirit of prophecy, have scattered or colonized "the people" of Israel to the ends of the earth. The multitude of nations coming from Ephraim have become as the dust of the earth, stars of heaven, and sand of the sea; and Manasseh has also become a great multitude of people, but smaller than Ephraim.

Deuteronomy 33:17 His [Joseph's] glory is like the firstling of his bullock, and **his horns** are like **the horns of unicorns** [Ephraim and Manasseh shall be strong nations]: with them [with the horns of their strength] **he** [Joseph] **shall push the people together to the ends of the earth**: and they are the **ten thousands of Ephraim**, and they are the **thousands of Manasseh**.

The blessing that Moses spoke over Joseph is that he, through his sons Ephraim and Manasseh, would "push the people" to the ends of the earth ... what people?... God's people? ... all people[5]??? Moses defines "the people" as the 12 tribes of Israel standing before him. To "push" means "to thrust forward", and implies the use of war. The "ends of the earth" means the whole of the earth, as opposed to a part. In the Hebrew text it is a term of completeness or finality. The end of the earth in context, then, would also have to include the "isles of the Gentiles[6]"; and the "isles of the sea[7]".

How did "the people" get to the "ends of the earth"—on foot, by ship, by swimming, covered wagon, airplane, or some other means? And what did "the people" do when they got to the "ends of the earth"? Did they turn around and come back? Did they conquer peoples, establish colonies and remain? Or did they do something else? **I have a question**: What "people", nation, and "company of nations" in the "middle of the earth" can fit this prophecy—and also has great material prosperity as a result of having taken Israel to the ends of the earth?

Therefore, by the Spirit of God and simple deduction, Ephraim and the 10 tribes of Israel not only are scattered throughout the earth, but in so doing they have increased in number to become as the dust of the earth, stars of heaven, and sand of the sea. They have already blessed every family on the earth with the spin-offs of their material prosperity. God has thus already fulfilled His promises of **Genesis 12:1-3** to Abraham **and his heirs through Isaac, Jacob and Joseph**—and has done it with a people who, through the generations, have lost their Hebrew identity. Amazing!

Israel: Find Joseph

---

5   C/p. Isaiah 41:1.
6   Genesis 10:5.
7   Ester 10:1; Psalms 97:1; Isaiah 24:15; 41:1 and 4; 49:1; 51:5; 60:9; Jeremiah 22:25; 31:10 and 11.

CHAPTER 9

THE BIRTHRIGHT AND THE BLESSING

It is the purpose of this book to establish through the writings of the Hebrew prophets that the nation of Israel is in a prophetic season in which her security and very survival requires her people and her leaders to determine where the descendants of Joseph through time have come to live. Israel must determine who their nations have become in order for there to be a reuniting of the Jewish Hebrews of Israel with the non-Jewish Hebrews hidden in the nations of Joseph and Ephraim. Stated differently, **it is time on God's prophetic clock for Joseph and Ephraim to be joined with Judah** in fulfillment of **Ezekiel 37:15-22**.

Central to the revelation of this book is an understanding that the Hebrew prophets of the Bible clearly reveal that:

- The **birthright** and the **blessing** of Abraham are the birthright and the blessing of Israel. Both were given by Jehovah to Joseph, and not to Judah.

- The greater manifestation of Joseph's birthright and blessing is to be found in the descendants of Ephraim, rather than Manasseh.

- **Ephraim** has become **a company of nations**[1] in the **middle of the earth**: the location of which we must discover.

- **Ephraim** has also become **a numberless multitude of people**[2] in the center of the earth, whose people have the characteristics of dust, stars and sand.

- **Manasseh**, too, has become **a great people**, also in the center

---

1 Genesis 35:11 and 48:19.
2 Genesis 48:4.

of the earth.

■ The future generations of Abraham have possessed or will **possess the gate³** of their enemies.

■ The **ten thousands** of Ephraim and **thousands** of Manasseh have **pushed the people** [of Israel] to the **ends of the earth.**

■ It is time on God's prophetic calendar to join the **stick⁴ of Joseph** with the **stick of Judah**. These two sticks shall become one nation upon the mountains of Israel, in the literal fulfillment of the prophesy of **Ezekiel 37:15-22**.

■ The stick of Joseph is to be found in the hand of Ephraim.

■ All of the descendants of the twelve tribes of Israel [Jacob] have the same right to occupy the land of Israel.

■ God has not promised a "Jewish state" to the tribe of Judah, nor to the modern nation of Israel. It is time (prophetically speaking) for the Jewish political and religious leadership, as well as the people of Israel, and Jews around the world, to recognize that they are a Hebrew nation; and to invest the time and resources necessary to locate the whereabouts of the descendants of Ephraim and Manasseh, and invite them back into their land—back into Israel.

■ The descendants of Ephraim that are alive in the world today vastly outnumber the entire population of Israel, including the population of the proposed Palestinian state. They also outnumber all Arab nations in the region put together.

■ To invite this multitude of Hebrew brethren back into the land would be in fulfillment of the numerous Scriptures that reference the regathering of the **remnant of Israel**, that are repeatedly prophesied by the Hebrew prophets of the Old Testament.

---

3 _Gate_ or _gateways_; entrances into or exiting from enemy nations ... passageways or ports (Genesis 22:17 and 24:60). I cannot find fulfillment of this promise anywhere in the history of the tribe of Judah, although I acknowledge that a very weak case could be made for the fulfillment of this promise during the reign of David and Solomon.

4 _Stick_: tree, wood, timber, stock, plank, stalk, stick, gallows. The Spirit of God by use of this word is indicating that all of the branches of Israel have the same root.

- To return Israel to the revealed will of God for His nation as is revealed in His written Word is no threat to the viability of Israel as a Hebrew nation: for the sceptre—the right to rule—was not given to Joseph or to his descendants, but is to remain with Judah, the Jews, until Shiloh (the Messiah) comes[5].

I thank God for the Jewish **remnant** that has returned to the land of Israel since 1948, in fulfillment of Bible prophecy. But, most of the sons of Jacob in the world today have lost their Hebrew identity, and must re-discover their heritage and inheritance as the natural descendants of Abraham. God does not intend nor desire this re-awakening to be a process of adversaries between the **Judah that is seen** in the land and the **Israel that is hidden** and remains scattered throughout the earth. To avoid this potential rivalry between siblings, the necessary call and summons for Joseph to return to the land, therefore, should be initiated by the Jewish populations of Israel and the world.

Like it or not, from one source or another, Joseph will eventually re-discover who he is and will reclaim his inheritance in the land of Israel. We know this with absolute certainty because **Israel's history is recorded in advance of its occurrence**; and no word of God will ever fail (Isaiah 55:11). When God says through His prophet that the stick of Joseph shall be joined with Judah to become one nation again on the mountains of Israel (Ezekiel 37:16-17), then this is a prophecy that is pre-Messianic and must and will be fulfilled now in this time.

If Jews do not begin to seek out and discover where their Hebrew brethren are in the world today, then God will wake up Joseph and Ephraim from another source; and they, as an adversary, will still demand their birthright in the land—because the **Messiah cannot come except** the dry bones of Ezekiel 37 wake up, live, and become one nation again on the West Bank mountains of Israel. Then, and only when Joseph has returned to the land, will **the third temple be rebuilt**. This is also a prerequisite to the Messiah's appearing (Ezekiel 37:26-27).

PEACE AND PROSPERITY WILL FOLLOW JOSEPH TO THE LAND

The Bible records the struggles between Jacob and Esau partly to give us an appreciation as to how vitally important and eternally valuable both the **birthright** and the **blessing** are to its recipient. God has bestowed his

5 Genesis 49:10.

blessing and honor on the twelve tribes of Israel in spite of Jacob's trickery. Esau was Isaac's firstborn and should have received the blessing of his father. Once Isaac had spoken his blessing over Jacob, however, Esau's tears were of no consequence. They could not change the effects of that blessing spoken over what was to become the **12 tribes** of the **house of Jacob**.

Likewise, both the birthright and the blessing of Israel [Jacob] that was spoken over Joseph and his sons are also eternal—with Ephraim (the younger) given the greater portion. When Joshua divided the land of Canaan, the tribe of Joseph received a double portion, as both Manasseh and Ephraim[6] received their own parcel of land. After David's kingdom was divided because of Solomon's sin, the 10 tribes of the northern kingdom reverberated to its previous name of *Israel,* and the southern kingdom to its former name of *Judah.* Jeroboam, of the half-tribe of Ephraim, was chosen by God as king over the ten tribes of Israel. In fact, the entire northern kingdom became known as *Ephraim, Samaria,* as well as *Israel.*

God became so angry because of the sins of Ephraim and the northern kingdom that he sowed them into the earth, and removed them as a nation from His sight. God did not kill them—He sowed them. The Lord's *sowing of His people* was in the same manner that a farmer scatters seed in a field. They were initially carried away as captives by Assyria. God, even today, knows where every one of His multitudinous people are on the earth. Every blessing that He has ever spoken over Joseph, Ephraim, Manasseh or Judah has already come to pass, or will yet come to pass: because God has both spoken and recorded His will. *I will hasten my word to perform it[7].*

For our purposes here we must remember again that the "stick of Joseph is in the hand of Ephraim[8]", and that Ephraim is still a blessed and immensely populous people. This blessing would not be a *blessing* in today's world, if it did not also include the additional technological and material prosperity that can greatly profit today's Israel.

Further, in the supreme councils and courts of the kingdom of heaven, **Ephraim** and the **house of Joseph** have "spiritually enforceable rights" to their portion of the physical land of Israel, because **Joseph is as much an heir to the Abrahamic Covenant as is Judah**. This is the prophetic season

6 The whole house of Jacob [Israel] is technically thirteen tribes and not twelve; because God has divided the tribe of Joseph into the half-tribes of Ephraim and Manasseh. [See map pg. 34]

7 Jeremiah 1:12.

8   Ezekiel 37:19.

for fulfillment of God's promises uttered in the writings of His Hebrew prophets—promises that are hidden within the *words* of Ezekiel 38—that **Israel "in the latter years" is promised by God a season of great material prosperity and peace**. This promise is to be fulfilled before the remainder of the events that are also prophesied in Ezekiel 38 and 39.

> **Ezekiel 38:8-14** After many days thou shalt be visited: **in the latter years** thou shalt come into **the land that is brought back from the sword**, and is **gathered out of many people**, against the **mountains of Israel**, which have been always waste: but it is brought forth out of the nations, and they shall **dwell safely** all of them. ... the **land of unwalled villages** ... that **dwell safely** ... **dwelling without walls**, and having **neither bars nor gates** ... the **desolate places that are now inhabited**, and upon the **people[9]** that are **gathered out of the nations**, which have **gotten cattle and goods**, that dwell in the midst of the land ... **silver and gold** ... **cattle and goods** ... a **great spoil** ... Thus saith the Lord God; In that day **when my people of Israel dwelleth safely**, shalt thou not know it?.

In this passage, all I have done is to leave out the ***words of war and persecution***: which leaves only the ***words of peace and prosperity*** that the armies of Gog will at some future date come to seize or destroy. In this coming season of peace and material prosperity, Israel is promised by God to become a land:

- Brought back from the sword.

- Gathered out of many people.

- Against the mountains of Israel.

- Dwelling in safety, with villages that are without walls or gates.

- With desolate places that are now inhabited.

- With a people that are gathered out of the nations.

- With people that have gotten cattle and other forms of material prosperity.

---

9 "People": more than just Jews.

- Whose people dwell in the midst of the land.

- Whose people are possessed with silver, gold, cattle, goods, and great spoil; and

- Where God's people of Israel dwell in safely.

These hidden blessings of **Ezekiel 38:8-14**, and a nation at rest, cannot manifest for Israel until the prophecy of Ezekiel 37 has been fulfilled, and the heirs of Joseph and Ephraim are back in the land.

Israel: Find Joseph

THESE DRY BONES OF A NATION OF 12 TRIBES MUST LIVE

Ezekiel 37:1 The hand of the LORD was upon me, and carried me out in the spirit of the LORD, and set me down in the midst of the **valley which was full of bones**, 2 And caused me to pass by them round about: and, behold, there were very many in the open valley; and, lo, they were very dry [Israel and Judah separated for over 2700 years]. 3 And he said unto me, Son of man, **can these bones live**? And I answered, O Lord GOD, thou knowest.

4 Again he said unto me, **Prophesy upon these bones**, and say unto them, O ye dry bones, hear the word of the LORD. 5 Thus saith the Lord GOD unto these bones; Behold, I will cause breath to enter into you, and **ye shall live** [as one nation]: 6 And I will lay sinews upon you, and will bring up flesh upon you, and cover you with skin, and put breath in you, and **ye shall live**; and ye shall know that I am the LORD. ... **10 So I prophesied** as he commanded me, and the **breath came into them,** and **they lived,** and **stood up upon their feet, an exceeding great army** [interesting phraseology given the times that are upon us].

When a prophet of God hears, reads, or discerns the word of the Lord, he or she speaks that *word* into the atmosphere so that God may hear Himself, and then bring to pass His own words spoken a second time out of the mouth of one of His prophets. God gives the prophet a glimpse of the future, so that He may return him or her to the present so that the people and land may return back to their future—to their destiny. *Surely the Lord GOD will do nothing, but he revealeth His secret unto his servants the prophets[10].*

Who are these dry bones of **the latter years** that God is showing to Ezekiel? Israel is trying to negotiate a solution to the Palestinian problems that plague the nation by establishing a Palestinian state alongside a Jewish state inside the present borders of Israel. She has yet to realize that her own Hebrew prophets have already prophesied God's solution for this hour. This God-ordained plan for Israel is to rejoin the northern kingdom of Israel with the southern kingdom of Judah—reuniting each into one nation upon the West Bank mountains of Israel—just as Ezekiel prophesied.

> **Ezekiel 37:11** Then he said unto me, Son of man, **these bones are the whole house of Israel** [the fullness of the twelve tribes of Jacob] behold, they say [the bones themselves have a voice], Our bones are dried, and our hope is lost: we are cut off for our parts [Judah is cut off from Joseph and Ephraim]. **12** Therefore **prophesy and say** unto them, Thus saith the Lord GOD; Behold, O my people, I will open your graves [the graves of the lost knowledge of their Hebrew heritage], and cause you to come up out of your graves, and **bring you into the land of Israel** [Judah is already in the land; it is Joseph and Ephraim that must now be found].

These dry bones represent Judah and the multitudes of Ephraim's descendants scattered throughout the earth. Ephraim has lost his Hebrew identity and does not know that his multitudes are the heirs of Abraham—through Isaac and Jacob—and that his people are as much heirs to the Abrahamic Covenant as any from the tribe of Judah. They have a blood-covenant right to possess their portion of the land of Israel, and carry the blessing of Joseph that's upon their lives as they return to the land.

> **Ezekiel 37:15** The word of the LORD came again unto me, saying, **16** Moreover, thou son of man, take thee **one stick**, and write upon it, For **Judah**, and for the **children of Israel his companions:** then take **another stick**, and write upon it, For **Joseph, the stick of Ephraim**, and **for all the house of Israel his companions** [the ten tribes of Israel … scattered]: **17** And join them one to another into one stick; and they shall become one in thine hand.

> **18** And when the children of thy people shall speak unto thee,

10 Amos 3:7.

saying, Wilt thou not shew us what thou meanest by these? **19** Say unto them, Thus saith the Lord GOD; Behold, **I will take** the **stick of Joseph, which is in the hand of Ephraim**, and **the tribes of Israel his fellows**, and **will put them** [the ten tribes of Israel] **with him** [Ephraim], even **with** the **stick of Judah**, and **make them** [Joseph, Ephraim and Judah] **one stick** [one nation], and they shall be **one in mine hand** [the hand of God]. **20** And the sticks whereon thou writest shall be in thine hand before their eyes.

21 And say unto them, Thus saith the Lord GOD; Behold, I will take the **children of Israel**[11] **from among the heathen** [the nations], whither they be gone, and **will gather them on every side,** and **bring them into their own land: 22** And I will make them **one nation in the land upon the mountains of Israel**; and **one king** shall be king to them all: and they shall be **no more two nations, neither** shall they be divided into **two kingdoms** [Israel and Judah] any more at all.

The prophetic pathway for Israel to reach this season of peace and prosperity of **Ezekiel 38:8-14** can only be attained by the fulfillment of the prerequisite prophecies of Ezekiel 37—that the branch of Joseph in the hand of Ephraim must be joined with the branch of Judah and the two branches shall become one nation again in the hand of the Lord. Jehovah's eternal foreknowledge has provided the plan for His chosen people in this unique hour. The "one king" that shall preside when all 12 tribes are returned to the land is a president and prime minister now, and the Messiah later. **This is a pre-messianic promise from God.**

The Israel of today is representative of all of the twelve tribes of Israel [Jacob]; but, the "Israel" that God said would be as the "dust of the earth, stars of heaven, and sand of the sea" is not only not in Israel proper, but they are **the "Josephs" of Israel** who have lost their Hebrew identity, and have been scattered throughout the earth—and, they are not Jews: who in their Diaspora have never lost their identity as a Hebrew people.

HOSEA CONFIRMS THIS READING OF EZEKIEL 37 AND 38

The prophet Hosea confirms this reading as to the impending timing

---

11 The term "children of Israel" here is a primary reference to the 10 tribes, which are the dry bones of Joseph and Ephraim ... as Judah is already in the land.

of the prophecy of Ezekiel 37 and 38.

> **Hosea 1:2** The beginning of the word of the LORD by Hosea. And the LORD said to Hosea, Go, take unto thee a wife of whoredoms and children of whoredoms: for the land hath committed great whoredom, departing from the LORD. **3** So he went and took Gomer the daughter of Diblaim; which conceived, and bare him a son. **4** And the LORD said unto him, Call his name **Jezreel**[12]; for yet a little while, and <u>**I will ... cause to cease the kingdom of the house of Israel**</u>. **5** And it shall come to pass at that day, that I will break the bow of Israel in the **valley of Jezreel**.

Ephraim and the 10 tribes of the northern kingdom of Israel have ceased to exist as a nation because of their idolatry and disobedience to the commandments of God. The Lord caused the **house of Israel** to be carried off into Assyrian captivity ... unto this day. While scattered, He has not been their God; and they have not been known as His people. However, because of David's life, His mercy was extended to the **house of Judah**, who a century later would be carried off to Babylon for 70 years: but allowed to return to the land. They were scattered again by the Romans in 70 CE; but, again by the mercy of God, Jews were restored to the land in 1948. Although God has sown the so-called lost tribes of Israel into the earth, He fully intends to receive them back as a bountiful harvest. Thousands of years ago Ezekiel 37 prophesied the appointed time for this God-ordained harvest.

> **Hosea 1:6** And she conceived again, and bare a daughter. And God said unto him, Call her name **Loruhamah**: for **I will no more have mercy upon the house of Israel** [the 10 tribes of Israel]; **but I will utterly take them away** [into Assyrian captivity]. **7** But I will have **mercy upon the house of Judah**, and will save them by the LORD their God ...

> **8** Now when she had weaned Loruhamah, she conceived, and bare a son. **9** Then said God, Call his name Loammi: for <u>**ye are not my people, and I will not be your God**</u>.

Yet, in spite of disobedience and the passage of several thousand years, God will still fulfill or has already fulfilled each and every promise that He

---

12 God scatters or sows.

made to Abraham, Isaac, Jacob and Joseph—that their descendants would grow to become as the dust of the earth, stars of heaven, and sand of the sea. They would also become a company of nations in the center of the earth. This is the "place" where Ephraim is today, where he shall be found, and where it shall be said unto him that he is a son of the living God.

> **Hosea 1:10** <u>Yet the number of the children of Israel shall be as the sand of the sea, which cannot be measured nor numbered</u> [the primary reference here is Ephraim]; and it shall come to pass, that <u>**in the place**</u> [the company of Ephraimic nations] **where it was said unto them, Ye are not my people, there it shall be said unto them, Ye are the sons of the living God.**

Many Christians argue that these "sons of the living God" is a reference to the church of Jesus Christ. I accept this as a **spiritual fulfillment** of this passage of Scripture. One common mistake of the prophetic teachers in the Church, however, is that they look for fulfillment in the Church what was promised by God to the nation of Israel. To rightly divide or understand every prophesy in both the Old and New Testaments, each passage must first be understood and its fulfillment discerned in its local application, before one searches out a spiritual application of the passage.

God promised the natural heirs of Abraham by whatever reference— the **house of Jacob, house of Judah, house of Joseph, children of Israel,** and many other references—to give them the land of Israel as an eternal possession: with a resurrected King David as their earthly king. He did this by the oath that He swore when He cut a blood-covenant with Abraham. The Church is promised a heavenly city, the New Jerusalem, as our eternal dwelling place with the Messiah reigning as King. But, this book is about Israel and not the Church. God will have no problem fulfilling all of His promises to both Israel and the Church at the same time.

> **Hosea 1:11** Then shall the <u>children of Judah</u> and the <u>children of Israel</u> be gathered together, and <u>appoint</u> themselves one head, and they shall come up out of the land: for great shall be the day of Jezreel.

When Messiah come, no one will "appoint" Him … so this passage of Scripture simply must have a pre-messianic fulfillment in the day of Jezreel, the day when God regathers the 10 tribes that He has sown.

THE BIRTHRIGHT AND BLESSING ON ISRAEL

When the descendants of Joseph and Ephraim return to the land of Israel, the **birthright and blessing of Joseph** on these Hebrews will add population and material prosperity to the nation of Israel. Unlike many of the Jews that have returned to the land impoverished, the descendants of Joseph and Ephraim are materially blessed like Joseph. They have not been persecuted over the centuries the way that Jews have. Some may even have been, or may now be persecutors of their Jewish brethren. Some real tangible forgiveness—like the story of Joseph—may be in order once they are found and reunited with Israel's Jews in the days and years to come.

What if some of these lost Hebrews were discovered to be in Germany with affiliations with the Nazis? What if many were found to be Iranians, Iraqis, or radical Muslims or factions of the Palestinians, themselves? In any such eventuality, the story of how Joseph dealt with his own personal betrayal should serve as **the primary example** of how God wants His Jewish children of today to minister to any of their repentant brethren found to be wayward towards Israel and Jews over the past millennia.

We should all remember that **the master law** of the Kingdom of God is first found in the Hebrew Scriptures in Genesis 1:11-12 … *"[T]he seed of a thing is in the thing; and everything reproduces after its own kind"*. Thus, because Judah was as responsible as any of his brothers in selling Joseph into Egyptian slavery, it would be no small thing thousands of years later for the descendants of Joseph to be found to have persecuted the descendants of Judah. This, simply put, would be another manifestation of the eternal and ever present spiritual law of sowing and reaping that none of us can escape.

What is clear, however, is that the inspired writings of the Hebrew prophets teach us that Ezekiel 37 is the pathway that Israel must take in order to experience this season of peace, prosperity, wealth and blessing that is promised in **Ezekiel 38:8-14**; and that this season of abundance shall transpire before the chaos which is also promised in Ezekiel 38 and 39, and from which Israel also shall be delivered.

Let us return, now, to our tracing of the Abrahamic Covenant and the Kingdom of Israel.

List Of Illustrations

PART II

THE DIVIDED KINGDOM

A King of Judah

Krieger.   Jüdischer König.

90

CHAPTER 10

THE ETERNAL THRONE OF DAVID

In making a determination of where Israel is today on God's prophetic clock, one of the more interesting questions to consider is what has happened to the eternal throne that God promised to David.

THE KINGDOM OF ISRAEL BECOMES UNITED

After the death of King Saul, God united the southern kingdom of Judah with the northern kingdom of Israel under David's rule. David, who is Jewish, had reigned over the kingdom of Judah for 7 years, when his Hebrew brethren of the 10 tribes of Israel in the north came to him to submit all Israel and Judah to him as king.

> **2 Samuel 5:1** Then came **all the tribes of Israel** to David unto Hebron, and spake, saying, Behold, **we are thy bone and thy flesh** [non-Jewish brothers: sons of our father Jacob]. **2** Also in time past, when Saul was king over us, thou wast he that leddest out and broughtest in Israel: and the LORD said to thee, Thou shalt feed **my people Israel**, and thou shalt be a captain over Israel.
>
> **3** So all **the elders of Israel** [the 10 tribes] came to the king to Hebron; and king David made a league with them in Hebron before the LORD: and they anointed David king over Israel. **4** David was thirty years old when he began to reign, and he reigned forty years. **5 In Hebron he reigned over Judah** seven years and six months: and **in Jerusalem he reigned** thirty and three years over **all Israel and Judah**.

When the kingdom is united, because the 12 tribes of Jacob are the 12 tribes of Israel [Jacob's new name], the name **Israel** becomes the common reference for the 12 sons of Israel. However, in a divided kingdom, a reference to Israel is more often than not a reference to the northern kingdom of the 10 tribes of Israel and Ephraim [also known as Samaria]. Any reference to Judah commonly includes the tribe of Benjamin and the priestly tribe of Levi, who have become merged with the Jews of Judah. Joseph became the dominant tribe in the northern kingdom, with his sons Ephraim and Manasseh each receiving sizable parcels of ground.

In 1948, God uses the tribe of Judah to resurrect the nation of Israel. Ephraim and the 10 tribes of Israel (including Manasseh) were not a visible part of the 1948 restoration of Israel, because each has lost his identity as being Hebrew. But, both Ephraim and Manasseh have yet grown up to become a multitude of nations in the center of the earth, fulfilling God's promises to Abraham, Isaac, Jacob and Joseph. They have the blessing of Joseph upon them; and their people have become as the dust of the earth, stars of heaven, and sand of the sea.

DAVID BRINGS THE ARK OF THE COVENANT TO JERUSALEM

Once the kingdom is united, David brings the Ark of the Covenant to Jerusalem.

> **2 Samuel 6:13** And it was so, that when they that bare the ark of the LORD had gone six paces, he sacrificed oxen and fatlings. **14** And **David danced before the LORD with all his might**; and David was girded with a linen ephod [garment of the high priest]. **15** So David and **all the house of Israel** brought up the ark of the LORD with shouting, and with the sound of the trumpet. **16** And as the ark of the LORD came into the **city of David** … **17** And they brought **in the ark of the LORD**, and set it in his place, in the midst of the tabernacle that David had pitched for it: and **David offered** burnt offerings and peace offerings before the LORD.

GOD GIVES DAVID AN ETERNAL KINGDOM, HOUSE AND THRONE

God gives David a promise that He would establish David's kingdom, his house, and his throne forever. Unlike the promises that He would later give to David's son, King Solomon, God's promises to David are unconditional. Their fulfillment is something that God, Himself, will perform.

> **2 Samuel 7:1** And it came to pass, when the king [David] sat in his house, and the LORD had given him rest round about from

all his enemies; **2** That the king said unto Nathan the prophet, See now, I dwell in an house of cedar, but the ark of God dwelleth within curtains. **3** And Nathan said to the king, Go, do all that is in thine heart; for the LORD is with thee.

4 And it came to pass that night, that the word of the LORD came unto Nathan, saying, **5** Go and tell my servant David, Thus saith the LORD, Shalt thou build me an house for me to dwell in? **6** Whereas I have not dwelt in any house since the time that I brought up the **children of Israel** out of Egypt, even to this day, but have walked in a tent and in a tabernacle. **7** In all the places wherein I have walked with all the children of Israel spake I a word with any of the tribes of Israel, whom I commanded to feed **my people Israel**, saying, Why build ye not me an house of cedar?

8 Now therefore so shalt thou say unto my servant David, Thus saith the LORD of hosts, I took thee from the sheepcote, from following the sheep, to be ruler over my people, over **Israel**: **9** And I was with thee whithersoever thou wentest, and have cut off all thine enemies out of thy sight, and have made thee a great name, like unto the name of the great men that are in the earth …

12 And when thy days be fulfilled, and thou shalt sleep with thy fathers, **I will set up thy seed after thee**, which shall <u>**proceed out of thy bowels**</u>[1], and **I will establish his kingdom. 13 He shall build an house** for my name, and **I will stablish the throne of his kingdom for ever. 14** I will be his father, and he shall be my son. <u>**If he commit iniquity**</u> [this cannot possibly be the Messiah], I will chasten him with the rod of men, and with the stripes of the children of men: **15** But my mercy shall not depart away from him, as I took it from Saul, whom I put away before thee.

God's mercy never left King Solomon; but His promises to Solomon were conditional. As for David, however, the Lord has said:

2 Samuel 7:16 And <u>thine house</u> and <u>thy kingdom</u> shall <u>be established for ever</u> before thee: <u>thy throne</u> shall be <u>established for ever</u>. 17 According to all these words, and according to all this vision, so did Nathan speak unto David.

---

1   *Bowels* speak of one's direct seed: the next generation. David at this point has not yet met Bathsheba, so Solomon has not been born.

The **house of David** is the house of Judah. The **kingdom of David** is the kingdom of Israel and Judah. The **throne of David** is the **scepter**: the eternal right to rule over the 12 tribes of Israel. In a divided kingdom, the throne of David remains with Judah because ... *The scepter shall not depart from Judah until Shiloh (the Messiah) comes*[2]. Since Judah has had no earthly king since its Babylonian captivity, where is the throne of David today?

THE 10 TRIBES SHALL HAVE THEIR OWN RESTING PLACE

2 Samuel 7:10 Moreover **I will** [future from David's kingdom] **appoint** [set, ordain, establish] **a place** [a fixed location] **for my people Israel, and will plant** [establish] **them**, that they may dwell [settle down to abide] in **a place**[3] **of their own**, and **move no more**; neither shall the **children of wickedness** afflict them any more, as beforetime, **11** And as since the time that I commanded judges to be over my people Israel, and have caused thee to rest from all thine enemies. Also the LORD telleth thee that **he will make thee an house** [the house of David].

1 Chronicles 17:9 Also I will ordain **a place** for my people Israel, and will plant them, and they shall dwell in their place, and shall be moved no more, neither shall the children of wickedness waste them any more, as at the beginning.

The above verse of Scripture, **2 Samuel 7:10**, makes absolutely no sense if the Lord is speaking of David's united kingdom of the 12 tribes of Israel and Judah when He tells David, through the prophet Nathan, that He would appoint "my people Israel" a "place of their own"—for them to be planted in a fixed location, and "move no more". Why? Because the united kingdom of Israel was at this very moment everything that God said that He would bring into manifestation for them in the future—in Israel.

"My people Israel" in verse 10, rather, has to be a reference to the "Israel" of the divided kingdom of 10 tribes that would be reestablished after the death of Solomon, who is yet unborn. God is speaking in verse 10 of **Ephraim**, who would grow into a company of nations in the middle of the earth; and who by the plans, purposes and foreknowledge of God would be planted and take root in new lands. That the Lord subtly shifts the meaning of "Israel" in verse 10 is further witnessed, because when God plants

---

2 Genesis 49:10.

3 See: 1 Chronicles 17:9; Hosea 1:10; Zechariah 10:6-10 and Isaiah 14:1-2.

the 10 tribes of Israel in their new "place", there will still be "children of wickedness" in the earth: as when they were carried off into captivity by Assyria. So this has to be a **pre-messianic promise of God**—one which has already been fulfilled in the "hidden Israel" of Ephraim.

THE MESSIAH HAS AN ETERNAL KINGDOM, HOUSE AND THRONE

In **2 Samuel 7:12** [pg. 93] God speaks of establishing David's eternal kingdom out of his "bowels", his direct offspring, King Solomon. But, in **1 Chronicles 17:11** God tells David that He will establish this kingdom through one of his sons—which appears be a reference to Solomon—but a closer reading indicates God is speaking of the Messiah, and the fourth temple of Ezekiel 40 through 48.

> **1 Chronicles 17:11** And it shall come to pass, when thy days be expired that thou must go to be with thy fathers, that I will raise up **thy seed** after thee, which shall be **of thy sons** [not … "out of your bowels" … as in 2 Samuel 7:12 [pg. 93]; but … "of thy sons" … which is a reference to future generations]; and **I will establish his kingdom. 12 He shall build me an house** [the temple of Ezekiel 40-48], and **I will stablish his throne for ever**. **13** I will be his father, and he shall be my son: and I will not take my mercy away from him, as I took it from him that was before thee [King Saul]: **14** But I will settle him **in mine house** [God's house, not David's] and **in my kingdom** [the kingdom of heaven] **for ever**: and **his throne shall be established for evermore**.

The Bible has very subtle distinctions in seemingly parallel passages. In **2 Samuel 7:12-14**, God speaks of a king from David's next generation (his bowels) who could commit iniquity and be chastened … "with the rod of men, and the stripes of the children of men". Here in **1 Chronicles 17:11-14**, God speaks of the "seed" of David which shall be "of thy sons", with no mention of iniquity or stripes. The first passage is a reference to King Solomon. The second speaks of the Messiah as He sits upon His throne in the temple of God, in the coming kingdom of heaven upon the earth.

DAVID HAS AN ETERNAL COVENANT WITH GOD

David's covenant with God is wholly God-initiated. It is everlasting and unbreakable. It covers the **two families of the house of Jacob**: the **house of Israel** and the **house of Judah**.

Jeremiah 33:19 And the word of the LORD came unto Jeremiah, saying, **20** Thus saith the LORD; If ye can break **my covenant of the day**, and **my covenant of the night**, and that there should not be day and night in their season; **21** Then may also <u>my covenant</u> be broken <u>with David my servant</u>, **that he should not have <u>a son to reign upon his throne</u>**; and with the Levites the priests, my ministers. **22** As the **host of heaven** cannot be numbered, neither the **sand of the sea** measured: **so will I multiply the <u>seed of David</u> my servant**, and the Levites that minister unto me [Levites in the third and fourth temples].

23 Moreover the word of the LORD came to Jeremiah, saying, **24** Considerest thou not what this people have spoken, saying, **The <u>two families</u>** [Israel and Judah] <u>**which the LORD hath chosen,**</u> **he hath even <u>cast them off?</u>** thus they have despised my people, **that they should be no more a nation** before them. **25** Thus saith the LORD; If my covenant be not with day and night, and if I have not appointed the ordinances of heaven and earth; **26** Then will I cast away the **seed of Jacob** [12 tribes], and David my servant [God's promises to David], so that I will not take any of his seed to be rulers over the **seed of Abraham, Isaac, and Jacob** [12 tribes]: for **I will cause their captivity to return**, and have mercy on them.

The captivity of both Israel and Judah shall return when they are rejoined back into one nation on the mountains of Israel as Ezekiel 37 is fulfilled.

DAVID RECEIVES HIS ETERNAL HOUSE

2 Samuel 7:18 Then went king David in, and sat before the LORD, and he said, Who am I, O Lord GOD? and what is my house, that thou hast brought me hitherto? … **25** And now, O LORD God, the word that thou hast spoken concerning thy servant, and **concerning his house, establish it for ever**, and do as thou hast said. **26** And let thy name be magnified for ever, saying, The LORD of hosts is the God over Israel: and **let the house of thy servant David be established before thee.**

27 For thou, O LORD of hosts, God of Israel, hast revealed to thy servant, saying, **I will build thee an house**: therefore hath thy servant found in his heart to pray this prayer unto thee. **28** And now, O Lord GOD, thou art that God, and thy words be true, and thou hast promised this goodness unto thy servant: **29** Therefore now **let it please thee to bless the house of thy servant, that it may continue for ever before thee**: for thou, O Lord GOD, hast spoken it: and with thy blessing **let the house of thy servant be blessed for ever.**

David understood that when God reveals something to you, or makes a promise to you: you receive it, settle it, pray it out, speak it forth out of the abundance of your heart, and then walk it out—and it will, and did, become a reality in King David's life.

SOLOMON PRAYS BEFORE THE LORD

Solomon, as soon as he became king, gave an offering, and prayed a prayer that touched the heart of God. As a result, God gave him wisdom, knowledge, riches, wealth and honor above all other kings upon the earth.

2 Chronicles 1:6 And Solomon went up thither to the brasen altar before the LORD, which was at the tabernacle of the congregation, and **offered a thousand burnt offerings** upon it. **7** In that night did **God appear unto Solomon**, and said unto him, Ask what I shall give thee. **8** And Solomon said unto God, Thou hast shewed great mercy unto David my father, and hast made me to reign in his stead. **9** Now, O LORD God, let thy promise unto David my father be established: for **thou hast made me king over a <u>people like the dust of the earth</u> in multitude. 10** Give me now wisdom and knowledge, that I may go out and come in before this people: for who can judge this thy people, that is so great?

11 And God said to Solomon, Because this was in thine heart, and thou hast not asked riches, wealth, or honour, nor the life of thine enemies, neither yet hast asked long life; but hast asked wisdom and knowledge for thyself, that thou mayest **judge my people**, over whom I have made thee king: **12 Wisdom and knowledge is granted unto thee; and I will give thee riches, and wealth, and honour**, such as none of the kings have had that have been before thee, neither shall there any after thee have the like.

God's Promises To Solomon Are Conditional

In the parallel passages of **2 Samuel 7:12-16** [pg.93] and **1 Chronicles 17:11-14** [pg. 95; see also 1 Chronicles 22:9-10], it appears that the LORD is promising Solomon an unconditional throne in the same manner that He promised David an eternal kingdom, house and throne. But, in **1 Kings 9:1-9** [below; see also 1 Chronicles 28:7 and 9], it is clear that God's promises to Solomon are conditional upon his obedience, and the obedience of his sons after him. The eternal aspects of the promises given to Solomon, however, are promises to the Messiah, and will be fulfilled in the coming of the greater Son of David.

1 Kings 9:1 And it came to pass, when Solomon had finished the building of the house of the LORD, and the king's house, and all Solomon's desire which he was pleased to do, **2** That the **LORD appeared to Solomon the second time**, as he had appeared unto him at Gibeon. **3** And the LORD said unto him, I have heard thy prayer and thy supplication, that thou hast made before me: **I have hallowed this house**, which thou hast built, **to put my name there for ever**; and mine eyes and mine heart shall be there perpetually.

4 And **if thou wilt walk before me** [this is a conditional promise], as David thy father walked, in integrity of heart, and in uprightness, to do according to all that I have commanded thee, and wilt keep my statutes and my judgments: **5** **Then I will establish the throne of thy kingdom upon Israel for ever,** as I promised to David thy father, saying, There shall not fail thee a man upon the **throne of Israel**.

In a united kingdom, reference is made to the **throne of Israel**. When the kingdom becomes divided, **the scepter** of the throne is called the **throne of David** or **throne of Judah**.

1 Kings 9:6 But **if ye shall at all turn from following me, ye or your children** [if the conditions are not met], and will not keep my commandments and my statutes which I have set before you, but go and serve other gods, and worship them [which Solomon did when he was old]: **7** **Then will I cut off Israel out of the land; and this house** [the temple Solomon had built], which I have hallowed for my name, **will I cast out of my sight**; and Israel shall be a proverb and a byword among all people:

When the Lord says that He will "cut of Israel" here, it is a reference to the 12 tribes, as all 12 eventually went into captivity. God has destroyed His temple twice: first by the Babylonians in 586 BCE, and then by the Romans in 70 CE. He caused all Israel to become a "proverb and a byword[4]", until God honored His promises to Abraham by recreating Israel as a nation in 1948.

1 Kings 9:8 And at **this house** [Solomon's temple], which is high, every one that passeth by it shall be astonished, and shall hiss; and they shall say, **Why hath the LORD done thus unto this land, and to this house?** 9 And they shall answer, **Because they forsook the LORD their God**, who brought forth their fathers out of the land of Egypt, and have taken hold upon other gods, and have worshipped them, and served them: therefore hath the LORD brought upon them all this evil.

Behold the goodness and severity of God.

GOD RENDS THE NORTHERN KINGDOM FROM THE THRONE OF DAVID

God is always faithful to His Word: for evil, as well as for good. Because Solomon with all his wisdom failed to take heed to the commandments of God spoken by Moses concerning multiplying wives[5], and marriages to foreign women[6] who would turn away his heart toward foreign gods, God takes the united kingdom away from Solomon, and the **throne of David** is left with only the **tribe of Judah**.

1 Kings 11:1 But king **Solomon loved many strange women**, together with the daughter of Pharaoh, women of the Moabites, Ammonites, Edomites, Zidonians, and Hittites; 2 Of the nations concerning which the LORD said unto the children of Israel, Ye shall not go in to them, neither shall they come in unto you: **for surely they will turn away your heart after their gods**: Solomon clave unto these in love. 3 And he had seven hundred wives, prin-

---

4 Deuteronomy 28:7;1 Kings 9:7; and 2 Chronicles 7:20.
5 Deuteronomy 17:17.
6 Exodus 34:15-16.

cesses, and three hundred concubines: and his wives turned away his heart.

4 For it came to pass, **when Solomon was old, that his wives turned away his heart after other gods**: and his heart was not perfect with the LORD his God, as was the heart of David his father. **5** For Solomon went after Ashtoreth the goddess of the Zidonians, and after Milcom the abomination of the Ammonites. **6** And **Solomon did evil in the sight of the LORD, and went not fully after the LORD, as did David his father**. **7** Then did Solomon build an high place for Chemosh, the abomination of Moab, in the hill that is before Jerusalem, and for Molech, the abomination of the children of Ammon. **8** And likewise did he for all his strange wives, which burnt incense and sacrificed unto their gods.

9 And the LORD was angry with Solomon, because his heart was turned from the LORD God of Israel, which had appeared unto him twice, **10** And had commanded him concerning this thing, that he should not go after other gods: but he kept not that which the LORD commanded. **11** <u>Wherefore the LORD said unto Solomon, Forasmuch as this is done of thee, and thou hast not kept my covenant and my statutes</u>, which I have commanded thee, <u>I will surely rend the kingdom from thee, and will give it to thy servant</u> [Jeroboam of the tribe of Ephraim].

Judah And Jerusalem Receive God's Mercy

The **southern kingdom of Judah and Jerusalem** are to remain with the royal line of David, because of God's mercy and His promises to David.

1 Kings 11:12 Notwithstanding in thy days I will not do it for David thy father's sake: but I will rend it out of the hand of thy son [Rehoboam]. **13** Howbeit I will not rend away all the kingdom; but will give <u>one tribe</u> to thy son **for David my servant's sake,** and **for Jerusalem's sake** which I have chosen.

14 And <u>the LORD stirred up an adversary</u> unto Solomon, Hadad the Edomite: he was of the king's seed in Edom [remember: Esau is Edom]. **...** **23** And <u>God stirred him up another adversary</u>, Rezon the son of Eliadah, which fled from his lord Hadadezer king of Zobah: …

The Lord has a very definite pattern of how He deals with His people when they get into prolonged disobedience of what He has commanded in His Word. First, He speaks forth His Word or commandment; and if it is not obeyed, He will usually send a prophet or preacher of righteousness to remind His people of what He has already spoken to them. If they are still disobedient, He will "stir up an adversary" in hopes that persecution and affliction will drive His people back to Him. How many times is it recorded in the Old Testament that when the people of God cried out to the Lord in their affliction, they were heard and delivered[7] of Him?

Here are **two prophetic questions** to consider as you read the remainder of this book. **First**, based upon the pattern of how God deals with His people [p. 142] when they miss the mark—both by commission and by omission—what is **the root cause** of the Palestinian problems concerning the land of Israel that the nation of Israel is experiencing today?

Second, is it not at least possible, if not likely, that the outright intransigence of the Palestinian leadership concerning the formation of a Palestinian state inside the borders of Israel has at its roots the same *hardening process* that God used with Pharaoh in the first 12 chapters of Exodus? What did God do in the Book of Exodus? Because the LORD had **a higher purpose** to perform than His people could understand, He hardened the neck of Pharaoh until He had accomplished the 10 plagues upon the land of Egypt—for His honor and glory—as judgment upon the gods of Egypt[8]. Because His people could have never been secure in the promise land in the shadow of the wealth and might of the Egypt that was before the plagues, He destroyed the mightiest nation on the earth … not because he hated Egypt, but because He loves the people that He had chosen to bear His name. What, then, is God's higher purpose for today's Israeli-Palestinian conflict that His people have yet to discern?

Israel: Find Joseph

GOD GIVES THE 10 TRIBES OF ISRAEL TO JOSEPH

As a result of Solomon's disobedience to the commandments of God, the Lord gives Jeroboam of the **house of Joseph**, an Ephraimite of the

7 C/p. 2 Chronicles 20:9.
8 Exodus 12:12.

101

half-tribe of **Ephraim**, of the northern kingdom of the 10 tribes of Israel.

1 Kings 11:31 And he [the prophet Ahijah] said to Jeroboam, **Take thee <u>ten pieces</u>: for thus saith the LORD, the God of Israel, Behold, I will rend the kingdom out of the hand of Solomon, and will give <u>ten tribes</u> to thee: 32 (But he shall have one tribe for my servant David's sake, and for Jerusalem's sake, the city which I have chosen out of all the tribes of Israel:)**

THE 10 TRIBES ARE CALLED ISRAEL

God remembers His promise of mercy to David's natural son.

1 Kings 11:34 Howbeit I will not take the whole kingdom out of his hand [Solomon's]: but I will make him prince all the days of his life for David my servant's sake, whom I chose, because he kept my commandments and my statutes: **35 But <u>I will take the kingdom out of his son's hand</u>** [Rehoboam]**, and will give it unto thee** [Jeroboam]**, <u>even ten tribes</u>. 36 And <u>unto his son will I give one tribe</u>[9]** [the tribe of Judah]**, that David my servant may have a light alway before me in Jerusalem**, the city which I have chosen me to put my name there.

God makes the same conditional promise to Jeroboam concerning obedience to His commandments that He made to Solomon.

1 Kings 11:37 And I will take thee, and thou shalt reign according to all that thy soul desireth, and shalt be **<u>king over Israel</u>** [the northern kingdom of 10 tribes]. **38 And it shall be, <u>if thou wilt hearken unto all that I command thee</u>**, and wilt walk in my ways, and do that is right in my sight, to keep my statutes and my commandments, as David my servant did; that I will be with thee, and build thee a sure house, as I built for David, and will give Israel unto thee. **39 And <u>I will for this afflict the seed of David, but not for ever</u>[10]** [Judah is promised a future redemption].

Hear the word of the Lord: The house of Judah (seed of David) shall be afflicted, but not forever; but the house [seed] of David, kingdom of David, and

9 The **tribe of Judah** includes Jews, plus the tribe of Benjamin, and the priestly tribe of Levi.

10 These are the *sure mercies of David* (Psalms 89 and Isaiah 55:3).

throne of David remain eternal and faithful prom-
ises of God.

God Curses The Royal Line Of David

The Lord God Jehovah became so grieved with the northern kingdom of Israel [Ephraim] that He cast it out of His sight as He had promised. He would not do the same for Judah, which committed the same abominations as did Israel, because of His sworn oath to David; **but He did curse the kingly line of David, so that no man of the royal line of David, through Solomon, would ever again sit on the throne of David**. At the time of this prophecy of Jeremiah, the northern kingdom of Israel has been carried into captivity by Assyria. Jeremiah is God's final witness to Judah prior to its soon coming 70 years of Babylonian captivity. Although the kingdom is divided, the throne of David is to remain with Judah.

> **Jeremiah 22:1** Thus saith the LORD; Go down to the **house of the king of Judah,** and speak there this word, **2** And say, Hear the word of the LORD, **O king of Judah, that sittest upon the throne of David**, thou, and thy servants, and thy people that enter in by these gates: **3** Thus saith the LORD; Execute ye judgment and righteousness, and deliver the spoiled out of the hand of the oppressor: and do no wrong, do no violence to the stranger, the fatherless, nor the widow, neither shed innocent blood in this place.

> **4** For if ye do this thing indeed, then shall there enter in by the gates of this house **kings sitting upon the throne of David**, riding in chariots and on horses, he, and his servants, and his people. **5** But if ye will not hear these words, **I swear by myself** [God swears by Himself because there is none greater], saith the LORD, that **this house shall become a desolation** [the house of the kings of Judah].

Jechoniah [also called Jehoiachin] was the last king of Judah in the royal line of David through Solomon to sit upon the throne of David, before Jeremiah utters his curse[11] on the kingly line of David. He was carried away by the king of Babylon, and freed after 37 years in prison[12]. The last actual king of Judah before its final deportation into Babylon was Jehoiachin's uncle, named Zedekiah, appointed by the king of Babylon. His

---

11   Jeremiah 22:30.
12   2 Kings 24:15 and 25:27; 2 Chronicles 36:9.

sons were slain before him and his eyes put out[13].

Jeremiah 22:24 As I live, saith the LORD, though **Coniah**[14] **the son of Jehoiakim king of Judah** were the signet upon my right hand, yet would I pluck thee thence; **25** And **I will give thee into the hand of them that seek thy life**, and into the hand of them whose face thou fearest, **even into the hand of Nebuchadrezzar king of Babylon**, and into the hand of the Chaldeans. **26** And I will cast thee out, and thy mother that bare thee, into another country, where ye were not born; and there shall ye die.

27 But to the land whereunto they desire to return, thither shall they not return. **28** Is this man Coniah a despised broken idol? is he a vessel wherein is no pleasure? wherefore are they cast out, he and his seed, and are cast into a land which they know not? **29** O earth, earth, earth, hear the word of the LORD. **30** Thus saith the LORD, **Write ye this man childless**, a man that shall not prosper in his days: <u>**for no man of his seed**</u> [Solomon's seed] <u>**shall prosper, sitting upon the throne of David, and ruling any more in Judah**</u>[15].

GOD WILL REESTABLISH THE THRONE OF DAVID

As God has promised, He will not afflict the offspring of David forever. The throne of David shall be reestablished because of **God's unbreakable Covenant with David**. These are the *sure mercies of David*[16].

Jeremiah 33:14 Behold, **the days come**, saith the LORD, that **I will perform** that good thing which I have promised unto the <u>**house of Israel**</u> and to the <u>**house of Judah**</u> [the divided kingdom has two houses ... unto this day]. **15** **In those days**, and **at that time** [in the days and time God restores the two houses of Israel together as one nation ... beginning with the fulfillment of the prophecy of Ezekiel 37], will I cause the **Branch of righteousness**

---

13 Jeremiah 39:1-7; 52:10-11; and 2 Kings 25:7.

14 God here takes His name away from the king of Judah. He leaves off the "Je" of King Jechoniah's [or Jehoiachin's] name—"Je" is the abbreviation of *Jehovah* in his name—indicating that God had left him.

15 Since its Babylonian captivity, the kingdom of Judah, and now national Israel, have been ruled by governors and not kings ... even unto this day.

16 Psalms 89:1-4, 17-37; 132:10-12; and Isaiah 55:3.

to grow up unto David [in the passage of time the Messiah shall reign over both houses of Israel, as well as the earth]; and he shall execute judgment and righteousness in the land.

16 In those days shall **Judah be saved**, and **Jerusalem shall dwell safely**: and this is the name wherewith she shall be called, The LORD our righteousness. **17** For thus saith the LORD; <u>**David shall never want a man to sit upon the throne of the house of Israel**</u> [in those days and at that time of the Messiah (verse 15) … this Scripture must be kept in its context]; **18** Neither shall the priests the Levites want a man before me to offer burnt offerings, and to kindle meat offerings, and to do sacrifice continually [and the third and fourth temples shall be built].

19 And the word of the LORD came unto Jeremiah, saying, **20** Thus saith the LORD; **If ye can break my covenant of the day**, and my covenant of the night, and that there should not be day and night in their season; **21** <u>**Then may also my covenant be broken with David my servant, that he should not have a son to reign upon his throne**</u>; and with the Levites the priests, my ministers. **22** As the host of heaven cannot be numbered, neither the sand of the sea measured: **so will I multiply the seed of David my servant**, and the Levites that minister unto me.

23 Moreover the word of the LORD came to Jeremiah, saying, **24** Considerest thou not what this people have spoken, saying, The <u>**two families**</u> [Israel and Judah] which <u>**the LORD hath chosen**</u>, he hath even cast them off? thus they have despised my people, that they should be no more a nation before them. **25** Thus saith the LORD; **If my covenant be not with day and night**, and if I have not appointed the ordinances of heaven and earth; **26** <u>**Then will I cast away the seed of Jacob**</u> [all 12 tribes], and David my servant, so that I will not take any of his seed to be rulers over **the seed of Abraham, Isaac, and Jacob** [all Israel]: for **I will cause their captivity to return**, and have mercy on them.

The captivity of both families of the Hebrew nation shall return to the land. It began with Judah in 1948, and will conclude with Joseph and Ephraim as Ezekiel 37 is fulfilled.

When Joseph is back in the land, the LORD will begin to restore worship as it was in the days of David, the sweet psalmist of Israel.

Amos 9:11 In that day will <u>I raise up the tabernacle of David that is fallen</u>, and close up the breaches thereof; and I will raise up his ruins, and <u>I will build it as in the days of old</u>: 12 That they may possess the **remnant of Edom** [Esau], and of all the **heathen**, which are **called by my name** [this speaks of the hidden multitude and nations of Joseph and Ephraim; the restoration of Esau; and probably speaks of much more], saith the LORD that doeth this.

13 Behold, the days come, saith the LORD, that the plowman shall overtake the reaper, and the treader of grapes him that soweth seed; and the mountains shall drop sweet wine, and all the hills shall melt. **14** And <u>**I will bring again the captivity of my people of Israel**</u> [all 12 tribes], and they shall build the waste cities, and inhabit them; and they shall plant vineyards, and drink the wine thereof; they shall also make gardens, and eat the fruit of them. **15** And **I will plant them upon their land**, and they shall no more be pulled up out of their land which I have given them, saith the LORD thy God.

In the days when the Lord completes the fulfillment of His promises to the **house of Israel** and to the **house of Judah, Judah will be saved**, and **Jerusalem will dwell in safety**—because the Messiah has come. But **Ezekiel 38:8-14 records an earlier time of Israel's peace, prosperity and safety**. Does this earlier breakthrough come because the Hebrew nation of Israel has reached agreement with the Palestinians and the world for recognition of Israel as a Jewish state, in return for giving away almost half of the land that God gave to Abraham and his descendants forever? **No**, but rather, Israel's present security will be realized when the stick of Joseph which in the hand of Ephraim is joined with the branch of Judah back into one nation on the mountains of Israel in fulfillment of **Ezekiel 37:15-22**. Then and only then shall Judah be saved and Jerusalem dwell safely ... now, in this time.

Israel: Find Joseph

CHAPTER 11

THE KINGDOM IS DIVIDED

God is always faithful to His Word, both in blessing and cursing[1]. As He promised both David and Solomon, after Solomon's death and because of his sin, He divides the **kingdom of Israel** from the **kingdom of Judah**.

I do not wish to intentionally offend Israel, Jews, Christians, Muslims, or other Arabs, but I must say what must be said. The Israel of today is a Jewish nation (actually a Hebrew nation) to everyone but Arabs. Jewish culture predominates in Israel—not because this is God's perfect will—but because of the sins of King Solomon: from which Judah has never fully recovered. One of the events that needs to happen is that Israel, as a nation, needs to repent in "sackcloth and ashes" for the sins of Solomon—a day of atonement for the nation's sins—because whenever a nation turns away from God, judgment will eventually follow. A time of national repentance is required for any nation to gain total freedom from its sins of the past.

The present political situation in Israel has not "just happened". The harvest that any person or nation receives on the earth is a direct result of the seed sown in the past—good or bad. Israel would have never been divided into the northern kingdom of the 10 tribes of Israel and the southern kingdom of Judah except for what ... ? Neither Solomon's temple nor Herod's temple would have been destroyed except for what ... ? There would have been no Babylonian captivity nor Roman Diaspora except for what ... ? Without a Diaspora, there would be no Palestinian issues to plague the nation of Israel today ... and the list goes on.

This book may offend those who do not believe God's Word; those who do not want to obey God's Word; and those who, for whatever reason, fear the consequences of God's Word coming to pass concerning the join-

1   *I call heaven and earth to record this day against you, that I have set before you life and death, choose life, that both thou and thy seed may live. (Deuteronomy 30:19)*

ing of Joseph and Ephraim with Judah. Moses said in Exodus, *Who is on the LORD'S side²?* Those who went with what God was doing at that given moment received a blessing. Those who did not received a curse.

If God says that Ephraim shall be joined with Judah ... then Ephraim shall be joined with Judah. There is nothing that any of us can do to stop this event from coming to pass. The very best that anyone could do would only be to delay what is inevitable. Therefore, the only valid question becomes ... *Is this the season and time for the prophecy of Ezekiel 37 to come to pass?* If it is, or if it might be, then the next issue has to be:

Israel: Find Joseph

ISRAEL IS TORN FROM THE THRONE OF DAVID

God rends the **kingdom of Israel** from the **throne of David** and the **kingdom of Judah**.

> **1 Kings 11:9** And **the LORD was angry with Solomon**, because his heart was turned from the LORD God of Israel, which had appeared unto him twice, **10** And had commanded him concerning this thing, that he should not go after other gods: but he kept not that which the LORD commanded. **11** Wherefore **the LORD said unto Solomon**, Forasmuch as this is done of thee, and thou hast not kept my covenant and my statutes, which I have commanded thee, **I will surely rend the kingdom from thee**, and will give it to thy servant [Jeroboam].

> **12** Notwithstanding in thy days I will not do it for David thy father's sake: but I will rend it out of the hand of thy son. **13** Howbeit I will not rend away all the kingdom; but will give <u>one tribe</u> to thy son for David my servant's sake, and for Jerusalem's sake which I have chosen

The southern kingdom of Judah and Jerusalem is to remain with the royal line of David. For a time, the **kings of Judah** will be seated on the **throne of David**.

---

2 Exodus 32:26.

GOD GIVES THE THRONE OF ISRAEL TO JOSEPH

Here is a continuation of the fulfillment that **Abraham** [through Isaac and Jacob] would be **the father of many nations** [not just Israel]; that **Sarah** would be **the mother of nations**; that **Rebekah** would become **the mother of billions**; that **Jacob** would become **a company of nations**; that **Ephraim** would become **a multitude of nations in the middle of the earth**, with **populations as** the **dust of the earth**, **stars of heaven**, and **sand of the sea**; and that **Manasseh** would become **a great people**[3], also in the middle of the earth.

1 Kings 11:26 And **Jeroboam** the son of Nebat, **an Ephrathite** of Zereda, Solomon's servant... **28** And the man Jeroboam was a mighty man of valour: and **Solomon** seeing the young man that he was industrious, **he made him ruler over all the charge of the house of Joseph**[4]. **29** And it came to pass at that time when Jeroboam went out of Jerusalem, that the prophet Ahijah the Shilonite found him in the way; and he had clad himself with a new garment; and they two were alone in the field:

30 And Ahijah caught the new garment that was on him [representing David's united kingdom], and **rent it in twelve pieces** [representing the 12 tribes of Israel]: **31** And he said to Jeroboam, **Take thee ten pieces** [the northern kingdom of Israel]: for **thus saith the LORD**, the God of Israel, Behold, **I will rend the kingdom out of the hand of Solomon, and will give ten tribes to thee**: **32** (But he [Solomon] **shall have one tribe** for my servant David's sake, and for Jerusalem's sake, the city which I have chosen out of all the tribes of Israel:) **33** Because that they have forsaken me, and have worshipped Ashtoreth the goddess of the Zidonians, Chemosh the god of the Moabites, and Milcom the god of the children of Ammon, and have not walked in my ways, to do that which is right in mine eyes, and to keep my statutes and my judgments, as did David his father.

TEN TRIBES FOR ISRAEL; ONE TRIBE FOR JUDAH

The **northern kingdom** of the 10 tribes is again called **Israel**.

---

3 Genesis 17:4 and 15; 24:60; 35:11 and 48:19.
4 The half-tribes of Ephraim and Manasseh.

1 Kings 11:34 Howbeit I will not take the whole kingdom out of his hand [King Solomon's]: but I will make him prince all the days of his life for David my servant's sake, whom I chose, because he kept my commandments and my statutes: **35 But I will take the kingdom out of his son's hand** [Rehoboam], **and will give it unto thee** [Jeroboam], **even <u>ten tribes</u>**.

36 And **unto his son will I give <u>one tribe</u>, that David my servant may have a light alway before me in Jerusalem**, the city which I have chosen me to put my name there.   **37** And I will take thee, and **thou shalt reign according to all that thy soul desireth, and shalt be <u>king over Israel</u>** [the 10 tribes].

Judah And Benjamin Face Israel And Ephraim

2 Chronicles 25:5 Moreover **Amaziah** [the king] **gathered Judah** together, and made them captains over thousands, and captains over hundreds, according to the houses of their fathers, throughout **all Judah and Benjamin**: and he numbered them from twenty years old and above, and found them three hundred thousand choice men, able to go forth to war, that could handle spear and shield.   **6** He hired also an hundred thousand mighty men of valour **out of Israel** [the northern kingdom] for an hundred talents of silver.   **7** But there came a man of God to him, saying, O king, let not **the army of Israel** go with thee; **for the LORD is not with Israel**, to wit, **with all the children of Ephraim.**

In the days of the divided kingdom, the terms *Ephraim* and *Israel* came to be used interchangeably to reference the northern kingdom of the 10 tribes.

Isaiah 7:1 And it came to pass in the days of **Ahaz…<u>king of Judah</u>**, that Rezin **the king of Syria**, and Pekah…**<u>king of Israel</u>**, went up toward Jerusalem to war against it, but could not prevail against it.   **2** And it was told **the house of David** [another name for Judah], saying, **Syria is confederate with Ephraim.**

Samaria Becomes The Capital Of Israel

Samaria becomes the capital city of Israel and **Jerusalem** remains the capital of Judah. Like Washington, London or Moscow, the kingdom of Israel also becomes known after the name of its capital city, Samaria.

> **2 Chronicles 28:7** And Zichri, a mighty man **of Ephraim**, slew Maaseiah the king's son, and Azrikam the governor of the house, and Elkanah that was next to the king. **8** And the **children of Israel** [Ephraim] carried away captive of **their brethren** [Judah] two hundred thousand, women, sons, and daughters, and took also away much spoil from them, and **brought the spoil to Samaria.**

EPHRAIM HAS BECOME NOT A PEOPLE

Here is the hard evidence of what this book is all about. The foundation that I have laid in tracing the Abrahamic Covenant in the first half of this book is to reach this point in the Holy Scriptures. In their Diaspora, the northern kingdom of the 10 tribes of Israel have become *not a people*. In other words, the people of Ephraim have lost their identity as Hebrews as they have grown to become a multitude of nations in the middle of the earth, with the blessing of Joseph upon them. The people of these nations, in fulfillment of prophecy, have also become as the dust of the earth, stars of heaven, and sand of the sea.

> **Isaiah 7:7** Thus saith the Lord GOD, It shall not stand, neither shall it come to pass. **8** For the **head of Syria is Damascus** [its capital city], and the head of Damascus is Rezin [its king]; and **within threescore and five years shall Ephraim be broken** [carried off into Assyrian captivity], **that it be <u>not a people</u>. 9** And **the head of Ephraim is Samaria** ...

The Lord God has just said that within 65 years the 10 tribes of **Ephraim** shall become **<u>not a people</u>**. Below, the Lord calls **Ephraim** and the **kingdom of the house of Israel** ... *not a people* ... because in the places where He will scattered them, they will lose their Hebrew identity.

> **Hosea 1:4** And the LORD said unto him, **Call his name Jezreel** [God will scatter or sow]; for yet a little while, and **I will** ... **cause to cease <u>the kingdom of the house of Israel</u>** ... **6** for **I will no more have mercy upon the house of Israel** [Ephraim]; **but I will utterly take them away** ... **9** Then said God ... for ye are **<u>not my people</u>**, and I will not be your God.

10 Yet **the <u>number of the children of Israel</u>** shall be as the <u>**sand of the sea**</u>**, which cannot be measured nor numbered**; and it shall come to pass, that **in the place** [pg. 94] where it was said unto them, Ye are **not my people**, here it shall be said unto them, **Ye are the sons of the living God.**

In this context, the **children of Israel**, who shall become as the sand of the sea, is a reference to Ephraim: who shall lose his Hebrew identity as a son of the living God—**in the place** where God has scattered him. Then, the Lord will send prophets and preachers unto them in the latter years with the message of their lost heritage … that they may rediscover their destiny in today's Israel.

Hosea 2:23 And <u>**I will sow her unto me**</u> [unto God] in the earth; and **I will have mercy** upon her that had not obtained mercy; and I will say to them which were <u>**not my people**</u>, **Thou art my people**; and they shall say, **Thou art my God.**

God has sown the 10 tribes of Ephraim and Israel unto Himself, so that He may have mercy upon them in the latter years and times. He will speak to Ephraim who has ceased to be a Hebrew nation and people, but is not lost in the eyes of God. Ephraim will awaken and acknowledge his God. The prophet Amos calls Ephraim "the sinful kingdom" that God would destroy "from off of the face of the earth"—**as a kingdom or nation**. The Lord did this concerning Ephraim, while for David's sake He had mercy upon Judah and Jerusalem. The 10 tribes of the house of Israel have been sifted as corn in a sieve, but with not one of His people unknown to God. Ephraim is now to be reaped as a harvest of nations in the center of the earth, that carry the blessing of Joseph upon them.

Amos 9:7 … **O children of Israel?** [Ephraim] … **8** Behold, the eyes of the Lord GOD are upon the sinful kingdom, and **I will destroy it from off the face of the earth; saving that I will not utterly destroy the house of Jacob, saith the LORD. 9** For, lo, I will command, and **I will sift the house of Israel** [the 10 tribes of Ephraim] **among all nations**, like as corn is sifted in a sieve, **yet shall not the least grain** [of His people] **fall upon the earth.**

Israel Has Two Houses

The **house of Jacob** or **house of Israel** in the divided kingdom has **two houses**: first, the **house of Israel**, which is also known as the **house of Joseph** or **house of Ephraim**; and second, the **house of Judah** or **house of David**.

> Isaiah 8:13 Sanctify the LORD of hosts himself; and let him be your fear, and let him be your dread. **14** And he shall be for a sanctuary; but for a stone of stumbling and for a rock of offence to **both the houses of Israel**[5], for a gin [a noose for catching animals] and for a snare to the inhabitants of Jerusalem.

The House Of Jacob Is Still Called Israel

Yet, the **house of Jacob** is still called by the **name of Israel**. Ephraim was sustained by the fountain of the nation, Judah, but their relationship with the true and living God was not from the heart and became religion: whose root word means *bondage*.

> Isaiah 48:1 Hear ye this, O **house of Jacob, which are called by the name of Israel**, and are **come forth out of the waters of Judah**, which swear by the name of the LORD, and make mention of the **God of Israel**, but not in truth, nor in righteousness. **2** For they call themselves of the holy city, and stay themselves upon **the God of Israel; The LORD of hosts is his name**.

Israel Receives A Famine In Hearing The Word Of God

There comes a time in the life of a disobedient person or nation when God finally stops talking.

> Amos 8:1 Thus hath the Lord GOD shewed unto me: and behold a basket of summer fruit. **2** And he said, Amos, what seest thou? And I said, A basket of summer fruit. Then said the LORD unto me, **The end is come upon my people of Israel** [the 10 tribes]; I will not again pass by them any more …

---

5 The northern kingdom of Israel was carried into captivity by Assyria during the lifetime of Isaiah, so that from this point forward in the Hebrew Scriptures the distinction between Israel and Judah takes on an even greater sygnificance.

113

11 Behold, the days come, saith the Lord GOD, that I will send **a famine** in the land, not a famine of bread, nor a thirst for water, but **of hearing the words of the LORD**: **12** And **they shall wander from sea to sea**, and wander **from the north even to the east**, they shall run to and fro to seek the word of the LORD, and shall not find it [until finally they stop seeking the Jehovah of Israel at all].

The 10 tribes were last seen in the first century in the area of Assyria, Babylon, and the Euphrates River [northern Iraq, pg. 125]. But the above text says that ... "they shall wander from sea to sea". There are no seas in northern Iraq. The text also says that they shall ... "wander from the north even to the east". They shall wander from the north of what to the east of where ... perhaps as a company of seafaring nations? God knows.

A Final Judgment On Ephraim While In The Land

The Lord said through his prophets that Ephraim shall soon be a nation no more. The Lord did not say, however, that Ephraim's condition in the nations would last forever ... because He has spoken other prophesies over Ephraim through Joseph, which must also be fulfilled.

Hosea 9:11 As for **Ephraim, their glory shall fly away like a bird**, from the birth, and from the womb, and from the conception. **12** Though they bring up their children, yet will I bereave them, that there shall not be a man left: yea, **woe also to them when I depart from them!** **13** Ephraim, as I saw Tyrus, is planted in a pleasant place: but Ephraim shall bring forth his children to the murderer. **14** Give them, O LORD: what wilt thou give? give them a miscarrying womb and dry breasts. **15** All their wickedness is in Gilgal: for there I hated them: for the wickedness of their doings I will drive them out of mine house, I will love them no more: all their princes are revolters.

16 **Ephraim is smitten**, their root is dried up, they shall bear no fruit: yea, though they bring forth, yet will I slay even the beloved fruit of their womb. **17** **My God will cast them away, because they did not hearken unto him: and they shall be wanderers among the nations.**

114

Hidden in the foreknowledge of God is that in the passage of time in the places to where they would migrate to, the people of Ephraim even with their lost Hebrew identity would actually become the heads of state in the company of nations in the middle of the earth that they were to become. The knowledge of this Bible fact should also help in locating Ephraim.

> **Isaiah 14:1** For the LORD will have **mercy on Jacob**, and **will yet choose Israel**, and **set them in their own land** [in a place]: and the strangers shall be joined with them, and they shall cleave to the **house of Jacob.**

Jacob and **Israel**, in Isaiah's day, is **a reference to the 10 tribes which were taken into Assyrian captivity during Isaiah's lifetime and ministry.** The 10 tribes of Israel were to be given **a new land ... a place ... a company of nations in the midst of the earth**[6]. In intermingling and intermarrying with Gentiles of these nations, the people in these new lands would become one with the 10 tribes: as these Hebrew people lose their identity with Israel.

> **Isaiah 14:2** And the people shall take them [the Gentiles of these new lands], and bring them to **their place**: and the **house of Israel** shall possess them in the **land of the LORD** for servants and handmaids: and **they shall take them captives, whose captives they were**; and **they shall rule over their oppressors**.

God here claims for Himself, and for Israel, these new lands which were populated by His people who unto this day do not know they are His. This numberless multitude of Joseph and Ephraim have come to rule in these new kingdoms to which they have been dispersed.

Isaiah Did Not Prophesy Solely To Judah

It is inaccurate to say, as do many commentators, that Isaiah prophesied exclusively to the kingdom of Judah. Isaiah's ministry as prophet was from approximately 760 to around 710 BCE. The northern kingdom of Israel went into Assyrian captivity about 721 BCE.

---

6 C/p. 2 Samuel 7:10 [pg. 94]; see also Chapter 7..

Isaiah 1:1 **The vision of Isaiah** the son of Amoz, which he **saw concerning Judah and Jerusalem** in the days of Uzziah, Jotham, Ahaz, and Hezekiah, kings of Judah. ...

Isaiah 7:1 And it came to pass in the days of Ahaz the son of Jotham, the son of Uzziah, **king of Judah**, that Rezin the king of Syria, and Pekah the son of Remaliah, **king of Israel**, went up toward Jerusalem to war against it, but could not prevail against it. 2 And it was told the **house of David** [Judah], saying, **Syria is confederate with Ephraim**. ...

3 Then said the LORD unto Isaiah, Go forth now to meet Ahaz ... 4 And say unto him, Take heed, and be quiet; fear not, neither be fainthearted for ... 7 Thus saith the Lord GOD, It shall not stand ... and **within threescore and five years shall Ephraim be broken, that it be not a people**.

Compare other nations that Isaiah prophesied to:

Isaiah 15:1 The burden of **Moab** ...
Isaiah 18:1 Woe to the land shadowing with wings, which is beyond the rivers of **Ethiopia** ...
Isaiah 19:1 The burden of **Egypt** ...
Isaiah 23:1 The burden of **Tyre** ...
Isaiah 34:1 Come near **ye nations** to hear and hearken ye people: let the earth hear, and all that is therein; the world, and all things that become forth of it.
Isaiah 47:1 Come down, and sit in the dust, O virgin daughter of **Babylon** ...

The Isaiah's prophesies, therefore, do not solely concern the southern kingdom of Judah. He had much to say concerning the northern kingdom of Ephraim, Israel, and many other nations.

JUDAH REPRESENTS ISRAEL BUT IS NOT ALL ISRAEL

Once David's united kingdom of Israel became two kingdoms, "all Israel was in Judah and Benjamin". In other words, the people of the southern kingdom of Judah in the territories of Judah and Benjamin were representative of all of the 12 tribes of Israel [Jacob]. But, although **all Israel**

116

was in Judah and Benjamin, all Israel **was not of** Judah and Benjamin.

Both in the days of the divided kingdoms of Israel and Judah, and the days when the northern kingdom of Israel had ceased to exist, down to the re-birth of the nation of Israel in 1948—the great multitude of Ephraim [the Diaspora of the 10 tribes of Israel] are not to be found among Jews of the tribe of Judah. Yet, the 10 tribes of Israel and Jews of the tribe of Judah **remain brethren** unto this day.

It is the same God that created the kingdom of Israel and the kingdom of Judah that has also divided them ... unto this day.

> **2 Chronicles 11:1** And when Rehoboam [King Solomon's son] was come to Jerusalem, he gathered of the **house of Judah and Benjamin** an hundred and fourscore thousand chosen men, which were warriors, **to fight against Israel** [the 10 tribes of Ephraim], that he might bring the kingdom again to Rehoboam.

> **11:2** But the word of the LORD came to Shemaiah the man of God, saying, **3** Speak unto Rehoboam the son of Solomon, king of Judah, and to **all Israel in Judah and Benjamin**, saying, **4** Thus saith the LORD, Ye shall not go up, **nor fight against your brethren** [their Hebrew brethren]: return every man to his house: for **this thing is done of me**. And they obeyed the words of the LORD, and returned from going against Jeroboam [king of Israel].

REPRESENTATIVES OF ALL ISRAEL WERE PRESENT WITH JUDAH

There was significant post-exile contact between Jews of the southern kingdom and those who had escaped from Assyrian captivity and returned to the land. Also, many of the poor were left in the land by the Assyrians; and they were still of the house of Jacob. None of this post-exile contact between the two kingdoms, however, changes the fact of where the multitude of the people of Ephraim were carried to, or where the descendants of Ephraim are today.

> **2 Chronicles 31:1** Now when all this was finished, **all Israel that were present** [with Judah] went out to the cities of Judah, and brake the images in pieces, and cut down the groves, and threw

117

down the high places and the altars out of **all Judah and Benjamin**, in **Ephraim** also and **Manasseh**, until they had utterly destroyed them all. ...

6 And concerning the **children of Israel** and **Judah**, that dwelt in the cities of Judah, they also brought in the tithe of oxen and sheep, and the tithe of holy things which were consecrated unto the LORD their God, and laid them by heaps.

2 Chronicles 34:1 Josiah was eight years old when he began to reign, and he reigned in Jerusalem one and thirty years. **2** And he did that which was right in the sight of the LORD, and walked in the ways of David his father, and declined neither to the right hand, nor to the left. **3** For in the eighth year of his reign, while he was yet young, he began to seek after the God of David his father: and in the twelfth year he began to **purge Judah and Jerusalem** from the high places, and the groves, and the carved images, and the molten images. ... **6** And so did he in the cities of **Manasseh**, and **Ephraim**, and **Simeon**, even unto **Naphtali**, with their mattocks round about. ...

9 And when they came to Hilkiah the high priest, they delivered the money that was brought into the house of God, which the Levites that kept the doors had gathered of the hand of **Manasseh** and **Ephraim**, and of **all the remnant of Israel** [escaped from Assyrian captivity], and of **all Judah and Benjamin**; and they returned to Jerusalem.

2 Chronicles 35:16 So all the service of the LORD was prepared the same day, to keep the passover, and to offer burnt offerings upon the altar of the LORD, according to the commandment of king Josiah. **17** And **the children of Israel** [from the 10 tribes] <u>**that were present**</u> **kept the passover** at that time, and the feast of unleavened bread seven days.

18 And there was no passover like to that kept in Israel from the days of Samuel the prophet; neither did all the kings of Israel keep such a passover as Josiah kept, and the priests, and the Levites, and <u>**all Judah and Israel that were present**</u>, and the **inhabitants of Jerusalem.**

THE PRIESTHOOD RETURNS TO JERUSALEM

The priesthood of the tribe of Levi came to Jerusalem after King Jeroboam begins to lead Israel into apostasy by rejecting the commandments of God.

2 Chronicles 11:5 And Rehoboam dwelt in Jerusalem, and built cities for defence in Judah. **... 13** And **the priests and the Levites that were in all Israel** [the northern kingdom] resorted to him out of all their coasts. **14** For the Levites left their suburbs and their possession, and came to Judah and Jerusalem: for **Jeroboam** and his sons had **cast them off from executing the priest's office** unto the LORD: **15** And he ordained him priests for the high places, and for the devils, and for the calves which he had made.

THE RIGHTEOUS OF THE NATION ALSO COME TO JERUSALEM

Many of the righteous in the northern kingdom whose walk was according to the Torah also came to Jerusalem. But, after only three years, King Rehoboam begins to turn himself and the people of Judah away from keeping the Torah.

2 Chronicles 11:16 And after them **out of all the tribes of Israel such as set their hearts to seek the LORD God of Israel came to Jerusalem**, to sacrifice unto the LORD God of their fathers. **17** So they strengthened the kingdom of Judah, and made Rehoboam the son of Solomon strong, three years: for three years they walked in the way of David and Solomon.

Israel as a nation was born in Egypt, where the 12 sons of Jacob became the 12 tribes of Israel. Probably several million Israelites came out of Egypt to enter the land of Canaan: that God promised to give to Abraham, Isaac and Israel [Jacob] for **an everlasting possession**. We are living today in the day of the recovery of *the whole house of Israel* spoken of in **Ezekiel 37:11** where God will restore all 12 tribes of His chosen earthly people back into the land of Israel again as one nation. It is the "righteous" Jew and Gentile of today who perceive from God's Word what the Lord is intending to accomplish in Israel that will truly seek the Lord for His wisdom in locating the identity and location of Ephraim, so that *all Israel* may again return to Jerusalem.

119

The Divided Kingdom of Israel and Judah

CHAPTER 12

GOD CEASES THE KINGDOM OF ISRAEL

Jehovah is the author of **the spiritual law of offerings**:

What is given or sown in abundance will return back to God [or us] in the same measure in which it was given out—multiplied—thirty, sixty, and a hundredfold[1].

God sowed the 10 tribes of Israel unto Himself. He fully intends to reap them back unto Himself. Over the passage of time, God will recover His Hebrew sons and daughters that He has sown: multiplied an hundredfold—as the dust of the earth, stars of heaven, and sand of the sea. To the descendants of Ephraim, who the Lord says are "not my people" because of their lost Hebrew identity, God will embrace as sons and be received as a Father. These are Joseph's half of the dry bones of **Ezekiel 37:15-22**: the **branch of Joseph** which is in the **hand of Ephraim** that is to be joined with the **branch of Judah** to become one nation again in Israel. **The fulfillment of the prophecy of Ezekiel 37 is the pathway to Hosea 2:23.**

Israel: Find Joseph

Hosea 2:23 And **I will sow her unto me** in the earth; and **I will have mercy** upon her that had not obtained mercy; and I will say to them which were not my people, **Thou art my people**; and they shall say, **Thou art my God.**

EPHRAIM SHALL BE BROKEN

God sent many witnesses to Israel [the northern kingdom] that He was going to cast it from off the face of the earth.

Isaiah 7:1 And it came to pass in the days of **Ahaz … king of**

---

1 C/p. Genesis 26:12 and Proverbs 3:9-10.

Judah, that Rezin **the king of Syria**, and Pekah ... **king of Israel**, went up toward Jerusalem to war against it, but could not prevail against it. **2** And it was told the **house of David** [Judah], saying, **Syria is confederate with Ephraim** ... **7** Thus saith the Lord GOD, It shall not stand, neither shall it come to pass. **8** ... and **within threescore and five years shall Ephraim be broken**, that it be not a people.

Ephraim Is Cast Out And Shall Be Regathered

The Hebrew prophets also foretold repeatedly that God would destroy and then rebuild the "**whole house of Israel**" [2]—that is all 12 tribes of Jacob. He would begin with the **house of Israel**. The **house of Judah** would follow in time. Hosea, a prophet to the northern kingdom, describes Ephraim as: the "**children of whoredoms**" (a picture of the backsliding Israel), and the "**kingdom of the house of Israel**". The prophet had a son whom God named **Jezreel** (God will scatter or sow). He then had a daughter whose name was **Loruhamah** (I will have mercy no more; or I will not have compassion). Finally, the prophet had another son who God named **Loammi** (not my people).

> **Hosea 1:2** The beginning of the word of the LORD by Hosea. And the LORD said to Hosea, Go, **take unto thee a wife of whoredoms** and **children of whoredoms**: for the land hath committed great whoredom, departing from the LORD. **3** So he went and took Gomer the daughter of Diblaim; which conceived, and bare him a son.

> **4** And the LORD said unto him, **Call his name Jezreel**; for yet a little while, and I ... **will cause to cease the kingdom of the house of Israel**. **5** And it shall come to pass at that day, that I will break the bow of Israel in the **valley of Jezreel** [the scattered ones].

> **6** And she conceived again, and bare a daughter. And God said unto him, **Call her name Loruhamah**: for **I will no more have mercy upon the house of Israel; but I will utterly take them away**.

Israel is deported into Assyrian captivity; but God remembers His cov-

---

2 Ezekiel 36:10 and 37:11.

enant of mercy with David[3]. He will save Judah by a sovereign act of God.

Hosea 1:7 But I will have mercy upon the <u>house of Judah</u>, and will save them by the LORD their God [Judah's salvation is by a sovereign act of God], **and will not save them by bow, nor by sword, nor by battle, by horses, nor by horsemen.**

"Ephraim likewise", saith the LORD, "will also not be redeemed by war, but by an equally sovereign act of God."

Israel: Find Joseph

JOSEPH AND EPHRAIM BECOME A NUMBERLESS MULTITUDE

The promises of God to Joseph will be fulfilled in the people of Ephraim, who have become numberless and have lost their Hebrew identity. There have never been too many Jews in the world to count (only something over 13 million now), but the Hebrew people of God that we cannot see are numberless. The "place" where they are nested is in a community of nations in whatever God has determined to be the middle of the earth. It is in this place they will discover that they are sons of the living God.

Hosea 1: 8 Now when she had weaned Loruhamah, she conceived, and bare a son. **9** Then said God, Call his name **Loammi** [not my people]: **for ye are <u>not my people</u>, and I will not be your God. 10 <u>Yet the number of the children of Israel</u>** [the 10 tribes] **<u>shall be as the sand of the sea, which cannot be measured nor numbered</u>**; and it shall come to pass, that **in <u>the place</u>**[4] where it was said unto them, Ye are not my people, here it shall be said unto them, Ye are the sons of the living God.

EPHRAIM IS SIFTED BUT NOT LOST

The progeny of Israel and Ephraim have been sifted like flour among the nations, but none shall be lost even though the prophet Amos calls Ephraim ... "the sinful kingdom" whom God would ... "destroy ... from off the face of the earth". [The kingdom was destroyed: but not the people.]

---

3 Psalms 89:20, 24 and 28.
4 2 Samuel 7:10; 1 Chronicles 17:9 and Isaiah 14:1-2.

Amos[5] 9:7 Are ye not as children of the Ethiopians unto me, **O children of Israel** [10 tribes]? saith the LORD. Have not I brought up Israel out of the land of Egypt? ... **8 Behold, the eyes of the Lord GOD are upon the sinful kingdom, and I will destroy it from off the face of the earth; saving that I will not utterly destroy the house of Jacob** [12 tribes]**, saith the LORD.**

Only 10 of the 12 tribes of Jacob would be banished out of God's sight, yet not one person of the 10 tribes of Israel is hidden or lost from the eyes or mercy of God. [Israel is technically 13 tribes, and not 12, because Joseph was given a double portion represented by the half-tribes of Ephraim and Manasseh. God gave the priestly tribe of Levi no inheritance in the land. After the kingdom divided, Levi has merged with the tribe of Judah.]

Amos 9:9 For, lo, **I will command,** and **I will sift the house of Israel** [Ephraim] **among all nations,** like as corn is sifted in a sieve, **yet shall not the least grain fall upon the earth.**

The 10 tribes of the northern kingdom of Israel have been sifted, scattered and sown among nations. They have carried with them the **blessing** and the **birthright of Joseph.** They also carry the **promises of God** made to **Ephraim and Manasseh.** God knows where all of the descendants of Ephraim are, even unto this day.

ISRAEL IS CARRIED INTO CAPTIVITY BY ASSYRIA

God now honors His Word and casts Israel out of His sight. Israel was carried into Assyrian captivity in 721 BCE, and has been out of the land since this date. But the promises of God are eternal; and He will yet fulfill all of His promises concerning the land of Israel and the destinies of the **two houses of Israel**—Israel (Ephraim), and **Judah** (the Jewish people of today's Israel). ... *For I will hasten my word to perform it[6].*

2 Kings 17:1 In the twelfth year of Ahaz king of Judah began Hoshea the son of Elah **to reign in Samaria over Israel** nine years. **2** And he did that which was evil in the sight of the LORD, but not as the kings of Israel that were before him [he did greater evil than ever before in Israel]. **3** Against him came up **Shalmaneser**

---

5 Amos was a prophet to the 10 tribes of the northern kingdom of Israel.
6 Jeremiah 1:10.

king of Assyria; ...

5 Then the king of Assyria came up throughout all the land, and went up to Samaria, and besieged it three years. 6 In the ninth year of Hoshea **the king of Assyria took Samaria**, and **carried Israel away into Assyria**, and placed them in Halah and in Habor by the **river of Gozan**[7], and in the **cities of the Medes** (Persia / Iran).

JOSEPHUS RECORDS THE MULTITUDES OF EPHRAIM

God still has a multitude of His people in the lands formerly ruled by Assyria. The Jewish historian, Josephus, has said that as late as 100 CE ... **"The Ten Tribes are beyond the Euphrates till now, and are an immense multitude, not to be estimated by numbers"**[8].

EPHRAIM AND ISRAEL ARE REJECTED BY GOD

As God had promised, He rejects the **seed of Ephraim** and **throne of Israel**.

2 Kings 17:7 For so it was, that the **children of Israel had sinned against the LORD their God**, which had brought them up out of the land of Egypt, from under the hand of Pharaoh king of Egypt, and had feared other gods, 8 And walked in the statutes of the heathen, whom the LORD cast out from before the **children of Israel**, and of the **kings of Israel**, which they had made.

9 And the **children of Israel** did secretly those things that were not right against the LORD their God, and they built them high places in all their cities, from the tower of the watchmen to the fenced city. 10 And they set them up images and groves in every high hill, and under every green tree: 11 And there they burnt incense in all the high places, as did the heathen whom the LORD carried away before them; and wrought wicked things to provoke the LORD to anger: 12 For they served idols, whereof the LORD had said unto them, Ye shall not do this thing.

The writer of Second Kings continues to distinguish Israel from Judah.

---

7 The Gozan River is one of the tributaries of the Euphrates River in northern Iraq.

8 Antiquities, XI, V, 2.

2 Kings 17:13 Yet **the LORD testified <u>against Israel</u>**, and <u>**against Judah**</u>, by all the prophets, and by all the seers, saying, **Turn ye from your evil ways**, and keep my commandments and my statutes, according to all the law which I commanded your fathers, and which I sent to you by my servants the prophets. **14** Notwithstanding they would not hear, but hardened their necks, like to the neck of their fathers, **that did not believe in the LORD their God**.

15 And they [the northern kingdom] <u>**rejected his statutes, and his covenant**</u> that he made with their fathers [Abraham, Isaac and Jacob], and <u>**his testimonies**</u> which he testified against them; and they followed vanity, and became vain, and went after the heathen that were round about them, concerning whom the LORD had charged them, that they should not do like them.

16 And they left all the commandments of the LORD their God, and made them molten images, even two calves, and made a grove, and worshipped all the host of heaven, and served Baal. **17** And they **caused their sons and their daughters to pass through the fire**, and **used divination and enchantments**, and sold themselves to do evil in the sight of the LORD, to provoke him to anger.

18 Therefore the <u>**LORD was very angry with Israel**</u>, and <u>**removed them out of his sight**</u>: there was <u>**none left**</u> [in His sight] <u>**but the tribe of Judah**</u> only. **19** Also <u>**Judah**</u> kept not the commandments of the LORD their God, but <u>**walked in the statutes of Israel**</u> which they made.

The writer clearly has reference to Ephraim and the 10 tribes when he makes reference to Israel's sins. The tribe of Judah that remained in the land included the tribes of Judah, Benjamin and Levi. Judah followed in the sins of Israel, and a century later is carried off into captivity by Babylon. For David's sake, God has had mercy on Judah and the Jews have been allowed to return twice to the land of Israel—first after 70 years of Babylonian captivity, and second in 1948. It is now time for the heirs of Joseph and Ephraim to also return to the land. Although the Lord cast them out of His sight, He did not cast them off the earth. He will fulfill all of His promises to Joseph and Ephraim, as well as to Judah.

1 Kings 17:20 And the **LORD rejected all the seed of Israel** [including the kingly line of Ephraim], and afflicted them, ard delivered them into the hand of spoilers, until **he had cast them out of his sight. 21** For **he rent Israel from the house of David**; and they made Jeroboam the son of Nebat king: and **Jeroboam drave Israel from following the LORD**, and made them sin a great sin.

22 For the children of Israel walked in all the sins of Jeroboam which he did; they departed not from them; **23** Until the **LORD removed Israel out of his sight**, as he had **said by all his servants the prophets[9]**. So was **Israel carried away out of their own land to Assyria unto this day**.

Unto this day is a technical term used in the Bible to indicate a condition which will last at least until the coming of the Messiah to reign on the earth. Here, by listening to the writer of Second Kings (believed to be Jeremiah) as if it were commentary on the internet or evening news, the message is clear—a multitude of hidden Hebrew descendants of the 10 tribes of Israel are still in the lands formerly ruled by Assyria *unto this day*. But the greater portion are in the company of nations of Joseph and Ephraim.

A New Wave Of Idolatry Infects The Remnant Of Israel

The people sent back by the king of Assyria into the lands of the northern kingdom of Israel brought with them their gods.

2 Kings 17:24 And the **king of Assyria brought men from Babylon**, and from Cuthah, and from Ava, and from Hamath, and from Sepharvaim, and **placed them in the cities of Samaria instead of the children of Israel**: and **they possessed Samaria** [Israel's former capital], and dwelt in the cities thereof.

25 And so it was at the beginning of their dwelling there, that **they feared not the LORD: therefore the LORD sent lions** among them, which slew some of them. **26** Wherefore they spake to the king of Assyria, saying, The nations which thou hast removed, and placed in the cities of Samaria, know not the manner of the God of the land: therefore **he hath sent lions** among them,

---

9   God does not do anything unless He first reveals His secret to His servants, the prophets (Amos 3:7).

and, behold, they slay them, because **they know not the manner of the God of the land[10]**.

27 Then the king of Assyria commanded, saying, Carry thither **one of the priests** whom ye brought from thence; and let them go and dwell there, and let him teach them the manner of the God of the land. **28** Then one of the priests whom they had carried away from Samaria came and dwelt in Bethel, and **taught them how they should fear the LORD.**

29 Howbeit every nation [in the lands of the northern kingdom] **made gods of their own**, and **put them in the houses of the high places which the Samaritans had made**, every nation in their cities wherein they dwelt. **30** And the men of Babylon made Succothbenoth, and the men of Cuth made Nergal, and the men of Hamath made Ashima, **31** And the Avites made Nibhaz and Tartak, and the Sepharvites burnt their children in fire to Adrammelech and Anammelech, the gods of Sepharvaim.

32 So they feared the LORD [they were afraid of the LORD because of the lions]**, and made unto themselves of the lowest of them priests** of the high places, which sacrificed for them in the houses of the high places. **33** They feared the LORD [they knew God], and served their own gods [yet they served other gods], after the manner of the nations whom they carried away from thence.

34 <u>Unto this day</u> they do after the former manners: they fear not the LORD neither do they after their statutes, or after their ordinances, or after the law and commandment which **the LORD commanded** the <u>children of Jacob, whom he named Israel</u>; **35** With whom the LORD had made a covenant, and charged them, saying, Ye shall not fear other gods, nor bow yourselves to them, nor serve them, nor sacrifice to them:

36 But the LORD, who brought you up out of the land of Egypt with great power and a stretched out arm, him shall ye fear, and him shall ye worship, and to him shall ye do sacrifice. **37** And the statutes, and the ordinances, and the law, and the commandment, which he wrote for you, ye shall observe to do for evermore;

10 Sometime the heathen know more than the people of God.

and ye shall not fear other gods. **38 And the covenant that I have made with you ye shall not forget; neither shall ye fear other gods**.

39 But the LORD your God ye shall fear; and he shall deliver you out of the hand of all your enemies. **40 <u>Howbeit they did not hearken, but they did after their former manner</u>**. **41** So these nations feared the LORD [they knew of God], and served their graven images, both their children, and their children's children: as did their fathers, **so do they <u>unto this day.</u>**

Israel Serves Other Gods In The Lands Of Assyria

Although the greater portion of the 10 tribes of Ephraim [Israel] have emigrated to distant lands, there is a large Hebrew remnant with a lost identity that remain in the lands formerly ruled by Assyria (including the territories of Babylon) who are still worshiping other gods—Islam, most likely. But, before sitting in judgment for the sins of its brethren, the Jews of today should remember their own idolatry[11] that took them into Babylon captivity for 70 years.

2 Kings 18:11 And **the king of Assyria did carry away Israel unto Assyria, and put them** in Halah and in Habor by the **river of Gozan[12]**, and **<u>in the cities of the Medes</u>**: **12** Because they obeyed not the voice of the LORD their God, but transgressed his covenant, and all that Moses the servant of the LORD commanded, and would not hear them, nor do them.

1 Chronicles 5:26 And the **God of Israel** stirred up the spirit of Pul **king of Assyria**, and the spirit of Tilgathpilneser **king of Assyria**, and he **carried them away**, even the **Reubenites** [the tribe of Reuben], and the **Gadites** [the tribe of Gad], and the **half tribe of Manasseh**, and brought them unto Halah, and Habor, and Hara, and to **the river Gozan, <u>unto this day</u>**.

It is a very interesting Bible study to superimpose maps of the kingdoms of Assyria, Babylon, and Medo-Persia on top of one another because, according to this and other passages of Scripture, there is a significant rem-

11   2 Kings 17:19.
12   See footnote #7, pg. 125.

nant of Israelites with lost identities in all of these territories ... worshiping other gods.

Israel: Find Joseph

JUDAH IS WARNED OF ITS COMING CAPTIVITY

Jeremiah also warns Judah that what has happened to Israel is about to happen to them—that Judah shall also be cast out of God's sight.

> **Jeremiah 7:15 And <u>I will cast you out of my sight, as I have cast out all your brethren, even the whole seed of Ephraim</u>.**

All the **seed of Ephraim** are the natural brothers of the Jews of today's Israel. All the descendants of Joseph and Ephraim, likewise, have the same blood-covenant right to possess their portion of the land of today's Israel, because they are also the promised heirs of Abraham, Isaac, Jacob and Joseph.

JUDAH SHALL ALSO BE SCATTERED THROUGHOUT THE EARTH

God also said that He would and has scattered Jews into all nations of the earth. For David's sake, however, Jews have never lost their identity as Jews nor their historical connection with the land of Israel and their Covenant with God and Abraham. Because God has promised that David's light[13] will always shine in Jerusalem, He has used the Diaspora of Jews to reestablish the nation of Israel. He now also intends to bring the children of Joseph and Ephraim back to the land to live as one nation with children of Judah, in fulfillment of **Ezekiel 37:15-22.**

> **Jeremiah 15:1** Then said the LORD unto me, Though Moses and Samuel stood before me, yet my mind could not be toward this people: cast them out of my sight, and let them go forth. ... **4** And <u>**I will cause them to be removed into all kingdoms of the earth**</u>, **because of Manasseh** the son of Hezekiah **king of Judah,** for that which he did in Jerusalem. ... **7** And ... <u>**I will destroy my people**</u>, since they return not from their ways. **8 Their widows are increased to me above the sand of the seas.**

---

13 1 Kings 11:35.

130

JUDAH IS CARRIED INTO BABYLONIAN CAPTIVITY

God honors His Word to the Jews of the southern kingdom, which are exiled for 70 years in Babylon. **Since this period in history, the throne of David has been without a king**. Zedekiah was the last king of Judah to sit on the throne of David. Zedekiah's fate demonstrates that a lack of spiritual vision in an individual, king, people or nation will eventually lead to a loss of natural vision: also required to function at every level of life.

Where there is no vision the people perish[14].

2 Kings 25:1 And it came to pass in the ninth year of his reign, in the tenth month, in the tenth day of the month, that **Nebuchadnezzar king of Babylon came**, he, and all his host, against Jerusalem, and pitched against it; and they built forts against it round about. **2** And **the city was besieged** unto the eleventh year of **king Zedekiah**. ... **7** And **they slew the sons of Zedekiah before his eyes**, and put out the eyes of Zedekiah, and bound him with fetters of brass, and **carried him to Babylon.**

2 Kings 25:8 And in the fifth month, on the seventh day of the month, which is the nineteenth year of king Nebuchadnezzar king of Babylon, came Nebuzaradan, captain of the guard, a servant of the king of Babylon, unto Jerusalem: **9** And **he burnt the house of the LORD[15]**, and the king's house, and all the houses of Jerusalem, and every great man's house burnt he with fire. **10** And all the army of the Chaldees, that were with the captain of the guard, **brake down the walls of Jerusalem** round about.

This was the third and last invasion and deportation of Jews to Babylon, where they remained for 70 years. When the 70 years were expired, the Persian king Cyrus was stirred[16] by God to allow the Jews to return to Jerusalem. Cyrus was named by the prophet Isaiah 150 years before he was born[17]. He was the son of Queen Esther and the Persian King Ahasuerus.

During the rebuilding of Jerusalem under Zerubbabel, Ezra and Nehemiah, only about 50,000 of the Jews who were in Babylonian captivity

14 Proverbs 29:18.
15 This fulfills Jeremiah's prophecy that Solomon's temple would be destroyed (Jeremiah 7:15).
16 Ezra 1:1-4; 2 Chronicles 36:22-23.
17 Isaiah 44:28; 45:1.

actually returned to rebuild the walls of Jerusalem. This is further evidence that there is a remnant of Jewish Hebrews to this day that remain in the former territories of ancient Babylon: which is present day Iraq.

GOD'S PEOPLE WILL REMEMBER HIM IN DISTANT LANDS

God has scattered and sown unto Himself both the **house of Joseph** [Ephraim, Manasseh and the 10 tribes of Israel] and **house of Judah** into foreign lands. There they have intermarried with the people of these lands. But God has promised that they will remember Him in these distant lands. For the house of Joseph, the fulfillment of Ezekiel 37 is crucial to this process ... for the Lord delights in His mercies: which are new every morning[18]. He is the **God of Ephraim**, as well as the **God of Judah**.

> **Zechariah 10:6** And I will **strengthen** the **house of Judah**, and I will **save** the **house of Joseph**, and I will bring them again **to place them**; for **I have mercy upon them: and they shall be as though I had not cast them off**: for **I am the LORD their God**, and will hear them.

> **7** And they of **Ephraim** shall be like a mighty man, and their heart shall rejoice as through wine: yea, their children shall see it, and be glad; their heart shall rejoice in the LORD ... **8** I will hiss [whistle] for them, and gather them; for I have redeemed them: and they shall increase as they have increased ... **9** And **I will sow them among the people**: and **they shall remember me in far countries**; and they shall live with their children, and turn again.

> **Jeremiah 31:27** Behold, the days come, saith the LORD, that **I will sow** the **house of Israel** and the **house of Judah** with the seed of man [intermarriage], and with the seed of beast [war]. **28** And it shall come to pass, that like as [in the same manner] **I have watched over them** [the God of Israel speaking], to **pluck up**, and to **break down**, and to **throw down**, and to **destroy**, and to **afflict**; so will I watch over them, to build, and to plant them even in the lands where they are sown, saith the LORD.

The descendants of both Israel and Judah have prospered in their Diaspora. Jews have accumulated wealth in almost every land in which they

18 Micah 7:18; Lamentations 2:22-23.

have been sown, though their numbers have been few. Ephraim, when he is discovered, has prospered in secret; and has become an immense multitude with the blessing of Joseph upon his people.

ISRAEL SHALL BE WITHOUT THE TEMPLE UNTIL THE LATTER DAYS

The 10 tribes of Israel shall live without the Temple until the latter days. King Solomon's Temple was destroyed in 586 BCE by the Babylonians. Herod's Temple was thrown down in 70 CE by the Roman general Titus. The Temple Institute in Jerusalem has made almost all the preparations that would be needed to construct the third temple, including the priestly garments, robe of the high priest, articles of worship, and has the red heifer needed to cleanse the priesthood. Also, the sons of the priestly tribe of Levi have been located by their DNA, and have been trained to reinstitute animal sacrifices under the restored Law of Moses.

One of several major impediments to building the third temple is that Israel does not control the Temple Mount. Although East Jerusalem was taken in the Six-Day War of 1967, the government of Israel caused the Temple Mount remaining in Arab control. The other major impediments are: that the Temple Mount is occupied by the Dome of the Rock mosque; there is some disagreement as to exactly where the footprints of Solomon and Herod's Temples are located; and whether the Dome of the Rock must be torn down in order for temple construction to take place.

> **Hosea 3:4** For the **children of Israel** [the 10 tribes of Israel] shall abide many days without a **king**, and without a **prince** [high priest], and without a **sacrifice** [animal sacrifice under the law of Moses], and without an **image**, and without an **ephod** [clothing of the high priest], and without **teraphim**: 5 Afterward [after many days] shall the children of Israel return [Ephraim rejoined to Judah], and seek the LORD their God, and David their King; and shall fear the LORD and his goodness **in the latter days** [latter days, not last days].

THE THIRD TEMPLE SHALL ONLY BE BUILT WHEN JOSEPH RETURNS TO THE LAND

<u>**Here is an interesting question**</u>: Is not the joining of Ephraim with Judah in fulfillment of **Ezekiel 37:15-22** perhaps the last prerequisite to

Israel's building the third temple ... expressed in the balance of the the Chapter?

> **Ezekiel 37:23** Neither shall they defile themselves any more with their idols, nor with their detestable things, nor with any of their transgressions: but **I will save them out of all their dwelling places**, wherein they have sinned, and will cleanse them: **so shall they be my people, and I will be their God**.

> **24** And **David my servant** [the Messiah] **shall be king over them**; and they all shall have one shepherd: they shall also walk in my judgments, and observe my statutes, and do them. **25** And they shall dwell in the land that I have given unto Jacob my servant, wherein your fathers have dwelt; and they shall dwell therein, even they, and their children, and their children's children for ever: and my servant **David shall be their prince for ever**.

> **26** Moreover **I will** make a covenant of peace with them; it shall be an everlasting covenant with them: and I will place them, and multiply them, and will **set <u>my sanctuary in the midst of them for evermore</u>**, and they shall be my people. **28** And the heathen shall know that I the LORD do sanctify Israel, **when <u>my sanctuary shall be in the midst of them for evermore</u>**.

One may expound in good faith that **Ezekiel 37:23-28** is entirely a messianic passage, and that the sanctuary of verse 26 is the sanctuary of Ezekiel 40-48. I see this. I accept this. However, God has not placed Himself "in a box", so that He is required to fulfill every passage of Scripture **sequentially**.

What I see in this passage, respectfully, is that when verses 26 through 28 are read in conjunction with verses 15-22—where the houses of Judah and Joseph [Ephraim] are joined as one nation again in the land of Israel—then the "sanctuary" referenced speaks of the third temple. However, when verses 23-28 are read independent of Ezekiel's "dry bones" in the rest of the chapter, then the sanctuary that is referenced is the fourth temple which is to be built by the Messiah.

Israel: Find Joseph

CHAPTER 13

ALL ISRAEL SHALL BE REGATHERED

God has sown the most precious seed of His people into the earth; but as the master of all creation and the establisher of the laws of *seed*, *time*, and *harvest*[1], He will not rest until He has received a bountiful harvest of His people back unto Him.

> **Psalms 126:1** When the LORD turned again the captivity of Zion, we were like them that dream. **2** Then was our mouth filled with laughter, and our tongue with singing: then said they among the heathen, The LORD hath done great things for them. **3** The LORD hath done great things for us; whereof we are glad. **4** Turn again our captivity, O LORD, as the streams in the south. **5 They that sow in tears shall reap in joy.** **6** He that goeth forth and weepeth, bearing precious seed, shall doubtless come again with rejoicing, bringing his sheaves with him.

How much more shall God receive for Himself of what He has promised each of us, that when we sow our most precious seed even with tears, we shall reap again with rejoicing? Was not the Lord in tears when He sowed Ephraim into the earth, because for Him judgment is a *strange work*[2]? It is contrary to His character of love. But when Ephraim is rejoined again to Judah in one nation upon the mountains of Israel[3], the Lord shall rejoice because His 12 tribes are back in the land.

Israel: Find Joseph

EPHRAIM SHALL WANDER FROM SEA TO SEA

As a result of being cast off, Ephraim has been scattered across the face

---

1 Genesis 8:22.
2 Isaiah 28:21.
3 Ezekiel 37:15-22.

of the entire earth.

Amos 8:1 Thus hath the Lord GOD shewed unto me: and behold a basket of summer fruit. **2** And he said, Amos, what seest thou? And I said, A basket of summer fruit. Then said the LORD unto me, **The end is come upon <u>my people of Israel</u>**; I will not again pass by them any more ... **12** And **they shall <u>wander from sea to sea</u>**, and wander **<u>from the north even to the east</u>** ...

ISRAEL SHALL RULE OVER THEIR OPPRESSORS

Hidden in the foreknowledge of God was that in His sowing the 10 tribes of house of Israel, that in the passage of time [*seed+time=harvest*] in the places where they would become a company of nations in the middle of the earth, His people with their lost Hebrew identity would actually become the heads of state in these foreign lands. The knowledge of this fact should help in locating Ephraim.

Isaiah 14:1 For the LORD will have **mercy on Jacob**, and **will yet choose Israel**, and **set them in <u>their own land</u>**: and the strangers shall be joined with them, and they shall cleave to the **house of Jacob**.

Jacob and Israel in Isaiah's day is a reference to the 10 tribes which were taken into Assyrian captivity during Isaiah's lifetime. Ephraim was to be given a new land ... a place ... a company of nations in the middle of the earth[4]. The people in these new lands would become one with the 10 tribes as these Hebrew people lose their identity with Israel by assimilation and intermarriage with the people of these lands. The Lord refers to company of nations in the middle of the earth as .. "the land of the Lord." These lands have been populated by "not a people[5]" who have lost there Hebrew identity; but as prophesied by the Lord they are His people who would also come to rule over those who had oppressed them.

Isaiah 14:2 And the people shall take them, and bring them to **<u>their place</u>**: and the **<u>house of Israel</u> shall possess them in the <u>land of the LORD</u>** for servants and handmaids: and **<u>they shall take them captives, whose captives they were</u>**; and **<u>they shall rule over their oppressors</u>**.

---

4 Genesis 35:11; 48:16-19; 2 Samuel 7:10; Hosea 1:10.
5 Isaiah 7:7; Hosea 1:9, 2:23.

Israel And Ephraim Are A Twice Sown Seed

The Lord, indeed, will watch over to gather what He has watched over to sow. When the loving heavenly Father, Jehovah, was forced by disobedience of Ephraim to sow him: that He sowed him in tears [standing in His own tears]. I am even surer that when He gathers His people He will reap them in joy. Jeremiah speaks of God's process of the sowing and reaping of His people. But, a careful reading hereof will indicate that **Israel and Ephraim are each to become a twice sown seed**.

> **Jeremiah 31:27** Behold, the days come, saith the LORD, that **I will sow** the <u>house of Israel</u> and the <u>house of Judah</u> **with the seed of man**, and with the seed of beast. **28 And it shall come to pass,** that **like as** [in the same manner] I have watched over them, to pluck up, and to break down, and to throw down[6], and to destroy, and to afflict; **so will I watch over them, to build,** and **to plant, saith the LORD**.

This has to be **a second and future sowing** of the **house of Israel**, because at the time of Jeremiah's prophecy the northern kingdom of Ephraim is already in Assyrian captivity. In these new lands they would intermingle and intermarry with the "seed of men". They would also overcome and prosper because of the blessing of Joseph that is upon them as they are sown with the "seed of beast" through wars, famines, pestilence and the like in order to become planted in these new lands. Concerning the **house of Judah**, at the time of Jeremiah's prophecy the southern kingdom has not yet been taken into slavery by Babylon.

Judah Is Also Sown A Second Time

Zechariah was a prophet to Judah after its return from Babylon. It is most significant, therefore, that he also prophesies both to the <u>Jews who have returned to the land</u>, as well as to the <u>far greater number of Jews who remained in Babylon</u>, that God would both **save the <u>house of Joseph</u>** and **sow <u>Ephraim</u> a second time**—but that Ephraim would remember Him later while in far countries. This passage, however, can also be read more broadly to indicate that God is foretelling Judah that he also shall be sown a second time into the nations of the earth.

> **Zechariah 10:6** And I will **strengthen** the <u>house of Judah</u>,

6 C/p. Jeremiah 1:10.

and I will **save** the **house of Joseph**, and I will bring them again **to place them**; **for I have mercy upon them: and they shall be as though I had not cast them off**: for I am the LORD their God [the God of Joseph as well as Judah], and will hear them.

7 And **they of Ephraim**[7] shall be like a mighty man [become strong nations], and their heart shall rejoice as through wine [wealth / affluence]: yea, their children shall see it, and be glad; their heart shall rejoice in the LORD. **8** I will hiss [whistle] for them, and gather them; for **I have redeemed them**: and they shall increase as they have increased [far, far more of Ephraim will return than was scattered].

Zechariah's prophecy of a future event after the return of Jews from Babylonian captivity clearly speaks of a second sowing of Ephraim who is already in Assyrian captivity; but it can also indicate a second sowing of Judah by the Romans.

Zechariah 10:9 And I will sow them among the people: and they shall remember me in far countries [Ephraim shall discover his Hebrew heritage; and Judah shall remember his covenant with God]; **and they shall live with their children, and turn again** [to God]. **10 I will bring them again also out of** the land of **Egypt**, and gather them out of **Assyria**; and I will bring them into the land of Gilead and Lebanon; and place shall not be found for them [because of their multitude].

From the point of Zechariah's prophesy, Judah indeed was sown into the earth a second time by the Romans beginning in 70 CE. But, because we know absolutely that God is faithful to His Word, Ephraim and Israel have also been sown a second time from wherever they were to **the place**[8] where they are now: and where they have grown into a company of nations in the midst of the earth, carrying the blessing of Joseph—whose people have become as the dust of the earth, stars of heaven, and sand of the sea.

Isaiah also speaks of a second recovery of the outcasts of Israel and the disbursed of Judah.

Isaiah 11:10 And in that day [when the Messiah comes] there

7 The *stick of Joseph* is in the *hand of Ephraim* (Ezekiel 37:16 and 19)
8 2 Samuel 7:10; Isaiah 14:1-2; and Hosea 1:10.
138

shall be **a root of Jesse**, which shall stand for an ensign [flag or banner] of the people; **to it Him shall the Gentiles seek**: and his rest shall be glorious. **11** And it shall come to pass **in that day**, that **the Lord shall set his hand again the <u>second time</u> to recover the remnant of his people, which shall be left, from Assyria** [Iraq and southern Turkey], and from **Egypt**, and from **Pathros** [upper Egypt], and from **Cush** [Ethiopia], and from **Elam** [Iraq / western Iran], and from **Shinar** [Babylon / Iraq], and from **Hamath** [upper Syria / perhaps parts of southern Turkey], and **from the <u>islands of the sea</u>** [originally settled by the sons of Japheth[9]].

11:12 And he shall set up an ensign [a sign] for the nations, and shall **assemble the <u>outcasts of Israel</u>**, and gather together the **<u>dispersed of Judah</u>** from the four corners of the earth. ... **16** And there shall be **an highway[10] for the remnant of his people**, which shall be left, **from Assyria**; like as it was to Israel in the day that he came up out of the land of Egypt.

It is clear that even when the Messiah [the anointed one] comes, there will still be a distinction between Israel [the 10 tribes] and Judah (verse 12).

GOD WILL SET HIS SANCTUARY IN THE MIDST OF ISRAEL

Jews in their Diaspora have been able to carry with them and teach their children both their Hebrew language and the Torah. Joseph and Ephraim have not only lost their Hebrew language and the Torah, but they have also lost the very knowledge of their Hebrew blood and heritage. In this passage of Hosea, God speaks of a system of animal sacrifices under the restored Law of Moses, which requires the building of a third temple. Ezekiel fixes the time for this sanctuary as coming after Joseph and Ephraim are back in the land of Israel.

Hosea 3:4 For the **children of Israel** [the 10 tribes of Israel] shall abide many days without a **king**, and without a **prince** [high priest], and without a **sacrifice** [animal sacrifice under the law of Moses], and without an **image**, and without an **ephod** [clothing of the high priest], and without **teraphim**: **5** Afterward [after many days] shall the children of Israel return [Ephraim rejoined to

9 Genesis 10:5.

10 The kings highway which came up from Sini to Jordan, and down from Iraq (Babylon) through Syria to Jordan and the mountains of Israel.

Judah], and seek the LORD their God, and David their King; and shall fear the LORD and his goodness **in the latter days** [latter days, not last days].

Ezekiel 37:26 Moreover **I will** make a covenant of peace with them; it shall be **an everlasting covenant** with them: and I will place them, and multiply them, and will **set <u>my sanctuary in the midst of them for evermore</u>**. 27 <u>**My tabernacle also shall be with them**</u>: yea, I will be their God, and they shall be my people. 28 And the heathen shall know that I the LORD do sanctify Israel, **when <u>my sanctuary shall be in the midst of them for evermore</u>**.

THE LATTER RAIN IS A CRY OF GOD TO EPHRAIM

The former and latter rain for Israel speak of seed, time and harvest. The former rain fell in October to prepare the ground for the planting of seed. The latter rain or spring rain fell in March and April to cause the grain to mature and ripen for harvest. God has planted His people into the earth, and like a good farmer will harvest them as all will eventually return to Him.

The passage of Scripture, below, was given by Hosea to the northern kingdom of Israel before its Assyrian captivity. From this perspective we can see that this latter rain prophecy is a very special call of God to Ephraim: who is now a multitude of Abrahamic nations that have grown up in the middle of the earth with the blessing of Joseph upon them. Second, it has application to the land of Israel: to Jews of today's Israel, and to Jews who are still scattered throughout the world. And third, the latter rain is a call to Manasseh and any other of the children of God to return to their Creator, and to the land which the Lord has also given unto them.

Hosea 5:5 And the pride of Israel doth testify to his face: therefore shall **<u>Israel</u>** and **<u>Ephraim</u>** fall in their iniquity; **<u>Judah</u>** also shall fall with them. .... **5:15 I will go and return to my place, till they acknowledge their offence**, and **seek my face: in their affliction** [the ***time of Jacob's trouble***[11] shall cause Israel, Ephraim, and Judah to seek the Lord] **they will seek me early**.

Hosea 6:1 Come, and let us [Israel, Ephraim and Judah] **<u>return unto the LORD</u>**: for he hath torn, and he will heal us; he

11 Jeremiah 30:7.
140

hath smitten, and he will bind us up. **2 After two days** [after 2,000 years] **will he revive us: in the third day** [during the 3rd millennium] **he will raise us up, and we shall live in his sight. 3** Then shall we know, if we follow on to know the LORD: his going forth is prepared as the morning; and **he shall come unto us as the rain, as the latter and former rain** unto the earth. **4 O Ephraim,** what shall I do unto thee? **O Judah,** what shall I do unto thee? for your goodness is as a morning cloud, and as the early dew it goeth away.

THERE SHALL BE PERFECT UNDERSTANDING IN THE LATTER DAYS

Our knowledge and understanding of the wisdom of God that is hidden in the Scriptures will increase as we move into the latter days. This book is a partial fulfillment of this prophecy.

Jeremiah 23:13 And I have seen folly in the **prophets of Samaria**; they prophesied in Baal, and caused my people Israel to err. **14** I have seen also in the **prophets of Jerusalem** an horrible thing: they commit adultery, and walk in lies: they strengthen also the hands of evildoers, that none doth return from his wickedness: they are all of them unto me as Sodom, and the inhabitants thereof as Gomorrah. ... **18** For who hath stood in the counsel of the LORD, and hath perceived and heard his word? who hath marked his word, and heard it?

19 Behold, a whirlwind of the LORD is gone forth in fury, even a grievous whirlwind: it shall fall grievously upon the head of the wicked. **20** The anger of the LORD shall not return, until he have executed, and till he have performed the thoughts of his heart: **in the latter days ye shall consider it perfectly**.

PERSECUTION WILL DRIVE ALL ISRAEL TO GOD

The LORD God Jehovah is very hard-nosed and unchangeable about some things. He is saying in love to all of His people—the natural seed of Abraham—that He wants them back now. But, He is also saying in love to both Israel and Judah ... *You can choose to return to me now; but you will return unto me later.* The final remnant of God's people, however, will not return unto Him until a period of extreme affliction and persecution has come upon them. Yet, the whole house of Jacob who have returned to the land in fulfillment of Ezekiel 37 shall be saved out of all that shall transpire during this *time of Jacob's trouble.*

> **Jeremiah 30:4** And these are the **words that the LORD spake concerning <u>Israel</u>** [10 tribes] **and concerning <u>Judah</u>**. **5** For thus saith the LORD; We have heard a voice of trembling, of fear, and not of peace. **6** Ask ye now, and see whether a man doth travail with child? wherefore do I see every man with his hands on his loins, as a woman in travail, and all faces are turned into paleness? **7** Alas! for that day is great, so that none is like it: it is even **<u>the time of Jacob's trouble</u>**; but **he** [12 tribes] shall be **saved out of it**.

THE PATTERN OF HOW GOD DEALS WITH HIS PEOPLE

The Lord, first by the mouth of a prophet, speaks His will into the earth[12]. Then, He will send to His people, and sometimes another nation, **a prophet** to warn the king and His people that it is time to repent and to seek the Lord. Most often in His mercy he will send a series of prophets with the same message ... repent, change direction, have a new thought! Next, He will stir up **an adversary**[13] even against His own people, so that in their desperation they will cry out to Him. Then, when He eventually gives up on their disobedience, He will send **an enemy to conquer** them. He will even destroy His own holy temple and the city that He loves, and **will drive His people into captivity from the land that He gave them forever**. Finally, He will **judge the adversary** that He raised up to persecute His people for their disobedience—the who by this time is usually caught up in pride for having been able to conquer the people of God. *Pride goeth before destruction, and a haughty spirit before a fall*[14].

THE ASSYRIAN IS THE ROD OF GOD'S ANGER

By the authority of the Hebrew prophets, all Israel and Judah will simply not return unto the LORD that created them until the Lord stirs up **the Assyrian** who the Lord will "give a charge". This Assyrian is *the little horn* mentioned in **Daniel 7 and 8**: who **comes from Syria**. Christians refer to him as the *Antichrist*. He is the rod of God's anger against <u>His own people</u>. Finally, God will at last judge this Assyrian when He is

12 Amos 4:7.

13 1 Kings 11:14, 23 and 25 (pg. 100).

14 Proverbs 16:18.

142

through allowing him to drive the remainder of His people back to Him during this **time of Jacob's trouble** (Jeremiah 30:7; see also Zechariah 12 through 14, and other *day of the Lord* passages of Scriptures). This Assyrian charge was fulfilled in measure in the deportation of 10 tribes by the king of Assyria in 721 CE. It shall have a second and complete fulfillment at the end of the age for all Israel, including "the people that dwell in Zion"[15]—which are the Jews and Josephs now back in the land.

> **Isaiah 10:1** Woe unto them that decree unrighteous decrees, and that write grievousness which they have prescribed; **2** To turn aside the needy from judgment, and to take away the right from the poor of my people, that widows may be their prey, and that they may rob the fatherless! **3** And what will ye do in the **day of visitation**, and in the desolation which shall come from far? to whom will ye flee for help? and where will ye leave your glory? **4** Without me they shall bow down under the prisoners, and they shall fall under the slain. For all this his anger is not turned away, but his hand is stretched out still.

> **5 O Assyrian, the rod of mine anger**, and the staff in their hand is mine indignation. **6 I will send him against an hypocritical nation**, and against the people of my wrath [God's own people] will **I give him a charge**, to take the spoil, and to take the prey, and to tread them down like the mire of the streets.

After Joseph is back in the land along with Judah, both will again return to their idolatry.

> **Isaiah 10:11** Shall I not, as I have done unto Samaria [capital of the northern kingdom of Israel and Ephraim] and her idols, so do to Jerusalem [and Judah] and her idols? **12** Wherefore it shall come to pass, that **when the Lord hath performed his whole work upon mount Zion and on Jerusalem, I will punish the fruit of the stout heart of the king of Assyria, and the glory of his high looks.**

> **20** And it shall come to pass **in that day** [when the king of Assyria is judged], that the **remnant of Israel**, and such as are escaped of the **house of Jacob**, shall no more again stay upon him

15 Isaiah 10:20 and 24.

that smote them; but shall stay upon the LORD, the Holy One of Israel, in truth. **21 The remnant shall return, even the remnant of Jacob, unto the mighty God. 22 For** though thy people Israel be as the sand of the sea [a reference to Ephraim], **yet a remnant of them shall return** [from all 12 tribes]: the consumption decreed shall overflow with righteousness.

23 For the Lord GOD of hosts shall make a consumption, even determined, in the midst of all the land. **24** Therefore thus saith the Lord GOD of hosts, **O my people that dwellest in Zion**, be not afraid of **the Assyrian: he shall smite thee with a rod**, and shall lift up his staff against thee, after the manner of Egypt. **25** For yet a very little while, and the indignation shall cease, and mine anger in their destruction.

The latter rain anointing will bring with it such an increase in the tangible presence of God on His people that it will remove the burden and destroy the yoke of the Assyrian from all Israel.

Isaiah 10:26 And the LORD of hosts shall stir up a scourge for him according to the slaughter of Midian[16] at the rock of Oreb: and as his rod was upon the sea, so shall he lift it up after the manner of Egypt. **27** And it shall come to pass **in that day** [the time of Jacob's trouble], that **his burden shall be taken away from off thy shoulder**, and **his yoke from off thy neck**, and **the yoke shall be destroyed because of the anointing.**

THE CAPTIVITY OF ISRAEL AND JUDAH SHALL RETURN

Following this time of Jacob's trouble and rise and fall of the Assyrian little horn, all Israel and Judah shall return to the land and possess it.

Jeremiah 30:1 The word that came to Jeremiah from the LORD, saying, **2** Thus speaketh the LORD God of Israel, saying, Write thee all the words that I have spoken unto thee in a book. **3** For, **lo, the days come,** saith the LORD, that **I will bring again the captivity of my people Israel and Judah,** saith the LORD: and **I will cause them to return to the land** that I gave to their fathers, and **they shall possess it.**

4 And these are the **words that the LORD spake concerning Israel and concerning Judah**. **5** For thus saith the LORD; We have heard a voice of trembling, of fear, and not of peace. **6** Ask ye now, and see whether a man doth travail with child? wherefore do I see every man with his hands on his loins, as a woman in travail, and all faces are turned into paleness? **7** Alas! for that day is great, so that none is like it: it is even **the time of Jacob's trouble**; but **he** [all of the tribes] shall be saved out of it.

8 For it shall come to pass in that day [Jacob's trouble], saith the LORD of hosts, that I will break **his yoke** [the Assyrian] from off thy neck, and will burst thy bonds, and strangers shall no more serve themselves of him: **9** But **they** [12 tribes] **shall serve the LORD their God, and David their king**, whom I will raise up unto them.

God has sown and scattered the whole house of Israel over the entire earth; but He knows where each and every son of Jacob is—and most of them are not Jews. And so all Israel shall be gathered back unto the Lord.

Jeremiah 30:10 Therefore **fear thou not**, O my servant **Jacob**, saith the LORD; **neither be dismayed, O Israel**: for, lo, **I will save thee from afar**, and **thy seed from the land of their captivity**; and **Jacob shall return**, and shall be in rest, and be quiet, and none shall make him afraid.

11 For I am with thee, saith the LORD, to save thee: though I make a full end of all nations whither I have scattered thee, yet will I not make a full end of thee: but I will correct thee in measure, and will not leave thee altogether unpunished. ... **15** Why criest thou for thine affliction? thy sorrow is incurable for the multitude of thine iniquity: because thy sins were increased, I have done these things unto thee.

16 Therefore **all they that devour thee shall be devoured**; and all thine adversaries, every one of them, shall go into captivity; and they that spoil thee shall be a spoil, and all that prey upon thee will I give for a prey. **17** For I will restore health unto thee, and I will heal thee of thy wounds, saith the LORD; because they called thee an Outcast, saying, **This is Zion** [the 12 tribes of Jacob who are back in the land are called Zion], whom no man seeketh after.

18 Thus saith the LORD; <u>**Behold, I will bring again the captivity of Jacob's tents, and have mercy on his dwellingplaces; and the city**</u> [Jerusalem destroyed for a final time] <u>**shall be builded upon her own heap, and the palace shall remain after the manner thereof**</u>[17]. **19** And out of them shall proceed thanksgiving and the voice of them that make merry, and <u>**I will multiply them**</u> [as the dust of the earth, stars of heaven, and sand of the sea], and they shall not be few; I will also glorify them, and they shall not be small.

20 Their children also shall be as aforetime, and their congregation shall be established before me, and **I will punish all that oppress them**[18]. **21** And their nobles shall be of themselves, and their governor shall proceed from the midst of them; and I will cause him to draw near, and he shall approach unto me: for who is this that engaged his heart to approach unto me? saith the LORD.

22 And ye shall be my people, and I will be your God [compare the First Chapter of Hosea, where God says of the 10 tribes of Israel that they will not be his people]. **23** Behold, the whirlwind of the LORD goeth forth with fury, a continuing whirlwind: it shall fall with pain upon the head of the wicked. **24** The fierce anger of the LORD shall not return, until he have done it, and until he have performed the intents of his heart: in **the latter days** [not last days] ye shall consider it.

Jeremiah 31:1 At the same time [in the latter days], saith the LORD, will **I be the God of all the families of Israel** [because the 12 tribes back in the land in fulfillment of Ezekiel 37]**, and they shall be my people** ... **7** For thus saith the LORD; Sing with gladness **for Jacob**, and shout among the chief of the nations: publish ye, praise ye, and say, O LORD, **save thy people, the remnant of Israel** [all Israel]. **8** Behold, **I will bring them from the north country**, and **gather them from the coasts of the earth**, and with them the blind and the lame, the woman with child and

---

17 This passage has already had a double fulfillment: following Judah's return to the land after Babylonian captivity, and its return to the land in 1948. There will be at least a third fulfillment of this passage following the events of Zechariah 12 through 14.

18 Zechariah 12-14.

her that travaileth with child together: **a great company shall return thither**.

The **remnant** of the 12 tribes of Israel shall be gathered from:

- The north country (Babylon – Jeremiah 46:10)

- The coasts of the earth (Jeremiah 31:8)

- All nations (Amos 9:9)

- Assyria, Egypt, Pathros, Cush, Elam, Shinar, Hamath, and the islands of the sea (Isaiah 11:11)

EPHRAIM IS THE LORD'S FIRSTBORN

Because of the **blessing of Israel** [Jacob] passed on to the sons of Joseph, **Ephraim is the firstborn**[19] **of the Lord** and has **received the blessing**. The descendants of Ephraim are, likewise, the firstborn of the Lord. They carry the birthright and the blessing of Abraham, Isaac, Jacob, and Joseph upon their lives and their nations. They have become a multitude of nations in the middle of the earth whose people are as dust, stars, and sand.

Jeremiah 31:9 They shall come with weeping, and **with supplications will I lead them**: I will cause them to walk by the rivers of waters in a straight way, wherein they shall not stumble: for I **am a <u>father to Israel</u>** [all Israel], and **<u>Ephraim is my firstborn</u>**.

10 Hear the word of the LORD, **O ye nations**, and **declare it in the isles afar off** [Ephraim is in the nations and isles of the earth], and say, **He that scattered Israel will gather him**, and **keep him**, as a shepherd doth his flock. **11** For **the LORD hath redeemed Jacob** [God sees the 12 tribes of Israel as already redeemed], and **ransomed him from the hand of him that was stronger than he**.

The 12 tribes of Israel scattered throughout the earth will be afflicted in a future time of persecution, including the multitude of people and nations of Ephraim and Manasseh ... but they shall begin their return to the land now, in this time.

---

19 1 Chronicles 5:1-2.

147

Jeremiah 31:9-10 has more than a double fulfillment. It is written by God, who knows the end from the beginning, to cover not only the 70 years of Judah's captivity in Babylon, but also covers their absence from Israel between 70 CE and 1948: even unto the reestablishing of a Hebrew nation of 12 tribes when Joseph and Ephraim are returned to the land.

Jeremiah 33:6 Behold, I will bring it health and cure, and I will cure them, and will reveal unto them the abundance of peace and truth. 7 And **I will cause** the <u>**captivity of Judah**</u> and the <u>**captivity of Israel**</u> **to return**, <u>**and will build them, as at the first**</u> [as a unified nation beginning with the fulfillment of Ezekiel 37]. **8** And I will cleanse them from all their iniquity, whereby they have sinned against me; and I will pardon all their iniquities, whereby they have sinned, and whereby they have transgressed against me.

9 And it shall be to me a name of joy, a praise and an honour before all the nations of the earth, which shall hear all the good that I do unto them: and they shall fear and tremble **for all the goodness and for all the prosperity that I procure unto it.**

The season of Israel's prosperity, culminating in **Ezekiel 38:8-14**, is a direct result of the joining of Joseph, Ephraim and Judah that God has spoken in **Ezekiel 37:15-22**.

Jeremiah 33:10 Thus saith the LORD; Again there shall be heard in this place, which ye say shall be desolate without man and without beast, even **in the <u>cities of Judah</u>**, and **in the <u>streets of Jerusalem</u>**, that are desolate, without man, and without inhabitant, and without beast [the condition in Judah's return from Babylon and the nations], **11** The voice of joy, and the voice of gladness, the voice of the bridegroom, and the voice of the bride, the voice of them that shall say, Praise the LORD of hosts: for the LORD is good; for his mercy endureth for ever: and of them that shall bring the sacrifice of praise into the house of the LORD. For **I will cause to return the captivity of the land**, as at the first, saith the LORD.

12 Thus saith the LORD of hosts; Again in this place, which is desolate without man and without beast, and in all the cities thereof, shall be an habitation of shepherds causing their flocks to lie down. **13** In the cities of the mountains, in the cities of the vale, and in the cities of the south, and in the land of Benjamin, and in the places about Jerusalem, and in the cities of Judah, shall the flocks pass again under the hands of him that telleth them, saith the LORD.

Judah Returns To The Land With Repentance

National repentance is necessary for the sins of a nation against God ... then and now. God calls **Judah the *seed of Israel*** that separated themselves from strangers that entered the land during Judah's Babylonian captivity. **Ownership of the land did not change simply because the Jews were absent for 70 years ... or almost 2000 years.**

Nehemiah 9:2 And the <u>seed of Israel</u> [Judah] separated themselves from all strangers, and <u>stood and confessed their sins, and the iniquities of their fathers</u>. ... 7 <u>Thou art the LORD the God, who didst choose Abram</u>, and broughtest him forth out of Ur of the Chaldees, and <u>gavest him the name of Abraham</u>; 8 And foundest his heart faithful before thee, and <u>madest a covenant</u> [in blood] <u>with him to give the land</u> of the Canaanites, the Hittites, the Amorites, and the Perizzites, and the Jebusites, and the Girgashites, <u>to give it</u>, I say, <u>to his seed</u>, and hast performed thy words; for thou art righteous: ... **23 Their children also multipliedst thou as the stars of heaven**, and broughtest them into the land, concerning which thou hadst promised to their fathers, <u>that they should go in to possess it</u>.

Messiah Shall Sit Upon The Throne Of David

When God has finished restoring the whole house of Israel [Jacob], the Messiah will come to sit upon the **throne of David** to reign over the earth.

Jeremiah 33:14 Behold, **the days come**, saith the LORD, that **I will perform** that good thing which I have promised unto the <u>house of Israel</u> and to the <u>house of Judah</u>. **15 In those days, and at that time**, will I cause the **Branch of righteousness to grow up unto David**; and he shall execute judgment and righteousness in the land.

16 In those days shall **Judah be saved**, and **Jerusalem shall dwell safely**: and this is the name wherewith she shall be called, The LORD our righteousness. 17 For thus saith the LORD; <u>David shall never want a man to sit upon the throne of the house of Israel</u> [in those days and at that time (vs. 15)]; 18 Neither shall the priests the Levites want a man before me to offer burnt offerings, and to kindle meat offerings, and to do sacrifice continually.

But God does not intend the redemption of Israel and Judah back to the land as one nation on the mountains of Israel [the West Bank] to await the coming of the Messiah. It is to **begin now** with the joining of Joseph, Ephraim and Judah in the fulfillment of the prophecy of Ezekiel 37.

WITH JOSEPH GOD WILL BUILD AGAIN THE TABERNACLE OF DAVID

When Joseph is back in the land, the Lord will begin to restore worship as it was in the days of David, the sweet psalmist of Israel.

Amos 9:11 **In that day will <u>I raise up the tabernacle of David that is fallen</u>**, and close up the breaches thereof; and I will raise up his ruins, and <u>**I will build it as in the days of old**</u>: 12 That they may possess the **remnant of Edom** [Esau], and of all the heathen, which are called by my name [the hidden multitude and nations of Joseph and Ephraim], saith the LORD that doeth this.

13 Behold, the days come, saith the LORD, that the plowman shall overtake the reaper, and the treader of grapes him that soweth seed; and the mountains shall drop sweet wine, and all the hills shall melt. 14 And <u>**I will bring again the captivity of my people of Israel**</u> [all 12 tribes], and they shall build the waste cities, and inhabit them; and they shall plant vineyards, and drink the wine thereof; they shall also make gardens, and eat the fruit of them. 15 And I will plant them upon their land, and they shall no more be pulled up out of their land which I have given them, saith the LORD thy God.

Israel: Find Joseph

Chapter 14

Joseph Shall Be Joined To Judah

The passages of Scripture below are generally considered to be messianic; but a closer reading reveals that the Messiah cannot come prior to their fulfillment.

God's Promises To Not A People

The promises of God to Joseph will be fulfilled in a people who have lost their identity as Hebrews—who have become "not a people". These are the multitudes of Ephraim and Manasseh who have become a numberless multitude in the middle of the earth where they have been scattered (Isaiah 14:1-2). They cannot be Jews because at no time in history have the Jews ever been so many that they could not be counted. Since no one will appoint the Messiah, the fulfillment of this passage has to be pre-messianic.

Hosea 1:9 Then said God, Call his name Loammi [not my people]: **for ye are not my people, and I will not be your God. 1:10 <u>Yet the number of the children of Israel shall be as the sand of the sea, which cannot be measured nor numbered</u>**; and it shall come to pass, that **in <u>the place</u> where it was said unto them, Ye are not my people, there it shall be said unto them, Ye are the sons of the living God.**

11 Then shall the **children of Judah** and the **children of Israel** be gathered together, and **appoint themselves one head**, and they shall come up out of the land: for great shall be the day of Jezreel [the scattered ones].

Israel Has Been Sifted But Not Lost

Amos was a prophet to the 10 tribes of the northern kingdom of Israel. He prophesies that the northern kingdom of Israel will completely lose its identity, and that the 10 of the tribes of Jacob would be banished out of God's sight … but that Judah shall remain. He also prophesies that not one person of the 10 tribes is hidden or lost from the mercy of God.

Amos 9:7 Are ye not as children of the Ethiopians unto me, **O children of Israel?** saith the LORD. Have not I brought up Israel out of the land of Egypt?… **8 Behold, the eyes of the Lord GOD are upon the sinful kingdom, and I will destroy it from off the face of the earth; saving that I will not utterly destroy the house of Jacob, saith the LORD.**

9 For, lo, I will command, and **I will sift the house of Israel** [Ephraim] **among all nations,** like as corn is sifted in a sieve, **yet shall not the least grain fall upon the earth.**

The 10 tribes have been sifted among the nations, carrying with them the **blessing** and **birthright** of Joseph and the promises of God made to Ephraim and Manasseh. God knows where Ephraim is, even unto this day. Ephraim has already become a multitude of nations in the middle of the earth: whose people are as the dust of the earth, stars of heaven, and sand of the sea. Manasseh has already become a great people also in the middle of the earth[1].

It Is God's Time To Join Joseph To Judah

Ephraim and the 10 tribes of Israel shall be gathered and joined to the tribe of Judah … now in this time.

Ezekiel 37:15 The word of the LORD came again unto me, saying, **16** Moreover, thou son of man, **take thee one stick,** and write upon it, **For Judah,** and **for the children of Israel his companions** [a remnant of all the children of Israel have become part of Judah: the Jews of Israel]: then **take another stick,** and write upon it, **For Joseph, the stick of Ephraim,** and **for all the house of Israel his companions** [Ephraim is in the presence of the house of Israel, the 10 tribes carried into Assyrian captivity]: **17** And **join them** one to another **into one stick;** and they shall become one in thine hand.

---

1 Genesis 48:16-20.

18 And when the children of thy people shall speak unto thee, saying, Wilt thou not shew us what thou meanest by these? **19** Say unto them, Thus saith the Lord GOD; Behold, **I will take** the **stick of Joseph, which is in the hand of Ephraim** [Ephraim has become a multitude of nations in the middle of the earth], **and the tribes of Israel his fellows** [Ephraim has been joined with the 10 tribes of the northern kingdom], and will put them with him, even **with the stick of Judah** [the Jews of Israel], and **make them one stick** [one nation], and they shall be one in mine hand.

20 And the sticks whereon thou writest shall be in thine hand before their eyes. **21** And **say unto them** [prophesy unto the bones], Thus saith the Lord GOD; Behold, **I will take the children of Israel** [Ephraim and the 10 tribes] **from among the heathen** [the nations], whither they be gone, and will gather them on every side, and bring them into their own land: **22** And I will make them **one nation in the land upon the mountains of Israel**; and one king [prime minister now, Messiah later] shall be king to them all: and **they shall be no more two nations, neither shall they be divided into two kingdoms** any more at all.

The mountains of Israel is the West Bank: the same portion of Judea and Samaria which was captured by Israel in the 1967 Six-Day War. It is proposed by many including United Nations' Resolutions, Israeli leadership, the Palestinian National Authority, and three American Administrations to become a Palestinian state. But this is not at all what God has said.

Ephraim Shall Return As The Latter Rain

Ephraim shall cry out to God in the latter days. His harvest shall be as the latter rain.

Hosea 6:1 Come, and let us return unto the LORD: for he hath torn, and he will heal us; he hath smitten, and he will bind us up. **2 After two days** [after 2,000 years] **will he revive us: in the third day** [during the third millennium] **he will raise us up, and we shall live in his sight. 3** Then shall we know, if we follow on to know the LORD: his going forth is prepared as the morning; and **he shall come unto us** [Israel, Ephraim, and Judah] **as the rain, as the latter and former rain unto the earth**.

4 O Ephraim, what shall I do unto thee? **O Judah**, what shall I do unto thee? for your goodness is as a morning cloud, and as the early dew it goeth away.

Return unto me, and I will return unto you, saith the LORD of hosts[2].

Isaiah 10:20 And it shall come to pass in that day, that **the remnant of Israel, and such as are escaped of the house of Jacob**, shall no more again stay upon him that smote them; but shall stay upon the LORD, the Holy One of Israel, in truth. **21 The remnant shall return, even the remnant of Jacob, unto the mighty God. 22 For though thy people Israel be as the sand of the sea** [a reference to Ephraim]**, yet a remnant of them shall return**: the consumption decreed shall overflow with righteousness.

GOD WILL REAP WHAT HE HAS SOWN

God will watch over to gather what He watched over to sow.

Jeremiah 31:27 Behold, the days come, saith the LORD, that **I will sow** the **house of Israel** and the **house of Judah with the seed of man** [intermarriage], and with the seed of beast [wars, famine, persecution]. **28 And it shall come to pass, that like as** [in the same manner] I have watched over them, to pluck up, and to break down, and to throw down, and to destroy, and to afflict; **so will I watch over them, to build,** and **to plant** [plant them in the lands where they were sown], **saith the LORD.**

Zechariah 10:6 And I will strengthen the **house of Judah**, and I will save the **house of Joseph** [Ephraim, Manasseh, and the 10 tribes of Israel], and I will bring them again to place them [place them back in the land as one nation]; **for I have mercy upon them: and they shall be as though I had not cast them off: for I am the LORD their God, and will hear them.**

7 And they of **Ephraim** [the house of Joseph] shall be like a mighty man [a strong people will return to the land], and their heart shall rejoice as through wine: yea, their children shall see it, and be glad; their heart shall rejoice in the LORD... **8** I will hiss [whistle] for them, and gather them; for I have redeemed them: and they shall increase as they have increased [far more will return than were scattered] … **9 And I will sow them among the people: and they shall remember me in far countries**; and they shall live with their children, and turn again [turn again to God and their Hebrew heritage, when they discover who they really are].

Israel is about the size of the state of New Jersey in the United States. It could not even begin to hold the hundreds of millions (or more) of Ephraim. However, with Judah's cooperation, the Lord could double or triple the population of Israel with Hebrews who have rediscovered their heritage and destiny. The "settlement", "natural growth", and two-state issues that plague Israel would simply evaporate. In Ezekiel 37, the prophet Ezekiel calls the dry bones of Joseph and Judah "an exceeding great army": when they stand up upon their feet as one nation again of the 12 tribes of Israel [Jacob]. This will forever shift the course of history in the Middle East and world—back to what God already established thousands of years ago. **Israel is God's prophetic time clock. It is the only nation on the earth whose history is written in advance of its occurrence**, and then recorded in the Bible. We all must relate to Israel both **internally** and **externally** solely by … *It is written!*

> **Ezekiel 37:10 So I prophesied** as he commanded me [to the valley of the dry bones of Joseph and Judah], and the **breath came into them, and they lived, and stood up upon their feet, an exceeding great army** [as one nation again upon the mountains of Israel].

> **Numbers 23:9** … lo, **the people shall dwell alone, and shall not be reckoned among the nations**. **10 Who can count the dust of Jacob, and the number of the fourth part of Israel?**

"Joseph shall be joined with Judah now in this time", saith the Lord.

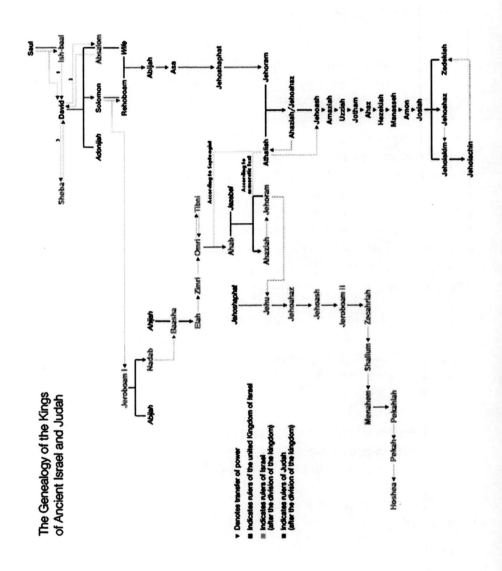

The Genealogy of the Kings
of Ancient Israel and Judah

▼ Denotes transfer of power

■ Indicates rulers of the united Kingdom of Israel

■ Indicates rulers of Israel
(after the division of the kingdom)

■ Indicates rulers of Judah
(after the division of the kingdom)

156

CHAPTER 15

THE BLESSING UPON EPHRAIM AND MANASSEH

I must continually reinforce the "why" of why it is the prophetic season and time for the Israel of today to seek out its fulfillment of **Ezekiel 37:15-22**—that the stick of Joseph that is in the hand of Ephraim be joined to the stick of Judah; and that the two sticks become one nation again on the mountains of Israel, which is the West Bank.

Israel needs people; Israel wants people—Jews of course—to move back into the land. As of 2010 the nation's total citizenship was 7,587,000, of which 75.7 percent (5,726,000) are Jewish, 20.4 percent (1,548,000) are Arab, and 4.1 percent (313,000) fall into a category referred to as "other," the majority of whom are immigrants not registered as Jewish by the Interior Ministry. Forecasts by the Israeli Bureau of Statistics indicate a huge potential increase in the number of Palestinians within these territories such that by 2030, the Palestinian population is expected to increase to 2.4 million citizens and will constitute about a quarter of the total population.

Add to these citizenship numbers there were approximately 2,500,000 Palestinian non-citizens living in the West Bank, and another 1,500,000 living in Gaza. Thus, in just the territory that Israel occupies, 5.7 million Jews are joined by almost an equal number of Palestinians: 1.5 million of which are citizens, and over 4 million of which are non-citizens.

This desire of Israeli Jews to fill Israel with other Jews from around the world is laudable, but unrealistic on any vast scale. I am informed that any Jewish person in the world can get his or her expenses paid to immigrate and receive a new financial start in Israel; but there are not enough Jews in the world to double or triple the size of the Jewish population of Israel.

There are only upwards of 13 million Jews in the world today. They are a people who have an enormous impact in the cultures and economy of every nation into which they have been scattered, though their numbers are few. But it is also unrealistic to expect a scattered nation of Jews around the world given to family, stability, and the successful accumulation of wealth—wherever they have gone—to leave their places of comfort and stability to become pioneers late in life in today's strife-torn Israel.

But, Jehovah has already provided the answers for Israel—in His Word—over 2,500 years before He caused the rebirth of Israel in 1948.

Israel: Find Joseph

THE WHOLE HOUSE OF ISRAEL MUST PERCEIVE ITS DESTINY

Joseph was a Hebrew[1]. Joseph's descendants are still Hebrew, and not Jewish. Even though Ephraim and the 10 tribes of the northern kingdom of Israel were disobedient and banished by God off the face of the earth as a nation, Ephraim nevertheless has been immensely blessed by God because of the blessing of Abraham. According to Scripture, Joseph's son Ephraim has grown into a multitude or company of nations in the middle of the earth, whose people have become as the dust of the earth, stars of the heavens, and sand of the sea. God's ways are simply higher than our ways.

Joseph received both the **birthright**[2] and the **blessing of Jacob**, which is the **birthright** and **blessing of Israel**: Jacob's new name from God. This **entitles all his descendants to the entire deposit of blessing** that God gave to **Abraham**, **Isaac** and **Jacob**. Joseph and his heirs are blessed materially, intellectually, and undoubtedly technologically. Israel knows how to excel in each.

God, 2,500 years ago, revealed His will for the Israel of the latter days and years[3]. The Lord, who declares the end from the beginning[4], has already confidently given **the sceptre**—the right to rule and govern—to Judah, and not to Joseph[5]. Has not the Lord commanded His priest[6], Ezekiel, to prophesy over the dry bones of a divided and half-dead nation … to be-

1   Genesis 39:14 and 17; 40:15.
2   1 Chronicles 5:1-2.
3   Ezekiel 38:8 and 16.
4   Isaiah 46:10.
5   Genesis 49:10.
6   Ezekiel 1:3.

158

come fully alive as an exceeding great army[7]? By joining the stick or branch of Joseph, that is in the hand of Ephraim, with the stick or branch of Judah back into one unified nation, the Lord will reestablish His nation of the 12 tribes of Israel: which was His will from the very beginning.

According to Ezekiel 37, both Judah and Israel [Ephraim] are spiritually dead to the destiny that God has preordained for them. God describes this condition to Ezekiel as a ... "valley of very dry bones" ... which He considers dead because He then asks Ezekiel **the question**, "Can these bones live?" [8] Thank God, the answer that God gives is ... Yes!

Let us stay with the Book of Ezekiel, however, and ask **the next question**. How can Israel reach the season of peace and immense prosperity outlined in **Ezekiel 38:8-14**, without meeting the prerequisite conditions already established **in Ezekiel 37:15-22**: which is the joining of Joseph through Ephraim back to Judah? Once this occurs, Israel will begin to amass so much God-given wealth that another company of nations[9] will eventually attempt to take it away, and will lose five-sixths of its armies[10] in the process.

Israel: Find Joseph

THE BLESSING HIDDEN IN EZEKIEL 38

Hidden in a chapter that foretells Israel's threatened destruction by the armies of Gog, **Ezekiel 38:8-14** outlines a coming season of great peace and material prosperity. One of the easier ways to determine that Ezekiel 38 and 39 is not what Christians call the battle of Armageddon is to view these chapters through the eyes of **Zechariah 12:1-2**, where the Lord says through His prophet that He would make Jerusalem a *cup of trembling* unto **all the people of the earth**. Listed in **Ezekiel 38:1-6** are many nations who in the future will come against Israel. But, there are some glaring omissions—**Egypt** is not present; and neither are the **kings of the East**[11].

Ezekiel 38:8-14 After many days thou shalt be visited: **in the**

---

7 Ezekiel 37:10.
8 Ezekiel 37:1-3.
9 Ezekiel 38:1-6; and perhaps Psalms 83:1-8.
10 Ezekiel 39:2.
11 Zechariah 12:11; Revelation 16:12, 16.

latter years [not last days] thou shalt come into **the land that is brought back from the sword**, and is **gathered out of many people**, against the **mountains of Israel**, which have been always waste: but it is brought forth out of the nations, and they shall **dwell safely** all of them. ... the **land of unwalled villages** ... that **dwell safely** ... **dwelling without walls**, and having **neither bars nor gates** ... the **desolate places that are now inhabited**, and upon the **people**[12] that are **gathered out of the nations**, which have **gotten cattle and goods**, that dwell in the midst of the land ... **silver and gold** ... **cattle and goods** ... a **great spoil** ... Thus saith the Lord God; In that day **when my people of Israel dwelleth safely**, shalt thou not know it [hardily the Israel of today]?

When one simply removes all the negative phraseology from the above text, it is easy to see what has transpired in the "Israel" that this company of nations is coming to liquidate. The Jewish portion of Israel is prospering today: but not like what is in this text.

> **Ecclesiastes 3:11 He hath made every thing beautiful in his time: also he hath set the world in their heart, so that no man can find out the work that God maketh from the beginning to the end. ...** 14 I know that, whatsoever God doeth, it shall be for ever: nothing can be put to it, nor any thing taken from it: and God doeth it, that men should fear before him. **15** That which hath been is now; and that which is to be hath already been; and God requireth that which is past.

The next question is: How can the Messiah come unless Ezekiel 36, 37, 38 and 39 are fulfilled in Israel, and the world? Let us look again at what God has already on deposit with Joseph through Ephraim and Manasseh.

JOSEPH HAS THE BIRTHRIGHT AND THE BLESSING

The **blessing of <u>Abraham</u>, <u>Isaac</u>** and <u>Israel</u> is on the <u>descendents of Joseph</u>. The **birthright of the firstborn is the right to receive the blessing of the father** ... from Abraham back to Adam.

> **Genesis 48:14** And Israel [Jacob] stretched out his right hand, and laid it upon **Ephraim's head**, who was **the younger**, and his

---

12 People—more than just Jews.

left hand upon **Manasseh's head**, guiding his hands wittingly; for **Manasseh was the firstborn. 15** And **he blessed Joseph**, and said, God, before whom my fathers Abraham and Isaac did walk, the God which fed me all my life long unto this day,

1 Chronicles 5:1 Now the **sons of <u>Reuben the firstborn of Israel</u>**, (for he was the firstborn; but, forasmuch as he defiled his father's bed, <u>**his birthright was given unto the sons of Joseph the son of Israel**</u>: and the genealogy is not to be reckoned after the birthright. **2** For <u>**Judah**</u> **prevailed above his brethren, and <u>of him came the chief ruler</u>** [the Messiah]; <u>**but the birthright was Joseph's**</u>:)

EPHRAIM AND MANASSEH ARE ISRAEL AND HAVE BECOME A MULTITUDE IN THE MIDDLE OF THE EARTH

Ephraim and Manasseh are blessed by Israel [Jacob] to become a multitude of people in the middle of the earth. They are to carry the name of Abraham, Isaac and Israel.

Genesis 48:16 The **Angel which redeemed me** [a reference to God] from all evil, **bless the lads**; and <u>**let my name be named on them**</u>, and the **name of my fathers Abraham and Isaac**; and <u>**let them grow into a multitude**[13] **in the midst**[14] **of the earth**</u>.

- Both Ephraim and Manasseh received the blessing of Israel that was upon Joseph

- Ephraim and Manasseh are called by the name of Israel.

- Ephraim and Manasseh—unto this day—are also to be known as sons of Abraham and Isaac, heirs to the Abrahamic Covenant.

- Ephraim and Manasseh have become a multitude of people in the middle of the earth.

---

13 Heb.. _rob_, abundance, greatness, multitude.

14 Heb., _qereb_, midst, among, inner part, middle; in the midst, among, from among (of a number of persons). What does "midst, middle, or center of the earth" mean? How about...land mass, longitude, latitude, or some other measure? Unlocking this mystery will also unlock the mystery of where Ephraim is today, and where Manasseh migrated to.

MANASSEH HAS BECOME A GREAT PEOPLE

Manasseh has been blessed over the years to become a great people in the middle or center of the earth.

> **Genesis 48:17** And when Joseph saw that his father laid his right hand upon the head of Ephraim, it displeased him: and he held up his father's hand, to remove it from Ephraim's head unto Manasseh's head. **18** And Joseph said unto his father, Not so, my father: for this is the firstborn [Manasseh]; put thy right hand upon his head. **19(a)** And his father refused, and said, I know it, my son, I know it: **he** [Manasseh] also **shall become a people**, and **he also shall be great:**

- **Manasseh** has become **a great people in the center of the earth.**

EPHRAIM HAS BECOME A MULTITUDE OF NATIONS

Ephraim has been blessed over the years to become **a multitude of nations, also in the middle or center of the earth.** This is in furtherance of the promises God gave to Abraham and Sarah that they would be the father and mother of nations[15]; and a company of nations[16]. God speaks here of more than just the nation of Israel. Also, the fulfillment of Ephraim will come before that of Manasseh, and at least initially shall be greater.

> **Genesis 48:19(b)**...but truly **his younger brother** [Ephraim] **shall be greater than he,** and **his seed shall become a multitude**[17] **of nations**[18] [in the midst or middle of the earth (verse. 16)]. **20** And **he blessed them** that day, saying, In thee **shall Israel bless,** saying, God make thee as Ephraim and as Manasseh: and **he set Ephraim before Manasseh.**

- Ephraim has become a multitude of both people and nations in the middle of the earth.

- Manasseh has become a great multitude of people in the mid-

---

15 Genesis 17:4-6, 16.

16 Genesis 35:11.

17 Heb., _melo_, fullness, that which fills, mass, multitude...as the dust of the earth, stars of heaven, and sand of the sea.

18 Heb., _gowy_ (_goyim_), nation, people, nations.

dle of the earth.

- Both Ephraim and Manasseh are called by the name of Israel; they are also the sons of Abraham and Isaac.

- Nowhere has this prophecy been fulfilled or can be fulfilled solely in the Jewish descendants of the tribe of Judah. But, because no Word from God shall ever fail, we simply must ascribe to Ephraim and / or Manasseh—not Ishmael, Esau or the sons of Keturah—these additional unfulfilled blessings of God's Covenant with Abraham, Isaac, and even Rebekah.

- Both Ephraim and Manasseh have become a blessing to all the families of the earth[19].

- Their seed has become as the dust of the earth, stars of heaven, and sand of the sea[20].

- They have possessed or will possess the gate[21] of their enemies.

- They have pushed the people [the children of Israel] to the ends of the earth[22].

- Rebekah has become the mother of billions[23].

- They shall possess the land of Canaan[24] [then as well as now].

Does anybody really believe that when God, even in His anger, sows or scatters both Israel and Judah throughout the earth, that He does not intend in time to reap a bountiful harvest? Not my God! In fact, I am persuaded that when Israel begins in earnest to search for Joseph, that the research will prove that God has set a mark of some kind in the hundreds of millions of Hebrew descendants scattered throughout the earth today [maybe more]—like the mark in the DNA of the Levites that identifies them as being of the priestly tribe, and capable of service in a rebuilt temple.

19 Genesis 12:3, 26:4 and 28:14.
20 *Dust* - Genesis 13:16 and 28:14; *stars* - Genesis 15:5, 22:17 and 26:4; *sand* - Genesis 22:17 and 32:12.
21 Genesis 22:17 and 24:60.
22 Deuteronomy 33:17.
23 Genesis 24:60.
24 Genesis 28:13.

Joseph Has Received The Double Portion

Both Ephraim and Manasseh received their own major parcels of land.

Genesis 48:21 And **Israel** [Jacob] **said unto Joseph**, Behold, I die: but God shall be with you, and bring you again unto the land of your fathers. **22** Moreover **I have given to thee one portion above thy brethren**, which I took out of the hand of the Amorite with my sword and with my bow.

The Sceptre Shall Remain With Judah

Judah is blessed by Israel with **<u>the sceptre</u>**: the right to rule.

Genesis 49:8 Judah, thou art he whom thy brethren shall praise: thy hand shall be in the neck of thine enemies; thy father's children shall bow down before thee ... **10** The **sceptre shall not depart from Judah, nor a lawgiver from between his feet, until Shiloh**[25] [the Messiah] **come**; and **unto him shall the gathering of the people be.**

Israel And Moses Expand Joseph's Blessing

What is said of Joseph is fulfilled in Ephraim and Manasseh. He has immense wealth awaiting his return to the land; together with his accumulations of wealth in the company of nations to which he has been scattered.

Genesis 49:22 Joseph is **a fruitful bough**, even a fruitful bough by a well; whose branches run over the wall: **23** The archers [his brothers] have sorely grieved him, and shot at him, and hated him: **24** But his bow abode in strength, and the arms of his hands were made strong by the hands of the mighty God of Jacob; (from thence is the shepherd, the stone of Israel:) **25** Even by the God of thy father, who shall help thee; and by **the Almighty**, who **shall bless thee with blessings** of heaven above, **blessings** of the deep that lieth under, **blessings** of the breasts, and of the womb [a multitude of children]:

26 The blessings of thy father [Jacob] **have prevailed above <u>the blessings</u> of my progenitors** [the blessings given to my fathers: Abraham and Isaac] unto the utmost bound of the everlasting hills: **they shall be on the head of Joseph**, and **on the crown of the head** of him that was separate from his brethren.

Moses adds to the blessing upon Ephraim and Manasseh. They shall become strong nations, and with their strength they shall "push the people" of Israel [colonize Israel?] to the ends of the earth. The multitude of nations coming from Ephraim shall have more people than Manasseh.

> **Deuteronomy 33:16** … [L]et the **blessing come upon the head of Joseph**, and **upon the top of the head** ["crown of his head" in Genesis 49:26] of him that was separated from his brethren. **17** His glory is like the firstling of his bullock, and **his horns are like the horns of unicorns**: with them he [they] **shall push the people together to the ends of the earth**: and they are the **ten thousands of Ephraim**, and they are **the thousands of Manasseh**.

- There is gargantuan financial blessing in the area of land that is the "crown of the head" or "top of the head" of the parcel of land Joshua gave to the tribe of Ephraim.

- Ephraim and Manasseh are a strong company of nations.

- Together with the national strengths they possess, they have carried the blessing of Joseph and the blood of Israel to the four corners of the earth … without knowing who they are.

- Ephraim has become as the dust of the earth, stars of heaven, and sand of the sea.

- Manasseh has become a multitude of a great people.

The blessing of both Israel [Jacob] and Moses upon Joseph both speak of a **blessing** coming upon the "**head of Joseph**", and upon the "**crown of the head**" or "**top of the head**" of Joseph. In a good map of the parcels of land that Joshua gave to the tribes of Israel, the parcel that was given to Ephraim actually looks like a king's profile with a crown on it. The area of the crown is adjacent to the city of Nābulus [biblical Shechem] and Mount Ebal—right in the middle of the area designated for a proposed Palestinian state—which Israel as of this writing would likely give away if its national recognition and security demands were met by the Palestinians.

165

But, as both Israel and Moses said by the power of the Spirit of God, there is indeed an immense blessing that is reserved for Joseph in the area of the crown of his head—be it oil, gas, gold or something else that God has reserved for Israel in these latter days.

"Therefore, I prophesy by the same Spirit of God that the economy of whatever nation owns this land whenever this blessing manifests will explode like a financial mushroom cloud of an Atomic Money Machine."

While I am on this subject, although this book deals with prophecy and not politics, it is interesting to note that the biggest portions of land for the proposed Palestinian state come from land that was previously the possession of Judah, Ephraim, and Manasseh. Judah has had a say in this. What does Joseph have to say about giving away his land?

GOD WILL BUILD HIS SANCTUARY WITH JOSEPH IN THE LAND

Here's my final point here concerning the blessing of Joseph. Consider:

> **Ezekiel 37:26** Moreover **I will make a covenant of peace** with them; it shall be an everlasting covenant with them: and I will place them, and multiply them, and will **set <u>my sanctuary in the midst of them for evermore</u>**. **27 <u>My tabernacle also shall be with them</u>**: yea, I will be their God, and they shall be my people. **28** And the heathen shall know that I the LORD do sanctify Israel, when **<u>my sanctuary shall be in the midst of them for evermore</u>**.

As a result of the joining of Joseph through Ephraim to Judah in fulfillment of **Ezekiel 37:15-22**, God almost immediately says that in addition to establishing an everlasting covenant of peace with His reunited nation, not only will He multiply them, but He will set His **sanctuary** and **tabernacle** in the midst of them for evermore. This passage of Scripture written by a Hebrew priest clearly reveals that the third temple cannot be constructed without the joining of Joseph with Judah. Or, phrased differently, the joining of Joseph with Judah is maybe the last event that must occur before God will release the construction of the third temple?

Israel: Find Joseph

Chapter 16

Persecution Shall Return All Israel To God

W**hile the whole house of Israel can choose to return to the LORD now, in this time, the children of Israel have always cried out to God when they experienced enough external pressure from an enemy. And so all Israel shall be saved.

Moses Speaks Of The Scattering Of Israel

All 12 tribes have been scattered among the nations. Judah has become few in number, but has been preserved as Jews because of God's sure mercies to David[1]. Joseph on the other hand, through his sons Ephraim and Manasseh have populated the ends of the earth[2]. Even in judgment, the Lord is still leading His people.

> **Deuteronomy 4:21** Furthermore the LORD was angry with me [Moses] for your sakes, and sware that I should not go over Jordan, and that I should not go in unto **that good land, which the LORD thy God giveth thee for an inheritance**: **22** But I must die in this land, I must not go over Jordan: but ye shall go over, and possess that good land. **23** **Take heed** unto yourselves, **lest ye forget the covenant of the LORD your God**, which he made with you, and make you a graven image, or the likeness of any thing, which the LORD thy God hath forbidden thee. **24** For the LORD thy God is a consuming fire, even a jealous God.
>
> **25** When thou shalt beget children, and children's children, and ye shall have remained long in the land, and shall corrupt yourselves, and make a graven image, or the likeness of any thing,

---

1 Isaiah 55:3; Psalms 89.
2 He literally has pushed the people of Israel to the ends of the earth (Deuteronomy 33:17).

and shall do evil in the sight of the LORD thy God, to provoke him to anger: **26 I call heaven and earth to witness against you this day, that <u>ye shall soon utterly perish from off the land</u>** [all 12 tribes] whereunto ye go over Jordan to possess it; ye shall not prolong your days upon it, but shall utterly be destroyed.

27 And <u>the LORD shall scatter you among the nations</u>, and ye shall **be left <u>few in number</u> among the heathen, <u>whither the LORD shall lead you</u>. 28 And there ye shall serve gods**, the work of men's hands, wood and stone, which neither see, nor hear, nor eat, nor smell.

The northern kingdom of Ephraim and Israel lost its identity as Hebrews, and with this have not known the God of Abraham. Its people have served other gods in foreign lands; and some likely no god.

Deuteronomy 4:29 But if from thence thou shalt seek the LORD thy God, thou shalt find him, if thou seek him with all thy heart and with all thy soul. **30 <u>When thou art in tribulation</u>**, and all these things are come upon thee, even **<u>in the latter days</u>**, if thou turn to the LORD thy God, and shalt be obedient unto his voice; **31** (For the LORD thy God is a merciful God;) he will not forsake thee, neither destroy thee, nor forget the covenant of thy fathers which he sware unto them.

Today's Israel [which is technically Judah] is in "great tribulation" right now. But, the tribulation of the latter days is not the great tribulation of the last days: which is the *time of Jacob's trouble*.

Deuteronomy 28:58 <u>If thou wilt not</u> observe to do all the words of this law that are written in this book, that thou mayest fear this glorious and fearful name, **THE LORD THY GOD** ... **62 And <u>ye shall be left few</u> in number, whereas <u>ye were as the stars of heaven</u> for multitude; because thou wouldest not obey the voice of the LORD thy God. 63 And it shall come to pass,** that as the LORD rejoiced over you to do you good, and to multiply you; so the LORD will rejoice over you to destroy you, and to bring you to nought; and ye shall be plucked from off the land whither thou goest to possess it.

64 And <u>the LORD shall scatter thee among all people, from the one end of the earth even unto the other</u>; and <u>there thou shalt serve other gods</u>, which neither thou nor thy fathers have known, even wood and stone. **65** And among these nations shalt thou find no ease, neither shall the sole of thy foot have rest: but the LORD shall give thee there a trembling heart, and failing of eyes, and sorrow of mind: **66** And thy life shall hang in doubt before thee; and thou shalt fear day and night, and shalt have none assurance of thy life: ... **68** And the **LORD shall bring thee into Egypt[3] again** with ships, by the way whereof I spake unto thee, Thou shalt see it no more again: and there ye shall be sold unto your enemies for bondmen and bondwomen, and no man shall buy you.

The prophecy in this paragraph has certainly been true for the Jewish people; but Joseph has been hidden because of the blessing spoken over him by Israel [Jacob].

THE TIME OF JACOB'S TROUBLE

Persecution and affliction by a future Assyrian[4] will cause the final remnant of the whole house of Israel [Jacob] to return to God. Some will come now in fulfillment of the prophecy of Ezekiel 37, while the remainder of both Israel and Judah will come later after a period of extreme persecution and affliction—at which time the Messiah shall come[5].

Jeremiah 30:4 And these are the **words that the LORD spake concerning <u>Israel</u> and concerning <u>Judah</u>. 5** For thus saith the LORD; We have heard a **voice of trembling**, of **fear**, and **not of peace. 6** Ask ye now, and see whether a man [all Israel] doth travail with child? wherefore do I see every man with his hands on his loins, as a woman in travail, and all faces are turned into paleness? **7** Alas! for that day is great, so that none is like it: it is even <u>**the time of Jacob's trouble**</u>; but <u>**he shall be saved out of it**</u>.

---

3   By the time of the Ptolemy kingdom in Egypt that succeeded the reign of Alexander the Great, a multitude of non-Hebrew speaking Jews were so flourishing in Egypt that the Septuagint was commissioned as a translation into Greek of the Tanaka (Hebrew Old Testament Scriptures) for the great library of Alexandria: so that Jews would be able to read Moses, the Psalms, and the Prophets.

4   Isaiah 10:5 and 27. The little horn of Daniel 7 and 8.

5   Zechariah 12-14.

8 For it shall come to pass in that day [the time of Jacob's trouble], saith the LORD of hosts, that I will break **his yoke** [of the Assyrian] from off thy neck, and will burst thy bonds, and strangers shall no more serve themselves of him: **9** But **they** [all Israel] **shall serve the LORD their God, and David their king**, whom I will raise up unto them.

These are the birth pains of the nation, in which all 12 tribes and the remainder of Joseph and Ephraim shall return to the Lord, and the land.

Jeremiah 30:10 Therefore fear thou not, <u>**O my servant Jacob**</u>, saith the LORD; neither be dismayed, <u>**O Israel**</u>: for, lo, **I will save thee from afar**, and **thy seed from the land of their captivity**; and **Jacob shall return**], and shall be in rest, and be quiet, and none shall make him afraid.

11 For I am with thee, saith the LORD, to save thee: <u>**though I make a full end of all nations whither I have scattered thee, yet will I not make a full end of thee**</u>: but I will correct thee in measure, and will not leave thee altogether unpunished. … **15 Why criest thou for thine affliction?** thy sorrow is incurable for the multitude of thine iniquity: because thy sins were increased, I have done these things unto thee.

16 Therefore <u>**all they that devour thee shall be devoured**</u>; and all thine adversaries, every one of them, shall go into captivity; and they that spoil thee shall be a spoil, and all that prey upon thee will I give for a prey. **17** For **I will restore health unto thee**, and I will heal thee of thy wounds, saith the LORD; because they called thee an Outcast, saying, <u>**This is Zion**</u>, whom no man seeketh after.

The 12 tribes of Israel [Jacob] are called **Zion** because Ezekiel 37 has been fulfilled … as well as Ezekiel 38 and 39.

THE ASSYRIAN IS THE ROD OF GOD'S ANGER

In the entire history of the Bible, God has repeatedly stirred up an enemy to His people after their prolonged disobedience, for the sole purpose of compelling them to cry out and to return back to Him. The final tyrant will be the **Assyrian little horn of Daniel 7 and 8** who Christians call the

170

Antichrist, and who comes from Syria. Isaiah was prophet in 722 BC when Assyria carried Israel into captivity. This prophecy of Isaiah would appear to be following their deportation, because he speaks of both a remnant such are escaped of the house of Jacob, and a remnant of Israel that has become as the sand of the sea (verse 20 and 21, below). Each of these remnants speak of Ephraim and Ezekiel 37. So, this "Assyrian" would, indeed, appear to be a future Assyrian, who shall rule for only a short time after Ezekiel 36 through 39 have been fulfilled and the third temple has been built. But, Israel after its coming unification is still not wholly following the God who created it, and must again be chastised by the Lord.

Isaiah 10:5 O Assyrian, the rod of mine anger, and the staff in their hand is mine indignation. **6 I will send him** against an hypocritical nation, and **against the people of my wrath will I give him a charge**, to take the spoil, and to take the prey, and to tread them down like the mire of the streets. ... **20** And it shall come to pass in that day, that **the remnant of Israel, and such as are escaped of the house of Jacob**, shall no more again stay upon him that smote them; but shall stay upon the LORD, the Holy One of Israel, in truth.

21 The remnant shall return, even the remnant of Jacob, unto the mighty God. 22 For though thy people Israel be as the sand of the sea [Ephraim]**, yet a remnant of them shall return** [beginning with Ezekiel 37 and continuing until the coming of the Messiah]: the consumption decreed shall overflow with righteousness.

23 For the Lord GOD of hosts shall make a consumption, even determined, in the midst of all the land. **24** Therefore thus saith the Lord GOD of hosts, **O my people that dwellest in Zion, be not afraid of the Assyrian: he shall smite thee with a rod** (verse 5), and shall lift up his staff against thee, after the manner of Egypt. **25** For yet **a very little while**, and the indignation shall cease, and mine anger in their destruction.

The Assyrian / little horn shall rule over Israel for only a short time ... the *time of Jacob's trouble*. His burden shall be removed and his yoke destroyed by the anointing of God (verse 27): which is His tangible presence on the earth, working in the midst of nations and people.

Isaiah 10:26 And the LORD of hosts shall stir up a scourge for him according to the slaughter of Midian[6] at the rock of Oreb: and as his rod was upon the sea, so shall he lift it up after the manner of Egypt. **27** And it shall come to pass **in that day,** that **his burden shall be taken away from off thy shoulder**, and **his yoke from off thy neck**, and **the yoke shall be destroyed because of the anointing**.

Jacob's Captivity Shall Return

The captivity of the whole house of Jacob shall return unto Israel. [We continue with Jeremiah 30 (from pg. 170).]

Jeremiah 30:18 Thus saith the LORD; Behold, I will bring again the **captivity of Jacob's tents**, and have mercy on his dwellingplaces; and the city shall be builded upon her own heap, and the palace shall remain after the manner thereof. **19** And out of them shall proceed thanksgiving and the voice of them that make merry, and I will multiply them, and they shall not be few; I will also glorify them, and they shall not be small.

20 Their children also shall be as aforetime, and their congregation shall be established before me, and **I will punish all that oppress them**. **21** And their nobles shall be of themselves, and their governor shall proceed from the midst of them; and I will cause him to draw near, and he shall approach unto me: for who is this that engaged his heart to approach unto me? saith the LORD.

22 And ye shall be my people, and I will be your God. 23 Behold, the whirlwind of the LORD goeth forth with fury, a continuing whirlwind: it shall fall with pain upon the head of the wicked. **24** The fierce anger of the LORD shall not return, until he have done it, and until he have performed the intents of his heart: **in the latter days** [not the last days] ye shall consider it.

God's Mercy In The North Country

God extends His hand of mercy in **the north country of Babylon**.

---

6 Judges 7:25.

Jeremiah 31:1 At the same time [the time of Jacob's trouble[7]], **saith the LORD, will I be the God of all the families of Israel** [Joseph, Ephraim and Judah]**, and they shall be my people. 2** Thus saith the LORD, The people which were left of the sword found grace in the wilderness; even Israel, when I went to cause him to rest. **3** The LORD hath appeared of old unto me, saying, Yea, **I have loved thee with an everlasting love: therefore with lovingkindness have I drawn thee.**

4 Again I will build thee, and thou shalt be built, O virgin of Israel: thou shalt again be adorned with thy tabrets, and shalt go forth in the dances of them that make merry. **5** Thou shalt yet plant vines upon the **mountains of Samaria**: the planters shall plant, and shall eat them as common things.

The West Bank has come alive with Joseph and Ephraim back in the land.

Jeremiah 31:6 For there shall be **a day**, that the **watchmen upon the mount Ephraim** shall cry, Arise ye, and let us go up to Zion unto the LORD our God. **7** For thus saith the LORD; Sing with gladness **for Jacob** [a unified Israel], and shout among the **chief of the nations**: publish ye, praise ye, and say, O LORD, save thy people, the **remnant of Israel** [Ephraim].

Chief of nations is a reference in Jeremiah's day to Babylon. For the latter days it means the mightiest nations of the world. The "coasts of the earth", below, is a reference to the isles of the sea or ends of the earth[8]. **Ephraim is the firstborn of the Lord** and carries with him the blessing of Joseph. When he returns, he shall return from every place that he has been scattered: not just from the company of nations in the middle of the earth.

Jeremiah 31:8 Behold, **I will bring them** from the **north country**, and gather them from **the coasts of the earth**, and with them the blind and the lame, the woman with child and her that travaileth with child together: **a great company shall return thither. 9** They shall come with weeping, and with supplications will I lead them: I will cause them to walk by the rivers of waters in a straight way, wherein they shall not stumble: for **I am a father to**

7 Jeremiah 30:7.
8 Deuteronomy 33:17.

Israel [the 10 tribes], and <u>**Ephraim is my firstborn**</u>.

Jeremiah says by the Lord that … "I [the Lord] will bring them [the remnant of the 10 tribes] from the north country [Babylon]" … which today is Iraq [and maybe Iran]. Contemporary Bible prophesy teachers routinely interpret any reference to the "north" as a reference to Russia; but we must understand Jeremiah's prophesy first within the context of the day he spoke it. Although Jeremiah makes repeated references to the vanquished and non-existent northern kingdom of Israel, **Jeremiah's primary mission was God's final warning to Judah of the 70 years of Babylonian captivity that was upon them.** We know from historical records that the Babylonian army came against Judah from the north [from Syria], and not from the east [today's Jordan].

Jeremiah prophesies …

Jeremiah 6:1 … [E]vil appeareth **out of the north**, and great destruction.

Jeremiah 6:22 Thus saith the LORD. Behold, a people cometh from **the north country**, and a great nation shall be raised from the sides of the earth.

In Jeremiah's day these are rather obvious references to the impending invasion from Babylon. In the latter days these are references to the little horn of Daniel 7 and 8, who comes from Syria. Jeremiah identifies **the exact location of the north country** as …

Jeremiah 46:10 " … <u>**[T]he north country by the river Euphrates**</u>."

In order to prophesy Babylon's destruction by the nations of the Medo-Persian Empire, Jeremiah makes a further reference to "an assembly of great nations from the north country[9]"—Medo-Persia [Iran] being even further to the "north" than Babylon. Immediately north of Israel is Syria. **Syria is the origin of the Assyrian: the king of the north of Daniel 11: the little horn of Daniel 7 and 8, and the Antichrist believed by Christians.**

The Bible makes it clear that a great harvest of Hebrews will eventually <u>return to the land</u> of Israel from these areas.

9 Jeremiah 50:9.

To finish our search for the *remnant of Israel*, let us consider a clearly Messianic prophecy:

> **Jeremiah 23:3** And **I will gather the remnant of my flock out of all countries whither I have driven them**, and will bring them again to their folds; and they shall be fruitful and increase. **4** And I will set up shepherds over them which shall feed them: and they shall fear no more, nor be dismayed, neither shall they be lacking, saith the LORD.
>
> **5** Behold, the days come, saith the LORD, that **I will raise unto David a righteous Branch, and a King shall reign and prosper,** and shall execute judgment and justice in the earth. **6 In his days** [days of the King] **Judah shall be saved**, and **Israel shall dwell safely:** and this is **his name** whereby he shall be called. **THE LORD OUR RIGHTEOUSNESS.**

Judah here is a clear reference to the **Jews of Judah** that Jeremiah is prophesying to—where they were then, and wherever in the world they are now. But, **Israel** in this passage has to be understood in the terms of how Jeremiah uses this term throughout his writings. In the days following the Assyrian captivity of the 10 tribes, **the northern kingdom was still commonly known as Israel**. When he spoke to Judah, Jeremiah undoubtedly knew exactly where his brethren had been scattered to. Consider further:

> **Jeremiah 23:7** Therefore, behold, **the days come**, saith the LORD, that they shall no more say, The LORD liveth, which brought up the children of Israel out of the land of Egypt; **8** But, The LORD liveth, **which brought up and which led the seed of the house of Israel out of the north country**[10], and **from all countries whither I had driven them**; and they shall dwell in their own land.

In this Messianic prophecy, the Messiah says that He is to become known for being alive and leading ... " ... [T]he seed of the house of Israel out of the north country". The "house of Israel" refers to the 12 tribes of Ja-

---

10 The million Jews that returned to Israel from Russia are not the primary reference here [c/p. Jeremiah 46:10].

cob; and "north country", as we have seen, refers to Babylon [greater Iraq]. God will also lead the whole house of Israel [Ephraim and Judah] out of all the additional countries to which He has driven them.

WHERE IS THE HEBREW NATION OF ISRAEL TODAY?

There are three critical points to remember concerning the Hebrew nation of Israel. First, a multitude of Jews went into Babylonian captivity, but only about 50,000 Jews returned from Babylon to rebuild the walls of Jerusalem and the temple under Zerubbabel, Ezra and Nehemiah. Where are the descendants today of those Jews who remained in Babylon? There is no doubt much Hebrew blood alive in this part of the world today, and which the Messiah intends to gather the final remnant thereof when He comes.

Second, when the 10 tribes went into captivity they were not Jews; and wherever their location is today, their descendants are still not Jews—they are the seed of "Abram the Hebrew"[11]: Hebrews who have lost their Hebrew identity. If the Messiah can re-gather these, His people, when He comes, why cannot the State of Israel of today, and its Jewish citizens, begin to search them out and initiate their exodus out of the nations and back into the land now: in the same fashion as the Ethiopian Jews have been returned to Israel? Just a thought ... but the greater point is that **until Ephraim is found and is joined again with Judah in fulfillment of the prophecy of Ezekiel 37, the world is not yet ready for the coming of the Messiah**.

Third, although there is a remnant of the "seed of the house of Israel" in the "north country" of Babylon, **the numberless multitude of Ephraim is to be found in a multitude of nations that have grown up in the middle or of the earth, with the anointing of Joseph upon them**.

Jeremiah 31:10 Hear the word of the LORD, O ye nations, and declare it in the isles afar off, and say, **He that scattered Israel will gather him**, and keep him, as a shepherd doth his flock. **11** For the **LORD hath redeemed Jacob** [12 tribes], and ransomed him from the hand of him that was stronger than he. ...

18 I have surely heard **Ephraim** bemoaning himself thus; Thou hast chastised me, and I was chastised, as a bullock unaccustomed to the yoke: turn thou me, and I shall be turned; for thou art the

11   Genesis 14:13.
176

LORD my God. **19** Surely after that I was turned, I repente; and after that I was instructed, I smote upon my thigh: I was ashamed, yea, even confounded, because I did bear the reproach of my youth.

20 Is **Ephraim my dear son**? is he a pleasant child? for since I spake against him, I do earnestly remember him still: therefore my bowels are troubled for him; **I will surely have mercy upon him**, saith the LORD. ... **23** Thus saith the LORD of hosts, the God of Israel; As yet **they shall use this speech in the land of Judah** [Jews of Israel shall speak the language of Ephraim] and in the cities thereof, **when I shall bring again their captivity**; The LORD bless thee, O habitation of justice, and mountain of holiness. **24** And there shall dwell in Judah itself, and in all the cities thereof together, husbandmen, and they that go forth with flocks. **25** For I have satiated the weary soul, and I have replenished every sorrowful soul. **26** Upon this I awaked, and beheld; and my sleep was sweet unto me.

27 Behold, the days come, saith the LORD, that **I will sow** the **house of Israel** and the **house of Judah** with the **seed of man** [intermarriage], **and with the seed of beast** [affliction, persecution, war, famine, etc.]. **28** And **it shall come to pass**, that like as I have watched over them, to pluck up, and to break down, and to throw down , and to destroy , and to afflict; **so will I watch over them, to build, and to plant**, saith the LORD. ...

GOD WILL ESTABLISH A NEW COVENANT WITH ISRAEL AND JUDAH

The LORD will make **a new covenant** with the **house of Israel** and the **house of Judah**.

Jeremiah 31:31 Behold, the days come , saith the LORD, that I will make **a new covenant** with the **house of Israel**, and with the **house of Judah**: **32** Not according to the covenant that I made with their fathers in the day that I took them by the hand to bring them out of the land of Egypt; which my covenant they brake, although I was an husband unto them, saith the LORD:

33 But this shall be the covenant that I will make with the house of Israel; After those days, saith the LORD, I will put my

law in their inward parts, and write it in their hearts; and will be their God, and they shall be my people. 34 And they shall teach no more every man his neighbour, and every man his brother, saying, Know the LORD: for they shall all know me, from the least of them unto the greatest of them, saith the LORD: for I will forgive their iniquity, and I will remember their sin no more. … **36** If those ordinances [sun, moon, stars, sea (vs. 35)] depart from before me, saith the LORD, then the <u>seed of Israel</u> [all 12 tribes] also shall cease from being a nation before me for ever.

Jeremiah uses the ordinances of the sun, moon, stars and the sea as examples of God's faithfulness to His Word, to Israel, and to Judah.

> **Jeremiah 31:37** Thus saith the LORD; If heaven above can be measured, and the foundations of the earth searched out beneath, I will also cast off all **the seed of Israel** for all that they have done, saith the LORD. **38** Behold, the days come, saith the LORD, that the city shall be built to the LORD from the tower of Hananeel unto the gate of the corner. …

THE TEMPLE SHALL BE REBUILT IN JERUSALEM

The Lord will also build again the tabernacle of David as part of a rebuilt temple, under the restored law of Moses with its animal sacrifices.

> **Amos 9:11 In that day will <u>I raise up the tabernacle of David that is fallen</u>,** and close up the breaches thereof; and I will raise up his ruins, and <u>**I will build it as in the days of old**</u>: **12** That they may possess the **remnant of Edom** [Esau], and of all **the heathen, which are called by my name**, saith the LORD that doeth this.

Who are "the heathen which are called by my name"? This speaks at a minimum of the hidden multitude and nations of Joseph and Ephraim; but probably speaks of much, much more.

> **Amos 9:13** Behold, the days come, saith the LORD, that the plowman shall overtake the reaper, and the treader of grapes him that soweth seed; and the mountains shall drop sweet wine, and all the hills shall melt. **14** And <u>**I will bring again the captivity of my people of Israel**</u> [all 12 tribes], and they shall build the waste

cities, and inhabit them; and they shall plant vineyards, and drink the wine thereof; they shall also make gardens, and eat the fruit of them. **15** And __I will plant them upon their land, and they shall no more be pulled up out of their land which I have given them__, saith the LORD thy God.

The Second Temple

The Second Temple and Jerusalem

CHAPTER 17

GOD'S PROPHETIC CLOCK HAS NOT CHANGED

While there was a good deal of contact between the kingdom of Judah and those escapees of Ephraim, Manasseh and others of the northern kingdom following their departure into Assyrian captivity, the contact was not great; and even if one argues that it was, it in no way invalidates the paramount conclusion of this book—that Ephraim and Manasseh have grown into a company of nations in the middle of the earth; that they have lost their identity as Hebrews; and that they have in the process of time grown to become as the dust of the earth, stars of heaven, and sand of the sea.

Let me state here that I am familiar with the arguments associated with **British Israelism**, and the writings of Herbert W. Armstrong, among others. British Israelism holds in essence that through a complicated set of suppositions and events, the throne of David has found its way to England, and is occupied at present by the Queen of England. These arguments are interesting; but I take no position on them, other than to say that the major error associated with this teaching is what has come to be known as **replacement theology**—that God has rejected the Jewish people.

A further error is that all of the promises of God to Israel will be fulfilled in and by Christians. To this conclusion I say, "Nonsense!" There is, however, one area of this study that I find potentially fruitful. If concerning the promises that God gave to Ephraim, one substituted for a "company of nations in the middle of the earth" a "commonwealth of nations in the middle of the earth", there may be something here to be discovered. The descendents of Ephraim are a multitude hidden somewhere in the earth. I will, however, leave this pursuit to others.

My assignment as a prophet of God, is to trace the Abrahamic Covenant, and determine—concerning the natural descendants of Abraham through Isaac, Jacob, and Jacob's sons (the 12 tribes of Israel)—what is missing and yet to be fulfilled before coming of the Messiah. The gaps and holes are numerous, wide, and deep. Whatever the extent of contact between Judah and Ephraim there was following the Assyrian captivity, or how many Israelites from the tribes of Ephraim, Manasseh, and the other northern kingdom tribes actually stayed with Judah when the kingdom divided (and there were a goodly number)—none of this can change the fulfillment of what God has said concerning Joseph—that through his sons he would:

- Grow to become a company of nations in the middle of the earth.

- Possess the gate of his enemies.

- Push the people of Israel to the end of the earth.

- Become a numberless multitude.

- Lose his Hebrew identity.

- In the latter years would come alive to his heritage; and

- Be joined with Judah in these latter years to become one nation again on the mountains of Israel ... which is the West Bank.

I am not so presumptuous as to tell Israel and its Jewish people how they should go about determining who and where Joseph's descendents are; but, again, as a prophet of God I will and do say to Israel—your very survival as a nation in these troublesome times is dependent upon rethinking and reconsidering where the God that created you has you on His prophetic clock, and then ...

Israel: Find Joseph

I also encourage Israelis, Jews, Christians, Muslims, as well as any other interested parties, to read or re-read the first 12 Chapters of the Book of Exodus. God had a higher purpose than the children of Israel could understand or see when He provoked the stubborn intransigence of Pharaoh, who would not let the nation go out into the desert to serve the true and living God.

I submit that at the root of why the Palestinian leadership has not been willing to take some rather attractive offers from the Israeli government over the past 20 years is because, like Pharaoh, it is God who is provoking their intransigence … again for a higher purpose. This higher purpose that the world Jewish community has yet to discern is that it is time on God's prophetic clock for the fulfillment of Ezekiel 37—with the joining of Joseph with Judah back into one Hebrew nation. I implore, again …

Israel: Find Joseph

JEREMIAH SAW THE DAY THAT WE ARE IN

Jeremiah 30:1 The word that came to Jeremiah from the LORD, saying, **2** Thus speaketh the LORD God of Israel, saying, Write thee all the words that I have spoken unto thee in a book. **3** For, lo**, the days come**, saith the LORD, that **I will bring again the captivity of my people <u>Israel</u>** [the 10 tribes] **and <u>Judah</u>**, saith the LORD: and <u>**I will cause them to return to the land that I gave to their fathers**</u>, and <u>**they shall possess it**</u>.

About 50,000 Jews around 516 BCE returned to the land after 70 years in Babylonian captivity. They were scattered again in 70 CE, and returned again in 1948. It is time now for Joseph and Ephraim to return and possess their portion of the land. I say this kindly but it must be said. The Jews of today's Israel appear to have only two choices concerning the future occupancy of the land of Israel. Their first choice to share the land with Palestinians, who have never had any national identity as a people; have no long-term historical connection with the Holy Land of the Bible; and have had no desire for a state before Israel was resurrected in 1948. The better choice for the Jewish people of Israel—and God's choice—is to share the land with Joseph and the 10 tribes of Israel: by locating Ephraim, and inviting Ephraim back into the land in fulfillment of Ezekiel 37.

THE PRIESTHOOD REMAINS WITH JUDAH

For the record, I will document again some of the contact that Judah had with Ephraim both before and after the 10 tribes were in Assyrian captivity. The priesthood all remain with Judah; as did many of the righteous in the northern kingdom.

2 Chronicles 11:5 And Rehoboam dwelt in Jerusalem, and built cities for defence in Judah. **...** **13** And **the priests and the Levites that were in all Israel** resorted to him out of all their coasts. **14** For the Levites left their suburbs and their possession, and came to Judah and Jerusalem: for **Jeroboam** [Israel's king] and his sons had **cast them off from executing the priest's office** unto the LORD [Israel begins its apostasy]: **15** And he ordained him priests for the high places, and for the devils, and for the calves which he had made.

THE RIGHTEOUS COME TO JERUSALEM

The righteous of the northern kingdom also come to Jerusalem.

2 Chronicles 11:16 And after them **out of all the** [10] **tribes of Israel such as set their hearts to seek the LORD God of Israel came to Jerusalem**, to sacrifice unto the LORD God of their fathers. **17** So they strengthened the kingdom of Judah, and made Rehoboam the son of Solomon strong, three years: for three years they walked in the way of David and Solomon.

ISRAEL AND JUDAH ARE BRETHREN

It is God that divided the kingdom of Israel from the kingdom of Judah.

2 Chronicles 11:1 And when Rehoboam [King Solomon's son] was come to Jerusalem, he gathered of the **house of Judah and Benjamin** an hundred and fourscore thousand chosen men, which were warriors, **to fight against Israel** [Ephraim], that he might bring the kingdom again to Rehoboam [a unified kingdom].

11:2 But the word of the LORD came to Shemaiah the man of God, saying, **3** Speak unto Rehoboam the son of Solomon, king of Judah, and to **all Israel in Judah and Benjamin** [all Israel physically present], saying, **4** Thus saith the LORD, Ye shall not go up, **nor fight against your brethren** [their Hebrew brethren]: return every man to his house: for **this thing is done of me** [God's dividing the kingdom of 12 brethren]. And they obeyed the words of the LORD, and returned from going against Jeroboam.

THE TRIBAL COMPOSITION OF MODERN ISRAEL

Once David's united kingdom of the 12 tribes of Israel was divided by God into **two kingdoms**—the **kingdom of Israel** and **kingdom of Judah**—"all Israel" was "in Judah and Benjamin". The Jews of the southern kingdom of "Judah" had three tribes merged together ... unto this day. They are the tribes of Judah, Benjamin and the priestly tribe of Levi. But Judah also contains a sampling of the remaining 10 tribes of Israel. So it is accurate to state that *all Israel was in Judah and Benjamin*. But, it is also accurate to state that *all Israel was not of Judah and Benjamin*—as both in the days of the divided kingdoms of Israel and Judah, and the days when the northern kingdom of Israel had ceased to exist down to the rebirth of the nation of Israel in 1948—the great multitude of Ephraim [the Diaspora of the 10 tribes of Israel] were never to be found among the tribe of Judah. Also, the multitudes of Ephraim and Manasseh were never Jewish in their ethnicity.

JUDAH REACHES OUT TO ISRAEL

After the northern kingdom of Israel was exiled into Assyrian captivity, there were some that escaped and returned to their lands. Hezekiah was one of the kings of Judah that reached out to them to come and participate in the feast of the Passover, that Judah had let slip in its own apostasy.

> **2 Chronicles 30:1** And Hezekiah sent to **all Israel** and **Judah**, and wrote letters also to **Ephraim** and **Manasseh**, that they should come to the house of the LORD at Jerusalem, to keep the passover unto the LORD God of Israel. **2** For the king had taken counsel, and his princes, and all the congregation in Jerusalem, to keep the passover in the second month. ... **5** So they established a decree to make proclamation throughout all Israel, from Beersheba even to Dan, that they should come to **keep the passover** unto the LORD God of Israel at Jerusalem: for **they had not done it of a long time in such sort as it was written.**
>
> **6** So the posts went with the letters from the king and his princes throughout **all Israel and Judah**, and according to the

commandment of the king, saying, **Ye children of Israel** [the 10 tribes], **turn again unto the LORD God of Abraham, Isaac, and Israel, and he will return to the <u>remnant</u> of you, that are <u>escaped</u> out of the hand of the kings of Assyria.**

7 And be not ye like your fathers, and like your brethren, which trespassed against the LORD God of their fathers, who therefore gave them up to desolation, as ye see. 8 Now **be ye not stiffnecked, as your fathers were,** but yield yourselves unto the LORD, and enter into his sanctuary [Solomon's temple in Jerusalem], which he hath sanctified for ever: and serve the LORD your God, that the fierceness of his wrath may turn away from you. **9 For if ye turn again unto the LORD, your brethren and your children shall find compassion before them that lead them captive, so that they shall come again into this land**: for the LORD your God is gracious and merciful, and will not turn away his face from you, **if ye return unto him** [the repentance of few can save a nation].

10 So the posts passed from city to city **through the country of Ephraim and Manasseh** even unto Zebulun: but they laughed them to scorn, and mocked them. 11 Nevertheless divers of **Asher** and **Manasseh** and of **Zebulun** [only some in the tribes of the northern kingdom] humbled themselves, and came to Jerusalem. 12 Also in **Judah the hand of God was to give them one heart to do the commandment of the king and of the princes, by the word of the LORD.** 13 And there assembled at Jerusalem much people to keep the feast of unleavened bread in the second month, a very great congregation.

14 And they arose and took away the altars that were in Jerusalem, and all the altars for incense took they away, and cast them into the brook Kidron. 15 Then they killed the passover on the fourteenth day of the second month: and the priests and the Levites were ashamed, and sanctified themselves, and brought in the burnt offerings into the house of the LORD. 16 And they stood in their place after their manner, according to the law of Moses the man of God: the priests sprinkled the blood, which they received of the hand of the Levites. 17 For there were many in the congregation that were not sanctified: therefore the Levites had the charge of the killing of the passovers for every one that was not clean, to

sanctify them unto the LORD.

18 For a multitude of the people, even many of **Ephraim**, and **Manasseh, Issachar**, and **Zebulun**, had not cleansed themselves, yet did they eat the passover otherwise than it was written. But Hezekiah prayed for them, saying, The good LORD pardon every one **19** That prepareth his heart to seek God, the LORD God of his fathers, though he be not cleansed according to the purification of the sanctuary. **20** And the LORD hearkened to Hezekiah, and healed the people.

21 And the **children of Israel that were present at Jerusalem** kept the feast of unleavened bread seven days with great gladness: and the Levites and the priests praised the LORD day by day, singing with loud instruments unto the LORD. ... **25** And all the **congregation of Judah**, with the priests and the Levites, and all the **congregation that came out of Israel** [the northern territories], and the strangers that came out of the land of Israel, and that dwelt in Judah, rejoiced.

26 So there was great joy in Jerusalem: for since the time of Solomon the son of David king of Israel there was not the like in Jerusalem. **27** Then the priests the Levites arose and blessed the people: and their voice was heard, and their prayer came up to his holy dwelling place, even unto heaven.

2 Chronicles 31:1 Now when all this was finished, **all Israel that were present** went out to the **cities of Judah**, and brake the images in pieces, and cut down the groves, and threw down the high places and the altars out of all **Judah** and **Benjamin**, in **Ephraim** also and **Manasseh**, until they had utterly destroyed them all. Then **all the children of Israel returned**, every man to his possession ...

2 Chronicles 34:8 Now in the eighteenth year of his reign [King Josiah], when he had purged the land, and the house, he sent ... to repair the house of the LORD his God. **9** And when they came to Hilkiah the high priest, they delivered the money that was brought into the house of God, which the Levites that kept the doors had gathered of the **hand of Manasseh** and **Ephraim**, and of **all the remnant of Israel** [escaped from Assyria], and of **all Judah**

and Benjamin; and they returned to Jerusalem.

Yes, there was much contact between Judah and the remnant of Israel escaped from Assyria. But the numbers here that we are acknowledging do not even remotely approach the dust of the earth, stars of heaven, or sand of the sea—which by the word of the Lord Ephraim has become.

God's prophetic clock has not changed.

"It is time for my Word to be fulfilled that I spoke by the prophet Ezekiel", saith the Lord; "that the dry bones of Judah be joined with the dry bones of Joseph", saith the Lord, "back into one nation again that I have established forever", saith the Lord.

"Trading land for peace will bring no peace, but only a curse upon your nation. Only I am wonderful. I am your Counselor. I am The mighty God. I am The everlasting Father. I am The Prince of Peace. Without me there can be no peace", saith the Lord.

"I know the end from the beginning", saith the Lord. "For I am the beginning and the end", saith the Lord. "When you do all that you can do", saith the Lord, "I will do what only the Prince of Peace can do", saith the Lord.

"The Palestinians are mine. I formed them for my glory", saith the Lord, "and like Pharaoh and the Egyptians, I am able to cause them to be conformed to my will for this time and for this hour", saith the Lord. "Has the arm of the LORD been shortened that He cannot save?", saith the Lord. "I say that it has not and will never be", saith the Lord.

"But to receive my grace in this matter that you know not of", saith the Lord, "my people of Judah must re-connect with my people of Ephraim; and re-establish the nation that I have created—and the road map for the peace and abundance that I have for you", saith the Lord, "is recorded in Ezekiel 37, saith the Lord."

Israel: Find Joseph

188

CHAPTER 18

WHERE IS ISRAEL TODAY?

So, where is the Hebrew nation of the 12 tribes of Israel today?

1. **Where were Israel and Judah during the reign of David and Solomon?**

   A. The 12 tribes were in one nation, undivided, called **Israel**.

2. **Where were Israel and Judah following the reign of Solomon?**

   A. The 12 tribes were divided into two nations: the **northern kingdom** of **10 tribes** was called **Israel** (also **Ephraim** and **Samaria**), and the **southern kingdom** of **2 tribes** (Judah and Benjamin) was called **Judah**. [The priestly tribe of Levi joined with Judah.]

3. **Which kingdom was ruled by the throne of David?**

   A. **Judah** was ruled by the throne of David. The northern kingdom had its own line of kings, beginning with Jeroboam of the half-tribe of Ephraim.

4. **Where was Israel** [the 10-tribe kingdom] **after being carried into captivity by Assyria in 721 BCE?**

   A. Beyond the Euphrates River in Assyrian captivity, in modern Iraq (and possibly Iran).

5. **Where was Judah during 70 years of Babylonian captivity beginning in 586 BCE?**

   A. Held captive in Babylon, in today's Iraq.

6. **Where was Judah following its Babylonian captivity?**

   A. A remnant of the southern kingdom, following its Babylonian captivity, returned to the land. It has been referred to as both **Judah** and **Israel**. The area to the north of Judah was called **Samaria**, and further to the north was **Galilee**.

7. **Where was Judah between 70 CE and 1948?**

   A. Scattered among the nations in the Diaspora of the Romans.

8. **Where is Judah today?**

   A. There are between 13 and 14 million Jews alive in the world today. Israel's 2010 Jewish population was 5,726,000, and approximately 6,500,000 Jews lived in the United States. The remainder are scattered among the nations. Of Israel's total population of 7,587,000, 75.7 percent (5,726,000) were Jewish, 20.4 percent (1,548,000) were Arab, and 4.1 percent (313,000) fell into a category referred to as "other," the majority of whom were immigrants not registered as Jewish by the Interior Ministry.

9. **Where is Ephraim and the 10 tribes of Israel today?**

   A. Hidden. They have grown up to be a **multitude of nations** in the **middle of the earth**, having the **blessing of Joseph upon them** through the **descendants of Ephraim.** In population they have become as the dust of the earth, stars of heaven, and sand of the sea. **Manasseh** has also become a great and populous people, also in the **middle of the earth.**

10. **Where is the throne of Israel** [the northern kingdom] **today?**

   A. Rejected since Ephraim and the 10 tribes of Israel were banished as a nation by the Lord in 721 BCE.

11. Where is the throne of David / the throne of Judah today?

    A. On hold for the Messiah at His soon coming: although the royal line of David through Solomon has been rejected since it was cursed of the Lord by the mouth of the prophet Jeremiah[1].

12. Where are the priests and Levites today?

    A. Waiting for the restoration of the Law of Moses and its animal sacrifices in a rebuilt temple. They have been identified and trained by the Temple Institute in Jerusalem.

13. When will the third temple be built on the Temple Mount?

    A. When the non-Jewish tribes of Joseph and Ephraim are back in the land of Israel[2] as one nation with the Jews of Judah: following the fulfillment of **Ezekiel 37:15-22**.

Mosaic Of The 12 Tribes

---

1 Jeremiah 22:30.
2 Ezekiel 37:26-28.

ISRAEL WITH THE
WEST BANK,
GAZA STRIP, AND
GOLAN HEIGHTS

○ National capital
◉ District (meḥoz) centre
○ City, town
✈ Airport
—··— International boundary
—·—· Boundary of former Palestine
      Mandate
— — — Armistice Demarcation Line
—···— District (meḥoz) boundary
——— Main road
——— Secondary road
—·—· Railroad
—·—· Oil pipeline

LEBANON
UNIFIL   UNDOF
Tyre
            Qiryat   SYRIA
            Shemona
                            Al Qunayṭirah
Nahariyya
'Akko   NORTHERN   GOLAN
         Lake Tiberias
Haifa   Tiberias
         Nazareth
HAIFA   Irbid   Dar
         Afula
Hadera
                          Jarash
Netanya   Ṭūlkarm
CENTRAL   Nābulus
Herzliyya   Az Zarqā'
TEL AVIV
Tel Aviv-Yafo   WEST BANK
Bat Yam   Rām
           Allāh
Ramla   ◎ Amman
         Jericho
Ashdod   Mādabā
         Jerusalem
Ashqelon   JERUSALEM
MEDITERRANEAN   Bethlehem
                          Dead
SEA   Sea   JORDAN
         Qiryat
Gaza   Gat
GAZA   Hebron
Khān Yūnis
                    Al Qaṭrānah
Al Arīsh   Beersheba
         SOUTHERN   Ak Karak
                Zefa'
Bi'r Lahfān   Aş Şāfi
         Dimona
Abū
Ujaylah
              Zin
'Ayn al
Quşaymah   NEGEV
                          Al Jafr
Bi'r Ḥasanah
         Mizpe
         Ramon
                    Ma'ān
EGYPT
S I N A I   Ra's
              an Naqb
An Nakhl
Al Kuntillah   Yotvata

0 10 20 30 40 50 60 km
0   10   20   30   40 mi

Ṭābā   Al 'Aqabah

192

CHAPTER 19

LET EPHRAIM NOW BE JOINED WITH JUDAH

Central to the revelation of this book, and what I have tracked in the proceeding pages, is an understanding that the Bible's Hebrew Scriptures clearly reveal:

- Abraham was Hebrew and not Jewish. So were Isaac, Jacob (who God named Israel), Joseph and Moses.

- God changed Jacob's name to Israel. The 12 sons of Israel became the 12 tribes of Israel.

- Israel always has been and always will be a Hebrew nation.

- All of the descendants of the twelve tribes of Israel are Hebrews. They are heirs according to all of the promises that God gave to Abraham, Isaac, and Jacob.

- All Jews are Hebrews, but not all Hebrews are Jews—and all Hebrews are of Israel.

- Rebekah has become the mother of billions of Hebrews, the vast multitude of which are hidden somewhere on the earth. These unseen Hebrews are not Jewish.

- The natural descendants of Abraham through Isaac have been given a perpetual right to possess the land of Canaan. This right of possession proceeds from Adonai-Jehovah, the God of Israel. The Lord God of Israel swore by Himself, while standing in blood, His Covenant to Abraham to give him and his offspring the land of Canaan / Palestine / Israel forever.

- These promises of God concerning the land of Israel are given to Abraham and flow through Isaac and Jacob, and not Ishmael, Esau or the sons of Abraham and Keturah.

- All of the descendants of each of the 12 tribes of Israel have the same right to possess the land of Israel: no matter where they are to be found in the world today, and irrespective of whether, at this writing, they have the knowledge that they are Hebrew.

- The descendants of Abraham, through Isaac and Jacob, have already blessed all of the families of the earth.

- Both the birthright and the blessing of Abraham were given by God to Joseph, and not to Judah.

- Ephraim, the youngest son of Joseph, is the Lord's firstborn.

- The greater manifestation of Joseph's birthright and blessing is to be found in the descendants of Ephraim, and secondly in those of Manasseh ... none of whom are Jewish.

- Ephraim and Manasseh, like Jacob, are called Israel.

- Ephraim and Manasseh, even today, are also to be known as sons of Abraham and Isaac. They are full-blooded heirs to the Abrahamic Covenant.

- Ephraim, through his descendants, has become a strong company of nations in the middle or center of the earth. They are a numberless multitude of people—who are as the dust of the earth, stars of heaven, and sand of the sea.

- Manasseh has become a great people, whose descendants are also in the middle of the earth.

- Ephraim has expanded ("pushed the people") to the ends of the earth the Hebrew children of Israel, carrying the blessing of Joseph that is upon them. His descendants have done so without knowing their true identity as Hebrew people.

- Ephraim (and possibly Manasseh) shall possess, possess now, or have possessed the gate [gateway] of his [or their] enemies.

- There is gargantuan blessing in the area of land that is the "top of the head" or crown[1] of the parcel of land given by Joshua to the tribe of Ephraim. This parcel of ground lies in an area of the West Bank: now designated as a proposed Palestinian state.

- Although Ephraim has lost his identity as Hebrew, in the latter years he will come alive to his lineage, and claim his inheritance in the nation and the land of Israel.

- It is time on God's prophetic calendar for the Jews of Israel to allow their Creator to rejoin the "stick of Joseph" with the "stick of Judah", in order to combine these two branches of the houses of Jacob back into one nation upon the mountains of Israel, in fulfillment of the prophecy of **Ezekiel 37:15-22**.

- The stick [heirs] of Joseph is [are] to be found in the hand [descendants] of Ephraim.

- The God of Israel has never promised a "Jewish state" to the tribe of Judah, or to the modern nation of Israel.

- For Israel to align itself with its Divinely inspired pre-recorded history, Jews of Israel and across the world simply must acknowledge that Judah is the smallest part of the hundreds of millions of Hebrews alive somewhere upon the earth: every one of which has the same *right of return* to Israel *as a citizen* as does any Jew; and this is what the God of Israel is requiring in the literal fulfillment of **Ezekiel 37:15-22** by rejoining Joseph and Ephraim again with Judah as the **whole house of Israel**.

- Such an invitation to return requires both the people of Israel and Jewry across the world to invest the time, energy, and resources to locate Ephraim (and Manasseh)—who vastly outnumber the entire population of Israel (and likely all of the Arab nations put together)—and invite their brethren back into the land: as is repeatedly prophesied in the Holy Scriptures written by God's Hebrew prophets.

- To return the nation of Israel to the revealed will of God by the pen of these Hebrew prophets is no threat to the viability of Israel as a Hebrew nation, for the sceptre—the right to rule—

---

1 The area of the crown is adjacent to the city of Nābulus [biblical Shechem] and Mount Ebal.

was not given to Joseph nor to his descendants, but is to remain with Judah until Shiloh (the Messiah) comes; and finally that

■ The fulfillment of Ezekiel 37—that Joseph and Ephraim will be joined again with Judah —appears to be the last prerequisite to the building of the third temple. I submit that God will not allow Herod's temple of a Jewish nation to be reconstructed, but only Solomon's temple of a unified Hebrew nation to be resurrected on the Temple Mount. There Abraham offered Isaac; and there David purchased the land from Araunah the Jebusite[2] in order to " ... build an alter unto the Lord ..." [3].

The Bible records the struggles between the twins, Jacob and Esau, partly to give us an appreciation as to how eternally valuable both the **birthright** and the **blessing** are to its recipient. It is called the law of the progenitor, or the right of inheritance of the firstborn son. Esau, as Isaac's firstborn, should have received the blessing of his father. Jacob stole it by trickery. Once Isaac had spoken his blessing over Jacob, however, Esau's tears were of no consequence; and the effects of that **blessing** spoken over what was to become the **house of Jacob** and **children of Israel** are eternal.

Likewise, both the **birthright** and the **blessing of Israel** [Jacob] were also spoken over Joseph and his sons, **Manasseh** and **Ephraim**, with Ephraim (like Jacob, the youngest) given the greater portion. In the dividing of the land of Canaan, the tribe of Joseph received the double portion spoken over his life by his father Israel[4]: as both Manasseh and Ephraim received their own parcels of land. Because Joseph became the half-tribes of Ephraim and Manasseh, Israel is technically thirteen tribes and not twelve.

When David's kingdom was divided because of Solomon's sin, the ten tribes of the northern kingdom became known as "Israel", and the southern kingdom "Judah", as it had been previously called. Jeroboam, of the half-tribe of Ephraim, was chosen by God to be king over the ten tribes of Israel. In fact, the entire northern kingdom became known as "Ephraim", as well as "Israel" [and even "Samaria"].

God became so angry because of the sins of Ephraim and the northern kingdom that he sowed them [Jezreel...scattered] into the earth, and

2 Genesis 10:16; and 2 Samuel 24:18-25.

3 2 Samuel 24:21.

4 Genesis 48:21-22.

196

removed them out of His sight as nation, but not as a people. They were initially carried away captive by Assyria. Even today God knows where every one of this multitudinous people have migrated to on the earth. **They have become as the dust of the earth, stars of the heaven, and sand of the sea**. Also, every blessing that He has ever spoken over Joseph, Ephraim, or Manasseh (as well as Judah, and all of the other tribes) has or will come to pass before the Messiah comes ... because according to the LORD ... *I will hasten my word to perform it[5]*; and ... *So shall my word be that goeth forth out of my mouth: it shall not return unto me void, but it shall accomplish that which I please, and it shall prosper in the thing whereto I sent it[6]*.

For our purposes here, we must be careful to remember that the "**stick [heirs] of Joseph is in the hand [descendants] of Ephraim**", and that Ephraim is still a blessed and immensely populous people. This blessing would not be a blessing in today's world, if it did not increase both the material and technological prosperity of Israel.

Further, in the supreme councils and courts of the kingdom of heaven, Ephraim and the house of Joseph have "spiritually enforceable rights" to their portion of the land of Israel, because Joseph is as much an heir to the Abrahamic Covenant as is Judah. This is the prophetic season for the leadership and people of Israel to return to their own Hebrew Scriptures and discern from the writings of their own Hebrew and Jewish prophets that Israel is in, as Ezekiel describes, "the latter years". Therefore, Israel is promised by the prophet Ezekiel a season of great peace and material prosperity.

> **Ezekiel 38:8-14** After many days thou shalt be visited: **<u>in the latter years</u>** thou shalt come into **the land that is brought back from the sword**, and is **gathered out of many people**, against the **mountains of Israel**, which have been always waste: but it is brought forth out of the nations, and they shall **dwell safely** all of them. ... the **land of unwalled villages** ... that **dwell safely** ... **dwelling without walls**, and having **neither bars nor gates** ... the **desolate places that are now inhabited**, and upon the **people[7]** that are **gathered out of the nations**, which have **gotten cattle and goods**, that dwell in the midst of the land **... silver and gold ... cattle and goods** ... a **great spoil** ... Thus saith the Lord God;

5 Jeremiah 1:12.

6 Isaiah 55:11.

7 People: more than just Jews.

In that day **when my people of Israel dwelleth safely**, shalt thou not know it?. [This profile hardly describes the Israel we see today.]

TODAY'S ISRAEL AS SEEN BY THE PROPHET EZEKIEL

Before we take another look at Ezekiel 37, let us turn on our favorite television or internet news program, and see how our anchorman, the prophet Ezekiel, describes what is happening in Israel today ... O, the amazing foreknowledge of God.

The mountains of Israel in Ezekiel's prophecy are the West Bank ... proposed to become a Palestinian state. The testimony of "the enemy" in verse 2 sounds just like the Palestinian leadership of the past decades. Israel, indeed, is surrounded on every side in order that he "might be a possession unto the residue of the heathen". **The God of Israel says** in verse 5, however, that **the land of Israel belongs to Him.**

> **Ezekiel 36:1** Also, thou son of man, **<u>prophesy</u> unto the mountains of Israel, <u>and say</u>**, Ye mountains of Israel, hear the word of the LORD: **2** Thus saith the Lord GOD; **Because the enemy hath said against you, Aha, even the ancient high places are ours in possession**: **3** Therefore prophesy and say, Thus saith the Lord GOD; Because they have made you desolate, and **swallowed you up on every side, that ye might be a possession unto the residue of the heathen**[8] [Palestinians], and ye are taken up in the lips of talkers, and are an infamy of the people:
>
> **4** Therefore, **ye mountains of Israel**, hear the word of the Lord GOD; **<u>Thus saith the Lord GOD to the mountains</u>**, and to **the hills**, to **the rivers**, and to **the valleys**, to the desolate wastes, and to the cities that are forsaken, which became a prey and derision to the **residue of the heathen** that are round about; **5** Therefore thus saith the Lord GOD; Surely in the fire of my jealousy have I spoken against the **residue of the heathen**, and against all **Idumea**[9] , which have **<u>appointed my land</u> into their possession** with the joy of all their heart, with despiteful minds, to cast it out for a prey.
>
> **6 Prophesy therefore concerning the land of Israel**, and say

8 A Bible *heathen* is a person without the God of Israel.

9 In Ezekiel's day, Idumea was the northern portion of Edom (Esau), just below Be'er Sheva (Beersheba): which was then Judah's southern border. Today it is a part of Israel.

unto the mountains, and to the hills, to the rivers, and to the valleys, Thus saith the Lord GOD; Behold, I have spoken in my jealousy and in my fury, because **ye have borne the shame of the heathen**: 7 Therefore thus saith the Lord GOD; I have lifted up mine hand, Surely **the heathen that are about you**, they shall bear their shame. **8** But ye, **O mountains of Israel**, ye shall shoot forth your branches, and **yield your fruit to my people of Israel**; for they are at hand to come.

The increase from the mountains of Israel belongs to the whole house of Israel, with its fulfillment in Ezekiel 37 when Joseph and Ephraim return to the land. There will be massive construction, not just "settlements". The Lord will do better for Israel in the latter days than during the reign of Solomon, where silver and gold became as plenteous as stones[10]. All 12 tribes shall be in the land. It shall begin with Ezekiel 37, and shall have its completion when the Messiah comes.

Ezekiel 36:9 For, behold, **I am for you** [mountains of Israel], and I will turn unto you, and ye shall be tilled and sown: **10** And I will multiply men upon you, <ins>all the house of Israel</ins>, even all of it: and the cities shall be inhabited, and the wastes shall be builded: **11** And I will multiply upon you man and beast; and they shall increase and bring fruit: and **I will settle you after your old estates, and will do better unto you than at your beginnings**: and ye shall know that I am the LORD. **12** Yea, I will cause men to walk upon you, even <ins>my people Israel</ins>; and **they shall possess thee, and thou shalt be their inheritance**, and thou shalt no more henceforth bereave [to cast out, miscarry, make childless] them of men.

Thus saith the Lord: "The land of Israel shall be possessed by the 12 tribes of Israel, and not by a Palestinian state ... And it shall be accomplished without the shedding of Palestinian blood", saith the Lord.

Ezekiel 36:13 Thus saith the Lord GOD; Because they say unto you, Thou land devourest up men, and hast bereaved thy nations; **14** Therefore thou shalt devour men no more, neither bereave thy nations any more, saith the Lord GOD. **15** Neither will I cause men to hear in thee the **shame of the heathen** any more, neither shalt thou bear the reproach of the people any more, neither shalt

---

10 2 Chronicles 1:15.

thou **cause thy nations** to fall any more, saith the Lord GOD.

The Lord begins to tell us here why He chastised the *Israel* He created. No other nation of people can long prosper that takes it upon themselves to chastise Israel when they are in the center of God's will. Ask Pharaoh.

Ezekiel 36:16 Moreover the word of the LORD came unto me, saying, **17** Son of man, when **the house of Israel** [10 tribes] dwelt in their own land, they defiled it by their own way and by their doings: their way was before me as the uncleanness of a removed woman. **18** Wherefore I poured my fury upon them for the blood that they had shed upon the land, and for their idols wherewith they had polluted it: **19** And **I scattered them among the heathen**, and they were dispersed through the countries: according to their way and according to their doings **I judged them**.

20 And **when they entered unto the heathen** [adopted the ways of the heathen], whither they went, **they profaned my holy name** [served other gods], when they said to them, **These are the people of the LORD**, and are gone forth out of his land. **21** But I had pity for mine holy name, which the **house of Israel had profaned among the heathen**, whither they went.

22 Therefore say unto the **house of Israel**, Thus saith the Lord GOD; I do not this for your sakes, O **house of Israel**, but for mine holy name's sake, which ye have profaned among the heathen, whither ye went. **23** And **I will sanctify**[11] **my great name**, which was **profaned among the heathen**, which ye have **profaned in the midst of them**; and **the heathen shall know** that I am the LORD, saith the Lord GOD, when **I shall be sanctified in you before their eyes**.

Because He delights in mercy, God will exhibit great joy when Joseph and Ephraim are joined again to Judah.

THE PEOPLE OF GOD DISCOVER WHO THEY ARE

God is determined to recover the people that He has lost, beginning with Ezekiel 37, until the Messiah comes.

---

11 *Sanctify*: to set apart for a holy purpose.

Ezekiel 36:24 For **I will take you** [10 tribes] **from among the heathen, and gather you out of all countries, and will bring you into your own land**. **25** Then will I sprinkle clean water upon you, and ye shall be clean: from all your filthiness, and from all your idols, will I cleanse you. **26** A new heart also will I give you, and a new spirit will I put within you: and I will take away the stony heart out of your flesh, and I will give you an heart of flesh. **27** And I will put my spirit within you, and cause you to walk in my statutes, and ye shall keep my judgments, and do them. **28** And ye shall **dwell in the land** that I gave to your fathers; and **ye shall be** [future tense] **my people** [c/p. Hosea 1:9-10, pg. 151], and **I will be** your God [again, future tense].

Verses 24-28 indicate that God is speaking of Ephraim, and that at present Ephraim is not present in the land of Israel. Also, because Ephraim has lost his identity as Hebrew, he is not yet known as the people of God.

Ezekiel 36:29 I will also save you from all your uncleannesses: and I will call for the corn, and will increase it, and lay no famine upon you. **30** And I will multiply the fruit of the tree, and the increase of the field [a great prosperity], that ye shall receive no more reproach of famine among the heathen. **31** Then shall ye remember your own evil ways, and your doings that were not good, and shall lothe yourselves in your own sight for your iniquities and for your abominations. **32** Not for your sakes do I this, saith the Lord GOD, be it known unto you: be ashamed and confounded for your own ways, O **house of Israel**.

33 Thus saith the Lord GOD; In the day that I shall have cleansed you from all your iniquities I will also cause you to dwell in the cities, and the wastes shall be builded. **34** And the desolate land shall be tilled, whereas it lay desolate in the sight of all that passed by. **35** And they shall say, **This land that was desolate is become like the garden of Eden** [this promise is already being fulfilled in Israel]; and the waste and desolate and ruined cities are become fenced, and are inhabited.

36 Then the **heathen that are left round about you** [the Palestinians as well as other Arab nations] **shall know** that I the LORD build the ruined places, and plant that that was desolate: I the LORD have spoken it, and I will do it. **37** Thus saith the Lord GOD; I will yet for this be enquired of by the **house of Israel**, to do it for them; I will increase them with men like a flock. **38** As the holy flock, as the flock of Jerusalem in her solemn feasts [in a restored Law of Moses]; so shall the waste cities be filled with flocks of men: and they shall know that I am the LORD.

THE STAGE OF EZEKIEL 36 HAS RELEASED EZEKIEL 37

The prophetic pathway for Israel to reach the season of peace and prosperity spoken of in **Ezekiel 38:8-14** can only be attained by fulfillment of the prerequisite prophecy of Ezekiel 37: which is the joining of the heirs of Joseph found in the descendants of Ephraim with the Jews of Judah, back into one nation upon the mountains of Israel ... again, the West Bank. The prophecy of Ezekiel 36 and 37 is Jehovah's eternal foreknowledge and plan for His chosen people in this prophetic hour. All 12 tribes of Israel, however, are His chosen natural seed—not just the tribe of Judah.

Who are these dry bones of the latter days that God is showcasing to the prophet in Ezekiel 37? First, Israel has been trying to reach a solution to the Palestinian question by establishing international recognition of Israel as a Jewish state. In so doing it has yet to discover or be willing to admit that its Hebrew prophets have already prophesied God's solution for this hour—the rejoining of the northern kingdom of Israel with the southern kingdom of Judah, into one Hebrew nation as Ezekiel has prophesied.

Second, the majority of these dry bones represent the multitudes of Ephraim disbursed throughout the earth, who have lost their Hebrew identity and do not know that they are the natural seed of Abraham—through Isaac, Jacob, and Joseph—and are heirs to the Abrahamic Covenant. They also do not realize that they have a blood-covenant right to possess their portion of the land of Israel, as they will in even greater manifestation continue to have the blessing of Joseph upon their lives if they return to the land. **The blessing of Joseph is the blessing of Abraham**.

Third, although the Israel of today is representative of all of the twelve tribes of Israel [Jacob], the "Israel" that God said would be as the "dust of the earth, stars of heaven, and sand of the sea" is not only not in Israel proper, but they are the "Josephs" of Israel: who have lost their Hebrew identity, and have become a multitudinous company of nations in the middle of the earth. Also, they cannot be Jews, who in their Diaspora have never lost their identity as being either Hebrew or Jewish.

Ezekiel 37:1 The hand of the LORD was upon me, and carried me out in the spirit of the LORD, and set me down in the midst of the **valley which was full of bones**, **2** And caused me to pass by them round about: and, behold, there were very many in the open valley; and, lo, **they were very dry** [spiritually dead for over 2700 years as a nation of 12 tribes]. **3** And he said unto me, Son of man, **can these bones live**? And I answered, O Lord GOD, thou knowest.

4 Again he said unto me, **Prophesy upon these bones**, and say unto them, O ye dry bones, hear the word of the LORD. **5** Thus saith the Lord GOD unto these bones; Behold, I will cause breath to enter into you, and ye shall live: **6** And I will lay sinews upon you, and will bring up flesh upon you, and cover you with skin, and put breath in you, and **ye shall live**; and ye shall know that I am the LORD. ... **10 So I prophesied** as he commanded me, and the **breath came into them, and they lived, and stood up upon their feet, an exceeding great army**.

11 Then he said unto me, Son of man, **these bones are the whole house of Israel** [the fullness of the twelve tribes of Jacob]: behold, they say, Our bones are dried, and our hope is lost [the dry bones themselves have a voice]: we are cut off for our parts [Joseph is separated from Judah]. **12** Therefore prophesy and say unto them, Thus saith the Lord GOD; Behold, O my people, I will open your graves [graves of the lost knowledge of their Hebrew heritage], and cause you to come up out of your graves, **and bring you into the land of Israel**. ...

15 The word of the LORD came again unto me, saying, **16** Moreover, thou son of man, take thee **one stick**, and write upon it, For **Judah**, and for the **children of Israel his companions**: then take **another stick**, and write upon it, For **Joseph, the stick of Ephraim**, and for **all the house of Israel his companions** [the 10 tribes of Israel ... scattered]: **17** And join them one to another into one stick; and they shall become one in thine hand [one in the hand of the prophet Ezekiel].

18 And when the children of thy people shall speak unto thee, saying, Wilt thou not shew us what thou meanest by these? **19** Say unto them, Thus saith the Lord GOD; Behold, **I will take** the **stick of Joseph, which is in the hand of Ephraim,** and the tribes of Israel his fellows [Ephraim is with the 10 tribes], and **will put them** [put the 10 tribes of Israel] **with him** [with Ephraim], even **with the stick of Judah** [with Jewish Hebrews], and **make them** [Joseph / Ephraim / the ten tribes / and Judah] **one stick** [one nation: before the Messiah comes], and they shall be one in mine hand [one in the hand of God]. **20** And the sticks whereon thou writest shall be in thine hand before their eyes.

21 And say unto them, Thus saith the Lord GOD; Behold, I will take the **children of Israel** [the primary reference is the ten tribes ... the dry bones of Joseph and Ephraim] from among the heathen [the nations], whither they be gone, and will gather them on every side, and bring them into their own land: **22** And I will make them **one nation in the land upon the mountains of Israel;** and one king [president or prime minister now; Messiah later] shall be king to them all: and they shall be **no more two nations, neither** shall they be divided into **two kingdoms** any more at all [this prophesy must be fulfilled before the coming of the Messiah].

HOSEA CONFIRMS THE HIDDEN ISRAEL

Hosea must be read in conjunction with the prophecies of Ezekiel 36 through 39. While the 10 tribes are sown or scattered, they will not be known as the people of God nor worship the God of Abraham. Hosea 1:11 is not a messianic prophecy, as no one will "appoint" the Messiah. The regathering of Joseph and Ephraim back into the land as one nation with Israel's Jews, therefore, must occur before Messiah's return, and not after.

Hosea 1:10 Yet the number of the children of Israel shall be as the sand of the sea, which cannot be measured nor numbered; and it shall come to pass, that **in the place** where it was said unto them, Ye are **not my people,** there it shall be said unto them, **Ye are the sons of the living God. 11** Then shall the children of Judah and the children of Israel be gathered together, and **appoint themselves one head,** and they shall come up out of the land: for great shall be the day of Jezreel.

The Third Temple Shall Be Built With Joseph In The Land

When Joseph is back in the land in fulfillment of Ezekiel 37, the LORD will begin to restore worship as it was in the days of David by constructing the third temple. God does not intend the redemption of Israel and Judah back into the land as one nation to await the coming of the Messiah; but that it is to begin now with the joining of Joseph, Ephraim and Judah in the fulfillment of the prophecy of Ezekiel 37.

Amos 9:11 In that day will <u>I raise up the tabernacle of David that is fallen</u>, and close up the breaches thereof; and I will raise up his ruins, and **<u>I will build it as in the days of old</u>**:

Ezekiel 37:26 Moreover **I will** make a **covenant of peace** with them; it shall be an everlasting covenant with them: and I will place them, and multiply them, and will **set <u>my sanctuary in the midst of them for evermore</u>**, and they shall be my people. 28 And the heathen shall know that I the LORD do sanctify Israel, **when <u>my sanctuary shall be in the midst of them for evermore</u>**.

God Will Establish A New Covenant With Israel And Judah

When God has finished His redemption of the whole house of Israel, the Messiah will come to sit upon the **throne of David**. The Lord will make **a new covenant** with the **house of Israel** and the **house of Judah**.

Jeremiah 31:31 Behold, the days come , saith the LORD, that I will make **a new covenant** with the **<u>house of Israel</u>** [10 tribes], and with the **<u>house of Judah</u>**: 32 Not according to the covenant that I made with their fathers in the day that I took them by the hand to bring them out of the land of Egypt; which my covenant they brake, although I was an husband unto them, saith the LORD:

33 But this shall be the covenant that I will make with the house of Israel; After those days, saith the LORD, I will put my law in their inward parts, and write it in their hearts; and will be their God, and they shall be my people. 34 ... for I will forgive their iniquity, and I will remember their sin no more. ... 37 Thus saith the LORD; If heaven above can be measured, and the foundations of the earth searched out beneath, I will also cast off all **the**

seed of Israel for all that they have done, saith the LORD.

ISRAEL SHALL BE EXALTED IN THE LAST DAYS

Jeremiah 33:14 Behold, **the days come**, saith the LORD, that **I will perform** that good thing which I have promised unto the **house of Israel** and to the **house of Judah**. **15 In those days**, and **at that time** [when God completes His restoration of the two families of Israel], will I cause the **Branch of righteousness to grow up unto David**; and he shall execute judgment and righteousness in the land.

16 In those days shall **Judah be saved**, and **Jerusalem shall dwell safely**: and this is the name wherewith she shall be called, **The LORD our righteousness. 17** For thus saith the LORD; **David shall never want a man to sit upon the throne of the house of Israel**.

Isaiah 2:1 The word that Isaiah the son of Amoz **saw concerning Judah and Jerusalem. 2** And it shall come to pass **in the last days** [last days verses latter days: before Messiah's reign], **that the mountain of the LORD'S house shall be established in the top of the mountains, and shall be exalted above the hills; and all nations shall flow unto it. 3** And many people shall go and say, Come ye, and let us go up to the mountain of the LORD, to the **house of the God of Jacob** [the 12 tribes]; and he will teach us of his ways, and we will walk in his paths: for out of Zion shall go forth the law, and the word of the LORD from Jerusalem.

4 And he shall judge among the nations, and shall rebuke many people: and they shall beat their swords into plowshares, and their spears into pruninghooks: nation shall not lift up sword against nation, neither shall they learn war any more. **5 O house of Jacob,** come ye, and let us walk in the light of the LORD. … **12** For the **day of the LORD of hosts**[12] shall be upon every one that is proud and lofty, and upon every one that is lifted up; and he shall be brought low: …

Israel: Find Joseph

12 The captain of the *God of Armies*.

CHAPTER 20

HOW TO PRAY FOR ISRAEL

LEARN TO PRAY THE WILL OF GOD OVER ISRAEL

The first step in successfully praying for Israel and the 13+ million Jews alive in the world today is to realize that from their Biblically recorded history, that their own Hebrew prophets by inspiration of the Spirit of God have spoken curses over the nation and people for their disobedience to the commandments and statutes of God. They have also spoken magnanimous blessings over the same nation and people during the times they walked in obedience to His commandments.

> **Deuteronomy 30:19** I call heaven and earth to record this day against you, that I have set before you life and death, blessing and cursing: therefore choose life, that both thou and thy seed may live.

These prophetic curses led to the banishment of the northern kingdom of the 10 tribes of Israel out of the sight of God as a nation: a nation whose people over the years would lose their Hebrew identity and heritage. Concerning the southern kingdom of Judah—the Jews of today—the prophets of Israel rightly foretold of Judah's 70 years of captivity in Babylon, and the nearly 2000 years of being in exile from the land by the Romans.

Beginning with the prophet Moses, anointed words were spoken over the nation that have been fulfilled in Judah: that the Jewish nation would stumble at the Law of Moses, the Torah, and the rest of the Old Testament writings. According to Moses, the *Israel* that consisted of the southern kingdom of Judah after Ephraim's deportation would become blinded to much of the revelation of God's plans, purposes, and ways that are hidden in the Hebrew portions of the Bible. [Don't throw any stones, I'm just reading the Bible. Political correctness has no place in this.]

Solely concerning the subject matter of this book, the Jews of Israel and the world, along with the United States and the other Arab and non-Arab nations, as well as Christians, apparently have almost no revelation whatsoever as to where God is on His prophetic time line for Israel and the nations of the world: who likewise must be measured by Israel's prophetic clock. It is the Lord's time for the fulfillment of **Ezekiel 37:15-22**—that the descendants of all the tribes of Jacob return to the West Bank to become one nation of 12 tribes again on the mountains of Israel.

If I have in any way misread these Scriptures, or you do not believe the Bible, any contrary response should simply point out based on some biblical or verifiable non-biblical evidence (substantiated as I have done by a host of Scripture and other data ... details, details, details) that the fulfillment of Ezekiel 37 is not for now in this time, but for some later period in Israel's future—and likely when Israel has bargained off the creation of a Palestinian state consuming 40% of her territorial borders. If it is not for now (or not at all), just tell me when; and let us continue to walk in love.

What I see unfolding daily in the media is that rather than seeking the plans and purposes of the God that created Israel, the Israeli government has been engaging in halfhearted attempts to swap land for peace in order to create a Palestinian state inside of Israel's borders—if its security concerns are met; and if it receives its desired recognition by the Arabs and the world that Israel has a right to exist and prosper as a Jewish state.

Where in the Holy Scriptures has God promised that Israel would become a Jewish state? My reading of these same Scriptures reveals that Israel is, and will always remain, a Hebrew nation under the God of Abraham, Isaac, Jacob, Joseph, Moses, David and all of the Hebrew prophets.

Successful prayer for Israel, then, requires our entreating the LORD Adonai-Jehovah:

- That God would remove any remaining curses of blindness spoken over Israel and the Jews of the world by its Hebrew prophets.

- That the Lord remove this same spiritual blindness, not only from Israel, but from the United States, Christians, and all nations of the world, so that we all may perceive and understand that Israel is a Hebrew nation and not just Jewish ... and may also perceive that there is a vast multitude of Hebrews in the world today [according to Scripture] that have lost their Hebrew identity.

■ That the Lord cause the world to be able to both see and verify that this multitude of Hebrews, with lost identities, have in Ephraim grown into a company of nations in the middle of the earth, with the blessing of Joseph upon them: whose people have become as the dust of the earth, stars of heaven, and sand of the sea.

■ That the Lord cause the world to become agreeable to His will for this prophetic season, in which the prophecy of **Ezekiel 37:15-22** must and shall be fulfilled.

■ That the descendents of Joseph and Ephraim (and even Manasseh), wherever they are in the world, be awakened to their Hebrew heritage and reclaim their inheritance in the nation and the land of Israel.

■ That the Lord give His appointed number of descendants of Joseph and Ephraim the desire to return to the land of Israel. And, like the Ethiopian Jews, that they be welcomed back into the land as citizens of Israel by the Jews of Israel and the world.

■ That God, Himself, will craft His will for the Palestinian people; and that He will turn their hearts, like Pharaoh's, to become agreeable with His will; and

■ That this entire process shall be accomplished without bloodshed or undue confrontation and confusion.

Jehovah is God. He can do all things that we release Him to do in prayer. This especially happens we are able to perceive from the Scriptures, themselves, His revealed will for a given situation and time, and pray according thereto—His will, and not necessarily our own. Let us look, then, at the curses that the Bible says have resulted in the spiritual blindness over Israel, Ephraim, and the Jews of the world.

A Prophet Can Speak Both Sight And Blindness Over A Nation And People

A prophet of God can command both spiritual as well as physical sight and blindness onto a nation and a people. We should all become prophets for whatever we see is clearly revealed in the Bible, whether we are Jewish, Christian, members of other religions or no religion—not for the purpose of cursing, but to speak a blessing. God's Hebrew prophets, beginning with Moses, have spoken words of blindness over the nation of Israel, as well as others.

> **2 Kings 6:16** And he [Elisha] answered [his servant Gehazi], Fear not: for they that be with us are more than they that be with them [speaking of the Syrian army]. **17** And Elisha prayed, and said, <u>**LORD, I pray thee, open his eyes, that he may see**</u>. And **the LORD opened the eyes of the young man; and he saw**: and, behold, **the mountain was full of horses and chariots of fire** round about Elisha. **18** And when they came down to him, <u>**Elisha prayed unto the LORD, and said, Smite this people, I pray thee, with blindness. And he smote them with blindness according to the word of Elisha**</u> [the LORD harkened to the voice of a man[1]]. ... **20** And it came to pass, when they were come into Samaria, <u>**that Elisha said, LORD, open the eyes of these men, that they may see**</u>. And <u>**the LORD opened their eyes, and they saw**</u> ...

We Are Also Commanded To Speak The Word Of The Lord

From the creation of man in the image and likeness of God[2], we have been given the dominion to decree a thing, and it shall be established [by God] unto us ... if the thing that we decree is something that He has promised us in His Word. The prophet Job understood this.

> **Job 22:21** Acquaint now thyself with him, and be at peace: thereby good shall come unto thee. **22** Receive, I pray thee, the law from his mouth, and lay up his words in thine heart. **23** If thou return to the Almighty, thou shalt be built up, thou shalt put away iniquity far from thy tabernacles. **24** Then shalt thou lay up gold as dust, and the gold of Ophir as the stones of the brooks. **25** Yea,

---

1 C/p. Ezekiel 22:30.
2 Genesis 1:26.

the Almighty shall be thy defence, and thou shalt have plenty of silver. **26** For then shalt thou have thy delight in the Almighty, and shalt lift up thy face unto God. **27 Thou shalt make thy prayer unto him**, and **he shall hear thee**, and thou shalt pay thy vows. **28 <u>Thou shalt also decree a thing, and it shall be established unto thee</u>**: and the light shall shine upon thy ways.

We are to both pray and speak the will of God into the earth. When God hears our words, He hears Himself, and delights in bringing what we say to pass. Here, then, are some of the curses that the Hebrew prophets have spoken over Israel and Judah, that must be kept in mind as we pray for God to lift the spiritual blindness off of all the descendants of Israel, Judah, Joseph, Ephraim and Manasseh. *For the Lord delights in mercy*[3].

CURSES SPOKEN OVER ISRAEL BY THE LORD'S PROPHETS

CURSES SPOKEN BY THE PROPHET MOSES

DEUTERONOMY 4:23 Take heed unto yourselves, **lest ye forget the covenant of the LORD your God**, which he made with you … **24 For the LORD thy God is a consuming fire**, even a jealous God. **25** When thou … shall do evil in the sight of the LORD thy God, to provoke him to anger : **26 I call heaven and earth to witness against you this day**, that <u>**ye shall soon utterly perish from off the land**</u> whereunto ye go over Jordan to possess it; ye shall not prolong your days upon it, but shall utterly be destroyed .

27 And <u>**the LORD shall scatter you among the nations**</u> [all 12 tribes], and ye shall **be <u>left few in number</u> among the heathen, <u>whither the LORD shall lead you</u>** [even in judgment, the Lord is still leading His people]. **28** And **there ye shall serve gods** … **29** But **if from thence thou shalt seek the LORD thy God, thou shalt find him, if thou seek him with all thy heart and with all thy soul. 30 <u>When thou art in tribulation</u>**, and all these things are come upon thee, even **<u>in the latter days</u>**, if thou turn to the LORD thy God, and shalt be obedient unto his voice; **31 (For the LORD thy God is a merciful God;) he will not forsake thee, neither destroy thee, <u>nor forget the covenant</u> of thy fathers <u>which he sware unto them</u>**.

3 Micah 7:18.

DEUTERONOMY 28:15 But it shall come to pass, if **thou wilt not hearken unto the voice of the LORD thy God, to observe to do all his commandments** and his statutes which I command thee this day; that **all these curses shall come upon thee, and overtake thee:** ... **28 The LORD shall smite thee with** madness, and **blindness,** and astonishment of heart: **29** And thou shalt grope at noonday, **as the blind gropeth in darkness,** and thou shalt not prosper in thy ways: and thou shalt be only oppressed and spoiled evermore, and no man shall save thee [curses from vs. 15 to 68].

DEUTERONOMY 30:17 But **if thine heart turn away** [spiritual blindness is a matter of the heart], **so that thou wilt not hear** [and obey], but shalt be drawn away, and worship other gods, and serve them; **18** I denounce unto you this day, that ye shall surely perish, and that ye shall not prolong your days upon the land, whither thou passest over Jordan to go to possess it. **19 I call heaven and earth to record this day against you, that I have set before you life and death, blessing and cursing: therefore choose life, that both thou and thy seed may live: 20** That thou mayest love the LORD thy God, and that thou mayest obey his voice, and that thou mayest cleave unto him: for he is thy life, and the length of thy days: that thou mayest dwell in the land which the LORD sware unto thy fathers, to Abraham, to Isaac, and to Jacob, to give them.

CURSES SPOKEN BY THE PROPHET DAVID

PSALMS 69:22 [Then spake David by the Spirit of God] **Let their table become a snare before them** [the Torah ... the Law of Moses, and other Hebrew Scriptures]: and that which should have been for their welfare, let it become a trap. **23 Let their eyes be darkened, that they see not** [cause them to become spiritually blind]; and make their loins continually to shake [a nation in constant fear ... this is the Israel of today; but it is not God's will for the Israel of today].

CURSES SPOKEN BY THE PROPHET ISAIAH

ISAIAH 6:8 Also I [Isaiah] heard the voice of the Lord, saying, Whom shall I send, and who will go for us? Then said I, Here am

I; send me. **9** And he [the LORD] said, <u>**Go, and tell this people, Hear ye indeed, but understand not; and see ye indeed, but perceive not. 10 Make the heart of this people fat, and make their ears heavy, and shut their eyes; lest they see with their eyes, and hear with their ears, and understand with their heart, and convert, and be healed**</u>. **11** Then said I, Lord, **how long**? And he answered, **Until** the cities be wasted without inhabitant, and the houses without man, and the land be utterly desolate [the curse of spiritual blindness is yet upon Israel and Judah].

ISAIAH **8:13** Sanctify the LORD of hosts himself; and let him be your fear, and let him be your dread. **14** And he shall be for a sanctuary; but <u>**for a stone of stumbling and for a rock of offence to both the houses of Israel**</u>, for a gin [a noose] and for a snare to the inhabitants of Jerusalem. **15** And many among them shall stumble, and fall, and be broken, and be snared, and be taken.

ISAIAH **29:10** For <u>**the LORD hath poured out upon you the spirit of deep sleep**</u>, and <u>**hath closed your eyes**</u>: the prophets and your rulers, the seers hath he covered. **11** And **the vision of all is become unto you <u>as the words of a book that is sealed</u>** [the Scriptures have become as a book that is sealed], which men deliver to one that is learned, saying, **Read this,** I pray thee: and he saith, **I cannot; for <u>it is sealed</u>**: **12** And the book is delivered to him that is not learned, saying, Read this, I pray thee: and he saith, I am not learned. **13** Wherefore the Lord said, Forasmuch as **this people draw near me with their mouth, and with their lips do honour me, <u>but have removed their heart far from me</u>** [spiritual blindness again is a matter of a heart turned from God], and their fear toward me is taught by the precept of men:

CURSES SPOKEN BY THE PROPHET DANIEL

DANIEL **12:4** But thou, O Daniel, **shut up the words, and <u>seal the book,</u> even to the time of the end**; many shall run to and fro, and knowledge shall be increased.

CURSES SPOKEN BY THE PROPHET JEREMIAH

JEREMIAH **6:21** Therefore thus saith the LORD, Behold, **I will**

lay stumbling blocks before this people, and the fathers and the sons together shall fall upon them; the neighbour and his friend shall perish.

CURSES SPOKEN BY THE PROPHET HOSEA

HOSEA 1:2 The beginning of the word of the LORD by Hosea. And the LORD said to Hosea, **Go, take unto thee a wife of whoredoms and children of whoredoms: for the land hath committed great whoredom, departing from the LORD**. **3** So he went and took Gomer the daughter of Diblaim; which conceived, and bare him a son. **4** And the LORD said unto him, Call his name **Jezreel** [God will scatter]; for yet a little while, and I will avenge the blood of Jezreel upon the house of Jehu, and **[I] will cause to cease the kingdom of the house of Israel** [the northern kingdom of 10 tribes]. ... **6** And she conceived again, and bare a daughter. And God said unto him, Call her name **Loruhamah** [I will have mercy no more]: for **I will no more have mercy upon the house of Israel; but I will utterly take them away**. ... **8** Now when she had weaned Loruhamah, she conceived, and bare a son. **9** Then said God, Call his name **Loammi** [not my people] **for ye are not my people** [while the northern kingdom of Joseph and Ephraim are scattered, they will lose their Hebrew identity], and I will not be your God.

CURSES SPOKEN BY THE PROPHET MALACHI

MALACHI 2:1 And now, **O ye priests, this commandment is for you**. **2** If ye will not hear, and if ye will not lay it to heart, to give glory unto my name, saith the LORD of hosts, **I will even send a curse upon you**, and I will curse your blessings: yea, I have cursed them already, because ye do not lay it to heart. ... **8** But ye are departed out of the way; <u>**ye have caused many to stumble at the law**</u>; ye have corrupted the covenant of Levi, saith the LORD of hosts.

Although this is not a New Testament book, the Jewish prophets of the New Testament, in quoting the Hebrew prophets, have re-spoken these same curses over Israel and its Jewish people. We must now in a frank and honest application of Bible history, and the way the LORD governs His

214

kingdom and people, seek the Lord to remove these curses because He truly delights in mercy: they are new every morning: they endure forever[4].

CURSES SPOKEN BY THE PROPHET JESUS

MATTHEW 13:14 And in them is fulfilled **the prophecy of Esaias** [Isaiah], which saith, By hearing ye shall hear [the Jews of Israel], and shall not understand; and seeing ye shall see, and shall not perceive: **15 For this people's heart is waxed gross, and their ears are dull of hearing, and their eyes they have closed; lest at any time they should see with their eyes, and hear with their ears, and should understand with their heart, and should be converted, and I should heal them**.

MATTHEW 15:7 Ye hypocrites [Jesus speaking to the scribes and Pharisees], well did Esaias [Isaiah] prophesy of you, saying, **8** This people draweth nigh unto me with their mouth, and honoureth me with their lips; but **their heart is far from me. 9** But in vain they do worship me, teaching for doctrines the commandments of men.

MARK 4:9 And he said unto them, He that hath ears to hear, let him hear. **10** And when he was alone, they that were about him with the twelve asked of him the parable. **11** And he said unto them, Unto you [Jesus' disciples] it is given to know the mystery of the kingdom of God: but unto them that are without [the Jews of Israel], all these things are done in parables: **12 That seeing they may see, and not perceive; and hearing they may hear, and not understand; lest at any time they should be converted, and their sins should be forgiven them**.

JOHN 9:39 And Jesus said, **For judgment I am come into this world, that they which see not might see; and that they which see might be made blind** [Israel's leaders remain blind to their Covenant, heritage, and Messiah]. **40** And some of the Pharisees which were with him heard these words, and said unto him, Are we blind also? **41** Jesus said unto them, If ye were blind, ye should have no sin: but now ye say, We see; therefore your sin remaineth.

JOHN 12:37 But though he had done so many miracles before

---

4 Micah 7:18; Lamentations 3:22-23; and Psalms 136.

them, yet they believed not on him: **38 That the saying of Esaias the prophet might be fulfilled,** which he spake, Lord, who hath believed our report? and to whom hath the arm of the Lord been revealed? **39** Therefore they could not believe, because that Esaias said again, **40 He hath blinded their eyes, and hardened their heart; that they should not see with their eyes, nor understand with their heart, and be converted, and I should heal them.**

CURSES SPOKEN BY THE PROPHET PAUL

ACTS **28:24** And some believed [the Jewish leadership in Rome] the things which were spoken, and some believed not. **25** And when they agreed not among themselves, they departed, after that Paul had spoken one word, <u>**Well spake the Holy Ghost by Esaias the prophet**</u> unto our fathers [the fathers of Israel], **26** Saying, <u>**Go unto this people, and say**</u>, **Hearing ye shall hear, and shall not understand; and seeing ye shall see, and not perceive: 27 For the heart of this people is waxed gross, and their ears are dull of hearing, and their eyes have they closed; lest they should see with their eyes, and hear with their ears, and understand with their heart, and should be converted , and I should heal them. 28** Be it known therefore unto you, that the salvation of God is sent unto the Gentiles, and that they will hear it.

ROMANS **9:31** But Israel, which followed after the law of righteousness, hath not attained to the law of righteousness. **32** Wherefore? Because they sought it not by faith, but as it were by the works of the law. **For they stumbled at that stumblingstone** [the law of Moses ... the Torah]; **33** As it is written, Behold, <u>**I lay in Sion a stumblingstone and rock of offence**</u>: and whosoever believeth on him shall not be ashamed.

ROMANS **11:7** What then? Israel hath not obtained that which he seeketh for; but the election hath obtained it, and the rest were blinded **8** (<u>**According as it is written, God hath given them the spirit of slumber, eyes that they should not see, and ears that they should not hear**</u>;) unto this day. **9** And <u>**David saith, Let their table be made a snare, and a trap, and a stumbling block, and a recompence unto them**</u>: **10** Let their eyes be darkened, that they may not see, and bow down their back alway. ...

25 For I would not, brethren, that ye should be ignorant of this mystery, lest ye should be wise in your own conceits; that **blindness in part is happened to Israel**, until the fulness of the Gentiles be come in. **26** And so **all Israel shall be saved**: as it is written, There shall come out of Sion [Zion] the Deliverer, and shall turn away ungodliness from Jacob: **27** For this is my covenant unto them, when I shall take away their sins.

Curses Spoken By The Prophet Peter

1 Peter 2:6 Wherefore also it is contained in the scripture, Behold, I lay in Sion a chief corner stone, elect, precious: and he that believeth on him shall not be confounded. **7** Unto you therefore which believe he is precious: but unto them which be disobedient, the stone which the builders disallowed, the same is made the head of the corner, **8** And **a stone of stumbling, and a rock of offence, even to them which stumble at the word**, being disobedient: whereunto also they were appointed.

THE SPIRITUAL CONDITION OF ISRAEL, JEWS AND JOSEPH

Based upon a simple reading of the above Scriptures from both the Old and New Testaments, here is the spiritual conditions of today's Israel, Joseph and Ephraim, and the Jews of the world—not because of what this writer thinks, but because of what the Bible says. Together we can change this ... *for the entrance of His Word giveth light*[5]. Here is a summary of the above Scriptures according to the Hebrew and Jewish prophets. Concerning the spiritual state of Israel and Jews of the world, in some aspects:

- They are spiritually blind [of their blood-covenant with God revealed in Scripture], groping in darkness [spoken by Moses].

- Their hearts are turned away from the Lord so that they will not hear His Word from the Scriptures [spoken by Moses].

- The Torah [the Law of Moses] has become a snare and a stumblingstone to them, and has darkened their spiritual eyes that they see not [spoken by David and Malachi; and quoted by the prophet Paul and paraphrased by Peter, who were both Jews].

---

5 Psalms 119:130.

- Hebrew people in Israel and across the world [Jews as well as Joseph, Ephraim and Manasseh] hear indeed [the written Word of God], but understand it not; see indeed, but perceive it not; the heart of this people is fat, their spiritual ears are heavy, and their spiritual eyes are shut [spoken by the prophets Isaiah, Hosea, Jesus and Paul].

- The Lord has given them a spirit of a deep slumber or sleep and has closed their eyes; and portions of the Holy Scriptures of the Old Testament are as the words of a sealed book—they lack sufficient revelation as to what these writings are actually saying by the Spirit of God [spoken by Isaiah and quoted by Paul].

- The people of Israel and Jews around the world draw near to the Lord with their mouth, and with their lips do honor Him, but have removed their heart far from Adonai-Jehovah [spiritual blindness is a heart turned from God that lacks perception of His Word], and their fear toward Him is taught by the precepts of men [spoken by Isaiah and quoted by Jesus].

- The multitudes of Joseph through his sons, Ephraim and Manasseh, have lost their Hebrew identity, and do not know who they truly are in the eyes of God [spoken by Hosea].

- By hearing they [the whole house of Israel] shall hear the Word of the Lord, and shall not understand it; and seeing they shall see the Word of the Lord, and shall not perceive its truth. For this people's heart is waxed gross, and their ears are dull of hearing, and their eyes they have closed; lest at any time they should see with their eyes, and hear with their ears, and should understand with their heart, and should be converted, and should be healed of their unbelief, and their sins forgiven [spoken by Isaiah; and quoted by the prophets Jesus and Paul].

OUR PRAYER AND CONFESSION FOR ISRAEL, JOSEPH AND JEWS OF THE WORLD

Father, Adonai-Jehovah, open the eyes of Israel, Jews, Joseph, Ephraim, Manasseh, the nations of the world, and the Palestinian people and Arab nations to the eternal knowledge that it is you who created the Hebrew nation of Israel; and that although you may, in your Omnipotence, chastise it according to your will, other nations and people may not.

The land that Israel occupies was given by you as an eternal possession to the 12 tribes of Jacob (who you renamed Israel). This land was and is given to your Hebrew nation for their per-petual possession, and that this land belongs to you. As such no people, nation, international body of nations, nor even the Jew-ish citizens of Israel, themselves, can take or even give away this land that you swore in blood to give to Abraham and his seed forever.

Lord, turn the hearts of the Jewish people in Israel, and both the Josephs and Jewish people of the world back to you and to your Word. Remove the stumbling blocks of the law that have blinded both kingdoms and their people to your clearly revealed will for this season and time that is expressed in Ezekiel 37:15-22.

Open our eyes also. Give us ears to hear and hearts to un-derstand your will for our lives in these perilous days and times. Pull down the spirits of slumber and sleep over Israel and over us. Unseal your Word and its revelation as an open book. As the en-trance of your Word brings spiritual light[6], flood us and the Jew-ish people of Israel and the world with the light of the knowledge of your Word.

Cause the descendants of Joseph, Ephraim and Manasseh— wherever they are—to become alive to their Hebrew inheritance. Give them the burning desire and intense hunger to return to Your land as members of a Hebrew nation of the 12 tribes of Is-rael. Turn the hearts of the leadership of Israel and Jews of the world to become agreeable and excited to invite their lost breth-ren back into the land of as non-Jewish Hebrew citizens of Israel.

For we are a people who are called by your name. We humble ourselves, and pray; we seek your face; we turn from our wicked and twisted ways. We hear from heaven, O LORD; forgive our sin; and heal the land of Israel[7]. Amen.

---

6   Psalms 119:89, 105 and 130.
7   2 Chronicles 7:14.

For the Jew: In the name of Adonai-Jehovah.
For the Christian: In the name of Jesus.
For those of other religions or no religion who want to see peace in the Middle East: In the name of the God of Israel.

Having both prayed and spoken (out loud) a spiritual awakening of Israel and her people, continue to pray and speak whatever your understanding is of the will of Jehovah for His nation—the nation of Israel.

ISRAEL IS CREATED FOR GOD'S GLORY

Here we are at the end of a book, but hopefully at the beginning of a Holy Spirit orchestrated move of God that will transform the nation of Israel. When Israel changes, the entire world will also have to make an adjustment. My final words, then, are not my words, but the words of God … who has said it all.

Isaiah 43:1 But now thus saith the LORD that created thee, **O Jacob**, and he that formed thee, **O Israel**, Fear not: for I have redeemed thee, I have called thee by thy name; thou art mine. **2** When thou passest through the waters, I will be with thee; and through the rivers, they shall not overflow thee: when thou walkest through the fire, thou shalt not be burned; neither shall the flame kindle upon thee.

3 For **I am the LORD thy God, the Holy One of Israel, thy Saviour**: I gave Egypt for thy ransom, Ethiopia and Seba for thee. **4** Since thou wast precious in my sight, thou hast been honourable, and I have loved thee: therefore will I give men for thee, and people for thy life. **5** Fear not: for I am with thee: **I will bring thy seed from the east**, and gather thee from **the west**; **6** I will say to **the north**, Give up; and to **the south**, Keep not back: bring my sons from far, and my daughters from the ends of the earth; **7** Even every one that is called by my name: for I have created him for my glory, I have formed him; yea, I have made him.

Shalom. Shalom.

APPENDIX

The West Bank and Gaza Strip

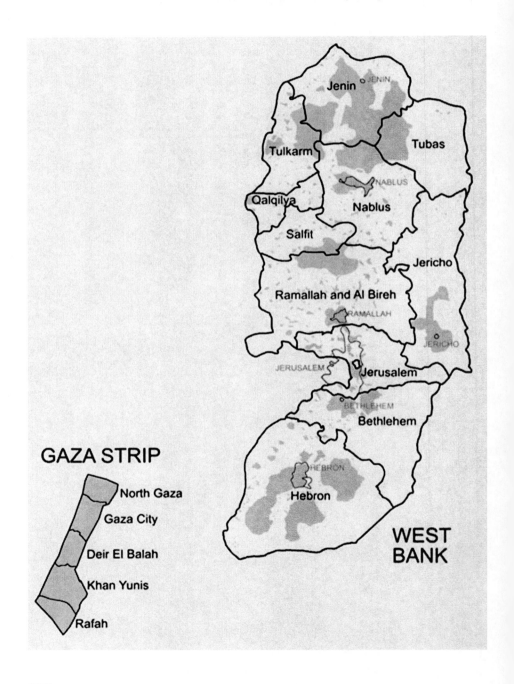

GAZA STRIP

North Gaza
Gaza City
Deir El Balah
Khan Yunis
Rafah

Jenin
Tulkarm
Tubas
Qalqilya
Nablus
Salfit
Jericho
Ramallah and Al Bireh
Jerusalem
Bethlehem
Hebron

WEST
BANK

PROPHECY

CHAPTER 1

"The land shall not be divided when Joseph is joined with Judah", saith the Lord.

CHAPTERS 8 AND 15

"Therefore, I prophesy by the same Spirit of God that the economy of whatever nation owns this land whenever this blessing manifests will explode like a financial mushroom cloud of an Atomic Money Machine."

CHAPTER 10

Hear the word of the Lord: "The house of Judah (seed of David) shall be afflicted, but not forever; but the house [seed] of David, kingdom of David, and throne of David remain eternal and faithful promises of God".

CHAPTER 12

"Ephraim likewise" , saith the LORD, "will also not be redeemed by war, but by an equally sovereign act of God."

CHAPTER 14

"Joseph shall be joined with Judah now in this time", saith the LORD.

CHAPTER 17

"It is time for my Word to be fulfilled that I spoke by the prophet Ezekiel", saith the Lord; "that the dry bones of Judah be joined with the dry bones of Joseph", saith the Lord, "back into one nation again that I have established forever", saith the Lord.

"Trading land for peace will bring no peace, but only a curse upon your nation. Only _I am_ wonderful. _I am_ your Counselor. _I am_ The mighty God. _I am_ The everlasting Father. _I am_ The Prince of Peace. Without me there can be no peace", saith the Lord.

"I know the end from the beginning", saith the Lord. "For _I am_ the beginning and the end", saith the Lord. "When you do all that you can do", saith the Lord, "I will do what only the Prince of Peace can do", saith the Lord.

"The Palestinians are mine. I formed them for my glory", saith the Lord, "and like Pharaoh and the Egyptians, I am able to cause them to be conformed to my will for this time and for this hour", saith the Lord. "Has the arm of the LORD been shortened that He cannot save?", saith the Lord. "I say that it has not and will never be", saith the Lord.

"But to receive my grace in this matter that you know not of", saith the Lord, "my people of Judah must re-connect with my people of Ephraim; and re-establish the nation that I have created—and the road map for the peace and abundance that I have for you", saith the Lord, "is recorded in Ezekiel 37, saith the Lord."

CHAPTER 19

"Thus saith the Lord: the land of Israel shall be possessed by the 12 tribes of Israel, and not by a Palestinian state ... And it shall be accomplished without the shedding of Palestinian blood", saith the Lord.

Key Scriptures – Abrahamic Covenant

SUMMARY OF SCRIPTURES

226

KEY SCRIPTURES - ABRAHAMIC COVENANT

ISRAEL'S SEASON OF GREAT PROSPERITY AND PEACE

Ezekiel 38:8-14[1] After many days thou shalt be visited: **in the latter years** thou shalt come into **the land that is brought back from the sword**, and is **gathered out of many people**, against the **mountains of Israel**, which have been always waste: but it is brought forth out of the nations, and they shall **dwell safely** all of them. ... the **land of un-walled villages** ... that **dwell safely** ... **dwelling without walls**, and having **neither bars nor gates** ... the **desolate places that are now inhabited**, and upon the **people**[2] that are **gathered out of the nations**, which have **gotten cattle and goods**, that dwell in the midst of the land ... **silver and gold** ... **cattle and goods** ... a **great spoil** ... Thus saith the Lord God; In that day **when my people of Israel dwelleth safely**, shalt thou not know it?. [Israel today has walls, bars, gates everywhere.]

ISRAEL'S PATHWAY TO GREAT PROSPERITY AND PEACE

Ezekiel 37:15[3] The word of the LORD came again unto me, saying, **16** Moreover, thou son of man, **take thee one stick**, and write upon it, **For Judah**, and **for the children of Israel his companions** [a remnant of all the children of Israel that are mingled with the Jews of Israel]: then **take another stick**, and write upon it, **For Joseph, the stick of Ephraim**, and **for all the house of Israel his companions** [Ephraim is in the presence of the house of Israel, which is the 10 tribes carried into Assyrian captivity]: **17** And **join them** one to another **into one stick**; and they shall become one in thine hand.

18 And when the children of thy people shall speak unto thee, saying, Wilt thou not shew us what thou meanest by these? **19** Say unto them, Thus saith the Lord GOD; Behold, **I will take** the **stick of Joseph, which is in the hand of Ephraim** [and has become a multitude of nations in the middle of the earth], **and the tribes of Israel his fellows** [Ephraim has been joined with the 10 tribes of Israel—also in the middle of the earth], and will put them with him, even **with the stick of Judah** [the Jews of Israel], and **make them one stick** [one nation], and

---

1   Ezekiel 38 and 39 also describe further attacks against the nation of Israel, but which result in devastating losses for its aggressors. But what is generally glossed over by the readers of these chapters is the prosperity and wealth that the intruders are coming to get that provokes this attack. Israel is doing very good economically these days, but not like what is described by a more careful reading of Ezekiel 38.

2   People: more than just Jews.

3   All Scripture is from the King James Version of the Bible.

228

they shall be one in mine hand.

20 And the sticks whereon thou writest shall be in thine hand before their eyes. **21** And say unto them, Thus saith the Lord GOD; Behold, **I will take the children of Israel** [Ephraim and the 10 tribes] **from among the heathen** [Ephraim is in the nations with a lost identity], whither they be gone, and will gather them on every side, and bring them into their own land: **22** And I will make them **one nation in the land upon the mountains of Israel**; and one king [prime minister for now; Messiah later] shall be king to them all: and they shall be no more two nations [Israel and Judah], neither shall they be divided into two kingdoms any more at all.

ISRAEL'S COVENANT OF BLESSING AND CURSING

Genesis 12:1 Now the **LORD had said** unto Abram, Get thee out of thy country, and from thy kindred, and from thy father's house, **unto a land** that I will shew thee: **2** And **I will make of thee a great nation**, and **I will bless thee**, and **make thy name great**; and **thou shalt be a blessing**: **3** And **I will bless them that bless thee, and curse him that curseth thee**: and **in thee shall all families of the earth be blessed**[4].

4 So Abram departed… and they went forth to go into the **land of Canaan**; and into the land of Canaan they came. **6** And Abram passed through the land unto the place of Sichem, unto the plain of Moreh. And **the Canaanite was then in the land. 7** And the **LORD appeared unto Abram**, and said, **Unto thy seed will I give this land**: and there builded he an altar unto **the LORD, who appeared unto him**.

GOD GIVES CANAAN TO ABRAHAM AND HIS SEED FOREVER

Genesis 13:12 Abram dwelled in the **land of Canaan**…**14** And the LORD said unto Abram, after that Lot was separated from him, **Lift up now thine eyes,** and look from the place where thou art northward, and southward, and eastward, and westward: **15 For all the land which thou seest, to thee will I give it, and to thy seed for ever.**

ABRAHAM'S SEED AS THE DUST OF THE EARTH

Genesis 13:16 And I will make thy seed as **the dust of the earth**: so that if a man can number the dust of the earth, then shall thy seed also be numbered. **17** Arise, walk through the land in the length of it and in

---

4   Genesis 26:4 and 28:14.

the breadth of it; for I will give it unto thee. **18** Then Abram removed his tent, and came and dwelt in the plain of Mamre, which is in Hebron, and built there an altar unto the LORD.

ABRAHAM'S SEED AS THE STARS OF HEAVEN

Genesis 15:1 After these things the word of the LORD came unto Abram in a vision, saying, Fear not, Abram: **I am thy shield, and thy exceeding great reward**. **2** And Abram said, Lord GOD, what wilt thou give me, seeing I go childless, and the steward of my house is this Eliezer of Damascus? **3** And Abram said, Behold, to me thou hast given no seed: and, lo, one born in my house is mine heir. **4** And, behold, the word of the LORD came unto him, saying, This shall not be thine heir; but he that shall come forth out of thine own bowels shall be thine heir.

5 And he brought him forth abroad, and said, **Look now toward heaven, and <u>tell the stars,</u> if thou be able to number them: and he said unto him, <u>So shall thy seed be</u>**. **6** And he believed in the LORD; and he counted it to him for righteousness.

GOD'S COVENANT IN BLOOD FOR THE LAND

Genesis 15:7 And he said unto him, **I am the LORD that brought thee out of Ur of the Chaldees, to give thee this land to inherit it**. **8** And he said, **Lord GOD, whereby shall I know** that I shall inherit it? **9** And he said unto him, Take me an heifer of three years old, and a she goat of three years old, and a ram of three years old, and a turtledove, and a young pigeon. **10** And he took unto him all these, and divided them in the midst [the shedding of blood ... which Abraham understood], and laid each piece one against another [a river of blood]: but the birds divided he not. **11** And when the fowls came down upon the carcases, Abram drove them away.

12 And when the sun was going down, a deep sleep fell upon Abram; and, lo, an horror of great darkness fell upon him. **13 And he said unto Abram, Know of a surety** that thy seed shall be a stranger in a land that is not theirs, and shall serve them; and they shall afflict them four hundred years; **14** And also that nation, whom they shall serve, will I judge: and afterward shall they come out with great substance. **15** And thou shalt go to thy fathers in peace; thou shalt be buried in a good old age. **16** But in the fourth generation they shall come hither again: for the iniquity of the Amorites is not yet full.

17 And it came to pass, that, when the sun went down, and it was dark, behold a smoking furnace, and a burning lamp [a lamp of fire] that passed between those pieces [in this ceremony, God walks a series of figure-eights through the blood of the sacrifice]. **18 In the same day the LORD made a covenant with Abram** [while standing in blood], saying, <u>**Unto thy seed have I given this land**</u>, from the river of Egypt unto the great river, the river Euphrates: **19** The Kenites, and the Kenizzites, and the Kadmonites, **20** And the Hittites, and the Perizzites, and the Rephaims, **21** And the Amorites, and the Canaanites, and the Girgashites, and the Jebusites.

THE HAGARIC COVENANT

Genesis 16:1 Now Sarai Abram's wife bare him no children: and she had an handmaid, an Egyptian, whose name was **Hagar**. **2** And Sarai said unto Abram, Behold now, the LORD hath restrained me from bearing: I pray thee, go in unto my maid; it may be that I may obtain children by her. And Abram hearkened to the voice of Sarai. **3** And Sarai Abram's wife took Hagar her maid the Egyptian, **after Abram had dwelt ten years in the land of Canaan**, and gave her to her husband Abram to be his wife [Abram is now 85 years old].

4 And he went in unto Hagar, and she conceived: and when she saw that she had conceived, her mistress was despised in her eyes. **5** And Sarai said unto Abram, My wrong be upon thee: I have given my maid into thy bosom; and when she saw that she had conceived, I was despised in her eyes: the LORD judge between me and thee. **6** But Abram said unto Sarai, Behold, thy maid is in thy hand; do to her as it pleaseth thee. And when Sarai dealt hardly with her, she fled from her face.

7 And **the angel of the LORD found her** by a fountain of water in the wilderness, by the fountain in the way to Shur. **8** And he said, Hagar, Sarai's maid, whence camest thou? and whither wilt thou go? And she said, I flee from the face of my mistress Sarai. **9** And the angel of the LORD said unto her, Return to thy mistress, and submit thyself under her hands.

10 And **the angel of the LORD said** unto her, **I will** [God Himself is speaking] **multiply thy seed exceedingly, that it shall not be numbered for multitude**[5]. **11** And the angel of the LORD said unto her, Behold, thou art with child, and shalt bear a son, and shalt **call his**

---

5 Although God promises that the seed of Abraham and Hagar shall also become a numberless multitude, Ishmael is not the seed of promise ... *[F]or in Isaac shall thy seed be called* (Genesis 17:21 and 21:12).

name Ishmael[6]; because the LORD hath heard thy affliction. **12** And **he will be a wild man; his hand will be against every man, and every man's hand against him; and he shall dwell in the presence of all his brethren** [Ishmael is unto this day everything that God said he would be].

Hagar Believed In The God Of Abraham

Genesis 16:13 And **she called the name of the LORD** that spake unto her, **Thou God seest me**: for she said, Have I also here looked after him that seeth me? **14** Wherefore the well was called Beerlahairoi [the well of living after seeing]; behold, it is between Kadesh and Bered. **15** And Hagar bare Abram a son: and Abram called his son's name, which Hagar bare, **Ishmael. 16** And **Abram was fourscore and six years old** [Abraham is 86 years old]**, when Hagar bare Ishmael to Abram**.

Abraham Is The Father Of All Abrahamic Nations

Genesis 17:1 And **when Abram was ninety years old and nine, the LORD appeared to Abram**, and said unto him, I am the Almighty God; walk before me, and be thou perfect. **2 And I will make my covenant between me and thee, and will multiply thee exceedingly**. **3** And Abram fell on his face: and God talked with him, saying,

4 As for me, behold, **my covenant** is with thee, and thou shalt be a **father of many nations** [Abraham is to be the father of many nations besides Israel … through Isaac and Jacob; this is not a reference to Ishmael]. **5** Neither shall thy name any more be called Abram, but **thy name shall be <u>Abraham</u>**; for a <u>**father of many nations**</u> have I made thee. **6** And I will make thee exceeding fruitful, and **I will make <u>nations</u> of thee**, and <u>**kings**</u> [kings of these many Abrahamic nations] shall come out of thee.

Canaan Given To Abraham For An Everlasting Possession

Genesis 17:7 And I will establish **my covenant** between me and thee and thy seed after thee in their generations for <u>**an everlasting covenant**</u>, to be a God unto thee, and to thy seed after thee. **8** And **I will give unto thee, and to thy seed after thee**, the land wherein thou art a stranger, **all the land of Canaan, for <u>an everlasting possession</u>**; and

---

6 *Ishmael* means *whom God hears*. Ishmael is the first of seven people in the Bible who God names before their birth. His genealogy is recorded at Genesis 17:20; 25:12-18 and 1 Chronicles 1:29-31.

I will be their God. **9** And God said unto Abraham, Thou shalt keep my covenant therefore, thou, and thy seed after thee in their generations [for a perpetual covenant].

CIRCUMCISION IS THE SIGN OF THE ABRAHAMIC COVENANT

Genesis 17:10 This is my covenant, which ye shall keep, between me and you and thy seed after thee; Every man child among you shall be circumcised. **11** And ye shall circumcise the flesh of your foreskin; and it shall be a token of the covenant betwixt me and you. **12** And he that is eight days old shall be circumcised among you, every man child in your generations, he that is born in the house, or bought with money of any stranger, which is not of thy seed. **13** He that is born in thy house, and he that is bought with thy money, must needs be circumcised: and **my covenant shall be in your flesh for an everlasting covenant**. **14** And the uncircumcised man child whose flesh of his foreskin is not circumcised, that soul shall be cut off from his people; he hath broken my covenant.

SARAH IS THE MOTHER OF ALL ABRAHAMIC NATIONS AND KINGS

Genesis 17:15 And God said unto Abraham, As for **Sarai** thy wife, thou shalt not call her name Sarai, but **Sarah shall her name be**. **16** And I will bless her, and give thee a son also of her: yea, I will bless her, and **she shall be a mother of nations** [many nations besides Israel: as she is unrelated to Ishmael]; **kings of people** [kings of the people of many nations ... whose people have become as the dust of the earth, stars of heaven, and sand of the sea] **shall be of her**.

17 Then Abraham fell upon his face, and laughed, and said in his heart, Shall a child be born unto him that is an hundred years old? and shall Sarah, that is **ninety years old** [with God, nothing is impossible], bear? **18** And Abraham said unto God, **O that Ishmael might live before thee!** **19** And God said, Sarah thy wife shall bear thee a son indeed; and thou shalt **call his name Isaac** [Isaac was also named by God before his birth]: and I will establish my covenant with him for **an everlasting covenant**, and **with his seed after him** [Isaac and his seed through Jacob have an everlasting covenant with God].

THE BLOOD COVENANT FLOWS THROUGH ISAAC

Genesis 17:20 And as for **Ishmael**, I have heard thee: Behold, **I have blessed him**, and will make him fruitful, and **will multiply him exceedingly**; **twelve princes** shall he beget, and I will make him **a great nation**. **21** But my covenant will I establish with **Isaac**, which Sarah shall bear unto thee at this set time in the next year. **22** And he left off talking with him, and God went up from Abraham.

23 And Abraham took Ishmael his son, and all that were born in his house, and all that were bought with his money, every male among the men of Abraham's house; and circumcised the flesh of their foreskin in the selfsame day, as God had said unto him. **24** And **Abraham was ninety years old and nine**, when he was circumcised in the flesh of his foreskin. **25** And **Ishmael his son was thirteen years old**, when he was circumcised in the flesh of his foreskin. **26** In the selfsame day was Abraham circumcised, and Ishmael his son. **27** And all the men of his house, born in the house, and bought with money of the stranger, were circumcised with him.

SARAH SHALL HAVE A SON

Genesis 18:1 And the LORD appeared unto him in the plains of Mamre: and he sat in the tent door in the heat of the day ... **9** And they said unto him, Where is Sarah thy wife? And he said, Behold, in the tent. **10** And he said, I will certainly return unto thee according to the time of life; and, lo, Sarah thy wife shall have a son. And Sarah heard it in the tent door, which was behind him.

11 Now Abraham and Sarah were old and well stricken in age [99 and 90]; and it ceased to be with Sarah after the manner of women. **12** Therefore Sarah laughed within herself, saying, After I am waxed old shall I have pleasure, my lord being old also? **13** And the LORD said unto Abraham, Wherefore did Sarah laugh, saying, Shall I of a surety bear a child, which am old? **14 Is any thing too hard for the LORD?** At the time appointed I will return unto thee, according to the time of life, and Sarah shall have a son. **15** Then Sarah denied, saying, I laughed not; for she was afraid. And he said, Nay; but thou didst laugh.

ABRAHAM SHALL SURELY BECOME A GREAT NATION

Genesis 18:17 And the LORD said, Shall I hide from Abraham that thing which I do; **18** Seeing that **Abraham shall surely become a great and mighty nation,** and **all the nations of the earth shall be blessed in him?** **19** For I know him, that he will command his children and his household after him [why Abraham was chosen by God], and they shall keep the way of the LORD, to do justice and judgment; that the LORD may bring upon Abraham that which he hath spoken of him.

Isaac Is The Son of Promise

Genesis 21:1 And the LORD visited Sarah as he had said, and the LORD did unto Sarah as he had spoken. **2** For Sarah conceived, and bare Abraham a son in his old age, at the set time of which God had spoken to him. **3** And Abraham called the name of his son that was born unto him, whom Sarah bare to him, **Isaac. 4** And Abraham circumcised his son Isaac being eight days old, as God had commanded him. **5 And Abraham was an hundred years old, when his son Isaac was born unto him.**

6 And Sarah said, God hath made me to laugh, so that all that hear will laugh with me. **7** And she said, Who would have said unto Abraham, that Sarah should have given children suck? for I have born him a son in his old age. **8** And the child grew, and was weaned: and Abraham made a great feast the same day that Isaac was weaned.

Ishmael Has Become A Great Nation

Genesis 21:8 And the child [Isaac] grew, and was weaned: and Abraham made a great feast the same day Isaac was weaned [3 to 5 years after birth]. **9** And Sarah saw the son of Hagar the Egyptian, which she had born unto Abraham, mocking. **10** Wherefore she said unto Abraham, Cast out this bondwoman and her son: for the son of this bondwoman shall not be heir with my son, even with Isaac. **11** And the thing was very grievous in Abraham's sight because of his son.

12 And God said unto Abraham, Let it not be grievous in thy sight because of the lad, and because of thy bondwoman; in all that Sarah hath said unto thee, hearken unto her voice; for **in Isaac shall thy seed be called. 13** And also of **the son of the bondwoman will I make a nation, because he is thy seed.**

14 And Abraham rose up early in the morning, and took bread, and a bottle of water, and gave it unto Hagar, putting it on her shoulder, and the child, and sent her away: and she departed, and wandered in the wilderness of Beersheba. **15** And the water was spent in the bottle, and she cast the child under one of the shrubs. **16** And she went, and sat her down over against him a good way off, as it were a bowshot: for she said, Let me not see the death of the child. And she sat over against him, and lift up her voice, and wept.

17 And God heard the voice of the lad [when Hagar lifted up her voice to God, God heard the voice of Ishmael's destiny]; and **the angel**

of God called to Hagar out of heaven, and said unto her, What aileth thee, Hagar? fear not; for God hath heard the voice of the lad where he is. **18** Arise, **lift up the lad**, and hold him in thine hand; for **I will make him a great nation**. **19** And God opened her eyes, and she saw a well of water; and she went, and filled the bottle with water, and gave the lad drink. **20** And God was with the lad; and he grew, and dwelt in the wilderness, and became an archer. **21** And he dwelt in the wilderness of Paran: and his mother took him a wife out of the land of Egypt.

ABRAHAM OFFERS ISAAC ON THE TEMPLE MOUNT

Genesis 22:1 And it came to pass after these things, that God did tempt [try or test] Abraham, and said unto him, Abraham: and he said, Behold, here I am. **2** And he said, Take now thy son, thine **only son Isaac**, whom thou lovest, and get thee **into the land of Moriah**; and of-**fer him** there for a burnt **offering upon one of the mountains** which I will tell thee of.

3 And Abraham rose up early in the morning, and saddled his ass, and took two of his young men with him, and Isaac his son, and clave the wood for the burnt offering, and rose up, and went unto the place of which God had told him. **4** Then on the third day Abraham lifted up his eyes, and saw the place afar off. **5** And Abraham said unto his young men, Abide ye here with the ass; and I and the lad will go yonder and worship, and come again to you. **6** And Abraham took the wood of the burnt offering, and laid it upon Isaac his son; and he took the fire in his hand, and a knife; and they went both of them together.

7 And Isaac spake unto Abraham his father, and said, My father: and he said, Here am I, my son. And he said, Behold the fire and the wood: but where is the lamb for a burnt offering? **8** And Abraham said, My son, **God will provide himself a lamb for a burnt offering** [God will provide Himself … a Lamb … for a burnt offering]: so they went both of them together.

9 And they came to the place which God had told him of; and Abra-ham built an altar there, and laid the wood in order, and **bound Isaac his son** [Abraham commanded his son, and Isaac was obedient to his father binding him on an alter where animals were killed], and laid him on the altar upon the wood. **10** And Abraham stretched forth his hand, and took the knife to slay his son.

11 And the angel of the LORD called unto him out of heaven, and said, Abraham, Abraham: and he said, Here am I. **12** And he said, Lay not thine hand upon the lad, neither do thou any thing unto him: for now I know that thou fearest God, seeing thou hast not withheld thy son, thine only son from me. **13** And Abraham lifted up his eyes, and looked, and behold behind him **a ram** caught in a thicket by his horns: and Abraham went and took the ram, and offered him up for a burnt offering in the stead of his son. **14** And Abraham called the name of that place Jeho-vahjireh [my God shall provide]: as it is said to this day, In the mount of the LORD it shall be seen.

GOD SWEARS BY HIMSELF HIS BLOOD COVENANT TO ABRAHAM

Genesis 22:15 And the **angel of the LORD** called unto Abraham out of heaven the second time, 16 And said, **By myself have I sworn** (Genesis 26:3), saith the LORD, for because thou hast done this thing, and hast not withheld thy son, thine only son: **17** That in **blessing** I will bless thee, and in **multiplying** I will multiply **thy seed as the <u>stars of the heaven</u>, and as the <u>sand which is upon the sea shore</u>; and thy seed shall <u>possess the gate</u>[7] of his enemies; 18 And <u>in thy seed</u> shall <u>all</u> the <u>nations</u> of the earth be <u>blessed</u>;** because thou hast obeyed my voice.

SARAH'S BONES POSSESS THE LAND

Genesis 23:1 And Sarah was an hundred and seven and twenty years old: these were the years of the life of Sarah. **2** And Sarah died in Kir-jatharba; the same is **Hebron in the land of Canaan**: and Abraham came to mourn for Sarah, and to weep for her.

3 And Abraham stood up from before his dead, and spake unto the sons of Heth[8], saying, **4** I am a stranger and a sojourner with you: give me a possession of a buryingplace with you, that I may bury my dead out of my sight. **5** And the children of Heth answered Abraham, saying unto him, **6** Hear us, my lord: **thou art a mighty prince among us**: in the choice of our sepulchres bury thy dead; none of us shall withhold from thee his sepulchre, but that thou mayest bury thy dead.

7 And Abraham stood up, and bowed himself to the people of the land, even to the children of Heth. **8** And he communed with them, say-ing, If it be your mind that I should bury my dead out of my sight; hear me, and intreat for me to Ephron the son of Zohar, **9** That he may give me the **cave of Machpelah**, which he hath, which is in the end of his

---

7 Gate or gateways; entrances into or exiting from enemy nations … passageways or ports (c/p. Genesis 24:60).

8 Heth is a son of Canaan (Genesis 10:15).

field; for as much money as it is worth he shall give it me for a possession of a buryingplace amongst you.

10 And Ephron dwelt among the children of Heth: and Ephron the Hittite answered Abraham in the audience of the children of Heth, even of all that went in at the gate of his city, saying, **11** Nay, my lord, hear me: the field give I thee, and the cave that is therein, I give it thee; in the presence of the sons of my people give I it thee: bury thy dead. **12** And Abraham bowed down himself before the people of the land. **13** And he spake unto Ephron in the audience of the people of the land, saying, But if thou wilt give it, I pray thee, hear me: I will give thee money for the field; take it of me, and I will bury my dead there. **14** And Ephron answered Abraham, saying unto him, **15** My lord, hearken unto me: the land is worth four hundred shekels of silver; what is that betwixt me and thee? bury therefore thy dead.

16 And Abraham hearkened unto Ephron; and Abraham weighed to Ephron the silver, which he had named in the audience of the sons of Heth, four hundred shekels of silver, current money with the merchant. **17** And the field of Ephron, which was in **Machpelah**, which was before Mamre, the field, and the cave which was therein, and all the trees that were in the field, that were in all the borders round about, were made sure **18** Unto Abraham for a possession in the presence of the children of Heth, before all that went in at the gate of his city.

19 And after this, **Abraham buried Sarah his wife** in the **cave** of the **field of Machpelah** before Mamre: the same is **Hebron** in the **land of Canaan**. **20** And the field, and the cave that is therein, were made sure unto Abraham for a possession of a burying place by the sons of Heth.

A Bride For Isaac

Genesis 24:1 And Abraham was old, and well stricken in age: and the LORD had blessed Abraham in all things. **2** And Abraham said unto his eldest servant[9] of his house, that ruled over all that he had, Put, I pray thee, thy hand under my thigh: **3** And I will make thee swear by the LORD, the God of heaven, and the God of the earth, that thou shalt not take a wife unto my son of the daughters of the Canaanites, among whom I dwell: **4** But thou shalt go unto my country [now living in Syria], and to my kindred, and take a wife unto my son Isaac. **5** And the servant said unto him, Peradventure the woman will not be willing to follow me unto this land: must I needs bring thy son again unto the land from whence thou camest?

9 Eliezer of Damascus (Genesis 15:2).

6 And Abraham said unto him, Beware thou that thou bring not my son thither again. **7 The LORD God of heaven,** which took me from my father's house, and from the land of my kindred, and which spake unto me, and that **sware unto me, saying, Unto thy seed will I give this land;** he shall send his angel before thee, and thou shalt take a wife unto my son from thence. **8** And if the woman will not be willing to follow thee, then thou shalt be clear from this my oath: only bring not my son thither again. **9** And the servant put his hand under the thigh of Abraham his master, and sware to him concerning that matter.

REBEKAH IS THE MOTHER OF BILLIONS

Genesis 24:33 And there was set meat before him to eat [Eliezer has reached his destination and believes he has spotted the LORD'S choice for Isaac's wife]: but he said, I will not eat, until I have told mine errand. And he said, Speak on. **34** And he said, I am Abraham's servant. **35** And the LORD hath blessed my master greatly; and he is become great: and he hath given him flocks, and herds, and silver, and gold, and menservants, and maidservants, and camels, and asses. **36** And Sarah my master's wife bare a son [Isaac] to my master when she was old: and unto him [Isaac] hath he [Abraham] given all that he hath. **37** And my master made me swear, saying, Thou shalt not take a wife to my son of the daughters of the Canaanites, in whose land I dwell: **38** But thou shalt go unto my father's house, and to my kindred, and take a wife unto my son ...

Genesis 24:51 Behold, Rebekah is before thee, take her, and go, and let her be thy master's son's wife, as **the LORD hath spoken** [they know the God of Abraham]...**60** And **they blessed Rebekah**, and said unto her, Thou art our sister, **be thou the <u>mother of thousands of millions</u>**[10], and <u>let thy seed possess the gate</u>[11] <u>of those which hate them</u> ...

64 And Rebekah lifted up her eyes, and when she saw Isaac, she lighted off the camel ... **67** And Isaac brought her into his mother Sarah's tent, and took Rebekah, and she became his wife; and he loved her: and Isaac was comforted after his mother's death.

ISAAC RECEIVES THE BIRTHRIGHT

Genesis 25:1 Then again [after Sarah's death] Abraham took a wife,

---

10 A thousand times a million is a billion. This is a literal promise, and not a primary reference to the Church of Jesus Christ.

11 Rebekah's family in Syria speaks the same blessing over Rebekah that God spoke over Abraham in Genesis 22:17.

and her name was **Keturah.** 2 And she bare him Zimran, and Jokshan, and Medan, and **Midian**, and Ishbak, and Shuah. **3** And Jokshan begat Sheba, and Dedan. And the sons of Dedan were Asshurim, and Letushim, and Leummim. **4** And the sons of Midian; Ephah, and Epher, and Hanoch, and Abida, and Eldaah. All these were the children of Keturah. **5 And Abraham gave all that he had unto Isaac** [the birthright of the firstborn son is given to Isaac, and not to Ishmael].

ABRAHAM'S BONES POSSESS THE LAND

Genesis 25:6 But unto the sons of the concubines, which Abraham had, Abraham gave gifts, and sent them away from Isaac his son, while he yet lived, eastward, unto the east country. **7** And these are the days of the years of **Abraham's life** which he lived, **an hundred threescore and fifteen years**. **8** Then Abraham gave up the ghost, and died in a good old age, an old man, and full of years; and was gathered to his people.

9 And his sons **Isaac** and **Ishmael** buried him in the **cave of Machpelah,** in the field of Ephron the son of Zohar the Hittite, which is before Mamre [in Hebron ... in the area of a proposed Palestinian state]; **10 The field which Abraham purchased of the sons of Heth: there was Abraham buried, and Sarah his wife. 11** And it came to pass after the death of Abraham, that **God blessed his son Isaac**; and Isaac dwelt by the well Lahairoi.

THE HAGARIC COVENANT IS PARTIALLY FULFILLED

Genesis 25:12 Now these are the **generations of Ishmael**, Abraham's son, whom Hagar the Egyptian, Sarah's handmaid, bare unto Abraham: **13** And these are the **names of the sons of Ishmael**, by their names, according to their generations: the firstborn of Ishmael, Nebajoth; and Kedar, and Adbeel, and Mibsam, **14** And Mishma, and Dumah, and Massa, **15** Hadar, and Tema, Jetur, Naphish, and Kedemah: **16** These are the sons of Ishmael, and these are their names, by their towns, and by their castles; <u>**twelve princes**</u>[12] **according to their nations.**

17 And these are the years of the life of Ishmael, an hundred and thirty and seven years: and he gave up the ghost and died; and was gathered unto his people. **18** And they dwelt from Havilah unto Shur, that is before Egypt, as thou goest toward Assyria: and he died in the presence of all his brethren.

---

12 Twelve princes, according to Genesis 17:20.

Two Nations Are Born Of Rebekah

Genesis 25:19 And these are the generations of Isaac, Abraham's son: Abraham begat Isaac: **20** And Isaac was forty years old when he took Rebekah to wife, the daughter of Bethuel the Syrian of Padanaram, the sister to Laban the Syrian. **21** And Isaac intreated the LORD for his wife, because she was barren: and the LORD was intreated of him, and Rebekah his wife conceived.

22 And **the children struggled together within her** [they are still struggling]; and she said, If it be so, why am I thus? And she went to enquire of the LORD. **23** And the LORD said unto her, **Two nations**[13] [only one of these nations can be Israel] are in thy womb, and **two manner of people** shall be separated from thy bowels; and the **one people shall be stronger** than the other people; and **the elder shall serve the younger.**

Esau Despises His Birthright

Genesis 25:24 And when her [Rachel's] days to be delivered were fulfilled, behold, there were **twins in her womb. 25** And **the first came out red**, all over like an hairy garment; and they called his name **Esau** [hairy, red]. **26** And **after that** came his brother out, and his hand took hold on Esau's heel; and his name was called **Jacob** [heel holder or supplanter]: and Isaac was threescore years old when she bare them. **27** And the boys grew: and Esau was a cunning hunter, a man of the field; and Jacob was a plain man, dwelling in tents. **28** And **Isaac loved Esau**, because he did eat of his venison: but **Rebekah loved Jacob.**

29 And Jacob sod pottage: and **Esau** came from the field, and he was faint: **30** And Esau said to Jacob, Feed me, I pray thee, with that same red pottage; for I am faint: therefore was his name called **Edom** [father of the Edomites]. **31** And Jacob said, **Sell me this day thy birthright. 32** And Esau said, Behold, I am at the point to die: and what profit shall this birthright do to me? **33** And Jacob said, Swear to me this day; and he sware unto him: and **he sold his birthright unto Jacob. 34** Then Jacob gave Esau bread and pottage of lentiles; and he did eat and drink, and rose up, and went his way: **thus Esau despised his birthright.**

Abraham's Seed As The Stars Of Heaven

Genesis 26:1 And there was a famine in the land, beside the first

---

13   Esau, the firstborn, became the nation of Edom (the Edomites, Genesis 36:1 and 8).

famine that was in the days of Abraham. And Isaac went unto Abimelech king of the Philistines unto Gerar. **2** And **the LORD appeared unto him**, and said, Go not down into Egypt; **dwell in the land** which I shall tell thee of: **3** Sojourn in this land, and I will be with thee, and will bless thee; for **unto thee,** and unto **thy seed, I will give all these countries,** and **I will perform the oath which I sware**[14] unto Abraham thy father; **4 And I will make thy seed to multiply as** <u>the stars of heaven,</u> and will <u>give unto thy seed all these countries</u>; and <u>in thy seed shall all the nations of the earth be blessed</u>[15]; **5** Because that Abraham obeyed my voice, and kept my charge, my commandments, my statutes, and my laws.

THE BLOOD COVENANT OF ABRAHAM IS RENEWED WITH ISAAC

Genesis 26:23 And he [Isaac] went up from thence to Beersheba. **24** And **the LORD appeared unto him** the same night, and said, I am the God of Abraham thy father: fear not, for **I am with thee,** and **will bless thee,** and **multiply thy seed** for my servant Abraham's sake. **25** And he builded an altar there, and called upon the name of the LORD, and pitched his tent there: and there Isaac's servants digged a well [Isaac gave an offering in the land of promise … he sowed into his destiny].

THE BLESSING OF ISAAC UPON JACOB

Genesis 27:1 And it came to pass , that **when Isaac was old**, and his eyes were dim, so that he could not see, he called Esau his eldest son, and said unto him, My son: and he said unto him, Behold, here am I. **2** And he said, Behold now, I am old, I know not the day of my death[16]: **3** Now therefore take, I pray thee, thy weapons, thy quiver and thy bow, and go out to the field, and take me some venison; **4** And make me savoury meat, such as I love, and bring it to me, that I may eat; that **my soul may bless thee before I die**.

5 And Rebekah heard when Isaac spake to Esau his son. And Esau went to the field to hunt for venison, and to bring it. **6** And Rebekah spake unto Jacob her son, saying, Behold, I heard thy father speak unto Esau thy brother, saying, **7** Bring me venison, and make me savoury meat, that I may eat, and bless thee before the LORD before my death. **8** Now therefore, my son, obey my voice according to that which I command thee [Rebekah knows the power of the blessing]. **9** Go now to the

---

14   Genesis 22:16.

15   Genesis 12:3 and 28:14.

16   Isaac lived to be 180 years old (Genesis 35:28). He also lived to see Jacob return to the land (Genesis 35:27), after 20 years of service with Laban in Syria.

flock, and fetch me from thence two good kids of the goats; and I will make them savoury meat for thy father, such as he loveth: **10** And thou shalt bring it to thy father, that he may eat, and **that he may bless thee before his death** [the coveted blessing of the firstborn].

11 And Jacob said to Rebekah his mother, Behold, Esau my brother is a hairy man, and I am a smooth man: **12** My father peradventure will feel me, and I shall seem to him as a deceiver; and I shall bring a curse upon me, and not a blessing. **13** And his mother said unto him, **Upon me be thy curse**, my son: only obey my voice, and go fetch me them.

14 And he went, and fetched, and brought them to his mother: and his mother made savoury meat, such as his father loved. **15** And Rebekah took goodly raiment of her eldest son Esau, which were with her in the house, and put them upon Jacob her younger son: **16** And she put the skins of the kids of the goats upon his hands, and upon the smooth of his neck: **17** And she gave the savoury meat and the bread, which she had prepared, into the hand of her son Jacob.

18 And he came unto his father, and said, My father: and he said, Here am I; who art thou, my son? **19** And **Jacob said unto his father, I am Esau thy firstborn**; I have done according as thou badest me: arise, I pray thee, sit and eat of my venison, **that thy soul may bless me**. **20** And Isaac said unto his son, How is it that thou hast found it so quickly, my son? And he said, Because the LORD thy God brought it to me.

21 And Isaac said unto Jacob, Come near, I pray thee, that I may feel thee, my son, whether thou be my very son Esau or not. **22** And Jacob went near unto Isaac his father; and he felt him, and said, The voice is Jacob's voice, but the hands are the hands of Esau. **23** And he discerned him not, because his hands were hairy, as his brother Esau's hands: **so he blessed him**. **24** And he said, Art thou my very son Esau? And he said, I am. **25** And he said, Bring it near to me, and I will eat of my son's venison, that my soul may bless thee. And he brought it near to him, and he did eat: and he brought him wine, and he drank.

JACOB STEALS ESAU'S BLESSING

Genesis 27:26 And his [Jacob's] **father Isaac said unto him**, Come near now, and kiss me, my son. **27** And he came near, and kissed him: and he smelled the smell of his raiment, and **blessed him**, and said, See, the smell of my son is as the smell of a field which the LORD hath blessed: **28** Therefore **God give thee of the dew of heaven,** and the **fatness of the earth,** and **plenty of corn and wine: 29 Let people serve thee,**

243

and **nations bow down to thee: be lord over thy brethren,** and **let thy mother's sons bow down to thee: cursed be every one that curseth thee,** and **blessed be he that blesseth thee**[17].

JACOB RECEIVES THE BIRTHRIGHT AND THE BLESSING OF ABRAHAM

Genesis 27:30 And it came to pass, as soon as Isaac had made an end of blessing Jacob, and Jacob was yet scarce gone out from the presence of Isaac his father, that Esau his brother came in from his hunting. **31** And he also had made savoury meat, and brought it unto his father, and said unto his father, Let my father arise, and eat of his son's venison, that thy soul may bless me. **32** And Isaac his father said unto him, Who art thou? And he said, I am thy son, thy firstborn Esau. **33** And Isaac trembled very exceedingly, and said, Who? where is he that hath taken venison, and brought it me, and I have eaten of all before thou camest, and have blessed him? yea, and **he shall be blessed**.

34 And when Esau heard the words of his father, he cried with a great and exceeding bitter cry, and said unto his father, Bless me, even me also, O my father. **35** And he said, Thy brother came with subtilty, and hath taken away thy blessing. **36** And he said, Is not he rightly named **Jacob** [heel holder or supplanter] for he hath supplanted me these two times: **he took away my birthright**; and, behold, **now he hath taken away my blessing**. And he said, Hast thou not reserved a blessing for me? **37** And Isaac answered and said unto Esau, **Behold, I have made him** [Jacob, who became Israel[18]] **thy lord**, and all his brethren have I given to him for servants; and with corn and wine have I sustained him: and what shall I do now unto thee, my son?

GOD'S PROPHECY OVER ESAU/EDOM

Genesis 27:38 And Esau said unto his father, Hast thou but one blessing, my father? bless me, even me also, O my father. And Esau [who became known as Edom[19]] lifted up his voice, and wept. **39** And Isaac his father answered and said unto him, Behold, thy dwelling shall be the fatness of the earth, and of the dew of heaven from above; **40** And **by thy sword shalt thou live**, and shalt **serve thy brother**; and it shall come to pass when thou shalt have the dominion, that **thou shalt break his yoke from off thy neck**.

---

17 Genesis 12:3.
18 Genesis 32:28.
19 Genesis 36:1 and 8.

Jacob Is The Heir To The Land Of Israel

Genesis 28:1 And Isaac called Jacob, and blessed him, and charged him, and said unto him, Thou shalt not take a wife of the daughters of Canaan. **2** Arise, go to Padanaram, to the house of Bethuel thy mother's father; and take thee a wife from thence of the daughters of Laban thy mother's brother. **3** And **God Almighty bless thee,** and **make thee fruitful,** and **multiply thee,** that thou mayest **be a <u>multitude of people; 4 And give thee the <u>blessing of Abraham,</u> to thee, and to thy seed with thee;</u>** that thou mayest <u>**inherit the land**</u> wherein thou art a stranger, which **God gave unto Abraham. 5** And Isaac sent away Jacob: and he went to Padanaram unto Laban, son of Bethuel the Syrian, the brother of **Rebekah: Jacob's and Esau's mother.**

Jacob Has Become A Multitude In All Four Directions

Genesis 28:10 And Jacob went out from Beersheba, and went toward Haran. **11** And he lighted upon a certain place, and tarried there all night, because the sun was set; and he took of the stones of that place, and put them for his pillows, and lay down in that place to sleep. **12** And he dreamed, and behold **a ladder** [the gate of heaven] set up on the earth, and the top of it reached to heaven: and behold the angels of God ascending and descending on it.

13 And, behold, the LORD stood above it, and said, <u>**I am the LORD God of Abraham thy father**</u>, and **the God of Isaac**: **the land** whereon thou liest, <u>**to thee will I give it, and to thy seed**</u>; **14** And <u>**thy seed shall be as the dust of the earth**</u>, and <u>**thou shalt spread abroad to the west**</u>, and <u>**to the east**</u>, and <u>**to the north**</u>, and <u>**to the south**</u> [Jacob's seed would become a numberless multitude in all four directions]: and <u>**in thee**</u> [in Jacob who became Israel] <u>**and in thy seed**</u> [in the whole house of Jacob which includes Israel, but is far greater than just the Jews of Israel] <u>**shall all the families of the earth be blessed**</u>[20].

15 And, behold, I am with thee, and will keep thee in all places whither thou goest, and will bring thee again into this land; for I will not leave thee [God's presence will be with Jacob through the next 20 years of persecution and affliction with Laban], until I have done that which I have spoken to thee of.

16 And Jacob awaked out of his sleep, and he said, Surely the LORD is in this place; and I knew it not. **17** And he was afraid, and said, How dreadful is this place! this is none other but **the house of God**, and this

20 Genesis 12:3 and 26:4.

is **the gate of heaven. 18** And Jacob rose up early in the morning, and took the stone that he had put for his pillows, and set it up for a pillar, and poured oil upon the top of it. **19 And he called the name of that place Bethel** [the house of God]: but the name of that city was called Luz at the first.

20 And Jacob vowed a vow, saying, If God will be with me, and will keep me in this way that I go, and will give me bread to eat, and raiment to put on, **21** So that I come again to my father's house in peace; then shall the LORD be my God: **22 And this stone, which I have set for a pillar, shall be God's house: and of all that thou shalt give me I will surely give the tenth** [a tithe before the law of Moses] **unto thee.**

GOD CALLS JACOB BACK TO CANAAN

Genesis 31:11 And the angel of God spake unto me in a dream, saying, Jacob: ... **13 I am the God of Bethel**, where thou anointedst the pillar, and where thou vowedst a vow unto me: now **arise, get thee out from this land,** and **return unto the land of thy kindred** [unto the land of Canaan].

JACOB REMINDS GOD OF HIS PROMISE

Genesis 32:11 Deliver me, I pray thee, from the hand of my brother, from the hand of Esau: for I fear him, lest he will come and smite me, and the mother with the children. **12 And thou saidst, I will surely do thee good, and <u>make thy seed as the sand of the sea</u>, which cannot be numbered for multitude.**

JACOB IS ISRAEL

Genesis 32:24 And Jacob was left alone; and there wrestled a man with him until the breaking of the day. **25** And when he saw that he prevailed not against him, he touched the hollow of his thigh; and the hollow of Jacob's thigh was out of joint, as he wrestled with him. **26** And he said, Let me go, for the day breaketh. And he said, **I will not let thee go, except thou bless me.**

27 And he said unto him, What is thy name? And he said, Jacob. **28** And he said, **<u>Thy name shall be called no more Jacob, but Israel</u>**[21]

21 Jacob = "heel holder" or "supplanter". Israel = "God prevails"—Prince with God; Soldier of God; God-wrestling, of God's Prince; for as a prince you have power with God and with man, and have prevailed (Genesis 35:10). "Israel" is used variously 2,229 times in the Old Testament. In each context, however, the meaning of the name "Israel" is not constant. It stands for at various

for as a prince hast thou power with God and with men, and hast prevailed. **29** And Jacob asked him, and said, Tell me, I pray thee, thy name. And he said, Wherefore is it that thou dost ask after my name? **And he blessed him there. 30** And Jacob called the name of the place **Peniel** [the face of God]: for I have seen God face to face, and my life is preserved.

Israel Returns To The House Of God

Genesis 35:1 And **God said unto Jacob**, Arise, go up to Bethel, and dwell there: and make there an altar unto God, that appeared unto thee when thou fleddest from the face of Esau thy brother. **2** Then Jacob said unto his household, and to all that were with him, Put away the strange gods that are among you, and be clean, and change your garments: **3** And let us arise, and go up to Bethel; and I will make there an altar unto God, who answered me in the day of my distress, and was with me in the way which I went. **4** And they gave unto Jacob all the strange gods which were in their hand, and all their earrings which were in their ears; and Jacob hid them under the oak which was by Shechem.

5 And they journeyed: **and the terror of God was upon the cities that were round about them, and they did not pursue after the sons of Jacob. 6** So Jacob came to **Luz**, which is in **the land of Canaan**, that is, **Bethel** [the house of God], he and all the people that were with him. **7** And he built there an altar, and called the place El-bethel: because there God appeared unto him, when he fled from the face of his brother.

God Confirms Jacob's Name Is Israel

Genesis 35:9 And God appeared unto Jacob again, when he came out of Padanaram, and blessed him. 10 And God said unto him, Thy name is Jacob: **thy name shall not be called any more Jacob, but Israel shall be thy name**[22]: and **he called his name Israel**.

Israel Has Become A Company Of Nations

Genesis 35:11 And God said unto him [Jacob], I am God Almighty: **be fruitful** and **multiply; a nation** [the nation of Israel] and **a company**

times: the 12 tribes of Jacob; the house of Jacob; the nation of Israel (before the kingdom was divided, and after a remnant returned from Babylonian captivity). It also stands for the 10 tribes of the northern kingdom of Israel after the kingdom was divided, and the southern kingdom became known as Judah. What is important to remember from this text is that the promises of the Abrahamic Covenant are resident in "all of Israel"—wherever located, and by whatever national or ethnic identity they are presently called.

22 Genesis 32:28.

of nations [the nations of Ephraim, and possibly Manasseh] shall be of thee, and kings [the kings, rulers, presidents, and prime ministers of Israel as well as this company of nations] shall come out of thy loins [out of the loins of the natural seed of Jacob];

GOD GIVES THE LAND OF CANAAN TO ALL OF SEED OF JACOB

Genesis 35:12 And **the land** which <u>I gave Abraham and Isaac, to thee I will give it, and to thy seed after thee will I give the land</u>. **13** And God went up from him in the place where he talked with him. **14** And **Jacob set up a pillar** in the place where he talked with him, even **a pillar of stone**: and he poured **a drink offering** thereon, and **he poured oil** thereon. **15** And Jacob called the name of the place where God spake with him, Bethel [the house of God].

THE 12 SONS OF JACOB ARE THE 12 TRIBES OF ISRAEL

Genesis 35:21 And **Israel** journeyed, and spread his tent beyond the tower of Edar. **22** And it came to pass, when Israel dwelt in that land, that <u>Reuben went and lay with Bilhah his father's concubine</u>[23]: and Israel heard it. **Now the sons of Jacob were twelve: 23** The **sons of Leah**; Reuben, Jacob's firstborn, and Simeon, and Levi, and Judah, and Issachar, and Zebulun: **24** The **sons of Rachel**; Joseph, and Benjamin: **25** And the **sons of Bilhah**, Rachel's handmaid; Dan, and Naphtali: **26** And the **sons of Zilpah**, Leah's handmaid; Gad, and Asher: **these are the sons of Jacob**, which were born to him in Padanaram.

27 And Jacob came unto Isaac his father unto Mamre, unto the city of Arbah, which is **Hebron**, where Abraham and Isaac sojourned. **28** And the **days of Isaac** were an hundred and fourscore years. **29** And Isaac gave up the ghost, and died, and was gathered unto his people, being old and full of days: and **his sons Esau and Jacob buried him**.

ESAU IS EDOM

Genesis 36:1 Now these are **the generations of Esau, who is Edom** [the Edomites]. ... **6** And Esau took his wives, and his sons, and his daughters, and all the persons of his house, and his cattle, and all his beasts, and all his substance, which he had got in the land of Canaan; and went into the country from the face of his brother Jacob. **7** For **their riches** were more than that they might dwell together; and the land wherein they were strangers could not bear them because of their cattle.

---

23   For this sin Reuben, Jacob's firstborn, lost his birthright: which was given to the sons of Joseph (Genesis 49:4 and 26; 1 Chronicles 5:1-2, pg. 66-67).

8 Thus dwelt Esau in mount Seir[24]: Esau is Edom.

ISRAEL REMAINS IN THE LAND OF CANAAN

Genesis 37:1 And **Jacob dwelt in the land** wherein his father was a stranger, **in the land of Canaan**.

JOSEPH IS SOLD INTO EGYPTIAN SLAVERY

Genesis 37:23 And it came to pass, when **Joseph** (the 11th son of Jacob, by Rachael) was come unto his brethren, that they stript Joseph out of his coat, his coat of many colours that was on him; **24** And they took him, and cast him into a pit: and the pit was empty, there was no water in it. **25** And they sat down to eat bread: and they lifted up their eyes and looked, and, behold, **a company of Ishmeelites** came from Gilead with their camels bearing spicery and balm and myrrh, going to carry it down to Egypt.

26 And **Judah** said [Judah has equal responsibility for selling Joseph … unto this day] unto his brethren, What profit is it if we slay our brother, and conceal his blood? **27** Come, and let us sell him to the **Ishmeelites**, and let not our hand be upon him; **for he is our brother and our flesh**. And his brethren were content [including Judah]. **28** Then there passed by **Midianites** merchantmen; and they drew and lifted up Joseph out of the pit, and **sold Joseph to the Ishmeelites for twenty pieces of silver: and they brought Joseph into Egypt** … **36** And the Midianites sold him into Egypt unto Potiphar, an officer of Pharaoh's, and captain of the guard.

JOSEPH PROSPERS IN SLAVERY

Genesis 39:1 And Joseph was brought down to Egypt; and Potiphar, an officer of Pharaoh, captain of the guard, an Egyptian, bought him of the hands of the Ishmeelites, which had brought him down thither. **2** And **the LORD was with Joseph, and he was a prosperous man[25]**; and he was in the house of his master the Egyptian. **3** And his master saw that the LORD was with him, and that the LORD made all that he did to prosper in his hand. **4** And Joseph found grace in his sight, and he served him: and he made him overseer over his house, and all that he had he put into his hand[26].

---

24 A range of mountains in southern Jordan.

25 The blessing of Abraham is upon Joseph even as a slave.

26 God is equipping Joseph with the management skills needed to fulfill his destiny even while in prison.

5 And it came to pass from the time that he had made him over-seer in his house, and over all that he had, that **the LORD blessed the Egyptian's house for Joseph's sake; and the blessing of the LORD was upon all that he had in the house, and in the field**. **6** And he left all that he had in Joseph's hand; and he knew not ought he had, save the bread which he did eat. And Joseph was a goodly person, and well favoured ...

Genesis 39:20 And Joseph's master [Potiphar] took him, and put him into the prison, a place where the king's prisoners were bound: and he was there in the prison. **21 But the LORD was with Joseph, and shewed him mercy, and gave him favour in the sight of the keeper of the prison**. **22** And the keeper of the prison committed to Joseph's hand all the prisoners that were in the prison; and whatsoever they did there, he was the doer of it. **23** The keeper of the prison looked not to any thing that was under his hand; because the LORD was with him, and that which he did, **the LORD made it to prosper**.

JOSEPH IS HEBREW AND NOT JEWISH

THE TESTIMONY OF POTIPHAR'S WIFE

Genesis 39:13 And it came to pass, when she [Potiphar's wife] saw that he [Joseph] had left his garment in her hand, and was fled forth, **14** That she called unto the men of her house, and spake unto them, saying, See, he [Potiphar] hath brought in **an Hebrew** unto us to mock us ... **17** And she spake unto him according to these words, saying, **The Hebrew servant**, which thou hast brought unto us, came in unto me to mock me ...

JOSEPH'S OWN TESTIMONY

Genesis 40:14 But think on me [spoken to Pharaoh's chief butler] when it shall be well with thee, and shew kindness, I pray thee, unto me, and make mention of me unto Pharaoh, and bring me out of this house: **15** For indeed **I was stolen away out of the land of the Hebrews** [Canaan was commonly identified with the Hebrew people]: and here also have I done nothing that they should put me into the dungeon.

THE TESTIMONY OF THE CHIEF BUTLER

Genesis 41:9 Then spake the chief butler unto Pharaoh, saying, I do remember my faults this day: **10** Pharaoh was wroth with his servants, and put me in ward in the captain of the guard's house, both me and the chief baker: **11** And we dreamed a dream in one night, I and he; we dreamed each man according to the interpretation of his dream. **12** And there was there with us a young man, **an Hebrew, servant** to the captain of the guard; and we told him, and he interpreted to us our dreams; to each man according to his dream he did interpret.

Testimony From Joseph's Home

Genesis 43:26 And when Joseph came home, they [his brothers] brought him the present which was in their hand into the house, and bowed themselves to him to the earth. ... **32** And they set on for him [Joseph] by himself, and for them by themselves, and for the Egyptians, which did eat with him, by themselves: **because the Egyptians might not eat bread with the Hebrews; for that is an abomination unto the Egyptians**[27].

Two Sons Are Born To Joseph In Egypt

Genesis 41:50 And **unto Joseph were born two sons** before the years of famine came, which Asenath the daughter of Potipherah priest of On bare unto him. **51** And Joseph called the name of the firstborn **Manasseh** [to forget]: For God, said he, hath made me forget all my toil, and all my father's house. **52** And the name of the second called he **Ephraim** [to be fruitful]: For God hath caused me to be fruitful in the land of my affliction.

Joseph Loves And Forgives His Brothers

Genesis 45:4 And Joseph said unto his brethren... I am Joseph your brother, whom ye sold into Egypt. **5** Now therefore be not grieved, nor angry with yourselves, that ye sold me hither: for **God did send me before you** to preserve life. **6** For these two years hath the famine been in the land: and yet there are five years, in the which there shall neither be earing nor harvest. **7** And God sent me before you **to preserve you a posterity in the earth, and to save your lives by a great deliverance**. **8** So now it was not you that sent me hither, but God: and he hath made me a father to Pharaoh, and lord of all his house, and a ruler throughout all the land of Egypt.

9 Haste ye, and go up to my father, and say unto him, Thus saith thy son Joseph, **God hath made me lord of all Egypt**: come down unto me, tarry not: **10** And thou shalt dwell in the land of Goshen, and thou

---

27 In Moses' struggles with Pharaoh in Egypt, he refers to "the God of the Hebrews" five times (Exodus 3:18; 5:3; 7:16; 9:1 and 10:3).

shalt be near unto me, thou, and thy children, and thy children's children, and thy flocks, and thy herds, and all that thou hast.

GOD MAKES JACOB THE NATION OF ISRAEL WHILE IN EGYPT

Genesis 46:1 And Israel took his journey with all that he had, and came to Beersheba, and offered sacrifices unto the God of his father Isaac. 2 And God spake unto Israel in the visions of the night, and said, **Jacob, Jacob.** And he said, Here am I. **3** And he said, **I am God, the God of thy father: fear not to go down <u>into Egypt</u>; for <u>I will there make of thee a great nation</u>: 4** I will go down with thee into Egypt; and I will also surely bring thee up again: and Joseph shall put his hand upon thine eyes.

THE ABRAHAMIC COVENANT IS KEPT ALIVE IN THE HOUSE OF JACOB/ISRAEL

Genesis 46:26 All the souls that came with Jacob into Egypt, which came out of his loins, besides Jacob's sons' wives, all the souls were **threescore and six**[28]; **27** And the sons of Joseph, which were born him in Egypt, were two souls: all the souls of the <u>**house of Jacob**</u>, which came into Egypt, were **threescore and ten. 28** And he sent Judah before him unto Joseph, to direct his face unto Goshen; and they came into the land of Goshen.

ISRAEL MULTIPLIES IN THE LAND OF EGYPT

Genesis 47:27 And **Israel** dwelt in the land of Egypt, in the country of Goshen; and they had possessions therein, and grew, and **multiplied exceedingly** [this is only the beginning of what God promised Abraham]. **28** And Jacob lived in the land of Egypt seventeen years: so the whole age of Jacob was an hundred forty and seven years.

ISRAEL MUST BE BURIED IN ISRAEL

Genesis 47:29 And the time drew nigh that Israel must die: and he called his son Joseph, and said unto him, If now I have found grace in thy sight, put, I pray thee, thy hand under my thigh, and deal kindly and truly with me; bury me not, I pray thee, in Egypt: **30** But I will lie with my fathers, and **thou shalt carry me out of Egypt**, and bury me in their burying place. And he said, I will do as thou hast said. **31** And he said, Swear <u>unto</u> me. And **he sware unto him**. And Israel bowed himself

28 These **70 souls** represent **the whole House of Jacob**, which represents **the whole house of Israel** ... heirs to the Covenant that God made with Abraham.

upon the bed's head.

Ephraim And Manasseh Belong To Israel

Genesis 48:1 And it came to pass after these things, that one told **Joseph,** Behold, thy father is sick: and he took with him **his two sons, Manasseh** and **Ephraim.** 2 And one told Jacob, and said, Behold, thy son Joseph cometh unto thee: and **Israel** strengthened himself, and sat upon the bed. 3 And **Jacob said unto Joseph, God Almighty** appeared unto me at Luz [Bethel] in the land of Canaan**,** and **blessed me, 4** And said unto me, Behold, **I will make thee fruitful,** and **multiply thee,** and **I will make of thee a multitude of people**; and **will give this land to thy seed** after thee **for an everlasting possession**.

[At no time in history, since the 70 souls of the whole house of Jacob, have Jews from the tribe of Judah been a [numberless] multitude of people—numberless by today's standards.]

Genesis 48:5 And now **thy two sons, Ephraim and Manasseh**[29], which were born unto thee in the land of Egypt before I came unto thee into Egypt, **are mine** [all of the descendants of Ephraim and Manasseh belong to Israel—even unto this day]; as **Reuben** and **Simeon** [Jacob's first two sons], **they shall be mine. 6 And thy issue,** which thou begettest after them, shall be thine, and **shall be called after the name of their brethren in their inheritance** [Israel gives his grandsons by Joseph the same status in their inheritance in God's Covenant with Abraham for blessing and the land as he does for his own natural sons, Reuben and Simeon]. ...

8 And **Israel beheld Joseph's sons**, and said, Who are these? 9 And Joseph said unto his father, They are my sons, whom God hath given me in this place. And he said, Bring them, I pray thee, unto me, and **I will bless them.** 10 Now the eyes of Israel were dim for age, so that he could not see. And he brought them near unto him; and he kissed them, and embraced them. 11 And Israel said unto Joseph, I had not thought to see thy face: and, lo, God hath shewed me also thy seed. 12 And Joseph brought them out from between his knees, and he bowed himself with his face to the earth. 13 And Joseph took them both, Ephraim in his right hand toward Israel's left hand, and Manasseh in his left hand toward Israel's right hand, and brought them near unto him.

---

29 Israel [Jacob] has already reversed the order of Genesis 48:1, and has placed Ephraim before Manasseh.

Ephraim Receives The Birthright And Blessing

Genesis 48:14 And Israel [Jacob] stretched out his right hand, and laid it upon **Ephraim's head**, who was **the younger**, and his left hand upon **Manasseh's head**, guiding his hands wittingly; for **Manasseh was the firstborn. 15** And **he blessed Joseph** [the blessings of the firstborn are given to Joseph instead of Reuben[30]], and said, God, before whom my fathers Abraham and Isaac did walk, the God which fed me all my life long unto this day,

1 Chronicles 5:1 Now the **sons of Reuben the firstborn of Israel**, (for he was the firstborn; but, forasmuch as he defiled his father's bed, **his birthright was given unto the sons of Joseph the son of Israel**: and the genealogy is not to be reckoned after the birthright. **2** For **Judah prevailed above his brethren, and of him came the chief ruler** [Messiah]; <u>but the birthright was Joseph's</u>:)

Joseph Is A Multitude In The Middle Of The Earth

Genesis 48:16 The **Angel which redeemed me** [a reference to God] from all evil, **bless the lads** [both Ephraim and Manasseh received the blessing of Israel and Abraham]; and <u>let my name be named on them</u> [let the name of Israel be on Ephraim and Manasseh], and **the name of my fathers Abraham and Isaac** [let the name of Abraham and Isaac also be on Ephraim and Manasseh]; and <u>let them grow</u> [growth over a period of time] <u>into a multitude</u>[31] <u>in the midst</u>[32] <u>of the earth</u>.

Manasseh Has Become A Great People

Genesis 48:17 And when Joseph saw that his father laid his right hand upon the head of Ephraim, it displeased him: and he held up his father's hand, to remove it from Ephraim's head unto **Manasseh's** head. **18** And Joseph said unto his father, Not so, my father: for this is **the firstborn** [Manasseh]; put thy right hand upon his head. **19(a)** And his father refused, and said, I know it, my son, I know it: **he** [Manasseh] also <u>shall become a people</u>, and **he also** <u>shall be great</u>: ...

---

30 1 Chronicles 5:1-2.

31 Heb.. _rob_, abundance, greatness, multitude.

32 Heb., _qereb_, midst, among, inner part, middle; in the midst, among, from among (of a number of persons). What does "midst or middle of the earth" mean? How about...land mass, longitude, latitude, or some other measure? Unlocking this mystery will also unlock the mystery of where Ephraim is today, and where Manasseh has migrated to.

254

Ephraim Has Become A Multitude Of Nations

Genesis 48:19(b) ... but truly **his younger brother** [Ephraim] **shall be greater than he**, and **his seed shall become a multitude[33] of nations[34]** [in the midst or middle of the earth (Genesis 48:16)]. **20** And **he blessed them** that day, saying, **In thee shall Israel bless**, saying, God make thee as Ephraim and as Manasseh: and **he set Ephraim before Manasseh** [the fulfillment of the promises given to Ephraim will come before those given to Manasseh, as well as be greater in magnitude].

Joseph Has Received The Double Portion

Genesis 48:21 And **Israel said unto Joseph**, Behold, I die: but God shall be with you, and **bring you again unto the land of your fathers**. **22** Moreover **I have given to thee one portion above thy brethren** [both Ephraim and Manasseh inherited their own plot of land in Israel], which I took out of the hand of the Amorite with my sword and with my bow.

Israel Prophesies Of The Last Days

Genesis 49:1 And **Jacob called unto his sons**, and said, Gather yourselves together, that I may tell you **that which shall befall you in the last days**. **2** Gather yourselves together, and hear, **ye sons of Jacob**; and hearken unto **Israel your father**.

The Sceptre Shall Remain With Judah

Genesis 49:8 Judah, thou art he whom thy brethren shall praise: thy hand shall be in the neck of thine enemies; thy father's children shall bow down before thee ... **10 The sceptre shall not depart from Judah** [the right to rule—the throne—is given to Judah], **nor a lawgiver from between his feet, until Shiloh come** [the Messiah shall also come from the tribe of Judah]; and **unto him shall the gathering of the people be**.

God's Promises To Joseph Are Fulfilled In Ephraim And Manasseh

Genesis 49:22 Joseph is **a fruitful bough** [what is said of Joseph

---

33 Heb., _melo_, fullness, that which fills, mass, multitude ... as the dust of the earth, stars of heaven, and sand of the sea.

34 Heb., _gowy_ (_goyim_), nation, people, nations. This is in furtherance of the promises God gave to Abraham and Sarah that they would be the father and mother of nations (Genesis 17:4-6, 16); and a company of nations (Genesis 35:11). God is speaking here of more than just the nation of Israel.

is to be fulfilled in Ephraim and Manasseh], even a fruitful bough by a well; whose branches run over the wall: **23** The archers [his brothers] have sorely grieved him, and shot at him, and hated him: **24** But his bow abode in strength, and the arms of his hands were made strong by the hands of the mighty God of Jacob; (from thence is the shepherd, the stone of Israel:)

Joseph Receives The Birthright And The Blessing

Genesis 49:25 Even by the God of thy father, who shall help thee; and by **the Almighty**, who shall bless thee with **blessings of heaven above, blessings of the deep** that lieth under, blessings of the breasts, and of the womb [a multitude of offspring]: **26 The <u>blessings of thy father</u> have prevailed above the blessings of my progenitors[35]** unto the utmost bound of the everlasting hills: **they shall be <u>on the head of Joseph</u>**, and <u>**on the crown of the head**</u> of him that was separate from his brethren.

1 Chronicles 5:1 Now the sons of Reuben the firstborn of Israel, (for he was the firstborn; but, forasmuch as he defiled his father's bed, **his birthright[36]** was <u>**given unto the sons of Joseph**</u> the son of Israel: and the genealogy is not to be reckoned after the birthright. 2 For **<u>Judah prevailed</u>** above his brethren, and **<u>of him came the chief ruler</u>** [the Messiah]; **but the birthright was Joseph's** [it is the birthright that establishes the right to the blessing of the father]:)

There Is Immense Wealth Hidden In The Crown Of Joseph

Genesis 49:26 … the <u>blessings</u> … they shall **<u>be on the head of Joseph</u>**, and on **the crown** top **of the head** of him that was separate from his brethren.

Deuteronomy 33:16b <u>**Let the blessing come upon the head of Joseph**</u>, and **<u>upon the top of the head</u>** of him that was separated from his brethren.

The Blessings Of Israel Is Upon All 12 Tribes

Genesis 49:28 All these are the <u>**twelve tribes of Israel**</u>: and this is

---

35 What Israel is saying to Joseph is this: "The blessings of your father [on you] are greater than the blessing of my forefathers [Abraham and Isaac on me]; and are as lasting as the utmost boundaries of the eternal hills."

36 Like Jacob, Joseph through his sons receives both the **birthright** and the **blessing** of Israel: which includes all of the promises that God made to Abraham, Isaac, Israel, Sarah and Rebekah.

it that their father spake unto them, and **blessed them**; **every one according to his blessing he blessed them**.

Genesis 49:29 And he [Israel] charged them, and said unto them, I am to be gathered unto my people: bury me with my fathers in the cave that is in the field of Ephron the Hittite, **30** In the cave that is in the **field of Machpelah**, which is before Mamre, **in the land of Canaan, which Abraham bought** with the field of Ephron the Hittite for a possession of a burying place [in Hebron].

31 There they buried Abraham and Sarah his wife; there they buried Isaac and Rebekah his wife; and there I buried Leah. **32** The purchase of the field and of the cave that is therein was from the children of Heth. **33** And when Jacob had made an end of commanding his sons, he gathered up his feet into the bed, and yielded up the ghost, and was gathered unto his people.

Genesis 50:4 And when the days of his [Jacob's] mourning were past, Joseph spake unto the house of Pharaoh, saying, If now I have found grace in your eyes, speak, I pray you, in the ears of Pharaoh, saying, **5** My father made me swear, saying, Lo, I die: in my grave which I have digged for me in the **land of Canaan**, there shalt thou bury me. Now therefore let me go up, I pray thee, and bury my father, and I will come again. **6** And Pharaoh said, Go up, and bury thy father, according as he made thee swear.

7 And Joseph went up to bury his father: and with him went up all the servants of Pharaoh, the elders of his house, and all the elders of the land of Egypt, **8** And **all the house of Joseph**, and his brethren, and his father's house: only their little ones, and their flocks, and their herds, they left in the land of Goshen.

9 And there went up with him both chariots and horsemen: and it was a very great company. **10** And they came to the threshing floor of Atad, which is beyond Jordan, and there they mourned with a great and very sore lamentation: and he made a mourning for his father seven days. **11** And when the inhabitants of the land, the Canaanites, saw the mourning in the floor of Atad, they said, This is a grievous mourning to the Egyptians: wherefore the name of it was called Abelmizraim, which is beyond Jordan.

12 And his sons did unto him according as he commanded them:

257

13 For his sons carried him into the **land of Canaan**, and buried him in the cave of the **field of Machpelah**, which Abraham bought with the field for a possession of a burying place of Ephron the Hittite, before Mamre. **14** And Joseph returned into Egypt, he, and his brethren, and all that went up with him to bury his father, after he had buried his father.

JOSEPH'S BONES POSSESS THE LAND

Genesis 50:22 And Joseph dwelt in Egypt, he, and his father's house: and Joseph lived an hundred and ten years. **23** And Joseph saw Ephraim's children of the third generation: the children also of Machir the son of Manasseh were brought up upon Joseph's knees. **24** And Joseph said unto his brethren, I die: and **God will surely visit you, and bring you out of this land unto the land which he sware to Abraham, to Isaac, and to Jacob**.

25 And Joseph took an oath of the children of Israel, saying, God will surely visit you, and ye shall **carry up my bones** from hence. **26** So Joseph died, being an hundred and ten years old: and they embalmed him, and he was put in a coffin in Egypt.

Exodus 13:19 And Moses took the **bones of Joseph** with him: for he had straitly sworn the children of Israel, saying, God will surely visit you; and ye shall carry up my bones away hence with you.

Joshua 24:32 And the **bones of Joseph**, which the children of Israel brought up out of Egypt, buried they in Shechem, in a parcel of ground which Jacob bought of the sons of Hamor the father of Shechem for an hundred pieces of silver: and it became the inheritance of the children of Joseph.

MOSES REMINDS GOD OF HIS BLOOD-SWORN PROMISES TO ABRAHAM

Exodus 32:7 And the LORD said unto Moses, Go, get thee down; for thy people, which thou broughtest out of the land of Egypt, have corrupted themselves: **8** They have ... made them a molten calf, and have worshipped it ... **11** And Moses besought the LORD his God, and said, LORD, why doth thy wrath wax hot against thy people, which thou hast brought forth out of the land of Egypt with great power, and with a mighty hand? ... **13** Remember Abraham, Isaac, and **Israel**, thy servants, to whom **thou swearest by thine own self**, and saidst unto them, **I will multiply your seed as the stars of heaven**, and **all this land** that I have spoken of **will I give unto your seed**, and they shall **inherit it for ever** [the unchangeable God of heaven and earth recognizes no Palestinian right to the land of Israel]. **14** And the LORD repented of the evil which he thought to do unto his people.

Even The Forth Part of Israel Cannot Be Numbered

Numbers 23:8 How shall I curse [the prophet Balaam is speaking], whom God hath not cursed ? or how shall I defy, whom the LORD hath not defied? **9** For from the top of the rocks I see him, and from the hills I behold him: lo, **the people shall dwell alone, and shall not be reckoned among the nations** [God has always intended Israel to be a distinct witness for Him in the earth ... which has only occurred briefly during the reign of David and Solomon]. **10 Who can count the dust of Jacob, and the number of the fourth part of Israel** [not even the fourth part of "**all Israel**" can be counted]?

Israel Has Become A Thousand Times More Than The Stars

Deuteronomy 1:6 The LORD our God spake unto us in Horeb, saying, Ye have dwelt long enough in this mount: **7** Turn you, and take your journey, and go to the mount of the Amorites, and unto all the places nigh thereunto, in the plain, in the hills, and in the vale, and in the south, and by the sea side, to the land of the Canaanites, and unto Lebanon, **unto the great river, the river Euphrates** [Israel never took all of the land that God had given them]. **8** Behold, I have set the land before you: **go in and possess the land which the LORD sware unto your fathers, Abraham, Isaac, and Jacob, to give unto them and to their seed after them.**

9 And I spake unto you at that time, saying, I am not able to bear you myself alone: **10** The LORD your God hath multiplied you, and, behold, **ye are this day as the stars of heaven for multitude** [this looks at first to be the fulfillment of God's promise to Abraham]. **11** (The LORD God of your fathers **make you a thousand times so many more as ye are** [but then the LORD God through the prophet Moses multiplies the stars of heaven by a thousand times more ... and which was to be fulfilled and has been fulfilled in the descendants of Joseph, and not Judah], and bless you, as he hath promised you!)

Deuteronomy 10:11 And the LORD said unto me, Arise, take thy journey before the people, that they may go in and possess the land, which I sware unto their fathers to give unto them. ... **22** Thy fathers went down into Egypt with threescore and ten persons; and **now the LORD thy God hath made thee as the stars of heaven for multitude.**

Deuteronomy 4:21 Furthermore the LORD was angry with me [Moses] for your sakes, and sware that I should not go over Jordan, and that I should not go in unto **that good land, which the LORD thy God giveth thee for an inheritance**: **22** But I must die in this land, I must not go over Jordan: but ye shall go over, and possess that good land. **23** Take heed unto yourselves, lest ye forget the covenant of the LORD your God, which he made with you, and make you a graven image, or the likeness of any thing, which the LORD thy God hath forbidden thee. **24** For the LORD thy God is a consuming fire, even a jealous God.

25 When thou shalt beget children, and children's children, and ye shall have remained long in the land, and shall corrupt yourselves, and make a graven image, or the likeness of any thing, and shall do evil in the sight of the LORD thy God, to provoke him to anger : **26 I call heaven and earth to witness against you this day,** that ye shall soon utterly perish from off the land whereunto ye go over Jordan to possess it; ye shall not prolong your days upon it, but shall utterly be destroyed .

27 And **the LORD shall scatter you among the nations** [all 12 tribes], and ye shall **be left <u>few in number</u> among the heathen, <u>whither the LORD shall lead you</u>** [even in judgment, the LORD is still leading His people]. **28** And **there ye shall serve gods** [in foreign lands], the work of men's hands, wood and stone, which neither see, nor hear, nor eat, nor smell [the northern kingdom lost its identity as Hebrews; Judah was preserved as Jews because of God's mercy to David].

29 But if from thence thou shalt seek the LORD thy God, thou shalt find him, if thou seek him with all thy heart and with all thy soul. **30** <u>**When thou art in tribulation**</u> [Israel is in "great tribulation" right now], and all these things are come upon thee, even **<u>in the latter days</u>** [tribulation of the latter days; not the great tribulation of the last days which is the *time of Jacob's trouble*], if thou turn to the LORD thy God, and shalt be obedient unto his voice; **31** (For the LORD thy God is a merciful God;) he will not forsake thee, neither destroy thee, nor forget the covenant of thy fathers which he sware unto them.

Disobedience Has Caused The Stars Of Judah To Become Few In Number

Deuteronomy 28:58 <u>If thou wilt not</u> observe to do all the words of this law that are written in this book, that thou mayest fear this glorious and fearful name, **THE LORD THY GOD ... 62** And <u>**ye shall**</u>

be left few in number, whereas ye were as the stars of heaven for multitude; because thou wouldest not obey the voice of the LORD thy God. 63 And it shall come to pass, that as the LORD rejoiced over you to do you good, and to multiply you; so the LORD will rejoice over you to destroy you, and to bring you to nought; and ye shall be plucked from off the land whither thou goest to possess it.

64 And the LORD shall scatter thee among all people [scatter all 12 tribes], from the one end of the earth even unto the other; and there thou shalt serve other gods [Joseph and Ephraim not only have lost their identity as Hebrews, but have not known the God of Abraham], which neither thou nor thy fathers have known, even wood and stone.

65 And among these nations shalt thou find no ease, neither shall the sole of thy foot have rest: but the LORD shall give thee there a trembling heart, and failing of eyes, and sorrow of mind: 66 And thy life shall hang in doubt before thee; and thou shalt fear day and night, and shalt have none assurance of thy life: ... 68 And the LORD shall bring thee into Egypt[37] again with ships, by the way whereof I spake unto thee, Thou shalt see it no more again: and there ye shall be sold unto your enemies for bondmen and bondwomen, and no man shall buy you [the prophecy in this paragraph has certainly been true for the Jewish people; but Joseph has another set of promises from God].

MOSES COMMANDS ONLY THE BEST FOR JOSEPH

Deuteronomy 33:1 And this is the blessing, wherewith Moses the man of God blessed the children of Israel before his death. 2 And he said, The LORD came from Sinai, and rose up from Seir unto them; he shined forth from mount Paran, and he came with ten thousands of saints: from his right hand went a fiery law for them. 3 Yea, he loved the people; all his saints are in thy hand: and they sat down at thy feet; every one shall receive of thy words. 4 Moses commanded us a law, even the inheritance of the congregation of Jacob. 5 And he was king in Jeshurun[38], when the heads of the people and the tribes of Israel were gathered together ...

13 And of Joseph he said, Blessed of the LORD be his land,

---

37 By the time of the Ptolemy kingdom that succeeded Alexander the Great, such a multitude of non-Hebrew speaking Jews were flourishing in Egypt that the Septuagint was commissioned as a translation into Greek of the Tanaka (Hebrew Old Testament Scriptures) for the great library in Alexandria, so that Jews would be able to read Moses, the Psalms, and the Prophets.

38 Heb. Yeshruwn, a symbolic name of Israel, meaning "the upright one".

for the **precious things** of heaven, for the dew, and for the deep that coucheth [lies or rests] beneath, **14** And for the **precious fruits** brought forth by the sun, and for the **precious things** put forth by the moon, **15** And for the **chief things** of the ancient mountains, and for the **precious things** of the lasting hills, **16** And for the **precious things** of the earth and fulness thereof, and for the **good will** of him that dwelt in the bush:

Joseph Has Populated The Entire Earth

Deuteronomy 33:16 ... [L]et the blessing come upon the head of Joseph, and upon the top of the head ("crown of head" in Genesis 49:26) of him that was separated from his brethren. **17** His [Joseph's] glory is like the firstling of his bullock, and **his horns** are like **the horns of unicorns** [Ephraim and Manasseh shall be strong nations]: with them [with the horns of their strength] <u>**he**</u> [Joseph] <u>**shall push the people together to the ends of the earth**</u> [the nations of both Ephraim and Manasseh have scattered or colonized "the people" of Israel to the ends of the earth]: and they are the **ten thousands of Ephraim** [the multitude of nations coming from Ephraim shall become as the dust of the earth, stars of heaven, and sand of the sea], and they are **the thousands of Manasseh** [Manasseh shall also become a great multitude of people].

Israel's Enemies Are Also Described As Sand

Joshua 11:4 And they went out [the enemies of Israel], they and all their hosts with them, **much people, even as the sand that is upon the sea shore in multitude**, with horses and chariots very many... to fight against Israel. **6** And the LORD said unto Joshua, Be not afraid because of them: for to morrow about this time will I deliver them up all slain before Israel: thou shalt hough their horses, and burn their chariots with fire. ... **16** So **Joshua took all that land**, the hills, and all the south country, and all the land of Goshen, and the valley, and the plain, and the mountain of Israel, and the valley of the same; ... **23 So Joshua took the whole land, according to all that the LORD said unto Moses; and Joshua gave it for an inheritance unto Israel according to their divisions by their tribes**. And the land rested from war.

Judges 7:12 And the Midianites and the Amalekites and all the children of the east lay along in the valley like grasshoppers for multitude; and their camels were **without number, as the sand by the sea side for multitude**.

1 Samuel 13:5 And the **Philistines gathered themselves together**

to fight with Israel, thirty thousand chariots, and six thousand horsemen, and **people as the sand which is on the sea shore in multitude**: and they came up, and pitched in Michmash, eastward from Bethaven.

SOLOMON'S WISDOM DESCRIBED AS SAND

1 Kings 4:20 Judah and **Israel were many, as the sand which is by the sea in multitude**, eating and drinking , and making merry. ... **29** And **God gave Solomon wisdom** and **understanding** exceeding much, and largeness of heart, even as the **sand that is on the sea shore**.

THE KINGDOM OF ISRAEL BECOMES UNITED

2 Samuel 5:1 Then came **all the tribes of Israel** [the 10 tribes of Israel, not the 2 tribes of Judah] to David unto Hebron, and spake, saying, Behold, **we are thy bone and thy flesh** [we are the non-Jewish sons of our father Jacob]. **2** Also in time past, when Saul was king over us, thou wast he that leddest out and broughtest in Israel: and the LORD said to thee, Thou shalt feed **my people Israel**, and **thou shalt be a captain over Israel** [David is already king over Judah].

3 So all the elders of Israel came to the king to Hebron; and king David made a league with them in Hebron before the LORD: and they anointed David king over Israel. **4** David was thirty years old when he began to reign, and he reigned forty years. **5 In Hebron he reigned over Judah** seven years and six months: and **in Jerusalem he reigned** thirty and three years **over all Israel and Judah** [even in the united kingdom there was still a distinction between Israel and Judah].

DAVID BRINGS THE ARK OF THE COVENANT TO JERUSALEM

2 Samuel 6:13 And it was so, that when they that bare the ark of the LORD had gone six paces, he sacrificed oxen and fatlings. **14** And David danced before the LORD with all his might; and David was girded with a linen ephod [the garment of the high priest]. **15** So David and **all the house of Israel** [*all the house of Israel* includes the 10 tribes of Israel as well as Judah (which includes Benjamin)] brought up the ark of the LORD with shouting, and with the sound of the trumpet. **16** And as the ark of the LORD came into the **city of David** ... **17** And they brought in the ark of the LORD, and set it in his place, in the midst of the tabernacle that David had pitched for it: and **David offered** burnt offerings and peace offerings before the LORD.

2 Samuel 7:1 And it came to pass, when the king [David] sat in his house, and the LORD had given him rest round about from all his enemies; **2** That the king said unto Nathan the prophet, See now, I dwell in an house of cedar, but the ark of God dwelleth within curtains. **3** And Nathan said to the king, Go, do all that is in thine heart; for the LORD is with thee.

7:4 And it came to pass that night, that the word of the LORD came unto Nathan, saying, **5** Go and tell my servant David, Thus saith the LORD, Shalt thou build me an house for me to dwell in? **6** Whereas I have not dwelt in any house since the time that I brought up the children of Israel out of Egypt [12 tribes came out of Egypt], even to this day, but have walked in a tent and in a tabernacle. **7** In all the places wherein I have walked with all the children of Israel spake I a word with any of the tribes of Israel, whom I commanded to feed **my people Israel**, saying, Why build ye not me an house of cedar?

8 Now therefore so shalt thou say unto my servant David, Thus saith the LORD of hosts, I took thee from the sheepcote, from following the sheep, to be ruler over my people, over Israel: **9** And I was with thee whithersoever thou wentest, and have cut off all thine enemies out of thy sight, and have made thee a great name, like unto the name of the great men that are in the the earth. ...

2 Samuel 7:12 And when thy days be fulfilled, and thou shalt sleep with thy fathers, **I will set up thy seed after thee**, which shall **proceed out of thy bowels**[39], and **I will establish his kingdom. 13 He shall build an house** for my name, and **I will stablish the throne of his kingdom for ever. 14** I will be his father, and he shall be my son. **If he commit iniquity** [this cannot possibly be the Messiah], I will chasten him with the rod of men, and with the stripes of the children of men: **15 But my mercy shall not depart away from him** [God's mercy never left Solomon; but as we shall see, God's promises to Solomon were conditional: His promises to David are eternal and without conditions], as I took it from Saul, whom I put away before thee.

16 And thine house[40] **and thy kingdom** shall **be established for**

---

39 *Bowels* speak of one's direct seed: the next generation. David at this point has not yet met Bathsheba, so Solomon has not been born.

40 The **house of David** is the house of Judah; the **kingdom of David** is the kingdom of Israel and Judah; and **the throne of David** is the scepter: which is the eternal right to rule over the 12 tribes of Israel (Genesis 49:10). But, when the kingdom becomes divided again, the

ever before thee: thy throne shall be established for ever [C/p. Jeremiah 33:21, below; Jeremiah 22:30, pg. 285]. **17** According to all these words, and according to all this vision, so did Nathan speak unto David.

DAVID RECEIVES HIS ETERNAL HOUSE

2 Samuel 7:18 Then went king David in, and sat before the LORD, and he said, Who am I, O Lord GOD? and what is my house, that thou hast brought me hitherto? ... **25** And now, O LORD God, the word that thou hast spoken concerning thy servant, and **concerning his house, establish it for ever**, and do as thou hast said. **26** And let thy name be magnified for ever, saying, The LORD of hosts is the God over Israel: and **let the house of thy servant David be established before thee.**

27 For thou, O LORD of hosts, God of Israel, **hast revealed to thy servant**, saying, I will build thee an house: therefore hath thy servant found in his heart to pray this prayer unto thee [when God reveals something to you, agree with it and pray it out]. **28** And now, O Lord GOD, thou art that God, and thy words be true, and thou hast promised this goodness unto thy servant: **29** Therefore now **let it please thee to bless the house of thy servant, that it may continue for ever** before thee: for thou, O Lord GOD, hast spoken it: and with thy blessing **let the house of thy servant be blessed for ever.**

DAVID HAS AN ETERNAL COVENANT WITH GOD

Jeremiah 33:19 And the word of the LORD came unto Jeremiah, saying, **20** Thus saith the LORD; If ye can break **my covenant of the day**, and **my covenant of the night**, and that there should not be day and night in their season; **21** Then may also **my covenant** be broken **with David my servant**, that he should not have **a son to reign upon his throne**-[C/p. 2 Samuel 7:16, above]; and with the Levites the priests, my ministers. **22** As the host of heaven cannot be numbered, neither the sand of the sea measured: **so will I multiply the seed of David my servant**, and the Levites that minister unto me [worshipers of God ... as well as the Levites in the third and fourth temples].

23 Moreover the word of the LORD came to Jeremiah, saying, **24** Considerest thou not what this people have spoken, saying, **The two families** [Israel and Judah] **which the LORD hath chosen, he hath even cast them off?** thus they have despised my people, **that they**

---

throne of David remained with Judah because ... "The scepter shall not depart from Judah ... until Shiloh (Messiah) comes" (Genesis 49:10). But again, since Judah has had no earthly king since returning from Babylonian captivity, where indeed is the throne of David today?

should be no more a nation before them. **25** Thus saith the LORD; If my covenant be not with day and night, and if I have not appointed the ordinances of heaven and earth; **26** Then will I cast away the **seed of Jacob** [12 tribes], and **David my servant** [God's promises to David], so that I will not take any of his seed to be rulers over the **seed of Abraham, Isaac, and Jacob** [12 tribes]: for **I will cause their captivity to return** [the captivity of both Israel and Judah in one nation on the mountains of Israel in fulfillment of Ezekiel 37], and have mercy on them.

The Messiah Has An Eternal Kingdom, House And Throne

1 Chronicles 17:11 And it shall come to pass, when thy days be expired that thou must go to be with thy fathers, that I will raise up **thy seed** after thee, which shall be **of thy sons** [not ... "out of your bowels" ... as in 2 Samuel 7:12 (pg. 264); but ... "of thy sons" ... which is a reference to future generations]; and <u>I will establish his kingdom</u>. **12** <u>He shall build me an house</u> [the temple of Ezekiel 40 to 48], and <u>I will stablish his throne for ever</u> [Messiah the Son of David]. **13** I will be his father, and he shall be my son: and I will not take my mercy away from him, as I took it from him that was before thee [King Saul]: **14** But I will settle him **in mine house** [God's house, not David's] and **in my kingdom** [the kingdom of heaven, not David's kingdom] **for ever**: and **his throne** [Messiah's throne in the temple and kingdom of God] **shall be established for evermore**.

Solomon Prays Before The LORD

2 Chronicles 1:6 And Solomon went up thither to the brasen altar before the LORD, which was at the tabernacle of the congregation, and **offered a thousand burnt offerings** upon it. **7** In that night did **God appear unto Solomon**, and said unto him, Ask what I shall give thee. **8** And Solomon said unto God, Thou hast shewed great mercy unto David my father, and hast made me to reign in his stead. **9** Now, O LORD God, let thy promise unto David my father be established: for **thou hast made me king over a <u>people like the dust of the earth</u> in multitude. 10** Give me now wisdom and knowledge, that I may go out and come in before this people: for who can judge this thy people, that is so great?

11 And God said to Solomon, Because this was in thine heart, and thou hast not asked riches, wealth, or honour, nor the life of thine enemies, neither yet hast asked long life; but hast asked wisdom and knowledge for thyself, that thou mayest **judge my people**, over whom I have made thee king: **12 Wisdom and knowledge is granted unto thee;**

and I will give thee riches, and wealth, and honour, such as none of the kings have had that have been before thee, neither shall there any after thee have the like.

God's Promises To Solomon Are Conditional

1 Kings 9:1 And it came to pass, when Solomon had finished the building of the house of the LORD, and the king's house, and all Solomon's desire which he was pleased to do, **2** That the **LORD appeared to Solomon the second time**, as he had appeared unto him at Gibeon. **3** And the LORD said unto him, I have heard thy prayer and thy supplication, that thou hast made before me: **I have hallowed this house**, which thou hast built, **to put my name there for ever**; and mine eyes and mine heart shall be there perpetually.

4 And **if thou wilt walk before me**, as David thy father walked [this is a conditional promise], in integrity of heart, and in uprightness, to do according to all that I have commanded thee, and wilt keep my statutes and my judgments: **5 Then I will establish the throne of thy kingdom upon Israel for ever,** as I promised to David thy father, saying, There shall not fail thee a man upon the **throne of Israel** [in a united kingdom reference is made to the **throne of Israel**; when the kingdom becomes divided the scepter of the throne is called the **throne of David** or **throne of Judah**].

6 But **if** [if the condition is not met] **ye shall at all turn from following me, ye or your children**, and will not keep my commandments and my statutes which I have set before you, but go and serve other gods, and worship them [which Solomon did when he was old]: **7 Then will I cut off Israel** [Israel here is a reference to 12 tribes, and all 12 eventually went into captivity] **out of the land; and this house** [the temple Solomon had built]**,** which I have hallowed for my name, **will I cast out of my sight** [God has destroyed His temple twice: first by the Babylonians and then by the Romans]; and Israel [all Israel] shall be a proverb and a byword among all people [which occurred between 70 CE and 1948]:

8 And at **this house** [Solomon's temple], which is high, every one that passeth by it shall be astonished, and shall hiss; and they shall say, **Why hath the LORD done thus unto this land, and to this house?** **9** And they shall answer, **Because they forsook the LORD their God**, who brought forth their fathers out of the land of Egypt, and have taken hold upon other gods, and have worshipped them, and served them: therefore hath the LORD brought upon them all this evil.

1 Kings 11:1 But king **Solomon loved many strange women**, together with the daughter of Pharaoh, women of the Moabites, Ammonites, Edomites, Zidonians, and Hittites; **2** Of the nations concerning which the LORD said unto the children of Israel, Ye shall not go in to them, neither shall they come in unto you: **for surely they will turn away your heart after their gods**: Solomon clave unto these in love. **3** And he had seven hundred wives, princesses, and three hundred concubines: and his wives turned away his heart.

4 For it came to pass, **when Solomon was old, that his wives turned away his heart after other gods**: and his heart was not perfect with the LORD his God, as was the heart of David his father. **5** For Solomon went after Ashtoreth the goddess of the Zidonians, and after Milcom the abomination of the Ammonites. **6** And **Solomon did evil in the sight of the LORD, and went not fully after the LORD, as did David his father**. **7** Then did Solomon build an high place for Chemosh, the abomination of Moab, in the hill that is before Jerusalem, and for Molech, the abomination of the children of Ammon. **8** And likewise did he for all his strange wives, which burnt incense and sacrificed unto their gods.

9 And **the LORD was angry with Solomon**, because his heart was turned from the LORD God of Israel, which had appeared unto him twice, **10** And had commanded him concerning this thing, that he should not go after other gods: but he kept not that which the LORD commanded. **11** Wherefore **the LORD said unto Solomon**, Forasmuch as this is done of thee, and thou hast not kept my covenant and my statutes, which I have commanded thee, **I will surely rend the kingdom from thee**, and will give it to thy servant [Jeroboam of the tribe of Ephraim].

JUDAH AND JERUSALEM RECEIVE GOD'S MERCY

1 Kings 11:12 Notwithstanding in thy days I will not do it for David thy father's sake: but I will rend it out of the hand of thy son [Rehoboam]. **13** Howbeit **I will not rend away all the kingdom; but will give <u>one tribe</u>** to thy son **for David my servant's sake**, and **for Jerusalem's**[41] **sake** which I have chosen.

14 And **the LORD stirred up an adversary** unto Solomon, Hadad

---

41 The southern kingdom of Judah and Jerusalem are to remain with the royal line of David because of God's mercy, and His promises to David.

the Edomite: he was of the king's seed in Edom [remember: Esau is Edom]. ... **23** And **God stirred him up another adversary**, Rezon the son of Eliadah, which fled from his lord Hadadezer king of Zobah: ...

God Gives The Throne Of Israel To Joseph

1 Kings 11:26 And **Jeroboam** the son of Nebat, **an Ephrathite** [of the tribe of Ephraim] of Zereda, Solomon's servant ... even he lifted up his hand against the king [King Solomon]. **27** And this was the cause that he lifted up his hand against the king: Solomon built Millo, and repaired the breaches of the city of David his father. **28** And the man Jeroboam was a mighty man of valour: and **Solomon** seeing the young man that he was industrious, **he made him ruler over all the charge of the house of Joseph**[42]. **29** And it came to pass at that time when Jeroboam went out of Jerusalem, that the prophet Ahijah the Shilonite found him in the way; and he had clad himself with a new garment [David's united kingdom]; and they two were alone in the field:

30 And Ahijah caught the new garment [David's united kingdom] that was on him, and **rent it in twelve pieces** [representing the 12 tribes of Israel]: **31** And he said to Jeroboam, **Take thee ten pieces** [the northern kingdom of Israel]: for **thus saith the LORD**, the God of Israel, Behold, **I will rend the kingdom out of the hand of Solomon, and will give ten tribes to thee**: **32** (But **he** [Solomon] **shall have one tribe** for my servant David's sake, and for Jerusalem's sake, the city which I have chosen out of all the tribes of Israel:)

Ten Tribes For Israel; One Tribe For Judah

1 Kings 11:34 Howbeit I will not take the whole kingdom out of his hand [Solomon's]: but I will make him prince all the days of his life for David my servant's sake, whom I chose, because he kept my commandments and my statutes: **35** But **I will take the kingdom out of his son's hand** [Rehoboam]**, and will give it unto thee** [Jeroboam]**, even ten tribes** [the 10 tribes of Israel]. **36** And **unto his son will I give one tribe**[43] [the tribe of Judah]**, that David my servant may have a light alway before me in Jerusalem**[44], the city which I have chosen me to put my name there.

37 And I will take thee, and thou shalt reign according to all that thy soul desireth, and shalt be **king over Israel** [the northern kingdom

---

42 The half-tribes of Ephraim and Manasseh.
43 The tribe of Judah includes the tribe of Benjamin and the priestly tribe of Levi.
44 The tribe of Judah exists today because of the life of one man—King David.

of 10 tribes]. **38** And it shall be, <u>**if** thou wilt hearken unto all that I command thee</u> [God makes the same conditional promise to Jeroboam that He made to Solomon], and wilt walk in my ways, and do that is right in my sight, to keep my statutes and my commandments, as David my servant did; that I will be with thee, and build thee a sure house, as I built for David, and will give Israel unto thee. **39** And <u>**I will for this afflict the seed of David, but not for ever**</u>[45] [Judah is promised a future redemption].

Judah And Benjamin Face Israel And Ephraim

2 Chronicles 25:5 Moreover **Amaziah** [the king] **gathered Judah** together, and made them captains over thousands, and captains over hundreds, according to the houses of their fathers, throughout **all Judah and Benjamin**: and he numbered them from twenty years old and above, and found them three hundred thousand choice men, able to go forth to war, that could handle spear and shield. **6** He hired also an hundred thousand mighty men of valour **out of Israel** [the northern kingdom] for an hundred talents of silver. **7** But there came a man of God to him, saying, O king, let not **the army of Israel** go with thee; **for the LORD is not with <u>Israel</u>**, to wit, **with all the <u>children of Ephraim</u>**.

Isaiah 7:1 And it came to pass in the days of **Ahaz…king of Judah**, that Rezin **the king of Syria**, and Pekah…**king of Israel**, went up toward Jerusalem to war against it, but could not prevail against it. **2** And it was told **the house of David** [another name for the southern kingdom of Judah], saying, **Syria is confederate with Ephraim** [the 10 tribe northern kingdom of Israel] …

Samaria Becomes The Capitol Of Israel

2 Chronicles 28:7 And Zichri, a mighty man **of Ephraim** [the 10 tribe kingdom], slew Maaseiah the king's son, and Azrikam the governor of the house, and Elkanah that was next to the king. **8** And the **children of Israel** [here the term children of Israel refers solely to the 10 tribes] carried away captive of **their brethren** [of Judah] two hundred thousand, women, sons, and daughters, and took also away much spoil from them, and **brought the spoil to Samaria**.

Israel Has Two Houses

Isaiah 8:13 Sanctify the LORD of hosts himself; and let him be

---

45 These are the *sure mercies of David* (Psalms 89 and Isaiah 55:3).

your fear, and let him be your dread. **14** And he shall be for a sanctuary; but for a stone of stumbling and for a rock of offence to **both the houses of Israel** [the **house of Jacob** or **house of Israel** has **two houses**: first, is the **house of Israel**, which is also known as the **house of Joseph** or **house of Ephraim**; and second, is the **house of Judah** or the **house of David**], for a gin [a noose for catching animals] and for a snare to the inhabitants of Jerusalem.

THE HOUSE OF JACOB IS STILL CALLED ISRAEL

Isaiah 48:1 Hear ye this, **O house of Jacob, which are called by the name of Israel** [the 12 tribes of Jacob are stilled called by name of Israel: Jacob's new God-given name], and are **come forth out of the waters of Judah** [Ephraim, carried into captivity in Isaiah's day, was sustained by the fountain of the nation: Judah], which swear by the name of the LORD, and make mention of the **God of Israel**, but not in truth [their relationship with the true and living God became religion (whose root word means *bondage*) ... and then nothing], nor in righteousness. **2** For they call themselves of the holy city, and stay themselves upon the **God of Israel; The LORD of hosts is his name.**

EPHRAIM HAS BECOME NOT A PEOPLE

Isaiah 7:7 Thus saith the Lord GOD, It shall not stand, neither shall it come to pass. **8** For the **head of Syria is Damascus** [its capital city], and the head of Damascus is Rezin [its king]; and **within threescore and five years shall Ephraim be broken** [the 10 tribes are to be carried off into Assyrian captivity within 65 years], **that it be not a people** [they will lose their Hebrew identity]. **9** And **the head of Ephraim is Samaria** [the capital city of the northern kingdom of Israel] ...

Hosea 1:4 And the LORD said unto him, **Call his name Jezreel** [God will scatter or sow]; for yet a little while, and **I will ... cause to cease the kingdom of the house of Israel** ... **6** for I will no more have mercy upon the house of Israel [Ephraim]; but I will utterly take them away ... **9** Then said God, Call his name Loammi [not my people]: for **ye are not my people, and I will not be your God.**

10 Yet the number of the children of Israel shall be as the sand of the sea, which cannot be measured nor numbered [these are the multitudes of Ephraim and Manasseh: because at no time in history have the Jews ever been so many that they could not be measured or numbered]; and it shall come to pass, that **in the place** [in the multitude of nations in the middle of the earth where they have been scattered (Isaiah

14:1-2, pg. 273; 1 Chronicles 17:9)] **where it was said unto them, <u>Ye are not my people</u>** [because their Hebrew identity has been lost], **<u>there it shall be said unto them, Ye are the sons of the living God</u>** [God will send prophets and preachers unto them in the latter years with the message of their lost heritage ... that they may rediscover their destiny].

Hosea 2:23 And **<u>I will sow her</u>** [Ephraim] **<u>unto me</u>** [God has sown His people unto Himself] in the earth; and **I will have mercy** upon her that had not obtained mercy; and **I will say** [at the appointed time God, Himself, will speak] **to them which were <u>not my people</u>, Thou art my people**; and they shall say, **Thou art my God** [when Ephraim rediscovers her identity in the latter days ... beginning with Ezekiel 37].

Amos 9:7 ... **O children of Israel?** [a reference to the 10 tribes] ... **8** Behold, the eyes of the Lord GOD are upon the sinful kingdom, and **I will destroy it from off the face of the earth** [Ephraim will completely lose its Hebrew identity]; **saving that I will not utterly destroy the house of Jacob** [the 10 tribes shall be destroyed as a nation while Judah shall be saved for David's sake]**, saith the LORD. 9** For, lo, I will command, and **I will sift the house of Israel** [the 10 tribes] **among all nations** [Ephraim scattered with his lost Hebrew identity has grown into a company of nations with the blessing of Joseph: whose people have become as dust of the earth, stars of heaven, and sand of the sea.]

ISRAEL RECEIVES A FAMINE IN HEARING THE WORD OF GOD

Amos 8:1 Thus hath the Lord GOD shewed unto me: and behold a basket of summer fruit. **2** And he said, Amos, what seest thou? And I said, A basket of summer fruit. Then said the LORD unto me, **The end is come upon <u>my people of Israel</u>** [the 10 tribes]; I will not again pass by them any more ... **11** Behold, the days come, saith the Lord GOD, that I will send **<u>a famine</u>** in the land, not a famine of bread, nor a thirst for water, but **<u>of hearing the words of the LORD</u>** [the 10 tribes have lost their Hebrew identity]:

ISRAEL SHALL WANDER FROM SEA TO SEA

Amos 8:12 And **they shall <u>wander from sea to sea</u>** [the 10 tribes were last seen in the areas of Assyria and Babylon (today's Iraq) ... but, there are no seas in this region of the earth], and [wander] **<u>from the north even to the east</u>** [wander from the north of what to the east of where ... perhaps as a company of seafaring nations?], they shall run to and fro to seek the word of the LORD, and shall not find it [until finally they stop seeking the Jehovah of Israel at all]

THE 10 TRIBES SHALL HAVE THEIR OWN RESTING PLACE

2 Samuel 7:10 Moreover **I will** [future tense] **appoint** [set, ordain, establish] **a place** [a fixed location ... the multitude of nations in the middle of the earth where they have been scattered **for my people Israel** [the **10 tribes** of the northern kingdom of Israel], **and will plant** [establish] **them**, that they may **dwell** [settle down to abide] **in a place** [Hosea 1:10; 1 Chronicles 17:9; Zechariah 10:6-10] **of their own**, and **move no more**; neither shall the children of wickedness [when the 10 tribes of Israel are planted in their "place", there will still be wicked children in the earth] afflict them any more, as beforetime, **11** And as since the time that I commanded judges to be over my people Israel, and have caused thee to rest from all thine enemies. Also the LORD telleth thee that **he will make thee an house** [the house of David].

1 Chronicles 17:9 Also I will ordain a place for my people Israel, and will plant them, and they shall dwell in their place, and shall be moved no more, neither shall the children of wickedness waste them any more, as at the beginning.

ISRAEL SHALL RULE OVER THEIR OPPRESSORS

Isaiah 14:1 For the LORD will have **mercy on Jacob**, and **will yet choose Israel** [a reference to the 10 tribes taken into Assyrian captivity during Isaiah's lifetime], and **set them in their own land** [a place ... a company on nations in the midst of the earth]: and the strangers shall be joined with them [intermarriage with Gentiles], and they shall cleave to the **house of Jacob** [the people in these new lands would become one with the 10 tribes, as these Hebrew people lose their identity with Israel].

2 And the people [Gentiles] shall take them, and bring them to **their place** [in these new nations]: and the **house of Israel shall possess them in the land of the LORD** [God here claims for Himself, and for Israel, this company of nations in the middle of the earth populated by His people without knowing they are His] for servants and handmaids: and **they shall take them captives, whose captives they were**, and **they shall rule over their oppressors** [Joseph and Ephraim will come to rule in the nations to which they are scattered].

EPHRAIM SHALL BE BROKEN

Isaiah 7:1 And it came to pass in the days of **Ahaz ... king of Judah**, that Rezin **the king of Syria**, and Pekah ... **king of Israel**, went up toward Jerusalem to war against it, but could not prevail against it. **2** And it was told the **house of David** [another name for the southern kingdom of Judah], saying, **Syria is confederate with Ephraim** [the 10 tribe nation of Israel]. ... **3** Then said the LORD unto Isaiah, Go forth now to meet Ahaz ... **4** And say unto him, Take heed, and be quiet; fear not, neither be fainthearted for ...

7 Thus saith the Lord GOD, It shall not stand, neither shall it come to pass. **8** For the **head of Syria is Damascus** [its capital city], and the head of Damascus is Rezin [its king]; and **within threescore and five years shall Ephraim be broken** [carried off into Assyrian captivity], **that it be not a people** [they will lose their Hebrew identity]. **9** And **the head of Ephraim is Samaria** [the capital city of the northern kingdom of Israel].

ISAIAH PROPHESIED TO MANY NATIONS

Isaiah 1:1 The vision of Isaiah the son of Amoz, which he saw **concerning Judah and Jerusalem** in the days of Uzziah, Jotham, Ahaz, and Hezekiah, kings of Judah. ...

Isaiah 15:1 The burden of **Moab** ...
Isaiah 18:1 Woe to the land shadowing with wings, which is beyond the rivers of **Ethiopia** ...
Isaiah 19:1 The burden of **Egypt** ...
Isaiah 23:1 The burden of **Tyre** ...
Isaiah 34:1 Come near **ye nations** to hear and hearken ye people: let the earth hear, and all that is therein; the world, and all things that become forth of it.
Isaiah 47:1 Come down, and sit in the dust, O virgin daughter of **Babylon** ...

A FINAL JUDGMENT ON EPHRAIM WHILE IN THE LAND

Hosea 9:11 As for **Ephraim, their glory shall fly away like a bird**, from the birth, and from the womb, and from the conception. **12** Though they bring up their children, yet will I bereave them, that there shall not be a man left: yea, woe also to them when I depart from them! **13** Ephraim, as I saw Tyrus, is planted in a pleasant place: but Ephraim shall bring forth his children to the murderer. **14** Give them, O LORD: what wilt thou give? give them a miscarrying womb and dry breasts. **15** All their wickedness is in Gilgal: for there I hated them: for the wickedness of their doings I will drive them out of mine house, I will love them no more: all their princes are revolters.

16 Ephraim is smitten, their root is dried up, they shall bear no fruit: yea, though they bring forth, yet will I slay even the beloved fruit of their womb. **17 My God will cast them away, because they did not hearken unto him: and they shall be wanderers among the nations** [but this Scripture does not say that Ephraim's condition in the nations shall last forever ... because God has spoken other prophesies over Ephraim which must also be fulfilled].

Ephraim Is Cast Out And Shall Be Regathered

Hosea 1:2 The beginning of the word of the LORD by Hosea. And the LORD said to Hosea, Go, **take unto thee a wife of whoredoms** [a picture of the backsliding northern kingdom of Israel] and **children of whoredoms**: for the land hath committed great whoredom, departing from the LORD. **3** So he went and took Gomer the daughter of Diblaim; which conceived, and bare him a son.

4 And the LORD said unto him, **Call his name Jezreel** [God will scatter or sow]; for yet a little while, and I will avenge the blood of Jezreel upon the house of Jehu, and **will cause to cease the kingdom of the house of Israel** [the term *house of Israel* here refers to Ephraim and the 10 tribes of Israel: which were to be carried into Assyrian captivity]. **5** And it shall come to pass at that day, that I will break the bow of Israel in the **valley of Jezreel** [valley of the scattered ones].

6 And she conceived again, and bare a daughter. And God said unto him, **Call her name Loruhamah** [I will have mercy no more; or I will not have compassion]: for **I will no more have mercy upon the house of Israel; but I will utterly take them away** [into Assyrian captivity].

7 But I will have mercy upon the house of Judah [God remembers His covenant of mercy with David[46]], **and will save them by the LORD their God** [Judah's salvation was by a sovereign act of God], and will not save them by bow, nor by sword, nor by battle, by horses, nor by horsemen. **8** Now when she had weaned Loruhamah, she conceived, and bare a son.

Joseph And Ephraim Become A Numberless Multitude

Hosea 1:9 Then said God, Call his name Loammi [not my people]: **for ye are not my people, and I will not be your God** [they would lose

---

46 Psalms 89:20, 24 and 28.

their Hebrew identity]. **10 Yet the number of the children of Israel** [here a reference to the descendants of the 10 tribe northern kingdom] **shall be as the sand of the sea, which cannot be measured nor numbered** [there have never been too many Jews in the world to count; but God's hidden Hebrew people are numberless]; and it shall come to pass, that **in the place**[47] [in the place where the 10 tribes have been scattered] where it was said unto them, Ye are not my people, here it shall be said unto them, Ye are the sons of the living God [when they discover their Hebrew identity].

GOD WILL HARVEST THE LOST SEED OF ISRAEL

Hosea 2:23 And **I will sow her unto me** [the northern kingdom of the 10 tribes of Israel] in the earth; and **I will have mercy** upon her that had not obtained mercy [in the passage of time, God will recover the Hebrew seed that He has sown ... multiplied an hundredfold]; and I will say to them which were not my people [not His people because they have lost their Hebrew identity], **Thou art my people**; and they shall say, **Thou art my God**.

EPHRAIM IS SIFTED BUT NOT LOST

Amos[48] **9:7** Are ye not as children of the Ethiopians unto me, **O children of Israel** [Amos was a prophet to the 10 tribes of the northern kingdom of Israel]? saith the LORD. Have not I brought up Israel out of the land of Egypt? ... **8 Behold, the eyes of the Lord GOD are upon the sinful kingdom, and I will destroy it from off the face of the earth** [the northern kingdom of Israel will completely lose its Hebrew identity]; **saving that I will not utterly destroy the house of Jacob** [only 10 of the 12 tribes of Jacob would be banished out of God's sight]**, saith the LORD.**

9 For, lo, **I will command**, and **I will sift the house of Israel** [the 10 tribes of the northern kingdom] **among all nations**, like as corn is sifted in a sieve, **yet shall not the least grain fall upon the earth** [not one person of the 10 tribes of Israel is hidden or lost from the eyes or mercy of God].

ISRAEL IS CARRIED INTO CAPTIVITY BY ASSYRIA

2 Kings 17:1 In the twelfth year of Ahaz king of Judah began Hoshea the son of Elah **to reign in Samaria over Israel nine years. 2**

---

47   2 Samuel 7:10 and Isaiah 14:1-2.

48   Amos was a prophet to the 10 tribes of the northern kingdom of Israel.

And he did that which was evil in the sight of the LORD, but not as the kings of Israel that were before him [he did greater evil than ever before in Israel]. **3** Against him came up **Shalmaneser king of Assyria**; ...

5 Then the king of Assyria came up throughout all the land, and went up to Samaria, and besieged it three years. **6** In the ninth year of Hoshea **the king of Assyria took Samaria**, and **carried Israel away into Assyria**, and placed them in Halah and in Habor by the river of Gozan, and in the cities of the Medes.

JOSEPHUS RECORDS THE MULTITUDES OF EPHRAIM

"The Ten Tribes are beyond the Euphrates till now, and are an immense multitude, not to be estimated by numbers"[49]

EPHRAIM AND ISRAEL ARE REJECTED BY GOD

2 Kings 17:7 For so it was, that the **children of Israel** [the northern kingdom is referred to here as the children of Israel] **had sinned against the LORD their God**, which had brought them up out of the land of Egypt, from under the hand of Pharaoh king of Egypt, and had feared other gods, **8** And walked in the statutes of the heathen, whom the LORD cast out from before the children of Israel, and of the kings of Israel, which they had made.

9 And the **children of Israel** did secretly those things that were not right against the LORD their God, and they built them high places in all their cities, from the tower of the watchmen to the fenced city. **10** And they set them up images and groves in every high hill, and under every green tree: **11** And there they burnt incense in all the high places, as did the heathen whom the LORD carried away before them; and wrought wicked things to provoke the LORD to anger: **12** For they served idols, whereof the LORD had said unto them, Ye shall not do this thing.

13 Yet the LORD testified **against Israel**, and **against Judah** [the Hebrew prophets knew the distinction between Israel and Judah], by all the prophets, and by all the seers, saying, **Turn ye from your evil ways**, and keep my commandments and my statutes, according to all the law which I commanded your fathers, and which I sent to you by my servants the prophets. **14** Notwithstanding they would not hear, but hardened their necks, like to the neck of their fathers, that did not believe in the LORD their God.

---

49 <u>Antiquities</u>, XI, V, 2.

15 And they [the northern kingdom] **rejected his statutes, and his covenant** that he made with their fathers [Abraham, Isaac and Jacob], and **his testimonies** which he testified against them; and they followed vanity, and became vain, and went after the heathen that were round about them, concerning whom the LORD had charged them, that they should not do like them.

16 And they left all the commandments of the LORD their God, and made them molten images, even two calves, and made a grove, and worshipped all the host of heaven, and served Baal. **17** And they **caused their sons and their daughters to pass through the fire**, and **used divination and enchantments**, and sold themselves to do evil in the sight of the LORD, to provoke him to anger.

18 Therefore the **LORD was very angry with Israel** [the 10 tribes], and **removed them out of his sight**: there was **none left** [in His sight] **but the tribe of Judah** only [Judah and Benjamin]. **19** Also **Judah** kept not the commandments of the LORD their God, but **walked in the statutes of Israel** which they made [Judah did all the sins of Israel; but for David's sake God had mercy on Judah].

20 And the **LORD rejected all the seed of Israel** [including the kingly line of Ephraim], and afflicted them, and delivered them into the hand of spoilers, until **he had cast them out of his sight**. **21** For **he rent Israel from the house of David** [the tribe of Judah]; and they made Jeroboam the son of Nebat king: and **Jeroboam drave Israel from following the LORD**, and made them sin a great sin.

22 For the children of Israel walked in all the sins of Jeroboam which he did; they departed not from them; **23** Until the **LORD removed Israel out of his sight**, as he had **said by all his servants the prophets**. So was **Israel** [the 10 tribes] **carried away out of their own land to Assyria unto this day**[50].

JUDAH REPRESENTS ISRAEL BUT IS NOT ALL ISRAEL

2 Chronicles 11:1 And when Rehoboam [King Solomon's son] was come to Jerusalem, he gathered of the **house of Judah and Benjamin** an hundred and fourscore thousand chosen men, which were war-

---

50 **Unto this day** is a technical term used in Bible history to indicate a condition which will last at least until the coming of the Messiah to reign on the earth. Here, by listening to the writer of Second Kings (Jeremiah) as if it were commentary on the evening news, the message is clear—a multitude of the descendants of the 10 tribes of Israel are still in the lands formerly ruled by Assyria.

278

riors, **to fight against Israel** [Israel or Ephraim], that he might bring the kingdom again to Rehoboam [to have a unified kingdom like David and Solomon].

11:2 But the word of the LORD came to Shemaiah the man of God, saying, **3** Speak unto Rehoboam the son of Solomon, king of Judah, and to **all Israel in Judah and Benjamin** [all of Israel that at this time was physically present in the territories of Judah and Benjamin], saying, **4** Thus saith the LORD, Ye shall not go up, <u>**nor fight against your brethren**</u> [their Hebrew brethren]: return every man to his house: for <u>**this thing is done of me**</u> [it is God that divided the kingdom of Israel from the kingdom of Judah]. And they obeyed the words of the LORD, and returned from going against Jeroboam.

REPRESENTATIVES OF ALL ISRAEL WERE PRESENT WITH JUDAH

2 Chronicles 31:1 Now when all this was finished, <u>**all Israel that were present**</u> [all Israel that were present at this time with Judah … not all Israel] went out to the cities of Judah, and brake the images in pieces, and cut down the groves, and threw down the high places and the altars out of **all Judah and Benjamin**, in **Ephraim** also and **Manasseh**, until they had utterly destroyed them all. … **6** And concerning the **children of Israel** and **Judah**, that dwelt in the cities of Judah, they also brought in the tithe of oxen and sheep, and the tithe of holy things which were consecrated unto the LORD their God, and laid them by heaps.

2 Chronicles 34:1 Josiah was eight years old when he began to reign, and he reigned in Jerusalem one and thirty years. **2** And he did that which was right in the sight of the LORD, and walked in the ways of David his father, and declined neither to the right hand, nor to the left. **3** For in the eighth year of his reign, while he was yet young, he began to seek after the God of David his father: and in the twelfth year he began to **purge Judah and Jerusalem** from the high places, and the groves, and the carved images, and the molten images. …

6 And so did he in the cities of **Manasseh**, and **Ephraim**, and **Simeon**, even unto **Naphtali**, with their mattocks round about. … **9** And when they came to Hilkiah the high priest, they delivered the money that was brought into the house of God, which the Levites that kept the doors had gathered of the hand of **Manasseh** and **Ephraim**, and of **all the remnant of Israel** [the remnant escaped from Assyrian captivity], and of **all Judah and Benjamin**; and they returned to Jerusalem.

2 Chronicles 35:16 So all the service of the LORD was prepared the same day, to keep the passover, and to offer burnt offerings upon the altar of the LORD, according to the commandment of king Josiah. **17** And **the children of Israel that were present kept the passover** at that time, and the feast of unleavened bread seven days. **18** And there was no passover like to that kept in Israel from the days of Samuel the prophet; neither did all the kings of Israel keep such a passover as Josiah kept, and the priests, and the Levites, and **all Judah and Israel that were present** [there was a representative sample of all Israel present ... but the multitude of the 10 tribes were in captivity and not present], and the **inhabitants of Jerusalem**.

THE PRIESTHOOD RETURNS TO JERUSALEM

2 Chronicles 11:5 And Rehoboam dwelt in Jerusalem, and built cities for defence in Judah. **... 13** And **the priests and the Levites that were in all Israel** resorted to him out of all their coasts. **14** For the Levites left their suburbs and their possession, and came to Judah and Jerusalem: for **Jeroboam** and his sons had **cast them off from executing the priest's office** unto the LORD [Israel begins its apostasy]: **15** And he ordained him priests for the high places, and for the devils, and for the calves which he had made.

THE RIGHTEOUS OF THE NATION ALSO COME TO JERUSALEM

2 Chronicles 11:16 And after them **out of all the tribes of Israel such as set their hearts to seek the LORD God of Israel came to Jerusalem**, to sacrifice unto the LORD God of their fathers. **17** So they strengthened the kingdom of Judah, and made Rehoboam the son of Solomon strong, three years: for three years they walked in the way of David and Solomon [and then Rehoboam begins to turn himself and the people of Judah away from God].

JUDAH REACHES OUT TO ISRAEL

2 Chronicles 30:1 And Hezekiah [king of Judah] sent to **all Israel** and **Judah**, and wrote letters also to **Ephraim** and **Manasseh**, that they should come to the house of the LORD at Jerusalem, to keep the passover unto the LORD God of Israel. **2** For the king had taken counsel, and his princes, and all the congregation in Jerusalem, to keep the passover in the second month. **... 5** So they established a decree to make proclamation throughout all Israel, from Beersheba even to Dan, that they should come to **keep the passover** unto the LORD God of Israel at Jerusalem: for **they had not done it of a long time in such sort as it was written**.

280

6 So the posts went with the letters from the king and his princes throughout **all Israel and Judah,** and according to the commandment of the king, saying, **Ye children of Israel, turn again unto the LORD God of Abraham, Isaac, and Israel, and he will return to the remnant of you, that are escaped out of the hand of the kings of Assyria** [there was a remnant back in the land that had escaped from Assyria].

7 And be not ye like your fathers, and like your brethren, which trespassed against the LORD God of their fathers, who therefore gave them up to desolation, as ye see. **8** Now **be ye not stiffnecked, as your fathers were,** but yield yourselves unto the LORD, and enter into his sanctuary, which he hath sanctified for ever: and serve the LORD your God, that the fierceness of his wrath may turn away from you. **9 For if ye turn again unto the LORD, your brethren and your children shall find compassion before them that lead them captive, so that they shall come again into this land:** for the LORD your God is gracious and merciful, and will not turn away his face from you, **if ye return unto him** [the repentance of a few could have delivered all of Israel.]

10 So the posts passed from city to city **through the country of Ephraim and Manasseh** even unto Zebulun: but they laughed them to scorn, and mocked them. **11** Nevertheless divers of **Asher** and **Manasseh** and of **Zebulun** [tribes of the northern kingdom] humbled themselves, and came to Jerusalem. **12** Also in Judah the hand of God was to give them one heart to do the commandment of the king and of the princes, by the word of the LORD. **13** And there assembled at Jerusalem much people to keep the feast of unleavened bread in the second month, a very great congregation.

14 And they arose and took away the altars that were in Jerusalem, and all the altars for incense took they away, and cast them into the brook Kidron. **15** Then they killed the passover on the fourteenth day of the second month: and the priests and the Levites were ashamed, and sanctified themselves, and brought in the burnt offerings into the house of the LORD. **16** And they stood in their place after their manner, **according to the law of Moses the man of God**: the priests sprinkled the blood, which they received of the hand of the Levites. **17** For there were many in the congregation that were not sanctified: therefore the Levites had the charge of the killing of the passovers for every one that was not clean, to sanctify them unto the LORD.

18 For a multitude of the people, even many of **Ephraim**, and **Manasseh, Issachar,** and **Zebulun**, had not cleansed themselves, yet did they eat the passover otherwise than it was written. But Hezekiah prayed for them, saying, The good LORD pardon every one **19** That prepareth his heart to seek God, the LORD God of his fathers, though he be not cleansed according to the purification of the sanctuary. **20** And the LORD hearkened to Hezekiah, and healed the people.

21 And the **children of Israel that were present at Jerusalem** kept the feast of unleavened bread seven days with great gladness: and the Levites and the priests praised the LORD day by day, singing with loud instruments unto the LORD. ... **25** And all the **congregation of Judah**, with the priests and the Levites, and all the **congregation that came out of Israel**, and the strangers that came out of the land of Israel, and that dwelt in Judah, rejoiced.

26 So there was great joy in Jerusalem: for since the time of Solomon the son of David king of Israel there was not the like in Jerusalem. **27** Then the priests the Levites arose and blessed the people: and their voice was heard, and their prayer came up to his holy dwelling place, even unto heaven.

2 Chronicles 31:1 Now when all this was finished, **all Israel that were present** [those from the northern kingdom that were resident in Judah, and the remnant that were escaped of Assyria] went out to the **cities of Judah**, and brake the images in pieces, and cut down the groves, and threw down the high places and the altars out of all **Judah** and **Benjamin**, in **Ephraim** also and **Manasseh**, until they had utterly destroyed them all. Then **all the children of Israel returned**, every man to his possession, into their own cities [in Judah and Israel].

2 Chronicles 34:8 Now in the eighteenth year of his reign [King Josiah], when he had purged the land, and the house, he sent Shaphan the son of Azaliah, and Maaseiah the governor of the city, and Joah the son of Joahaz the recorder, to repair the house of the LORD his God. **9** And when they came to Hilkiah the high priest, they delivered the money that was brought into the house of God, which the Levites that kept the doors had gathered of the **hand of Manasseh** and **Ephraim**, and of **all the remnant of Israel** [those that were escaped of Assyria], and of **all Judah and Benjamin**; and they returned to Jerusalem.

A New Wave Of Idolatry Infects The Remnant Of Israel

2 Kings 17:24 And the **king of Assyria brought men from Babylon**, and from Cuthah, and from Ava, and from Hamath, and from Sepharvaim, and **placed them in the cities of Samaria instead of**

the children of Israel: and **they possessed Samaria** [capital of the northern kingdom], and dwelt in the cities thereof.

25 And so it was at the beginning of their dwelling there, that **they feared not the LORD: therefore the LORD sent lions** among them, which slew some of them. **26** Wherefore they spake to the king of Assyria, saying, The nations which thou hast removed, and placed in the cities of Samaria, know not the manner of the God of the land: therefore he hath sent lions among them, and, behold, they slay them, because **they know not the manner of the God of the land**.

27 Then the king of Assyria commanded, saying, Carry thither **one of the priests** whom ye brought from thence; and let them go and dwell there, and let him teach them the manner of the God of the land. **28** Then one of the priests whom they had carried away from Samaria came and dwelt in Bethel, and **taught them how they should fear the LORD**.

29 Howbeit every nation made gods of their own [a new wave of idolatry in the lands of the northern kingdom], and put them in the houses of the high places which the Samaritans had made, every nation in their cities wherein they dwelt. **30** And the men of Babylon made Succothbenoth, and the men of Cuth made Nergal, and the men of Hamath made Ashima, **31** And the Avites made Nibhaz and Tartak, and the Sepharvites burnt their children in fire to Adrammelech and Anammelech, the gods of Sepharvaim.

32 So they feared the LORD [they were afraid of the LORD because of the lions]**, and made unto themselves of the lowest of them priests** of the high places, which sacrificed for them in the houses of the high places. **33** They feared the LORD [they knew the true and living God], and served their own gods [yet they served other gods], after the manner of the nations whom they carried away from thence.

34 <u>Unto this day</u> **they do after the former manners: they fear not the LORD** [their fear of God produces no change in their lives], neither do they after their statutes, or after their ordinances, or after the law and commandment which the LORD commanded the **children of Jacob, whom he named Israel**; **35** With whom the LORD had made a covenant, and charged them, saying, Ye shall not fear other gods, nor bow yourselves to them, nor serve them, nor sacrifice to them:

36 But the LORD, who brought you up out of the land of Egypt with great power and a stretched out arm, him shall ye fear, and him shall ye worship, and to him shall ye do sacrifice. **37** And the statutes, and the ordinances, and the law, and the commandment, which he wrote for you, ye shall observe to do for evermore; and ye shall not fear other gods. **38** And **the covenant that I have made with you ye shall not forget; neither shall ye fear other gods**.

39 But the LORD your God ye shall fear; and he shall deliver you out of the hand of all your enemies. **40** <u>**Howbeit they did not hearken, but they did after their former manner**</u>. **41** So these nations feared the LORD [they knew of God], and served their graven images, both their children, and their children's children: as did their fathers, **so do they** <u>**unto this day**</u> [and some of these are Hebrews of Ephraim with a lost knowledge of their Hebrew heritage].

ISRAEL SERVES OTHER GODS IN THE LANDS OF ASSYRIA

2 Kings 18:11 And **the king of Assyria did carry away Israel unto Assyria, and put them** in Halah and in Habor by the river of Gozan [northern Iraq], and **in the cities of the Medes**: **12** Because they obeyed not the voice of the LORD their God, but transgressed his covenant, and all that Moses the servant of the LORD commanded, and would not hear them, nor do them.

1 Chronicles 5:26 And the **God of Israel** stirred up the spirit of Pul **king of Assyria**, and the spirit of Tilgathpilneser **king of Assyria**, and he **carried them away**, even the **Reubenites** [the tribe of Reuben], and the **Gadites** [the tribe of Gad], and the **half tribe of Manasseh**, and brought them unto Halah, and Habor, and Hara, and **to the river Gozan**, <u>**unto this day**</u> [further evidence of where a portion of Joseph and Ephraim can be found today].

JUDAH IS WARNED OF ITS COMING CAPTIVITY

Jeremiah 7:15 And <u>**I will cast you out of my sight**</u> [Judah's captivity is coming], **as I have cast out all your brethren, even the whole seed of Ephraim**.

JUDAH SHALL ALSO BE SCATTERED THROUGHOUT THE EARTH

Jeremiah 15:1 Then said the LORD unto me, Though Moses and Samuel stood before me, yet my mind could not be toward this people: cast them out of my sight, and let them go forth. ... **4** And <u>**I will cause them to be removed into all kingdoms of the earth**</u> [this is the Diaspora of Jews], because of Manasseh the son of Hezekiah king of **Judah**, for

284

that which he did in Jerusalem. ... **7** And ... **I will destroy my people** [as a nation], since they return not from their ways. **8 Their widows are increased to me above the sand of the seas** ...

God Curses The Royal Line Of David

Jeremiah 22:1 Thus saith the LORD; Go down to the **house of the king of Judah**, and speak there this word, **2** And say, Hear the word of the LORD, <u>**O king of Judah, that sittest upon the throne of David**</u>[51], thou, and thy servants, and thy people that enter in by these gates: **3** Thus saith the LORD; Execute ye judgment and righteousness, and deliver the spoiled out of the hand of the oppressor: and do no wrong, do no violence to the stranger, the fatherless, nor the widow, neither shed innocent blood in this place.

4 For if ye do this thing indeed, then shall there enter in by the gates of this house **kings sitting upon the throne of David**, riding in chariots and on horses, he, and his servants, and his people. **5** But if ye will not hear these words, <u>**I swear by myself**</u>, saith the LORD, that **this house shall become a desolation** [the house of the kings of Judah].

Jeremiah 22:24 As I live, saith the LORD, though **Coniah**[52] the **son of Jehoiakim king of Judah** were the signet upon my right hand, yet would I pluck thee thence; **25** And **I will give thee into the hand of them that seek thy life**, and into the hand of them whose face thou fearest, **even into the hand of Nebuchadrezzar king of Babylon**, and into the hand of the Chaldeans. **26** And I will cast thee out, and thy mother that bare thee, into another country, where ye were not born; and there shall ye die.

27 But to the land whereunto they desire to return, thither shall they not return. **28** Is this man Coniah a despised broken idol? is he a vessel wherein is no pleasure? wherefore are they cast out, he and his seed, and are cast into a land which they know not? **29** O earth, earth, earth, hear the word of the LORD. **30** Thus saith the LORD, **Write ye this man childless**, a man that shall not prosper in his days: <u>**for no man of his seed**</u> [the seed of Solomon] <u>**shall prosper, sitting upon the throne of David, and ruling any more in Judah**</u>[53].

---

51 In the divided kingdom, the throne of David remained with Judah.

52 God here takes His name away from the king of Judah. He leaves off the "Je" of King Jechoniah's [or Jehoiachin's] name—"Je" is the abbreviation of *Jehovah* in his name—indicating that God had left him.

53 Since its Babylonian captivity, Judah and now Israel have been ruled by governors and not kings ... unto this day [c/p. 2 Samuel 7:16; Jeremiah 33:21, pg. 264-265].

Judah Is Carried Into Babylonian Captivity

2 Kings 25:1 And it came to pass in the ninth year of his reign, in the tenth month, in the tenth day of the month, that **Nebuchadnezzar king of Babylon came**, he, and all his host, against Jerusalem, and pitched against it; and they built forts against it round about. **2** And the city was besieged unto the eleventh year of king Zedekiah [the last king of Judah to sit on the throne of David, until this day] … **7** And **they slew the sons of Zedekiah before his eyes, and put out the eyes of Zedekiah**, and bound him with fetters of brass, and **carried him to Babylon.**

25:8 And in the fifth month, on the seventh day of the month, which is the nineteenth year of king Nebuchadnezzar king of Babylon, came Nebuzaradan, captain of the guard, a servant of the king of Babylon, unto Jerusalem: **9** And **he burnt the house of the LORD**, and the king's house, and all the houses of Jerusalem, and every great man's house burnt he with fire. **10** And all the army of the Chaldees, that were with the captain of the guard, **brake down the walls of Jerusalem** round about.

Israel And Ephraim Are A Twice Sown Seed

Jeremiah 31:27 Behold, the days come, saith the LORD, that **I will sow** the **house of Israel** [this is a second and future sowing of the 10 tribes of Israel: because at the time of Jeremiah's prophecy the northern kingdom is already in Assyrian captivity] and the **house of Judah with the seed of man** [intermarriage of both Israel and Judah with locals while in foreign lands], and with the seed of beast [wars, famines, pestilences, etc.]. **28 And it shall come to pass,** that **like as** [in the same manner] I have watched over them, to pluck up, and to break down, and to throw down[54], and to destroy, and to afflict; **so will I watch over them, to build,** and **to plant** [build and plant them in the lands where they are sown, and shall be sown], **saith the LORD.**

Judah Is Also Sown A Second Time

Zechariah 10:6 And I will **strengthen** the <u>house of Judah</u> [who has just returned from Babylonian captivity during the time of Zechariah's ministry], and I will **save** the <u>house of Joseph</u> [Ephraim, Manasseh, and the 10 tribes of Israel], and I will bring them again <u>to place them</u>[55]; for **I have mercy upon them: and <u>they shall be as though I had not</u>**

---

54 Jeremiah 1:10.

55 Hosea 1:10; 2 Samuel 7:10; 1 Chronicles 17:9; Isaiah 14:1-2.

cast them off: for I am the LORD their God [the God of Judah and Joseph], and will hear them.

7　And **they of Ephraim**[56] shall be like a mighty man [Ephraim in his new locations shall become strong nations], and their heart shall rejoice as through wine: yea, their children shall see it, and be glad; their heart shall rejoice in the LORD. **8** I will hiss for them [they of Ephraim, or they of Ephraim and Judah], and gather them; for I have redeemed them: and they shall increase as they have increased [far, far more of Ephraim will return than were scattered; but true also of Judah].

9　**And I will sow** [God speaks of a future event from the time of Zechariah's prophecy] **them among the people** [this is clearly a second sowing of Ephraim: because at the time of this prophecy Ephraim is already in Assyrian captivity; but it can also indicate a second sowing of Judah by the Romans]: **and they shall remember me in far countries** [Ephraim shall discover his Hebrew heritage; and Judah shall remember his covenant with God]; and they shall live with their children, and turn again [to God]. **10 I will bring them again also out of** the land of **Egypt,** and gather them out of **Assyria**; and I will bring them into the land of Gilead and Lebanon; and place shall not be found for them [because of their multitude].

Isaiah 11:10　And in **that day** [when Messiah comes] there shall be **a root of Jesse**, which shall stand for an ensign [flag or banner] of the people; **to it Him shall the Gentiles seek**: and his rest shall be glorious. **11**　And it shall come to pass **in that day**, that **the Lord shall set his hand again the second time to recover the remnant of his people**, **which shall be left, from Assyria** [Iraq and southern Turkey], and from Egypt, and from Pathros [upper Egypt], and from Cush [Ethiopia], and from Elam [Iraq / western Iran], and from Shinar [Babylon / Iraq], and from Hamath [upper Syria / perhaps parts of southern Turkey], and **from the islands of the sea** [originally settled by the sons of Japheth[57]].

11:12　And he shall set up an ensign [a sign] for the nations, and shall **assemble the outcasts of Israel**, and gather together the **dispersed of Judah** from the four corners of the earth. ... **16** And there shall be **an highway for the remnant of his people**, which shall be left, **from Assyria**[58]; **like as** it was to Israel in the day that he came up out of the land

---

56　The stick of Joseph is in the hand of Ephraim (Ezekiel 37:16 and 19)

57　Genesis 10:5.

58　God still has a multitude of His people in the lands formerly ruled by Assyria. The Jewish historian, Josephus, has said that as late as 100 A.D. ... **"The Ten Tribes are beyond the Euphrates till now, and are an immense multitude, not to be estimated by numbers."**

of Egypt [the kings highway which came up from Sini to Jordan, and down from Iraq (Babylon) through Syria to Jordan and the mountains of Israel].

The Lord Has Sown His Most Precious Seed

Psalms 126:1 When the LORD turned again the captivity of Zion, we were like them that dream. **2** Then was our mouth filled with laughter, and our tongue with singing: then said they among the heathen, The LORD hath done great things for them. **3** The LORD hath done great things for us; whereof we are glad. **4** Turn again our captivity, O LORD, as the streams in the south. **5 They that sow in tears shall reap in joy** [God sowed His precious people with tears; He will reap them back with joy]. **6** He that goeth forth and weepeth, bearing precious seed, shall doubtless come again with rejoicing, bringing his sheaves with him.

God Will Reap What He Sows

Jeremiah 31:27 Behold, the days come, saith the LORD, that **I will sow** the <u>house of Israel</u> and the <u>house of Judah</u> **with the seed of man** [intermarriage], and with the seed of beast [wars, famine, persecution]. **28 And it shall come to pass, that like as** [in the same manner] I have watched over them, to pluck up, and to break down, and to throw down, and to destroy, and to afflict; <u>**so will I watch over them, to build, and to plant them even in the lands where they are sown**</u> [they shall prosper in their Diaspora: as Jews have always done; and as Ephraim has done in secret], **saith the LORD.**

Judah Shall Return Before Israel

Jeremiah 33:6 Behold, I will bring it health and cure, and I will cure them, and will reveal unto them the abundance of peace and truth. **7** And **I will cause** the <u>captivity of Judah</u> and the <u>captivity of Israel</u> **to return** [Judah returned to the land first after 70 years of Babylonian captivity; and returned again in 1948], **and will build them, as at the first** [beginning as a unified nation with the fulfillment of Ezekiel 37]. **8** And I will cleanse them from all their iniquity, whereby they have sinned against me; and I will pardon all their iniquities, whereby they have sinned, and whereby they have transgressed against me.

9 And it shall be to me a name of joy, a praise and an honour before all the nations of the earth, which shall hear all the good that I do unto them: and they shall fear and tremble **for all the goodness and for all the prosperity that I procure unto it** [the season of Israel's prosperity

288

culminating in **Ezekiel 38:8-14** is a direct result of the joining of Joseph, Ephraim and Judah that God has spoken in **Ezekiel 37:15-22**].

10 Thus saith the LORD; Again there shall be heard in this place, which ye say shall be desolate without man and without beast, even **in the cities of Judah**, and **in the streets of Jerusalem**, that are desolate, without man, and without inhabitant, and without beast [while Judah was in Babylonian captivity], **11** The voice of joy, and the voice of gladness, the voice of the bridegroom, and the voice of the bride, the voice of them that shall say, Praise the LORD of hosts: for the LORD is good; for his mercy endureth for ever: and of them that shall bring the sacrifice of praise into the house of the LORD. For **I will cause to return the captivity of the land**, as at the first, saith the LORD.

12 Thus saith the LORD of hosts; Again in this place, which is desolate without man and without beast, and in all the cities thereof, shall be an habitation of shepherds causing their flocks to lie down. **13** In the cities of the mountains, in the cities of the vale, and in the cities of the south, and in the land of Benjamin, and in the places about Jerusalem, and in the cities of Judah, shall the flocks pass again under the hands of him that telleth them, saith the LORD.

JUDAH RETURNS TO THE LAND WITH REPENTANCE

Nehemiah 9:2 And the **seed of Israel** [here a reference to Judah] separated themselves from all strangers, and **stood and confessed their sins, and the iniquities of their fathers**. ... **7 Thou art the LORD the God, who didst choose Abram**, and broughtest him forth out of Ur of the Chaldees, and **gavest him the name of Abraham**; **8** And foundest his heart faithful before thee, and **madest a covenant** [in blood] **with him to give the land** of the Canaanites, the Hittites, the Amorites, and the Perizzites, and the Jebusites, and the Girgashites, **to give it**, I say, **to his seed**, and hast performed thy words; for thou art righteous: ... **23 Their children also multipliedst thou as the stars of heaven**, and broughtest them into the land, concerning which thou hadst promised to their fathers, **that they should go in to possess it** [ownership of the land did not change simply because Judah was absent for 70 years].

EPHRAIM IS THE LORD'S FIRSTBORN

Jeremiah 31:9 They shall come with weeping, and **with supplications will I lead them**: I will cause them to walk by the rivers of waters in a straight way, wherein they shall not stumble: for **I am a father to Israel** [all Israel], and **Ephraim is my firstborn** [the multitude of nations in the middle of the earth with the blessings of Joseph: whose people are as the dust of the earth, stars of heaven, and sand of the sea are of Ephraim—the firstborn of the LORD—because of the blessing].

10 Hear the word of the LORD, **O ye nations**, and **declare it in the isles afar off** [Ephraim is in the nations and isles of the earth], and say, **He that scattered Israel will gather him**, and **keep him**, as a shepherd doth his flock. **11** For **the LORD hath redeemed Jacob** [God sees the 12 tribes of Israel as already redeemed], and **ransomed him from the hand of him that was stronger than he** [all 12 tribes of Israel scattered throughout the earth will be afflicted in a future time of persecution, including the multitude of people and nations of Ephraim and Manasseh ... but they shall begin their return to the land now, in this time].

THE LATTER RAIN CRY IS TO EPHRAIM

Hosea 3:4 For the **children of Israel** [the 10 tribes] shall abide many days without a **king**, and without a **prince**, and without a **sacrifice**, and without an **image**, and without an **ephod**, and without **teraphim** [articles of worship under the Law of Moses]: **5 Afterward** [after many days] **shall the children of Israel return, and seek the LORD their God**, and David their King; and shall fear the LORD and his goodness in the **latter days** [latter days, not the last days ... this is not the season for the coming of Messiah].

Hosea 5:5 And the pride of Israel doth testify to his face: therefore shall <u>**Israel**</u> and <u>**Ephraim**</u> fall in their iniquity; <u>**Judah**</u> also shall fall with them. ... **5:15 I will go and return to my place, till they acknowledge their offence**, and **seek my face: in their affliction** [the *time of Jacob's trouble*[59] shall cause Israel, Ephraim, and Judah to seek the Lord] **they will seek me early**.

Hosea 6:1 Come, and let us return unto the LORD: for he hath torn, and he will heal us; he hath smitten, and he will bind us up. **2 After two days** [after 2,000 years] **will he revive us: in the third day** [during the third millennium] **he will raise us up, and we shall live in his sight**. **3** Then shall we know, if we follow on to know the LORD: his going forth is prepared as the morning; and <u>**he shall come unto us**</u> [Israel, Ephraim, and Judah] <u>**as the rain, as the latter and former rain unto the earth**</u>.

4 <u>O Ephraim</u> [when this Scripture is put back into its context, it is clear that this latter rain prophecy is directed primarily toward Ephraim: which has become a multitude of Abrahamic Hebrew nations in the middle of the earth with the blessing of Joseph; the latter rain is also a call to Judah to receive back as one her brothers from the places to which they have been scattered], what shall I do unto thee? **O Judah** [the Jews of present Israel and those scattered throughout the world], what shall I do unto thee? for your goodness is as a morning cloud, and as the early dew it goeth away [God says this about Judah … even unto this day].

Malachi 3:7 Return unto me, and I will return unto you, saith the LORD of hosts.

Isaiah 10:20 And it shall come to pass in that day, that **the remnant of Israel, and such as are escaped of the house of Jacob**, shall no more again stay upon him that smote them; but shall stay upon the LORD, the Holy One of Israel, in truth. **21 The remnant shall return, even the remnant of Jacob, unto the mighty God. 22 For though thy people Israel be as the sand of the sea** [the *sand of the sea* reference to the *remnant of Jacob* identifies this reference to be of Ephraim]**, yet a remnant of them shall return**[60]: the consumption decreed shall overflow with righteousness.

THERE SHALL BE PERFECT UNDERSTANDING IN THE LATTER DAYS

Jeremiah 23:13 And I have seen folly in the **prophets of Samaria**; they prophesied in Baal, and caused my people Israel to err. **14** I have seen also in the **prophets of Jerusalem** an horrible thing: they commit adultery, and walk in lies: they strengthen also the hands of evildoers, that none doth return from his wickedness: they are all of them unto me as Sodom, and the inhabitants thereof as Gomorrah. … **18** For who hath stood in the counsel of the LORD, and hath perceived and heard his word? who hath marked his word, and heard it?

19 Behold, a whirlwind of the LORD is gone forth in fury, even a grievous whirlwind: it shall fall grievously upon the head of the wicked. **20** The anger of the LORD shall not return, until he have executed, and till he have performed the thoughts of his heart: **in the latter days ye shall consider it perfectly** [this book partially fulfills this prophecy].

---

60   Israel is about the size of the state of New Jersey in the United States. It would not even begin to hold the hold the hundreds of millions (or more) of Ephraim. But, the LORD could with Judah's cooperation double or triple the population of Israel with Hebrews who have rediscovered their destinies … and the "settlement" and "natural growth" issues would evaporate; and **Ezekiel 37:10** calls them when they "stood up upon their feet, an exceeding great army"— which will forever shift the balance of power in the Middle East.

Ezekiel 37:15 The word of the LORD came again unto me, saying, **16** Moreover, thou son of man, **take thee one stick**, and write upon it, **For Judah**, and **for the children of Israel his companions** [a remnant of all the children of Israel have become part of Judah: the Jews of Israel]: then **take another stick**, and write upon it, **For Joseph, the stick of Ephraim**, and **[for] all the house of Israel his companions** [Ephraim is in the presence of the house of Israel: the 10 tribes first carried into Assyrian captivity]: **17** And **join them** one to another **into one stick**; and they shall become one in thine hand.

18 And when the children of thy people shall speak unto thee, saying, Wilt thou not shew us what thou [meanest] by these? **19** Say unto them, Thus saith the Lord GOD; Behold, **I will take** the **stick of Joseph, which is in the hand of Ephraim** [and has become a multitude of nations in the middle of the earth], **and the tribes of Israel his fellows** [Ephraim has been joined with the 10 tribes of Israel: in the middle of the earth], and will put them with him, [even] **with the stick of Judah** [the Jews of Israel], and **make them one stick** [one nation], and they shall be one in mine hand.

20 And the sticks whereon thou writest shall be in thine hand before their eyes. **21** And **say unto them** [prophesy], Thus saith the Lord GOD; Behold, **I will take the children of Israel** [Ephraim and the 10 tribes] **from among the heathen** [the nations], whither they be gone, and will gather them on every side, and bring them into their own land: **22** And I will make them **one nation in the land upon the mountains of Israel** [which is the West Bank: proposed by many including United Nations' Resolutions and Israeli leadership, to become a Palestinian state ... which is not at all what God says]; and one king [prime minister now; Messiah later] shall be king to them all: and they shall be no more two nations, neither shall they be divided into two kingdoms any more at all.

The Third Temple Shall Only Be Built With Joseph In The Land

Ezekiel 37:26 Moreover **I will** make a covenant of peace with them; it shall be an everlasting covenant with them: and I will place them, and multiply them, and will **set <u>my sanctuary in the midst of them for evermore</u>. 27 <u>My tabernacle also shall be with them</u>**: yea, I will be their God, and they shall be my people. **28** And the heathen shall know that I the LORD do sanctify Israel, **when <u>my sanctuary shall be in the midst of them for evermore</u>**.

Israel Shall Be Without The Temple Until The Latter Days

Hosea 3:4 For the **children of Israel** [the 10 tribes of Israel] shall abide many days without a **king**, and without a **prince** [high priest], and without a **sacrifice** [animal sacrifice under the law of Moses], and without an **image**, and without an **ephod** [clothing of the high priest], and without **teraphim**: **5** Afterward [after many days] shall the children of Israel return [Ephraim rejoined to Judah], and seek the LORD their God, and David their King; and shall fear the LORD and his goodness **in the latter days** [latter days, not last days].

With Joseph God Will Build Again The Tabernacle Of David

Amos 9:11 In that day [the day when the 12 tribes of Israel are restored to the land: beginning with the fulfillment of Ezekiel 37] **will I raise up the tabernacle of David that is fallen**, and close up the breaches thereof; and I will raise up his ruins, and **I will build it as in the days of old**: **12** That they may possess the remnant of Edom, and of all the heathen, which are called by my name [this speaks of the hidden multitude and nations of Joseph and Ephraim; but probably speaks of much, much more], saith the LORD that doeth this.

13 Behold, the days come, saith the LORD, that the plowman shall overtake the reaper, and the treader of grapes him that soweth seed; and the mountains shall drop sweet wine, and all the hills shall melt. **14** And **I will bring again the captivity of my people of Israel** [all 12 tribes], and they shall build the waste cities, and inhabit them; and they shall plant vineyards, and drink the wine thereof; they shall also make gardens, and eat the fruit of them. **15** And **I will plant them upon their land, and they shall no more be pulled up out of their land which I have given them**, saith the LORD thy God.

Today's Israel As Seen By The Prophet Ezekiel

Ezekiel 36:1 Also, thou son of man, **prophesy unto the mountains of Israel** [the mountains of Israel are its West Bank area ... proposed as a Palestinian state], and say, Ye mountains of Israel, hear the word of the LORD: **2** Thus saith the Lord GOD; **Because the enemy hath said against you, Aha, even the ancient high places are ours in possession** [some prophecies have a double fulfillment ... and this sounds just like the Palestinian leadership of today]: **3** Therefore prophesy and say, Thus saith the Lord GOD; Because they have made you desolate, and **swallowed you up on every side** [Israel, indeed, is surrounded on every side], **that ye might be a possession** [a Palestinian state] **unto**

the residue of the heathen [a Bible *heathen* is a person without the God of Israel ... most of the Palestinians], and ye are taken up in the lips of talkers, and are an infamy of the people:

4 Therefore, **ye mountains of Israel**, hear the word of the Lord GOD; **Thus saith the Lord GOD to the mountains**, and to **the hills**, to **the rivers**, and to **the valleys**, to the desolate wastes, and to the cities that are forsaken, which became a prey and derision to the **residue of the heathen** that are round about; **5** Therefore thus saith the Lord GOD; Surely in the fire of my jealousy have I spoken against the **residue of the heathen**, and against all **Idumea** [in Ezekiel's day the northern portion of Edom (Esau), just below Be'er Sheva, which was then Judah's southern border; today it is a part of Israel], which have <u>appointed my land</u> into their possession [God says the land belongs to Him] with the joy of all their heart, with despiteful minds, to cast it out for a prey.

6 Prophesy therefore concerning the land of Israel, and say unto the mountains, and to the hills, to the rivers, and to the valleys, Thus saith the Lord GOD; Behold, I have spoken in my jealousy and in my fury, because **ye have borne the shame of the heathen**: **7** Therefore thus saith the Lord GOD; I have lifted up mine hand, Surely **the heathen that are about you,** they shall bear their shame. **8** But ye, O mountains of Israel, ye shall shoot forth your branches, and yield your fruit to my people of Israel [the increase from the land belongs to Israel]; for they are at hand to come.

9 For, behold, I am for you [the mountains of Israel], and I will turn unto you, and ye shall be tilled and sown: **10** And I will multiply men upon you, <u>all the house of Israel</u> [which will be fulfilled in the next Chapter, Ezekiel 37, when Joseph and Ephraim return to the land], even all of it: and the cities shall be inhabited, and the wastes shall be builded [massive construction, not just settlements]: **11** And I will multiply upon you man and beast; and they shall increase and bring fruit: and I will settle you after your old estates, and will do better unto you than at your beginnings [better than in the reign of Solomon where silver and gold became as plenteous as stones[61]]: and ye shall know that I am the LORD.

12 Yea, I will cause men to walk upon you, even <u>my people Israel</u> [all 12 tribes ... beginning with Ezekiel 37, with its completion when Messiah comes]; and **they shall possess thee, and thou shalt be their inheritance**, and thou shalt no more henceforth bereave [to cast out; miscarry; make childless] them of men.

---

61 2 Chronicles 1:15.

13 Thus saith the Lord GOD; Because they say unto you, Thou land devourest up men, and hast bereaved thy nations; **14** Therefore thou shalt devour men no more, neither bereave thy nations any more, saith the Lord GOD. **15** Neither will I cause men to hear in thee the **shame of the heathen** any more, neither shalt thou bear the reproach of the people any more, neither shalt thou cause thy nations to fall any more, saith the Lord GOD.

16 Moreover the word of the LORD came unto me, saying, **17** Son of man, when **the house of Israel** [the 12 tribes] dwelt in their own land, they defiled it by their own way and by their doings: their way was before me as the uncleanness of a removed woman. **18** Wherefore I poured my fury upon them for the blood that they had shed upon the land, and for their idols wherewith they had polluted it: **19** And **I scattered them among the heathen**, and they were dispersed through the countries: according to their way and according to their doings **I judged them**.

20 And **when they entered unto the heathen** [when they adopted the ways of the nations into which they were scattered], whither they went, **they profaned my holy name** [all Israel served other gods], when they said to them, **These are the people of the LORD**, and are gone forth out of his land. **21** But I had pity for mine holy name, which the **house of Israel had profaned among the heathen** [Joseph and Ephraim have lost their identity as Hebrews of Israel; but how many Jews only give lip service to the God of Abraham?], whither they went.

22 Therefore say unto the **house of Israel**, Thus saith the Lord GOD; I do not this for your sakes, O **house of Israel**, but for mine holy name's sake, which ye have profaned among the heathen, whither ye went. **23** And **I will sanctify my great name**, which was **profaned among the heathen**, which ye have **profaned in the midst of them**; and **the heathen shall know** that I am the LORD, saith the Lord GOD, when **I shall be sanctified in you before their eyes** [Jehovah will show off when Joseph and Ephraim are joined with Judah].

THE PEOPLE OF GOD DISCOVER WHO THEY ARE

Ezekiel 36:24 For I will take you from among the heathen, and gather you out of all countries, and will bring you into your own land [beginning with Ezekiel 37 until Messiah comes]. **25** Then will I sprinkle clean water upon you, and ye shall be clean: from all your filthiness, and from all your idols, will I cleanse you. **26** A new heart also will I give you, and a new spirit will I put within you: and I will take away the stony heart out of your flesh, and I will give you an heart of flesh. **27** And I will put my spirit within you, and cause you to walk in my statutes, and ye shall keep my judgments, and do them. **28** And ye shall **dwell in the land** that I gave to your fathers; and **ye shall be** my people, and **I will be** your **God** [indicating that at present they are not in the land, and because they have lost their identity they are not yet known as the people of God].

29 I will also save you from all your uncleannesses: and I will call for the corn, and will increase it, and lay no famine upon you. **30** And I will multiply the fruit of the tree, and the increase of the field [great prosperity], that ye shall receive no more reproach of famine among the heathen. **31** Then shall ye remember your own evil ways, and your doings that were not good, and shall lothe yourselves in your own sight for your iniquities and for your abominations. **32** Not for your sakes do I this, saith the Lord GOD, be it known unto you: be ashamed and confounded for your own ways, O **house of Israel** [the 12 tribes of Ephraim and Judah].

33 Thus saith the Lord GOD; In the day that I shall have cleansed you from all your iniquities I will also cause you to dwell in the cities, and the wastes shall be builded. **34** And the desolate land shall be tilled, whereas it lay desolate in the sight of all that passed by. **35** And they shall say, **This land that was desolate is become like the garden of Eden** [this promise is already being fulfilled in Israel]; and the waste and desolate and ruined cities are become fenced, and are inhabited.

36 Then the **heathen that are left round about you** [the Palestinians as well as other Arab nations] shall know that I the LORD build the ruined places, and plant that that was desolate: I the LORD have spoken it, and I will do it. **37** Thus saith the Lord GOD; I will yet for this be enquired of by the **house of Israel**, to do it for them; I will increase them with men like a flock. **38** As the holy flock, as the flock of Jerusalem in her solemn feasts; so shall the waste cities be filled with flocks of men: and they shall know that I am the LORD.

THE STAGE OF EZEKIEL 36 HAS RELEASED EZEKIEL 37

Ezekiel 37:1 The hand of the LORD was upon me, and carried me out in the spirit of the LORD, and set me down in the midst of the **valley which was full of bones**, **2** And caused me to pass by them round about: and, behold, there were very many in the open valley; and, lo, they were very dry. **3** And he said unto me, Son of man, can these bones live? And I answered, O Lord GOD, thou knowest.

4 Again he said unto me, Prophesy upon these bones, and say unto them, O ye dry bones, hear the word of the LORD. **5** Thus saith the Lord GOD unto these bones; Behold, I will cause breath to enter into you, and ye shall live: **6** And I will lay sinews upon you, and will bring up flesh upon you, and cover you with skin, and put breath in you, and **ye shall live**; and ye shall know that I am the LORD. ... **10** So I prophesied as **he commanded me, and the breath came into them, and they lived, and stood up upon their feet, an exceeding great army** [an interesting phraseology by the Spirit of God].

11 Then he said unto me, Son of man, **these bones are the whole house of Israel** [the fullness of the twelve tribes of Jacob]: behold, they say, Our bones are dried, and our hope is lost: we are cut off for our parts [for 2700 years]. **12** Therefore prophesy and say unto them, Thus saith the Lord GOD; Behold, O my people, I will open your graves [the graves of the lost knowledge of their Hebrew heritage], and cause you to come up out of your graves, **and bring you into the land of Israel**. ...

Ezekiel 37:15 The word of the LORD came again unto me, saying, **16** Moreover, thou son of man, take thee **one stick**, and write upon it, For **Judah**, and for the **children of Israel his companions**[62]: then take **another stick**, and write upon it, For **Joseph, the stick of Ephraim**, and for **all the house of Israel his companions** [the ten tribes of Israel ... scattered]: **17** And join them one to another into one stick; and they shall become one in thine hand [one in the hand of the prophet].

18 And when the children of thy people shall speak unto thee, saying, Wilt thou not shew us what thou meanest by these? **19** Say unto them, Thus saith the Lord GOD; Behold**, I will take** the **stick of Joseph, which is in the hand of Ephraim**, and the tribes of Israel his fellows [Ephraim is with the 10 tribes], and **will put them** [the 10 tribes of Israel] **with him** [Ephraim], even **with the stick of Judah**, and **make them** [Joseph / Ephraim / the ten tribes / and Judah] **one stick** [one nation ... and before Messiah comes], and they shall be one in mine hand [one in the hand of God]. **20** And the sticks whereon thou writest shall be in thine hand before their eyes.

21 And say unto them, Thus saith the Lord GOD; Behold, I will take the **children of Israel** [the primary reference is the ten tribes... the dry bones of Joseph, Ephraim and the tribes of Israel] from among

---

62 The Israel of today is representative of all of the twelve tribes of Jacob / Israel; but, the "Israel" that God said would be as the "dust of the earth, stars of heaven, and sand of the sea" is not only not in Israel proper, but are the "Josephs" of Israel: who have lost their identity as Hebrews, and have become a multitudinous company of nations in the middle of the earth—and, they are not Jews (who in their Diaspora have never lost their identity).

the heathen [the nations], whither they be gone, and will gather them on every side, and bring them into their own land: **22** And I will make them **one nation in the land upon the mountains of Israel**; and one king [president or prime minister now; Messiah later] shall be king to them all: and they shall be **no more two nations**, **neither** shall they be divided into **two kingdoms** any more at all [again, this prophesy must be fulfilled before the coming of the Messiah, and not after].

23 Neither shall they defile themselves any more with their idols, nor with their detestable things, nor with any of their transgressions: but **I will save them out of all their dwelling places**, wherein they have sinned, and will cleanse them: **so shall they be my people, and I will be their God**.

24 And **David my servant** [the Messiah] **shall be king over them**; and they all shall have one shepherd: they shall also walk in my judgments, and observe my statutes, and do them. **25** And they shall dwell in the land that I have given unto Jacob my servant, wherein your fathers have dwelt; and they shall dwell therein, even they, and their children, and their children's children for ever: and my servant **David shall be their prince for ever**.

26 Moreover **I will** make a covenant of peace with them; it shall be an everlasting covenant with them: and I will place them, and multiply them, and will **set <u>my sanctuary in the midst of them for evermore</u>**, and they shall be my people. **28** And the heathen shall know that I the LORD do sanctify Israel, **when <u>my sanctuary shall be in the midst of them for evermore</u>**.

HOSEA CONFIRMS THE HIDDEN ISRAEL

Hosea 1:2 The **Hosea 1:2** The beginning of the word of the LORD by Hosea. And the LORD said to Hosea, Go, take unto thee a wife of whoredoms and children of whoredoms: for the land hath committed great whoredom, departing from the LORD. **3** So he went and took Gomer the daughter of Diblaim; which conceived, and bare him a son. **4** And the LORD said unto him, Call his name **Jezreel** [God sows... God sowed the entire northern kingdom of Israel into the earth—to receive them back as harvest at the appointed time]; for yet a little while, and **I will … cause to cease the kingdom of the house of Israel**. **5** And it shall come to pass at that day, that I will break the bow of Israel in the **valley of Jezreel** [the valley of the dry bones of Ezekiel 37].

6 And she conceived again, and bare a daughter. And God said unto him, Call her name Loruhamah: for **I will no more have mercy upon the house of Israel; but I will utterly take them away** [the 10 tribes of the northern kingdom of Israel]. **7** But **I will have mercy upon the house of Judah**[63], and will save them by the LORD their God …

8 Now when she had weaned Loruhamah, she conceived, and bare a son. **9** Then said God, Call his name Loammi: for **ye are not my people, and I will not be your God** [while the northern kingdom is sown or scattered, they will not be known as the chosen people of God: neither will they worship the God of Abraham, Isaac and Jacob].

10 Yet the number of the children of Israel shall be as the sand of the sea, which cannot be measured nor numbered [during the centuries during which the northern kingdom of Israel has lost its identity, they have grown to become in number as sand, stars, and dust in fulfillment of God's promises to Abraham; and of Jacob's (Israel's) blessing upon the sons of Joseph]; and it shall come to pass, that **in the place** [God knows who they and where they are] where it was said unto them, Ye are **not my people** [because they have lost their Hebrew identity], there it shall be said unto them, **Ye are the sons of the living God.**

11 Then shall the children of Judah and the children of Israel be gathered together, and appoint themselves one head [no one will appoint the Messiah]**, and they shall come up out of the land** [before Messiah's return, and not after]: **for great shall be the day of Jezreel** [when God re-gathers the 10 tribes that He has sown].

THE TIME OF JACOB'S TROUBLE

Jeremiah 30:1 The word that came to Jeremiah from the LORD, saying, **2** Thus speaketh the LORD God of Israel, saying, Write thee all the words that I have spoken unto thee in a book. **3** For, lo, **the days come**, saith the LORD, that **I will bring again the captivity of my people Israel** [the 10 tribe northern kingdom which had ceased to exist] **and Judah**, saith the LORD: and **I will cause them to return to the land that I gave to their fathers, and they shall possess it.**

4 And these are the **words that the LORD spake concerning Israel and concerning Judah**. **5** For thus saith the LORD; We have heard a **voice of trembling**, of **fear**, and **not of peace. 6** Ask ye now, and see whether a man [all Israel] doth travail with child [the birth pains of the final remnant of Israel and Judah returning to the God of their

---

63 Estimates of over 2 million Jews went into Babylonian captivity for 70 years; but only about 50,000 returned to the land under the ministries of Zerubbabel, Ezra and Nehemiah.

creation]? wherefore do I see every man with his hands on his loins, as a woman in travail, and all faces are turned into paleness? **7** Alas! for that day is great, so that none is like it: it is even **the time of Jacob's trouble** [a coming time of persecution for all 12 tribes of Jacob / Israel who have returned to the land in fulfillment of Ezekiel 37]; but **he** [the nation of Israel] **shall be saved out of it** [those who are left alive … although two-thirds shall perish (Zechariah 13:8-9)].

8 For it shall come to pass in that day [in the time of Jacob's trouble], saith the LORD of hosts, that I will break **his yoke** [the yoke of the Assyrian[64]] from off thy neck, and will burst thy bonds, and strangers shall no more serve themselves of him: **9** But **they** [the unified nation of Israel] **shall serve the LORD their God, and David their king**, whom I will raise up unto them.

10 Therefore fear thou not, **O my servant Jacob** [the whole house of Jacob], saith the LORD; neither be dismayed, **O Israel** [the remainder of Joseph and Ephraim scattered]: for, lo, **I will save thee from afar, and thy seed from the land of their captivity**; and **Jacob shall return** [all 12 tribes shall return to the LORD and the land], and shall be in rest, and be quiet, and none shall make him afraid.

11 For I am with thee, saith the LORD, to save thee: though I make a full end of all nations whither I have scattered thee, yet will I not make a full end of thee: but I will correct thee in measure, and will not leave thee altogether unpunished. … 15 Why criest thou for thine affliction? thy sorrow is incurable for the multitude of thine iniquity: because thy sins were increased, I have done these things unto thee.

16 Therefore **all they that devour thee shall be devoured**; and all thine adversaries, every one of them, shall go into captivity; and they that spoil thee shall be a spoil, and all that prey upon thee will I give for a prey. **17** For **I will restore health unto thee**, and I will heal thee of thy wounds, saith the LORD; because they called thee an Outcast, saying, **This is Zion** [the 12 tribes of Jacob are called Zion because Ezekiel 37 has been fulfilled … as well as Ezekiel 38 and 39], whom no man seeketh after.

JACOB'S CAPTIVITY SHALL RETURN

Jeremiah 30:18 Thus saith the LORD; Behold, I will bring again the **captivity of Jacob's tents** [the unified nation of Israel], and have mercy

64   Isaiah 10:5 and 27; the little horn of Daniel 7 and 8.

on his dwellingplaces; and the city shall be builded upon her own heap, and the palace shall remain after the manner thereof. **19** And out of them shall proceed thanksgiving and the voice of them that make merry, and I will multiply them, and they shall not be few; I will also glorify them, and they shall not be small.

20 Their children also shall be as aforetime, and their congregation shall be established before me, and **I will punish all that oppress them**. **21** And their nobles shall be of themselves, and their governor shall proceed from the midst of them; and I will cause him to draw near, and he shall approach unto me: for who is this that engaged his heart to approach unto me? saith the LORD.

22 **And <u>ye shall be my people, and I will be your God</u>** [a primary reference to Ephraim]. **23** Behold, the whirlwind of the LORD goeth forth with fury, a continuing whirlwind: it shall fall with pain upon the head of the wicked. **24** The fierce anger of the LORD shall not return, until he have done it, and until he have performed the intents of his heart: **in the latter days** [not the last days] ye shall consider it.

GOD'S MERCY IN THE NORTH COUNTRY

Jeremiah 31:1 At the same time [the *time of Jacob's trouble*[65]], **saith the LORD, will I be the God of all the families of Israel** [Joseph, Ephraim and Judah]**, and they shall be my people.** 2 Thus saith the LORD, The people which were left of the sword found grace in the wilderness; even Israel, when I went to cause him to rest. **3** The LORD hath appeared of old unto me, saying, Yea, **I have loved thee with an everlasting love: therefore with lovingkindness have I drawn thee.**

4 Again I will build thee, and thou shalt be built, O virgin of Israel: thou shalt again be adorned with thy tabrets, and shalt go forth in the dances of them that make merry. **5** Thou shalt yet plant vines upon the **mountains of Samaria** [the West Bank has come alive with Joseph and Ephraim back in the land]: the planters shall plant, and shall eat them as common things.

6 For there shall be **a day**, that the **watchmen upon the mount Ephraim** [the northern kingdom] shall cry, Arise ye, and let us go up to Zion unto the LORD our God. **7** For thus saith the LORD; Sing with gladness **for Jacob** [a unified Israel], and shout among the **chief of the nations** [a reference in Jeremiah's day to Babylon; but for the latter days it means the mightiest nations of the world]: publish ye, praise ye,

---

65 Jeremiah 30:7.

and say, O LORD, save thy people, the **remnant of Israel** [Joseph and Ephraim who have returned to the land].

8 Behold, **I will bring them from the north country**, and gather them from **the coasts of the earth** [the isles of the sea, or ends of the earth[66]], and with them the blind and the lame, the woman with child and her that travaileth with child together: **a great company shall return thither** [Ephraim shall return from every place that he has been scattered, not just the company of nations in the middle of the earth]. 9 They shall come with weeping, and with supplications will I lead them: I will cause them to walk by the rivers of waters in a straight way, wherein they shall not stumble: for **I am a father to Israel** [a unified Israel], and **Ephraim is my firstborn** [carrying the blessing of Joseph].

Jeremiah 6:1 ... [E]vil appeareth **out of the north**, and great destruction.

Jeremiah 6:22 Thus saith the LORD. Behold, a people cometh from **the north country**, and a great nation shall be raised from the sides of the earth.

Jeremiah 46:10 " ... **[T]he north country by the river Euphrates**.

Where Is The Hebrew Nation Of Israel Today?

Jeremiah 31:10 Hear the word of the LORD, O ye nations, and declare it in the isles afar off, and say, **He that scattered Israel will gather him**, and keep him, as a shepherd doth his flock. 11 For the **LORD hath redeemed Jacob** [12 tribes], and ransomed him from the hand of him that was stronger than he. **...**

18 I have surely heard **Ephraim** [the remainder of the lost tribes which have not accepted their Hebrew identity or returned to the land of Israel] bemoaning himself thus; Thou hast chastised me, and I was chastised, as a bullock unaccustomed to the yoke: turn thou me, and I shall be turned; for thou art the LORD my God. **19** Surely after that I was turned, I repente; and after that I was instructed, I smote upon my thigh: I was ashamed, yea, even confounded, because I did bear the reproach of my youth.

20 Is **Ephraim my dear son**? is he a pleasant child? for since I spake against him, I do earnestly remember him still: therefore my bowels are troubled for him; **I will surely have mercy upon him**, saith the LORD.

66 Deuteronomy 33:17.

... **23** Thus saith the LORD of hosts, the God of Israel; As yet they shall use this speech in the land of Judah and in the cities thereof, when I shall bring again their captivity; The LORD bless thee, O habitation of justice, and mountain of holiness. **24** And there shall dwell in Judah itself, and in all the cities thereof together, husbandmen, and they that go forth with flocks. **25** For I have satiated the weary soul, and I have replenished every sorrowful soul. **26** Upon this I awaked, and beheld; and my sleep was sweet unto me.

27 Behold, the days come, saith the LORD, that **I will sow the house of Israel and the house of Judah with the seed of man** [intermarriage], **and with the seed of beast** [affliction, persecution, war, famine, etc.]. **28** And **it shall come to pass**, that like as I have watched over them, to pluck up, and to break down, and to throw down , and to destroy , and to afflict; **so will I watch over them, to build, and to plant**, saith the LORD. ...

THE ASSYRIAN IS THE ROD OF GOD'S ANGER

Isaiah 10:1 Woe unto them that decree unrighteous decrees, and that write grievousness which they have prescribed; **2** To turn aside the needy from judgment, and to take away the right from the poor of my people, that widows may be their prey, and that they may rob the fatherless! **3** And what will ye do in the **day of visitation**, and in the desolation which shall come from far? to whom will ye flee for help? and where will ye leave your glory? **4** Without me they shall bow down under the prisoners, and they shall fall under the slain. **For all this his anger is not turned away, but his hand is stretched out still.**

5 O Assyrian, the rod of mine anger [the little horn of Daniel 7 and 8 from Syria], and the staff in their hand is mine indignation. **6 I will send him** against an hypocritical nation [Ezekiel 36 through 39 have been fulfilled and the third temple rebuilt; but the unified nation of Israel is still not wholly following the LORD who created it, and must again be chastised by the LORD], and **against the people of my wrath**

will I give him a charge, to take the spoil, and to take the prey, and to tread them down like the mire of the streets. ... **20** And it shall come to pass in that day, that **the remnant of Israel, and such as are escaped of the house of Jacob**, shall no more again stay upon him that smote them; but shall stay upon the LORD, the Holy One of Israel, in truth.

21 The remnant shall return, even the remnant of Jacob [the remnant of Joseph and Ephraim], **unto the mighty God. 22 For**

though thy people Israel be as the sand of the sea [this pinpoints the remnant as Ephraim], yet a remnant of them shall return [beginning with Ezekiel 37 and continuing until the return of Messiah]: the consumption decreed shall overflow with righteousness.

23 For the Lord GOD of hosts shall make a consumption, even determined, in the midst of all the land. 24 Therefore thus saith the Lord GOD of hosts, O my people that dwellest in Zion, be not afraid of the Assyrian: he shall smite thee with a rod (verse 5), and shall lift up his staff against thee, after the manner of Egypt. 25 For yet a very little while [a relatively short period of time], and the indignation shall cease, and mine anger in their destruction.

26 And the LORD of hosts shall stir up a scourge for him according to the slaughter of Midian at the rock of Oreb: and as his rod was upon the sea, so shall he lift it up after the manner of Egypt. 27 And it shall come to pass in that day, that his [the Assyrian's] burden shall be taken away from off thy shoulder, and his yoke from off thy neck, and the yoke shall be destroyed because of the anointing.

The Final Remnant Of Israel

Jeremiah 23:3 And I will gather the remnant of my flock out of all countries whither I have driven them, and will bring them again to their folds; and they shall be fruitful and increase. 4 And I will set up shepherds over them which shall feed them: and they shall fear no more, nor be dismayed, neither shall they be lacking, saith the LORD.

5 Behold, the days come, saith the LORD, that I will raise unto David a righteous Branch, and a King shall reign and prosper, and shall execute judgment and justice in the earth. 6 In his days [the days of the greater son of David] Judah shall be saved, and Israel shall dwell safely: and this is his name whereby he shall be called, THE LORD OUR RIGHTEOUSNESS.

7 Therefore, behold, the days come, saith the LORD, that they shall no more say, The LORD liveth, which brought up the children of Israel out of the land of Egypt; 8 But, The LORD liveth, which brought up and which led the seed of the house of Israel out of the north country[67], and from all countries whither I had driven them; and they shall dwell in their own land.

---

[67] The million Jews that returned to Israel from Russia are not the primary reference here.

Jeremiah 33:14 Behold, **the days come**, saith the LORD, that **I will perform** that good thing which I have promised unto the **house of Israel** and to the **house of Judah** [the divided kingdom has two houses ... unto this day]. **15 In those days**, and **at that time** [in the days and time God restores the two houses of Israel together as one nation ... beginning with the fulfillment of the prophecy of Ezekiel 37], will I cause the **Branch of righteousness to grow up unto David** [in the passage of time Messiah shall reign over both houses of Israel, as well as the earth]; and he shall execute judgment and righteousness in the land.

16 In those days shall **Judah be saved**, and **Jerusalem shall dwell safely**: and this is the name wherewith she shall be called, The LORD our righteousness. **17** For thus saith the LORD; **David shall never want a man to sit upon the throne of the house of Israel** [in those days and at that time (verse 15) ... this Scripture must be kept in its context]; **18** Neither shall the priests the Levites want a man before me to offer burnt offerings, and to kindle meat offerings, and to do sacrifice continually [and the third and fourth temples shall be rebuilt].

19 And the word of the LORD came unto Jeremiah, saying, **20** Thus saith the LORD; **If ye can break my covenant of the day**, and my covenant of the night, and that there should not be day and night in their season; **21 Then may also my covenant be broken with David my servant, that he should not have a son to reign upon his throne** [God's eternal covenant with David did not depend upon what David did or did not do ... the *sure mercies of David*[68]]; and with the Levites the priests, my ministers. **22** As the host of heaven cannot be numbered, neither the sand of the sea measured: **so will I multiply the seed of David my servant**, and the Levites that minister unto me.

23 Moreover the word of the LORD came to Jeremiah, saying, **24** Considerest thou not what this people have spoken, saying, The **two families** [Israel and Judah] which **the LORD hath chosen**, he hath even cast them off ? thus they have despised my people, that they should be no more a nation before them. **25** Thus saith the LORD; **If my covenant be not with day and night**, and if I have not appointed the ordinances of heaven and earth; **26 Then will I cast away the seed of Jacob** [all 12 tribes], and David my servant, so that I will not take any of his seed to be rulers over **the seed of Abraham, Isaac, and Jacob** [all Israel]: for **I will cause their captivity to return** [the captivity of both families of the Hebrew nation shall return to the land: beginning with

68   Psalms 89:1-4, 17-37; 132:10-12; and Isaiah 55:3.

Judah in 1948, and with Ephraim and Joseph as Ezekiel 37 is fulfilled], and have mercy on them:

Israel Is Created For God's Glory

Isaiah 43:1 But now thus saith the LORD that created thee, **O Jacob**, and he that formed thee, **O Israel**, Fear not: for I have redeemed thee, I have called thee by thy name; thou art mine. **2** When thou passest through the waters, I will be with thee; and through the rivers, they shall not overflow thee: when thou walkest through the fire, thou shalt not be burned; neither shall the flame kindle upon thee.

3 For **I am the LORD thy God, the Holy One of Israel, thy Saviour**: I gave Egypt for thy ransom, Ethiopia and Seba for thee. **4** Since thou wast precious in my sight, thou hast been honourable, and I have loved thee: therefore will I give men for thee, and people for thy life. **5** Fear not: for I am with thee: **I will bring thy seed from the east**, and gather thee from **the west**; **6** I will say to **the north**, Give up; and to **the south**, Keep not back: bring my sons from far, and my daughters from the ends of the earth; **7** Even **every one that is called by my name**: **for I have created him for my glory**, I have formed him; yea, I have made him.

God Will Establish A New Covenant With Israel And Judah

Jeremiah 31:31 Behold, the days come , saith the LORD, that I will make a **new covenant** with the **house of Israel**, and with the **house of Judah**: **32** Not according to the covenant that I made with their fathers in the day that I took them by the hand to bring them out of the land of Egypt; which my covenant they brake, although I was an husband unto them, saith the LORD:

33 But this shall be the **covenant** that I will make with the house of Israel; After those days, saith the LORD, I will put my law in their inward parts, and write it in their hearts; and will be their God, and they shall be my people. **34** And they shall teach no more every man his neighbour, and every man his brother, saying, Know the LORD: for they shall all know me, from the least of them unto the greatest of them, saith the LORD: for I will forgive their iniquity, and I will remember their sin no more. ... **36** If those ordinances [of the sun, moon, stars and the sea: all of which Jeremiah uses as examples of God's faithfulness to His Word, to Israel, and to Judah] depart from before me, saith the LORD, then the **seed of Israel** [all 12 tribes] also shall cease from being a nation before me for ever.

37 Thus saith the LORD; If heaven above can be measured, and the foundations of the earth searched out beneath, I will also cast off all **the seed of Israel** for all that they have done, saith the LORD. **38** Behold, the days come, saith the LORD, that the city shall be built to the LORD from the tower of Hananeel unto the gate of the corner ....

Israel Shall Be Exalted In The Last Days

Isaiah 2:1 **The word that Isaiah** the son of Amoz **saw concerning Judah and Jerusalem**. **2** And it shall come to pass **in the last days** [last days verses latter days], **that the mountain of the LORD'S house shall be established in the top of the mountains, and shall be exalted above the hills; and all nations shall flow unto it. 3** And many people shall go and say, Come ye, and let us go up to the mountain of the LORD, to the **house of the God of Jacob** [God of the 12 tribes of Israel]; and he will teach us of his ways, and we will walk in his paths: for out of Zion shall go forth the law, and the word of the LORD from Jerusalem.

4 And he shall judge among the nations, and shall rebuke many people: and they shall beat their swords into plowshares, and their spears into pruninghooks: nation shall not lift up sword against nation, neither shall they learn war any more. **5** O **house of Jacob**, come ye, and let us walk in the light of the LORD. ... **12** For the day of the LORD of hosts shall be upon every one that is proud and lofty, and upon every one that is lifted up; and he shall be brought low: ...

Prayer For Israel Must Remove The Curses Spoken By Its Prophets

A Prophet Speaks Both Sight And Blindness Onto A Nation

2 Kings 6:16 And he answered, Fear not: for they that be with us are more than they that be with them. **17** And Elisha prayed, and said, **LORD, I pray thee, open his eyes, that he may see**. And **the LORD opened the eyes of the young man; and he saw**: and, behold, the mountain was full of horses and chariots of fire round about Elisha. **18** And when they came down to him, **Elisha prayed unto the LORD, and said, Smite this people, I pray thee, with blindness. And he smote them with blindness according to the word of Elisha**. **19** And Elisha said unto them, This is not the way, neither is this the city: follow me, and I will bring you to the man whom ye seek. But he led them to Samaria. **20** And it came to pass, when they were come into Samaria, **that**

Elisha said, LORD, open the eyes of these men, that they may see. And **the LORD opened their eyes, and they saw** ...

WE ARE ALSO COMMANDED TO SPEAK THE WORD OF THE LORD

Job 22:21 Acquaint now thyself with him, and be at peace: thereby good shall come unto thee. **22** Receive, I pray thee, the law from his mouth, and lay up his words in thine heart. **23** If thou return to the Almighty, thou shalt be built up, thou shalt put away iniquity far from thy tabernacles. **24** Then shalt thou lay up gold as dust, and the gold of Ophir as the stones of the brooks. **25** Yea, the Almighty shall be thy defence, and thou shalt have plenty of silver. **26** For then shalt thou have thy delight in the Almighty, and shalt lift up thy face unto God. **27 Thou shalt make thy prayer unto him**, and **he shall hear thee**, and thou shalt pay thy vows. **28 Thou shalt also decree a thing, and it shall be established unto thee**: and the light shall shine upon thy ways.

CURSES SPOKEN BY THE PROPHET MOSES

Deuteronomy 28:15 But it shall come to pass, if **thou wilt not hearken unto the voice of the LORD thy God** [Adonai-Jehovah], **to observe to do all his commandments** and his statutes which I command thee this day; that **all these curses shall come upon thee, and overtake thee**: ... **28 The LORD shall smite thee with** madness, and **blindness**, and astonishment of heart: **29** And thou shalt grope at noonday, **as the blind gropeth in darkness**, and thou shalt not prosper in thy ways: and thou shalt be only oppressed and spoiled evermore, and no man shall save thee.

Deuteronomy 30:17 But **if thine heart turn away** [spiritual blindness is a matter of the heart], **so that thou wilt not hear** [and obey], but shalt be drawn away, and worship other gods, and serve them; **18** I denounce unto you this day, that ye shall surely perish, and that ye shall not prolong your days upon the land, whither thou passest over Jordan to go to possess it. **19 I call heaven and earth to record this day against you, that I have set before you life and death, blessing and cursing: therefore choose life, that both thou and thy seed may live: 20** That thou mayest love the LORD thy God, and that thou mayest obey his voice, and that thou mayest cleave unto him: for he is thy life, and the length of thy days: **that thou mayest dwell in the land which the LORD sware unto thy fathers, to Abraham, to Isaac, and to Jacob, to give them**.

Curses Spoken By The Prophet David

Psalms 69:22 [Then spake David by the Spirit of God] **Let their table become a snare before them** [the Torah ... the Law of Moses and other Hebrew Scriptures and writings]: and that which should have been for their welfare, let it become a trap. **23 Let their eyes be darkened, that they see not** [cause them to become spiritually blind]; and make their loins continually to shake [a nation in constant fear ... the Israel we see today.].

Curses Spoken By The Prophet Isaiah

Isaiah 6:8 Also I [Isaiah] heard the voice of the Lord, saying, Whom shall I send, and who will go for us? Then said I, **Here am I; send me**. 9 And he [the LORD] said, **Go, and tell this people, Hear ye indeed, but understand not; and see ye indeed, but perceive not. 10 Make the heart of this people fat, and make their ears heavy, and shut their eyes; lest they see with their eyes, and hear with their ears, and understand with their heart, and convert, and be healed**. 11 Then said I, Lord, **how long?** And he answered, **Until** the cities be wasted without inhabitant, and the houses without man, and the land be utterly desolate [the curse of spiritual blindness upon **Israel** and **Judah**].

Isaiah 8:13 Sanctify the LORD of hosts himself; and let him be your fear, and let him be your dread. 14 And he shall be for a sanctuary; but **for a stone of stumbling and for a rock of offence to both the houses of Israel**, for a gin and for a snare to the inhabitants of Jerusalem. 15 And many among them shall stumble, and fall, and be broken, and be snared, and be taken.

Isaiah 29:10 For **the LORD hath poured out upon you the spirit of deep sleep**, and **hath closed your eyes**: the prophets and your rulers, the seers hath he covered. 11 And **the vision of all is become unto you as the words of a book that is sealed** [the Scriptures have become as a book that is sealed], which men deliver to one that is learned, saying, **Read this,** I pray thee: and he saith, **I cannot; for it is sealed**: 12 And the book is delivered to him that is not learned, saying, Read this, I pray thee: and he saith, I am not learned . 13 Wherefore the Lord said, Forasmuch as **this people draw near me with their mouth, and with their lips do honour me, but have removed their heart far from me** [spiritual blindness again a matter of a heart turned from God], and their fear toward me is taught by the precept of men:

CURSES SPOKEN BY THE PROPHET JEREMIAH

Jeremiah 6:21 Therefore thus saith the LORD, Behold, **I will lay stumblingblocks before this people**, and the fathers and the sons together shall fall upon them; the neighbour and his friend shall perish.

CURSES SPOKEN BY THE PROPHET HOSEA

Hosea 1:2 The beginning of the word of the LORD by Hosea. And the LORD said to Hosea, **Go, take unto thee a wife of whoredoms and children of whoredoms: for the land hath committed great whoredom, departing from the LORD. 3** So he went and took Gomer the daughter of Diblaim; which conceived, and bare him a son. **4** And the LORD said unto him, Call his name **Jezreel** [God will scatter]; for yet a little while, and I will avenge the blood of Jezreel upon the house of Jehu, and **[I] will cause to cease the kingdom of the house of Israel** [the northern kingdom of 10 tribes]. ... **6** And she conceived again, and bare a daughter. And God said unto him, Call her name **Loruhamah** [I will have mercy no more]: for **I will no more have mercy upon the house of Israel; but I will utterly take them away.** ...

8 Now when she had weaned Loruhamah , she conceived , and bare a son. **9** Then said God, Call his name **Loamm** [not my people] **for ye are not my people** [while the northern kingdom of Joseph and Ephraim are scattered, they will lose their Hebrew identity], and I will not be your God.

CURSES SPOKEN BY THE PROPHET MALACHI

Malachi 2:1 And now, **O ye priests, this commandment is for you**. **2** If ye will not hear, and if ye will not lay it to heart, to give glory unto my name, saith the LORD of hosts, **I will even send a curse upon you**, and I will curse your blessings: yea, I have cursed them already, because ye do not lay it to heart. ... **8** But ye are departed out of the way; <u>ye have caused many to stumble at the law</u>; ye have corrupted the covenant of Levi, saith the LORD of hosts.

CURSES SPOKEN BY THE PROPHET JESUS

Matthew 13:14 And in them is fulfilled <u>the prophecy of Esaias</u> [Isaiah], which saith, **By hearing ye shall hear** [the Jews of Israel], **and shall not understand; and seeing ye shall see, and shall not perceive: 15 For this people's heart is waxed gross, and their ears are dull of hearing, and their eyes they have closed; lest at any**

310

time they should see with their eyes, and hear with their ears, and should understand with their heart, and should be converted, and I should heal them.

Matthew 15:7 Ye hypocrites [Jesus speaking to the scribes and Pharisees], well did Esaias prophesy of you, saying, **8** This people draweth nigh unto me with their mouth, and honoureth me with their lips; but **their heart is far from me**. **9** But in vain they do worship me, teaching for doctrines the commandments of men.

Mark 4:9 And he said unto them, He that hath ears to hear, let him hear. **10** And when he was alone, they that were about him with the twelve asked of him the parable. **11** And he said unto them, Unto you [Jesus' disciples] it is given to know the mystery of the kingdom of God: but unto them that are without [the Jews of Israel], all these things are done in parables: **12 That seeing they may see, and not perceive; and hearing they may hear, and not understand; lest at any time they should be converted, and their sins should be forgiven them.**

John 12:37 But though he had done so many miracles before them, yet they believed not on him: **38 That the saying of Esaias the prophet might be fulfilled,** which he spake, Lord, who hath believed our report? and to whom hath the arm of the Lord been revealed? **39** Therefore they could not believe, because that Esaias said again, **40 He hath blinded their eyes, and hardened their heart; that they should not see with their eyes, nor understand with their heart, and be converted, and I should heal them.**

John 9:39 And Jesus said, **For judgment I am come into this world, that they which see not might see; and that they which see might be made blind** [the spiritual leaders are blind to their Covenant, heritage, and Messiah]. **40** And some of the Pharisees which were with him heard these words, and said unto him, Are we blind also? **41** Jesus said unto them, If ye were blind, ye should have no sin: but now ye say, We see; therefore your sin remaineth .

CURSES SPOKEN BY THE PROPHET PAUL

Acts 28:24 And some believed [the Jewish leadership in Rome] the things which were spoken, and some believed not. **25** And when they agreed not among themselves, they departed, after that Paul had spoken one word, **Well spake the Holy Ghost by Esaias the prophet** unto our fathers [the fathers of Israel], **26** Saying, **Go unto this people, and say,** Hearing ye shall hear, and shall not understand; and seeing ye shall see, and not perceive: **27** For the heart of this people is waxed gross, and their ears are dull of hearing, and their eyes have they closed; lest they should see with their eyes, and hear with their ears, and understand with their heart, and should be converted, and I should heal them. **28** Be it known therefore unto you, that the salvation of God is sent unto the Gentiles, and that they will hear it.

Romans 9:31 But Israel, which followed after the law of righteousness, hath not attained to the law of righteousness. **32** Wherefore? Because they sought it not by faith, but as it were by the works of the law. For they stumbled at that stumblingstone [the law of Moses]; **33** As it is written, Behold, **I lay in Sion a stumblingstone and rock of offence**: and whosoever believeth on him shall not be ashamed.

Romans 11:7 What then? Israel hath not obtained that which he seeketh for; but the election hath obtained it, and the rest were blinded **8** (**According as it is written, God hath given them the spirit of slumber, eyes that they should not see, and ears that they should not hear**;) unto this day. **9** And **David saith, Let their table be made a snare, and a trap, and a stumblingblock, and a recompence unto them**: **10** Let their eyes be darkened, that they may not see, and bow down their back alway. ... **25** For I would not, brethren, that ye should be ignorant of this mystery, lest ye should be wise in your own conceits; that blindness in part is happened to Israel, until the fulness of the Gentiles be come in . **26** And so **all Israel shall be saved**: as it is written, There shall come out of Sion the Deliverer, and shall turn away ungodliness from Jacob: **27** For this is my covenant unto them, when I shall take away their sins.

Curses Spoken By The Prophet Peter

1 Peter 2:6 Wherefore also it is contained in the scripture, Behold, I lay in Sion a chief corner stone, elect, precious: and he that believeth on him shall not be confounded. **7** Unto you therefore which believe he is precious: but unto them which be disobedient, the stone which the builders disallowed, the same is made the head of the corner, **8** And **a stone of stumbling, and a rock of offence, even to them which stumble at the word**, **being disobedient**: whereunto also they were appointed.

312

Index

PRESS RELEASE / BIO

FOR IMMEDIATE RELEASE:

April 1, 2015—Introducing the fresh, dynamic, and prophetic ministry of **prophet, pastor, and teacher, Walter James Taylor**. Bro. Taylor preaches an insightful and powerful word on Israel in the light of Bible prophecy, the prophetic end times, the love of Jesus, the power of the cross, the authority of the Word of God, and how easy it is to heal the sick.

Come, hear, and see the Lord confirm His Word with signs, wonders, and notable miracles while souls, souls, and souls are being added into the kingdom of God.

Bro. Taylor is the President of **Walnut Harvest Media Group (www. securityofisrael.com)**. He is ordained under the watchful eye of Houston's Charles and Francis Hunter, who were known around the world as two of the most anointed and energetic evangelists in the Body of Christ. Over a period of 30 years the Hunters' ministry recorded a billion salvations. Millions of people were also healed by the power of God and gifts of the Holy Spirit (**www.happyhunters.org**).

Bro. Taylor has been a 24/7 student of the Word of God over the past 34 years. He has preached for the past 16 years to the world on the web concerning the **COMING EVENTS IN BIBLE PROPHECY** and the order of end time events that must proceed the second coming of Jesus to reign over the earth (**www.whattimeitis.org**). He is also an accomplished trumpet and guitar player, and incorporates his prophetic horn into his preaching, teaching, and healing ministry.

To schedule Bro. Taylor for a time of analysis of Israel in light of Bible prophecy, ministry, prophetic worship or healing in your church, synagogue, temple, mosque, business, civic or news group, he may be contacted at **whattimeblog@gmail.com**; or **@prophettaylor**. Enter the book's title and also find us on **Facebook**.

The following maps and graphics are offered solely for the purpose of giving the readers a place to start in any attempt to locate the multitudes of "Josephs" that are hidden somewhere in the earth today. They are scattered everywhere, but most are to be found in the nations that the descendants of Ephraim have become. Share with me your findings at whattimeblog@gmail.com.

Maps and Graphics Locating Joseph

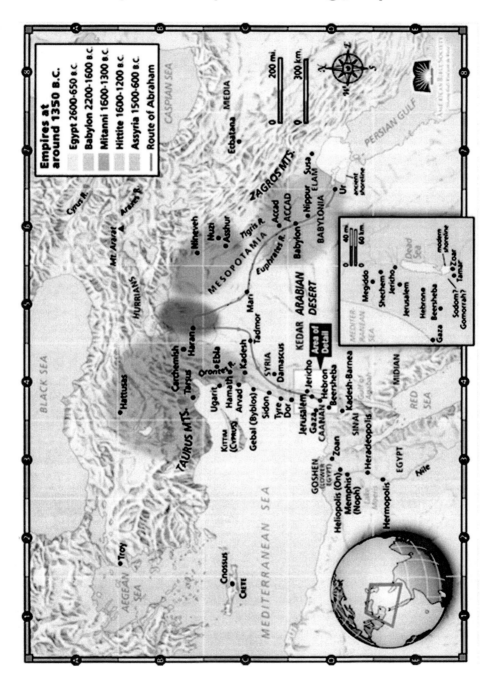

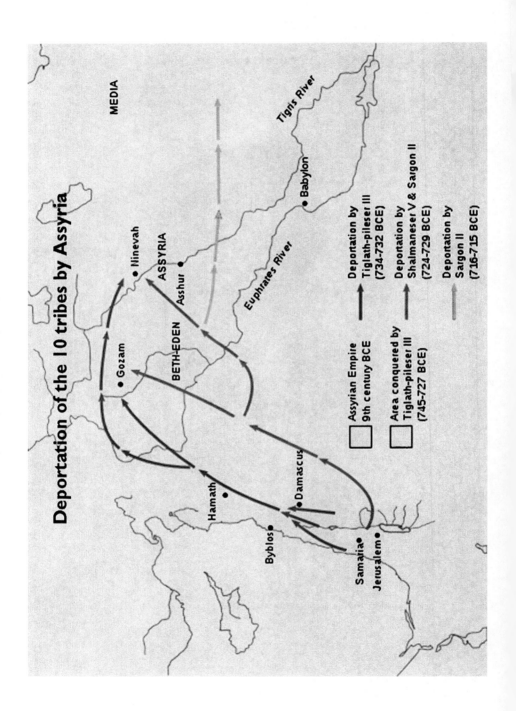

Deportation of the 10 tribes by Assyria

MEDIA

Tigris River

Babylon

Euphrates River

Ninevah

ASSYRIA

Asshur

BETH-EDEN

Gozam

Hamath

Damascus

Byblos

Samaria
Jerusalem

Assyrian Empire
9th century BCE

Area conquered by
Tiglath-pileser III
(745-727 BCE)

Deportation by
Tiglath-pileser III
(734-732 BCE)

Deportation by
Shalmaneser V & Sargon II
(724-729 BCE)

Deportation by
Sargon II
(716-715 BCE)

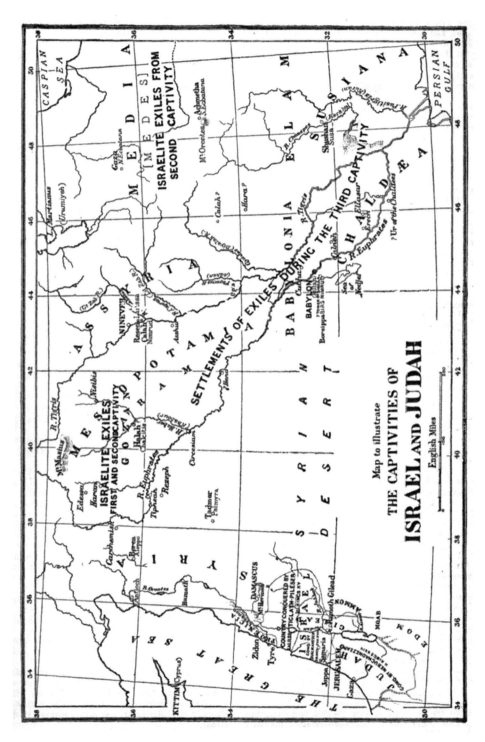

Map to illustrate

THE CAPTIVITIES OF

ISRAEL AND JUDAH

English Miles

325

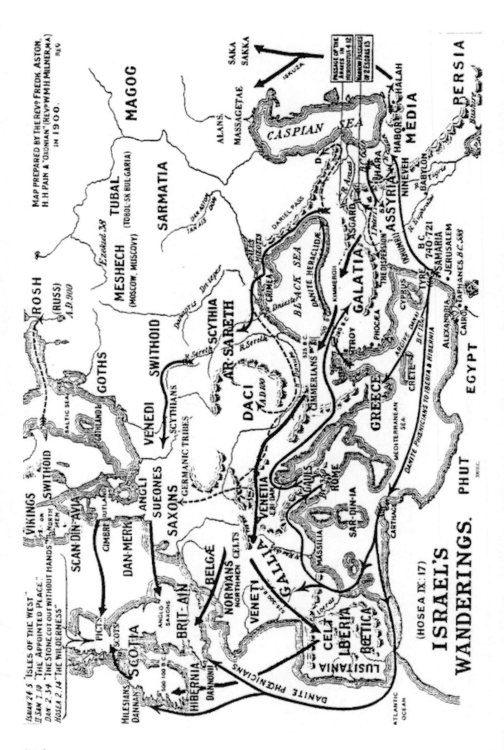

MAP PREPARED BY THE REV'D FREDK. ASTON,
H.H.PAIN & "OIDMAN" (REV W.M.H.MILNER,M.A.)
IN 1900.   REV.

ISRAEL'S WANDERINGS.

(HOSEA IX: 17)

Isaiah 24.5 "ISLES OF THE WEST"
II Sam. 7.10 "THE APPOINTED PLACE."
Dan. 2. 34 "THE STONE cut out WITHOUT HANDS"
Hosea 2.14 "THE WILDERNESS"

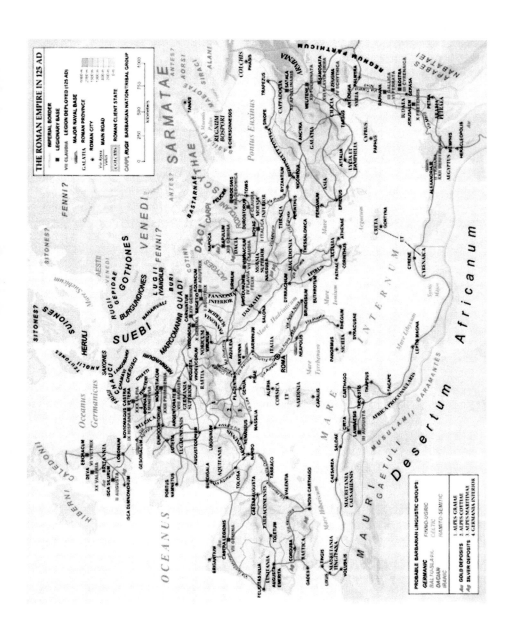

THE ROMAN EMPIRE IN 125 AD

IMPERIAL BORDER
LEGIONARY BASE
VII CLAUDIA LEGION DEPLOYED 125 AD
MAJOR NAVAL BASE
GALATIA ROMAN PROVINCE
ROMAN CITY
MAIN ROAD
ROMAN CLIENT STATE
CARP, RUGII BARBARIAN NATION/TRIBAL GROUP

PROBABLE BARBARIAN LINGUISTIC GROUPS
GERMANIC   FINNO-UGRIC
BALTO-SLAVIC CELTIC
DACIAN   HAMITO-SEMITIC
IRANIC

1 ALPES GRAIAE
2 ALPES COTTIAE
3 ALPES MARITIMAE
4 GERMANIA INFERIOR

Au GOLD DEPOSITS
Ag SILVER DEPOSITS

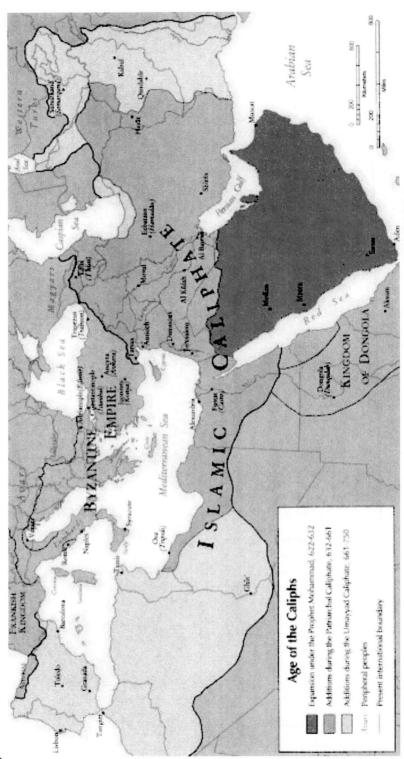

Age of the Caliphs

Expansion under the Prophet Muhammad, 622-632

Additions during the Patriarchal Caliphate, 632-661

Additions during the Umayyad Caliphate, 661-750

Peripheral peoples

Present international boundary

The Silk Route

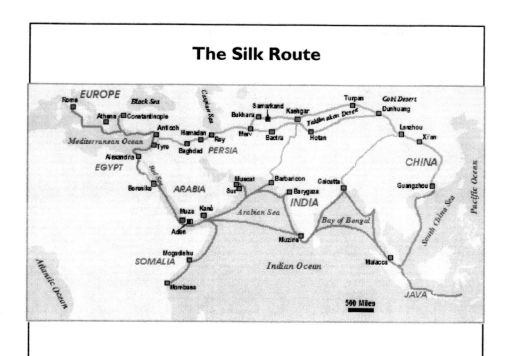

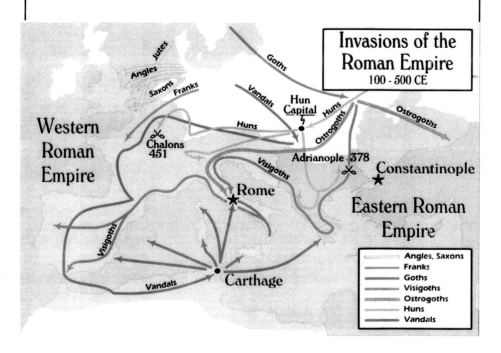

The 1040 Window - 1/3 of world's land; 2/3 world's people

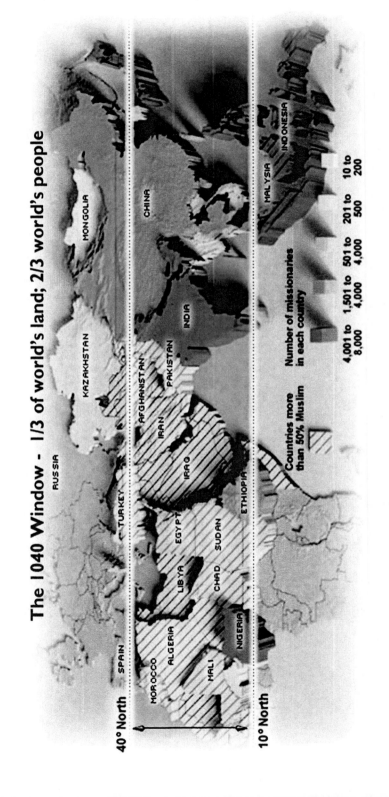

40° North

10° North

RUSSIA

SPAIN

MOROCCO

ALGERIA

MALI

LIBYA

CHAD

SUDAN

NIGERIA

ETHIOPIA

TURKEY

EGYPT

IRAQ

IRAN

AFGHANISTAN

PAKISTAN

KAZAKHSTAN

MONGOLIA

CHINA

INDIA

MALAYSIA

INDONESIA

Countries more
than 50% Muslim

Number of missionaries
in each country

4,001 to
8,000

1,501 to
4,000

501 to
4,000

201 to
500

10 to
200

330

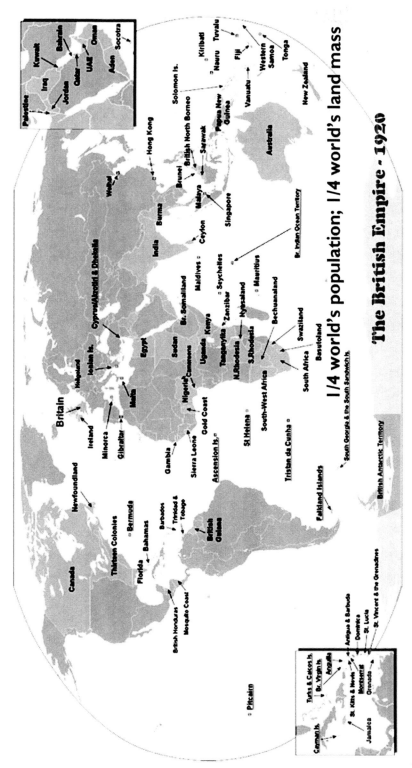

The British Empire - 1920

1/4 world's population; 1/4 world's land mass

CPSIA information can be obtained
at www.ICGtesting.com
Printed in the USA
FSOW01n0158090615
7716FS